Technical Report No. 25

# *A Gendered Past*
## *A Critical Bibliography of Gender in Archaeology*

*Edited by*
Elisabeth A. Bacus   Alex W. Barker   Jeffrey D. Bonevich
Sandra L. Dunavan   J. Benjamin Fitzhugh   Debra L. Gold
Nurit S. Goldman-Finn   William Griffin   Karen M. Mudar

*with contributions by*
Kurt F. Anschuetz   Elisabeth A. Bacus   Alex W. Barker
Jeffrey D. Bonevich   Sandra L. Dunavan   Starr Farr   Michael Finn
Lynn E. Fisher   J. Benjamin Fitzhugh   Debra L. Gold   Nurit S. Goldman-Finn
William Griffin   Karin Jones   Karen M. Mudar   Tineke Van Zandt

*and with a foreword by*
Alison Wylie

Ann Arbor
1993

©1993 The Regents of the University of Michigan
The Museum of Anthropology
All rights reserved

Printed in the
United States of America

ISBN 0-915703-31-9

The University of Michigan Museum of Anthropology currently publishes three monograph series: Anthropological Papers, Memoirs, and Technical Reports. We have over seventy titles in print. For a complete catalog, write to Museum of Anthropology Publications, 4009 Museums Building, Ann Arbor, MI 48109-1079, or call (313) 764-0485

*Cover design*: Katherine Clahassey. From "Theire sitting at meate," engraved by Theodor de Bry, after John White's original watercolor, published in the 1590 edition of *A Briefe and True Report of the New Found Land of Virginia*, by Thomas Hariot.

*The paper used in this publication meets the requirements of the
ANSI Standard Z39.48-1984 (Permanence of Paper)*

# Table of Contents

| | |
|---|---|
| **LIST OF CONTRIBUTORS** | iv |
| **LIST OF ILLUSTRATIONS** | v |
| **FOREWORD**<br>*Alison J. Wylie* | vii |
| **PREFACE**<br>*Alex W. Barker* | xiv |
| **ACKNOWLEDGMENTS** | xviii |
| **INTRODUCTION**<br>*Nurit Goldman-Finn, Sandra L. Dunavan and*<br>*J. Benjamin Fitzhugh* | 1 |
| **ANNOTATED REFERENCES** | |
|     Citations    A-B | 7 |
|     Citations    C-D | 26 |
|     Citations    E-F | 47 |
|     Citations    G-H | 54 |
|     Citations    I-J | 76 |
|     Citations    K-L | 79 |
|     Citations    M-N | 87 |
|     Citations    O-P | 100 |
|     Citations    Q-R | 105 |
|     Citations    S T | 115 |
|     Citations    U-V | 137 |
|     Citations    W-X | 139 |
|     Citations    Y-Z | 155 |
|     Additional References | 161 |
| **AUTHOR INDEX** | 163 |
| **SUBJECT INDEX** | 167 |

# List of Contributors

| | |
|---|---|
| Kurt F. Anschuetz | KFA |
| Elisabeth A. Bacus | EAB |
| Alex W. Barker | AWB |
| Jeffrey D. Bonevich | JDB |
| Sandra L. Dunavan | SLD |
| Starr Farr | SF |
| Michael R. Finn | MRF |
| Lynn E. Fisher | LEF |
| J. Benjamin Fitzhugh | JBF |
| Debra L. Gold | DLG |
| Nurit S. Goldman-Finn | NGF |
| William D. Griffin | WDG |
| Karin Jones | KJ |
| Karen M. Mudar | KMM |
| Tineke Van Zandt | TVZ |

# *List of Illustrations*

Mesolithic rock painting from Lakhajoar, India. Redrawn from *Prehistoric Indian Rock Painting* (1983), by Erwin Neumayer, Oxford University Press, Figure 44, p. 89. Drawn by J. Benjamin Fitzhugh. — 11

Effigy ear ornaments (gold, ca. 4.5 cm high), possibly Nasca, from Ica, Peru. Redrawn from *Indian Art in South America* (1967), by Frederic J. Dockstader, New York Graphic Society Publishers, Ltd., Plate 153. Drawn by J. Benjamin Fitzhugh. — 25

Ceramic figurines from the Evolved Preclassic period, Chupícuaro, Guanajuato. Redrawn from *Arts of Ancient Mexico* (1967), by Jacques Soustelle, Viking Press, Plate 23. Drawn by Laada Bilaniuk. — 58

Prehistoric petroglyphs from the Great Lakes Region (near Peterborough, Ontario). Redrawn from *Native Arts of North America, Africa, and the South Pacific* (1988), by George A. Corbin, Harper & Row Publishers, Figure 28, p. 107. Drawn by Laada Bilaniuk. — 106

Euro-American oil on composition board painting, "American Gothic" (1930), by Grant Wood. Redrawn from *Grant Wood: The Regionalist Vision* (1983), by Wanda M. Corn, Yale University Press, Figure 206, p. 142. Drawn by Katherine Clahassey. — 119

Indian painting, "Ragini Malkos" (Rajasthani, Raghogarh School, ca. 1700). Redrawn from *A Collector's Dream: Indian Art in the Collections of Basant Kumar and Saraladevi Birla and the Birla Academy of Art and Culture* (1987), by Karl Khandalavela and Saryv Doshi, Marg Publications, p. 135, accession number v3. Drawn by Nurit Goldman-Finn. — 129

Design in low relief of Tutankhamen and queen, back of king's throne, from Egyptian Museum, Cairo (New Kingdom, XVIIIth dynasty). Redrawn from *Egypt: The Art of the Pharoahs* (1965), by Irmgard Woldering, translated by Ann E. Keep, Methuen, Plate 31, p. 154. Drawn by Nurit Goldman-Finn. — 144

## Foreword
# Gender Archaeology/Feminist Archaeology

Alison Wylie
University of Western Ontario

When Sandra Morgen compiled a series of critical review essays and curriculum guidelines for publication just three years ago (the American Anthropological Association "Project on gender and the curriculum," *Gender and Anthropology: Critical Reviews for Research and Teaching*, 1989), she had to acknowledge that, for the most part, "a feminist archaeology is a vision for the future" (Morgen 1989:5). In this she echoed the assessment of Spector and Whelan who contributed an essay to *Gender and Anthropology* outlining the potential and value for "incorporating gender in archaeology courses" (the title of their contribution, 1989:65):

> Since there is as yet no body of literature that is both informed by recent feminist scholarship and also uses archaeological data and research strategies to study gender, we could not create our module utilizing current archaeological studies of prehistoric men and women. (Spector and Whelan 1989: 66)

Spector and Whelan, in turn, take as a benchmark Conkey and Spector's 1984 paper, the first systematic discussion of the need for and promise of archaeological research on gender to appear in the field; they report that, five years later, it "continues to accurately describe the general state of archaeology" (Spector and Whelan 1989: 66). In both articles, the authors note that, although "there is virtually no systematic work on the archaeological study of gender" (Conkey and Spector 1984:2; quoted by Spector and Whelan 1989:66), much *is* claimed or presumed, in extant interpretations of the record, about sexual divisions of labour, gender roles, gendered social structures, and the presence, role, or status of women in prehistory. Very often these interpretations depend upon, and reinforce, ethnocentric and presentist assumptions about gender relations and their stability over time and across cultural contexts; where Conkey and Spector document ways in which this limits the scope and compromises the integrity of primary research in archaeology (Conkey and Spector 1984: 2, 5-14), Spector and Whelan show how it translates into manifest androcentrism in many of the texts used to teach archaeology (1989:66-68). This lack of critical analysis of androcentrism and the silence on questions about gender as a focal topic for research is particularly striking, Spector and Whelan observe, given the interest and ingenuity that anthropological archaeologists have displayed in taking up questions about (other) social and cultural dimensions of past cultures (Spector and Whelan 1989: 65), and given the enormous expansion of research on gender in closely aligned fields, especially socio-cultural anthropology (Conkey and Spector 1984: 14).

Spector and Whelan do observe, hopefully, that by 1989 the situation of neglect described by them, and by Conkey and Spector before them, had begun to change (1989: 66). And, in fact, by the time their contribution to the AAA curriculum project appeared (in Morgen 1989), their detailed and optimistic assessment of the potential for gender research in archaeology had begun to be realized—with a vigor and enthusiasm that they could scarcely have anticipated when they set out to review existing curriculum resources in the area. Most visibly, an open and international call for papers on the topic "The Archaeology of Gender," issued by the organizers of the 1989 Chacmool Conference in Calgary, drew over a hundred submissions, from as far afield as New Zealand, Scandinavia, the U.K., western Europe, and all over North America. This was dramatic testimony that the "promise of a gender-conscious archaeology" was beginning to be widely recognized (to paraphrase Barker's introduction to this volume) and, given the scope of the submissions, that it was beginning to impinge on an extremely wide range of subfields, geographical and temporal interests, technical specialities and problem areas (for an analysis of the scope of these submissions, see Hanen and Kelley 1992, and the published proceedings, Walde and Willows 1991, abstracted below).

The 1989 Chacmool conference was by no means an isolated initiative. The previous spring (1988) a small working conference on "Women and Production in Prehistory" was convened by Gero and Conkey in South Carolina; it issued in a session on this topic at the 1989 annual meeting of the Society for American Archaeology and in the collection *Engendering Archaeology: Women and Prehistory* (Gero and Conkey 1991). In the same year, a special issue of *Archaeological Review from Cambridge* appeared on "Women and Archaeology" (Spring 1988), based in part on the "Cambridge Feminist Archaeology Workshops" in 1987-1988 and on presentations made at the annual Theoretical Archaeology Group Conferences held in the U.K. in 1987 (with antecedents in 1982 and 1985; see Arnold et al. in *ARC* 1988: 1, abstracted below). Also in this period, the Women's Caucus of the Society for Historical Archaeology organized a number of groundbreaking workshops and conference sessions for the SHA annual meetings that provided a forum for gender research and feminist theory in historical archaeology. In retrospect, the year Spector and Whelan's curriculum review appeared was something of a turning point, a watershed, in the fortunes of archaeological work on gender.

Since 1989 an increasing number of conferences, workshops, symposia, and annual meeting sessions have been devoted to research on women and gender in archaeology: a conference on "Women in Archaeology" was held at Charles Sturt University in Australia in January 1990 (the proceedings are now in press; du Cros and Smith 1992); two very successful open invitation conferences on gender research have been organized by Cheryl Claassen at Appalachian State University in North Carolina (proceedings of the first of these have just appeared; Claassen 1992a); and a number of prominent anthropology departments have sponsored curriculum development seminars and workshops on gender research in archaeology (e.g., the "Feminist Mainstreaming Project in Anthropology" at the University of Michigan which was responsible, in part, for the genesis of the bibliography that follows). Although I have focused here on developments in predominantly English language contexts, these are by no means the earliest or most vigorous initiatives in the areas. In fact, they were anticipated, by a decade, by a prescient group of Norwegian archaeologists who organized a conference called "Were They All Men?" in November 1979 (the proceedings, which were not published until 1987, are abstracted below: Bertelsen, Lillehammer, Naess 1987); this gave rise, subsequently, to "Norwegian Women in Archaeology" (the acronym is "KAN" in Norwegian), a group that has been meeting and producing a journal, *KAN*, since 1985 (much of this history of development is discussed in endnotes in Wylie 1992).

Although there was no very visible body of

literature on the "archaeology of gender" or on archaeological studies of women before 1988-1989—certainly there was nothing comparable to the dynamic programs of research which had emerged in socio-cultural anthropology and history by that time—a number of papers had appeared, or were circulating as the texts of conference presentations, which did address questions about gender relations and women in archaeological terms. Where publications are concerned, these include: archaeological contributions to region or culture-specific literatures where there existed a developed anthropological and historical interest in the status and roles of women (e.g., Barstow 1978, Kehoe 1983, and Rohrlich-Leavitt 1977); the work of some postprocessualists who endorse feminist initiatives and have, on occasion, explored gender as a dimension of cultural life relevant to their studies of the "insides" of prehistoric life and action (e.g., Hodder 1984, and Braithwaite 1984; but see Engelstad 1991); and the work of non-archaeologists who recognize the importance of archaeological research, and have attempted to integrate what they could learn of it into their own historical or anthropological research on the origins, evolution, and diversity of gender systems (e.g., Rapp 1977).

In addition, Claassen has compiled an on-line bibliography of papers on archaeology and gender that were delivered at archaeological conferences (and/or appeared in conference proceedings) from 1964-1992 in which, as she summarizes her results, 24 of a total of 284 entries were presented prior to January 1988 (Claassen 1992b: "Introduction"), only two of which have appeared in print (Kehoe 1976 and Spector 1983). But even given this evidence of antecedent interest in questions about women and gender, Claassen's analysis bears out the pessimistic assessments published by Conkey and Spector in 1984, and by Spector and Whelan in 1989. Over half of the conference papers she lists were presented at conferences between 1988 and 1990 (altogether 151; Claassen 1992b: Introduction), with another 98 presented in the last two years. And of this total, she finds that "there are 102 published conference papers, the vast majority of those published in 1991" (Claassen 1992b: Introduction).

It is, then, a very recent phenomenon that Morgen's "vision for the future" has begun to be realized. This is why the present bibliography is such an important and welcome contribution to the existing literature; it was unthinkable, even a few years ago, that anyone could compile such a rich offering of published archaeological research on women and gender.

The question whether this body of research constitutes a "feminist archaeology"—where Morgen's vision is of a "feminist archaeology" (1989: 5), and Spector and Whelan specifically regret the lack of archaeological work informed by feminist scholarship (1989: 66)—is a vexed one, and one which the editors of this bibliography identify as a point of disagreement which they themselves encountered. Certainly any answer to this question depends on how you define "feminism" as much as on your reading of the new work on gender in archaeology, and this is a notoriously controversial issue; contra the presumption of much media coverage, there is no party line here. Where archaeological practice is concerned, many of those now taking up questions about gender do not identify themselves as feminists and are not motivated by explicitly (or even implicitly) feminist concerns. Certainly many are wary of claiming any very close association with an overtly political movement—now famously the object of a widespread "backlash"—even if their interest in understanding the status of women and gender relations in the past arises, in part, from a politically grounded suspicion of contemporary gender stereotypes and a commitment to gender equity in the present and future. Strategically this stance of disengagement may be justified. But it is worth reiterating a point I have argued elsewhere (Wylie 1991): that feminist commitments by no means entail a systematic partiality, a retributive dogmatism, along gender lines.

For one thing, feminist commitments do not entail any one particular conclusion, or set of conclusions, about the significance of gender as an organizing principle (past or present), about the status of women relative to men, or about their relationship to public vs. private spheres, domestic contexts, productive or reproductive labour practices. Famously, "radical" feminists of the 1970s tended to view gender as a fundamental and quasi-autonomous organizing principle in social, political, and economic life and to presume that women are everywhere subdominant, while the liberal feminists they challenged took gender to be a much thinner and more variable construct, and expected to be able to identify contexts in which women exercise considerable power and privilege. These positions contrast in obvious ways with the stance of Marxist and socialist feminists of the period who often presumed that gender inequities would prove explicable in terms of, or in some sense dependent upon, more familiar political-economic structures and conditions. This is a crude characterization of the political and theoretical positions which emerged early on in the second wave women's movement and inspired much feminist research in the social and life sciences; the range of positions now in play has increased dramatically (in diversity and sophistication) since the days when it was possible to draw the straightforward distinctions I cite here with any precision (for one account of underlying differences in social, political theory; see Jaggar 1983). My point is simply that a feminist commitment to take gender structures seriously, and to problematize contemporary gender stereotypes—assumptions about the "naturalness," the inevitability and/or universality of familiar gender relations—leaves open the whole range of interesting questions that gender research in archaeology is beginning to take up: when and how (under what conditions) were sexual differences elaborated into gender roles and structures?; what different forms have "sex/gender" systems taken over time and across cultures?; and how have gender structures (including social relations, roles, identities) been affected by, and how have they affected, transformations in other dimensions of social, cultural life (e.g., "hominidization, cultural diversification, and the formation of food producing societies and urban states" [Spector and Whelan 1989: 71])?

A second and closely related point to be made in this connection is that when self-consciously *feminist* researchers entered their various fields in the 1960s and 1970s, armed with questions that reflected the political and theoretical commitments described above, they rarely returned with results they expected. In fact, the history of feminist research in the social sciences and, most visibly, in socio-cultural anthropology, is one of profound and continuous critical reassessment of framing presuppositions; gender structures, and their interconnections with class, race, national and other structuring systems, have proven much more complex than feminists, starting with a critical suspicion of our own "taken-for-granteds" about gender, could have anticipated. This literature is replete with auto-critiques which document ways in which feminist researchers have found their own frameworks and accounts flawed by an unwitting acceptance of entrenched androcentric assumptions or simple inversions of these assumptions; in this they have held even deeply entrenched presuppositions open to revision in light of the results of rigorous empirical and conceptual analysis (e.g., Rosaldo 1980, and the wide ranging critiques of "essentialism" that have emerged in virtually all areas of feminist research the decade since Rosaldo's discussion; see Wylie 1992 for a discussion of these transformations, specifically in feminist thinking about power). Time and again the commitment to understand how gender systems work, and how variable they are, has made feminist research one of the most dynamic and productive areas of inquiry to have emerged in the last several decades.

Feminist thinking is, then, not only multidimensional and diverse, but continually evolving, in the best tradition of scholarly practice, through critical engagement with the questions it raises and with the results of sustained investigation of its various subject matters. The new research on gender in archaeology could have no better model for its practice than this, however it names itself. Certainly, the archaeology of gender will be much impoverished if it fails to take advantage of the rich and sophisticated feminist literature on "sex/gender systems" that has resulted of these decades of inquiry in closely aligned fields. In the sense of being, at least, "informed by recent feminist scholarship" (Spector and Whelan 1989:6), the best of the new archaeological work on gender is clearly feminist.

The bibliography which follows is crucially important in fostering the development of this new research in archaeology, first for the reasons given by the editors themselves. They do an invaluable service in making visible and accessible the emerging (and scattered) literature in this area; it is critical that such research should proceed in all the various subfields and specialities of archaeology. As Strathern has argued, with respect to socio-cultural anthropology, a great deal is lost if the study of gender, and feminist research generally, comes to be viewed as just another approach or sub-speciality; this sort of "theoretical containment" (Strathern 1987: 200) blunts the critical import of such work, obscuring the fact that critiques of androcentrism and a detailed understanding of gender dynamics have relevance for virtually all research programs and subject areas in anthropology. And yet, it is also important that this not enforce a fragmentation which obscures common reference points and insights.

Even more important than broad cross-fertilizing coverage, however, is the sort of critical engagement of the issues raised by research on gender/feminist research that a bibliography of this kind makes possible. And what particularly distinguishes this bibliography is the fact that it begins this engagement directly. Its editors and compilers make it clear that their annotations are not simple summaries or abstracts; they mean to give the literature they assemble a close critical reading, to push its limits conceptually. In this they bring to bear a very wide range of backgrounds, sympathies, presuppositions, and expectations, with the result that the original literature is much enriched; they discern pitfalls and prospects for gender research, new questions and resources, that can only emerge through this sort of focused exchange. It is to be hoped that this level of engagement will continue, and that all parties will come away enriched: puzzled about things they had taken for granted; aware of a range of new ways of looking at cultural phenomena and of the resources afforded by feminist scholarship across the social sciences and humanities; intrigued by possibilities for reconceptualizing old problems and bodies of data they had not considered; and perhaps prepared to search out the data and background sources necessary to take up new questions about the emergence, evolution, and diversity of gender relations.

# *References Cited*

Arnold, K., R. Gilchrist, P. Graves, and S. Taylor (editors)
1988   Women in archaeology. *Archaeological Review from Cambridge* 7.1:2-8.

Barstow, A.
1978   The uses of archeology for women's history: James Mellaart's work on the Neolithic Goddess at Çatal Hüyük. *Feminist Studies* 4.3: 7-17.

Bertelsen, R., A. Lillehammer, and J. Naess (editors)
1987   *Were They All Men?: An Examination of Sex Roles in Prehistoric Society.* Arkeologist museum i Stavanger, Stavanger, Norway.

Claassen, Cheryl (editor)
1992a  *Exploring Gender Through Archaeology: Selected Papers from the 1991 Boone Conference.* Monographs in World Archaeology, no. 11. Prehistory Press, Madison.

1992b  Bibliography of archaeology and gender: Papers delivered at archaeology conferences 1964-1992. *Annotated Bibliographies for Anthropologists* 1(2).

Conkey, Margaret W., and Janet D. Spector,
1984.  Archaeology and the study of gender. In *Advances in Archaeological Method and Theory*, edited by Michael B. Schiffer, 7:1-38.

DuCros, Hilary and Laurajane Smith (editors)
1992    *Women in archaeology: A feminist critique*. Department of Prehistory, Australian National University, Canberra, Australia.

Gero, Joan
1992 (in press) The social world of Paleo-Indian prehistoric facts: Gender and power in knowledge construction. In *Women in Archaeology: A Feminist Critique*, edited by Hilary du Cros and Laurajane Smith. Occasional Papers, Australian National University, Department of Prehistory and Anthropology, Canberra.

Gero, J. M. and M. W. Conkey (eds.),
1991    *Engendering Archaeology: Women and Prehistory*. Basil Blackwell, Oxford.

Hanen, Marsha and Jane Kelley
1992 (in press) Gender and archaeological knowledge. In *Metaarchaeology*, edited by Lester Embree, 205-238. Boston Studies in the Philosophy of Science. Kluwer Academic Press, Boston.

Hodder, I.
1984    Burials, houses, women and men in the European Neolithic. In *Ideology, Power, and Prehistory*, edited by D. Miller and C. Tilley, 51-68. Cambridge University Press, Cambridge.

Jaggar, Alison M.
1983    *Feminist Politics and Human Nature*. Rowman and Allenheld, Totowa, New Jersey.

Kehoe, Alice
1976    Ethnicity at a pedlar's post in Saskatchewan. *Western Canadian Journal of Anthropology* 6(1): 52-60.

Morgen, Sandra
1989    Gender and anthropology: Introductory essay. In *Gender and Anthropology: Critical Reviews for Research and Teaching*, edited by Sandra Morgen, 1-20. American Anthropological Association, Washington, D.C.

Rapp, Rayna
1977    Gender and class: An archaeology of knowledge concerning the origin of the state. *Dialectical Anthropology* 2: 309-316.

Rosaldo, Michelle Z.
1980    The use and abuse of anthropology: Reflections on feminism and cross-cultural understanding. *Signs* 5: 389-417.

Spector, Janet D. and Mary K. Whelan
1989    Incorporating gender into archaeology courses. In *Gender and Anthropology: Critical Reviews for Research and Teaching*, edited by Sandra Morgen, 65-94. American Anthropological Association, Washington, D.C.

Strathern, Marilyn
1987    An awkward relationship: The case of feminism and anthropology. *Signs* 12: 276-292.

Walde, D., and N. Willows (editors)
1991   *The Archaeology of Gender*, Proceedings of the 22nd Annual Chacmool Conference. Calgary: The Archaeological Association of the University of Calgary.

Wylie, Alison
1991   Beyond objectivism and relativism: Feminist critiques and archaeological challenges. In *The Archaeology of Gender, Proceedings of the 22nd Annual Chacmool Conference*, edited by D. Walde and N. Willows, 17-23. Archaeological Association, The University of Calgary, Calgary.

1992   Feminist theories of social power: Some implications for a processual archaeology. *Norwegian Archaeological Review* 25(1):56-68.

# Preface
# Reflections on a Gendered Past

Alex W. Barker
University of Michigan

*We shall not cease from exploration
And the end of all our exploring
Will be to arrive where we started
And know the place for the first time.*

---T.S. Eliot

Few topics in the archaeological literature have witnessed so rapid a growth as studies of gender and gender relations in past societies. Gender represents one of the--perhaps *the*--most fundamental but underexamined axes of social differentiation. Only within the past decade, however, has the promise of gender studies in archaeology been appreciated widely within the discipline.

But the literature has expanded in many different directions at once, with research relevant to the study of gender in the human past appearing in a variety of contexts, informed by a variety of theoretical perspectives, and filtered through a variety of disciplinary vocabularies. Few archaeologists save those focusing solely on these topics can follow all the journals, all the volumes, and all symposia proceedings necessary to stay up-to-date on this burgeoning area of research. As a result, since theoretical treatments of gender are scattered across the literature of several disciplines they have received relatively less attention in anthropological archaeology than other central axes of social differentiation. While the role of androcentric bias in explaining resistance to studies consciously exploring the nature and roles of gender in past societies remains open to debate, the effects of the fundamentally cross-disciplinary nature of such research seems clear. Researchers already convinced of the theoretical importance and methodological utility of gender-conscious approaches follow the literature across disciplinary boundaries, and thus have access to a broad canon of studies complementing their own work. Researchers skeptical of the theoretical importance of gender in archaeology see only the occasional study outside the context of this cross-disciplinary corpus of theory, and may view such studies as marginal. Each is thus confirmed in his or her beliefs; each can point to the empirical basis for his or her contradictory conclusions.

In this volume we do not seek to provide an exhaustive summary of all the writings that are significant to the study of gender in prehistory. Such a task lies beyond both our abilities and our inclinations. At once constructed by society and one of the blocks whereby society constructs itself, gender and gender roles are implicit in virtually all interpersonal relations. Attempting to include all the works significant to such a topic would be an impossible task, amounting to all works significant to anthropology itself. Instead, we have assembled articles dealing specifically and for the most part consciously with gender in prehistory. We have largely restricted ourselves to English-language texts, but wish to note the long tradition of gender-conscious research in other parts of the world, notably Scandinavia.

For many archaeologists, the significance of these topics lies in their promise to inform and improve theoretical constructs for understanding the historical development of social institutions and the human past. The past is not the province of archaeologists alone, and many others travel there in search of authority-- whether the authority of historical precedent or the authority of "archaeological" vindication for their views of other times and other social arrangements. Sometimes these travelers see things we have overlooked; sometimes they imagine what they wished to see. But the immediacy of the past, its immanence in constructing theories in other disciplines largely separate from archaeology, must be recognized and its consequences reckoned. The past has become contested ground, and the contestants struggle for what Milan Kundera calls "access to the laboratories where photographs are retouched and biographies and histories rewritten."

As archaeologists we rarely confront the past directly. Rather than traveling to the past, we spy upon it using a variety of devices, catching glimpses of it in this lens or that mirror. Held one way we see the dim outlines of past social forms and institutions, held another we see the interplay of culture and environment, or the intricate web of relations spanning domestic and political economies, while held yet another way we see ourselves staring back. The power of gender studies to irritate us, to confound our accepted beliefs and comfortable assumptions, ultimately lies less in its ability to show us new and different pictures in the glass than to show us the chips and waves in the mirror itself.

In addition to examining articles or essays dealing with gender in the human past, we also have included studies of gender in the discipline of archaeology itself. More than evidence for a loose definition of "gender in archaeology," these studies are included as a necessary adjunct to the remaining literature. They provide a measure of biases within the discipline--an occasionally painful but necessary exercise if we are to gauge the success of archaeology's attempts to deal with questions of gender and gender relations. One way of assessing how well archaeology has dealt with these questions in the past is to see how well it deals with these problems in the present--in short, to look for irregularities in the mirror's surface.

At the same time, much of the rhetoric surrounding these studies suggests a radical newness that cannot be supported historically. One of the central debates in the early decades of anthropological inquiry involved the historical reality of matriarchy and its role in changing human social forms and institutions. Debates regarding the status of women in the rise of private property and the state, the changing relations between men and women in the origins of marriage and the family, and the historicity of patriarchy and agnatic descent all played significant roles in the theoretical development of the discipline. Many of the questions addressed here are not new, but newly appreciated. Like most questions of fundamental importance to archaeology, these are less new than unresolved, constantly calling for new approaches and new methods to address perennial questions of concern in understanding the human career.

All of this suggests that studies of gender, of the roles of men and women in past societies and in the evolution of social forms, are neither marginal nor purely a product of a radical critique of the discipline. They are mainstream, central, and in fact, can claim greater antiquity and precedence within the discipline than most other areas of study. Whether due to androcentric biases or the methodological difficulties of attributing gender to peoples in the past, however, discussion of many of these questions languished, or at best remained at the level of just-so hypotheses and scenarios, until relatively recently. The feminist critique returned these central issues to their original place in anthropological discourse, while at the same time providing a fresh theoretical perspective from which they could be viewed. This critique focused in large part not only on the just-so stories earlier archaeologists thought they saw reflected, but on the quality of the mirror itself. They challenged not merely type assignments but stereotypes, not just theories but the ways in which theories were built. They pointed to androcentric biases in the discipline and its theoretical constructions, and pointed accusingly to stereotypes built into many widely accepted and even celebrated archaeological interpretations. One indicator of the pervasiveness of these stereotypes is that many researchers--even within the context of the feminist critique--do not distinguish between gender and women's roles. Work done by men is seen as work, while work done by women is seen as women's work. Women remain a marked category, and while individual men or groups of men fill specific economic niches, there is still a tendency to discuss the economic niche-- and occasionally the archaeology--of women as a group, as though they represent an analytical unit on a par with tanners or merchants.

Most researchers would agree that in no extant society do women enjoy the same rights, statuses and powers as men. But what of extinct ones? For all their flaws--real or imagined--our disciplinary lenses and mirrors can be trained on just such questions. The unique ability of archaeology to pose social questions not across the *longue duree* of five hundred or even a thousand years but across millennia lets archaeology address questions of gender inequality by specifying how and not simply speculating why. In these heady days when the theoretical sophistication of many of the questions raised outstrips our methodological ability to address them, it may be well to recognize from the start the complexity inherent in such topics. Consider, then, what terms like *inequality* imply. On the face of it, the meaning is simple. Inequality is the want of equality, a condition of disparity between two things or groups. Yet this kind of bloc-regarding inequality is but one of a series of different kinds of inequality potentially crosscutting any society. Bloc-regarding equality presumes equality between groups, but says nothing about intragroup structures. Thus, different genders might enjoy relative equality, while the degree of disparity between the haves and the have-nots differs radically within each. One gender might have access to both the highest social ranks and the lowest, with both extremes denied to another. Yet by many measures these blocs would be seen as enjoying equal relative status. Then we must factor in other cross-cutting social domains. Is the relative disparity between or within blocs significantly different by social class? By age? By occupation? By wealth? Does the intergroup disparity appear to be static, or does it vary by situation and social context? What is the relative social mobility between groups? Are relative ranks measured against the same or different scales? And having considered all of these questions in constructing a research design, how to devise measurable variables that will monitor these significant dimensions? The promise of a gender-conscious archaeology has now been largely recognized. As the literature swells with appreciations of the importance of gender studies, the new challenge becomes the framing of middle range theory and bridging arguments to link the growing body of theoretical literature to past societies. Even the most elementary questions, such as how to identify and distinguish genders archaeologically, remain problematic. We do not mean to suggest that these questions are insoluble, but quite the opposite, that their solution must be a central concern in coming years.

This volume provides no direct solutions to these problems. It seeks only to provide an overview of the available English-language literature germane to such questions, in the hope that a broader range of archaeologists will attempt to address them and explore the existing body of literature. It also seeks to provide brief critiques of the available archaeological literature for the benefit of scholars in other disciplines. In both roles it is a research tool, aimed at furthering reflections on a gendered past rather than advancing answers to the questions raised, providing less a set of rules for the game than summarizing the state of play. We hope it will prove of value to scholars in archaeology and related disciplines as they take up these difficult but crucial questions, and pick their way through what has increasingly become a wilderness of mirrors.

# Acknowledgments

The editors are grateful to the many persons in the University community and elsewhere who contributed both to the success of the Gender in Archaeology seminar and to the compilation of this volume. Space considerations preclude our mentioning all, but several merit special note.

Gracia Clarke coordinated the Feminist Mainstreaming Project within the University of Michigan Department of Anthropology, and provided support and encouragement for the organization of the original seminar. The Feminist Mainstreaming Project is supported in part by funds provided by the University of Michigan. We gratefully acknowledge this support.

Carla Sinopoli, who taught an undergraduate seminar and led a graduate discussion group on gender in archaeology at the Museum of Anthropology in 1989, deserves credit for bringing the topic to the interest of many of our seminar participants. Her course syllabus provided the organizers and editors with many relevant works, as did syllabi and reading lists contributed by Margaret Conkey, Cheryl Claassen, and Elizabeth Brumfiel. A mid-term visit by Margaret Conkey brought alternative views and renewed interest on several hot discussion topics, as well as a wealth of new literature from her own courses at Berkeley and from several other institutions holding anthropological and archaeological courses emphasizing gender issues.

Cheryl Claassen, editor of *Exploring Archaeology and Gender* and that volume's publishing staff at Prehistory Press graciously permitted a pre-publication version of their work to be examined by our annotators. Joan Gero, Kenneth Sassaman, and Bruce Smith also replied to our requests for copies of their works in press in a timely manner, enabling us to keep our bibliography as current as possible. Many other authors also sent us copies of their conference papers, and although for the most part our volume does not cover these unpublished works, it must be acknowledged that these works stimulated many discussions and shaped our views on many issues.

Barbara Smuts deserves special thanks for her contributions to our seminar and patience under duress during our discussion on sex, sociobiology, and the biological bases of behavior. Holly Smith also gave freely from her insights from paleoanthropology.

John D. Speth volunteered to serve as faculty sponsor for the seminar, and attended many of the class meetings. Richard I. Ford also attended several class sessions, and encouraged us both in the organization of the seminar and in the publication of this work. Alison Wylie kindly agreed to contribute a foreword to the volume, and cheerfully met our all-but-impossible deadlines. The cover was designed by Kay Clahassey, and we wish to thank her for both her efforts and her good humor as she listened to our many conflicting suggestions and instructions. Sally Horvath ably directs the University of Michigan Museum of Anthropology publications series, and we are grateful to her for her patience, guidance and good counsel. We have always appreciated her sound advice, but have not always heeded it--hence whatever flaws remain in this volume.

# Introduction

Nurit S. Goldman-Finn, Sandra L. Dunavan, and J. Benjamin Fitzhugh
University of Michigan

## Origins

This bibliography evolved from a seminar in gender and archaeology organized by graduate students in archaeology in the Department of Anthropology at the University of Michigan. Although many of us had been discussing these issues at the Museum of Anthropology, our course had its origins in the Feminist Mainstreaming Project, a campus-wide program implemented through the Women's Studies program. When funding became available for a feminism-related project, it was agreed that a seminar addressing gender in archaeology would be the most productive outlet. The seminar was approved and encouraged by Gracia Clark, organizer of Feminist Mainstreaming in Anthropology, Richard Ford, Chair of the Department of Anthropology, and John Speth, Curator of North American archaeology, who agreed to sponsor the class.

What began as a feminist-related project quickly grew into a much larger collective effort. The seminar syllabus, put together by Sandy Dunavan, Nurit Goldman-Finn, Karen Mudar and Jeff Bonevich, used ideas, references and class syllabi contributed by many other students and faculty members, including several at other institutions. Student response to the course was overwhelming, despite the heavy reading load. Out of the 30 graduate students in residence in the Winter 1992 term, over half regularly participated in the weekly seminar, and many others came when compelled by a particular topic or their schedules permitted.

All involved shared a general interest in issues related to gender and a desire to incorporate these issues into their own research and teaching. To provide participants with a broad framework in gender studies, a diverse set of works from feminist theory, ethnology, primate studies and sociobiology was included in the syllabus (reprinted in the appendix to Claassen's 1992 edited volume, *Exploring Gender Through Archaeology*). Discussion in the first half of the seminar drew on this literature to examine the political ramifications of feminist theory, explore theories of gender, and survey gender relations in cultures of varying social complexity. In the latter half of the course, we focused exclusively on archaeology and gender. Many additional references to this part of the syllabus were added by seminar participants to form the nucleus of this bibliography.

## *Divergence and Definitions*

It was clear after the first session that our viewpoints differed a great deal and that discussion would be animated. Many exchanges were characterized by disagreements continuing through the seminar break, on walks and drives home, and sometimes intermittently through the next week. On several occasions, participants could only agree to disagree. Others confessed to feelings of ambiguity or were astonished at their ignorance of certain topics. Many of us considered new perspectives, or re-examined our own approaches to gender, in theory and practice.

Questions of meaning, especially for terms used in models and theoretical approaches, pushed their way into almost every class. Many of us were surprised that there was a sharp dichotomy between those of us who defined ourselves as feminists and those of us who didn't. Some perceived feminism as a movement committed to realizing equal opportunities for women and men, while others identified feminism with political undertones promoting male exclusion. This dichotomy led to heated discussions over feminist theory and the appropriateness of treating gender studies as a subset of feminist theory. Some of us argued that the seminar could have been titled "Feminist Archaeology" (its official title was "Gender in Archaeology"), but the issue remained far from a consensus. We did come to recognize that much of our disagreement stemmed from differences of definition and self identification, and not necessarily from radically diverging values or goals.

Defining gender itself proved to be an equally sticky topic. Surprisingly, this has been given little consideration in current archaeological literature. Conkey and Spector, while not offering an explicit definition *per se*, do move towards one. Following sociocultural anthropologists, they view gender as a culturally constructed division between women and men, and between femininity and masculinity:

"[Gender is] a multifaceted and important social phenomenon having several different dimensions, including gender role, gender identity, and gender ideology....[F]eminist scholars conceptualize gender as a complex system of meaning — that is, as a social category that lies at the core of how people in particular cultures identify who they are, what they are capable of doing, what they should do, and how they are to relate to others similar to and different from themselves" (Conkey and Spector 1984:15-16).

As a cultural construct, or a collective creation of cultural imagination, gender is an axis of both cultural meaning and social organization. Gender defines sex roles and sexuality, and thus structures relationships between people, organizes tasks, and shapes conceptual realities. But how is gender tied to sex? As much feminist work points out, gender cannot be simply reduced to biology. At the same time, most of us felt that biological sex is fundamentally implicated. Gender is draped over sex. An anthropological understanding of how and why gender ideologies and roles vary, and how these relate to sex, is still relatively undeveloped. This lack of research led us to question the appropriateness of using sex-based data to get at prehistoric gender (through mortuary studies, representational art, etc.). The validity of discussing "women" or "men" in prehistory was also challenged, since these are culture-bound categories. Most archaeologists begin with a working assumption of two clear-cut genders. As other anthropologists have pointed out, however, it is possible that some cultures recognize multiple gender categories, or that a single-gendered system, where differences in sexual roles and identities are devalued, may exist. Furthermore, the fact that gender represents a way of categorically structuring relationships comparable to ethnicity, kinship, economic class, and age groupings complicates matters. If gender cannot be equated with sex, how can it be archaeologically recognized as distinct from other organizational structures? Some of us felt an explicit theory of gender, specifying how gender organizes social relationships and can be identified

## Introduction

in the archaeological record, needs to be developed. Others felt that linking gender to sex is appropriate, at least for launching research.

We did agree that the assumptions that tie gender to sex must be made explicit, and that these assumptions may vary depending on the problem of interest. The importance of articulating definitions and assumptions in research projects and when teaching these issues was repeatedly emphasized. At the beginning of the semester we all had different definitions for feminism, gender, inequality, and science. At the end of the semester our definitions still differed, but our understanding of what these issues entail was enriched by the literature and our heated discussions of it. We hope that some of this has been passed on in our individual annotations.

Through all our debates, the idea that a gender conscious perspective can illuminate many archaeological problems, even those seemingly unrelated to gender, was a constant theme. As a fundamental organizing principle of human society, gender has undoubtedly been a central facet of prehistoric economies and divisions of labor, politics, and social life. An explicit focus on gender in archaeology, while posing many methodological challenges (presently being met with optimism and determination) holds great theoretical potential for anthropological theory. Studies of gender also promise to bring new understandings to a variety of issues within the realm of feminist theory by addressing such interesting central questions as the universality of gender ideologies and gender divisions of labor, how and why gender relations vary, how and why they evolved, whether or not truly egalitarian societies have existed, and the origins of gender inequalities. A gendered perspective goes beyond revealing women's roles in prehistory, elucidating interactions of people of different genders.

## *Organization*

This bibliography includes articles and books published in anthropological archaeology, historical archaeology, and some classical and ethnoarchaeological works that deal with gender. It also contains materials addressing gender as it relates to how archaeology is practiced. We anno-

tated materials published (or, in a few cases, presented at conferences) prior to September 1992. A list of several important publications in press or unavailable at the time of publication can be found at the back of this volume, and references to many more unpublished papers have recently been collected in Claassen's (1992 on disk) *Annotated Bibliographies for Anthropologists*. Although much of the literature covered is composed of revisionist works focusing on women in prehistory, or on prehistoric gender relations, the bibliography consciously includes many works emphasizing other related issues, including many written before the recent surge of interest in gender in archaeology. There is a heavy emphasis on female representations and roles, due to the nature of the literature.

Although a few relevant publications were undoubtedly missed, many sources outside the ken of most archaeologists have been uncovered. It is because this discussion of gender is so widely dispersed that we believe this bibliography will be particularly useful. An index of the authors of the literature annotated and a detailed subject index, including geographical areas, countries, states, archaeological time periods, authorities cited, and many different theoretical and material topics provides some interesting angles into the literature and will enable a wide audience to find particular interests.

The annotations are an opportunity to share our insights and to extend our discussions. All annotations are, however, individually authored. The contributors come from different genders and sexual orientations, and a variety of ages and ethnic, social and economic backgrounds. Their views on archaeology, anthropology, and science were influenced by myriad colleges, teaching experiences, excavation projects, and personal relationships. Although the seminar undoubtedly had some influence on our ideas, no single line emerged, as shown by the debates in class and the variety of reactions and approaches to the literature annotated. Contributors had the freedom to write what they thought relevant, and take individual responsibility for their annotations. Thus, authors' initials follow every annotation. Complete names for identifying initials are shown on page iv.

Although annotators were encouraged to write balanced critiques evaluating the literature in its appropriate context, some annotations are more critical than others, since our opinions on particular works' strengths and weaknesses differ significantly. Critical, in the sense used in our subtitle, does not mean negative, but indicates that some personal evaluation, as well as a summary of this important literature, occurred in each annotation. Undoubtedly, many readers will disagree with some annotations (perhaps as vehemently as we disagreed on the use of the word critical in the subtitle and with some of each other's annotations), but at the very least, these annotations will bring some new perspectives to readers, allowing them to make their own decisions on which of the original works they will find useful or interesting. Given the social pervasiveness of gender and the diversity of material annotated, most archaeologists and many others interested in prehistory will find something relevant here.

## *References Cited*

Conkey, Margaret, and Janet D. Spector,
1984   Archaeology and the Study of Gender. *Advances in Archaeological Method and Theory* 7:1-38. Academic Press, New York.

# *Annotated References*

1. ANATI, EMMAUEL 1986. The question of "fertility cults". In *Archaeology and Fertility Cult in the Ancient Mediterranean: Papers Presented at the First International Conference on Archaeology of the Ancient Mediterranean*, edited by A. Bonanno, 2-15. B.R. Grüner Publishing Co., Amsterdam.

This short review paper takes up the question of fertility cults in the ancient Mediterranean. Anati defines fertility cults as ritual performances intended to promote natural or human fertility, and rejects what he regards as common misuses of the term. The remainder of the paper briefly reviews evidence for fertility cults in the Mediterranean prior to the Bronze Age, beginning with a general review of "The Art of Hunters and its Content," and proceeding to examine "Early Post-Palaeolithic Evidence" and "The Birth of Agriculture and Connected Ideologies." For each of these broadly defined time periods, Anati concludes that there is no archaeological evidence for performance of fertility rituals, except in rare instances. Artistic representations often taken as evidence of a concern with fertility may be part of more complex fundamental paradigms or symbolic concepts of nature and the supernatural.

In general, Anati points out that fertility cult interpretations of pre-Bronze Age artistic representations tend to focus exclusively on specific objects that refer in some way to sex, reproduction, or women, without considering other related or associated images, or other aspects of the archaeological context of the art. The emphasis in the fertility cult literature has been on a perceived continuity of symbolic focus on women and fertility beginning with the "Venus" figures of the Upper Paleolithic. Anati uses a different approach that traces associations between fundamental symbolic paradigms and forms of subsistence economies. He argues that practices that could be termed fertility cults are rare among hunters and gatherers concerned with success in hunting and fishing activities, but that a "concern for the fertility of the land" (and to some extent human groups) is a universal feature of agricultural societies. Even in these cases, though, Anati emphasizes the more general concepts expressed in fertility-related symbols and images (e.g., genealogy, ancestors, sexual morality and control, and understanding of the natural world) and questions whether a fertility cult, as an isolated phenomenon, is an accurate or useful way of describing archaeological representations.

Anati's emphasis on a clear definition of fertility cults as ritual performances should prove extremely productive. The value of his emphasis on universal patterns at the expense of local practices is less clear. Anati's own interpretations of early religions focuses on the common ideological concerns of hunters versus those of agriculturalists, and on a series of "elementary mental processes of association." Although the treatment of these complex issues is necessarily brief, Anati summarizes views developed in several Italian publications (for example 1983a,b), and could briefly clarify a number of questions not addressed here. How, for example, should the link between subsistence systems (hunting and gathering versus horticulture) and religion or ideology be conceived, and how far will this take us? What is it that makes certain mental associations elementary rather than merely common? In choosing to pitch his argument on a universal scale, Anati rejects considerations of a Mediterranean sphere, which are dismissed as "local cultural and conceptual patterns" through which elementary patterns are filtered. While analysis at a very broad scale is probably necessary, it seems counter productive not to consider local patterns. Detailed analyses of local patterns might clarify the formation and operation of Anati's elementary associations. LEF

*References cited*
Anati, Emmanuel 1983a. *Gli Elementi Fondamentali della Cultura.* Jaca Book, Milano.

Anati, Emmanuel 1983b. Intelletualita dell'uomo preistorico: Una visione in prospettiva. *Studi in Onore di Dinu Ademesteanu,* 97-109.

*fertility cults/religion/Venus figurines/agriculture/gatherer-hunters/Paleolithic/Neolithic/Mediterranean*


2. ARNOLD, BETTINA 1991. The deposed Princess of Vix: The need for an engendered European prehistory. In *The Archaeology of Gender: Proceedings of the Twenty-Second Annual Conference of the Archaeological Association of the University of Calgary,* edited by Dale Walde and Noreen D. Willows, 366-374. Archaeological Association, The University of Calgary, Calgary.

Arnold's contribution to this volume argues that the role of elite women in central European Iron Age society has been neglected, and that a set of assumptions about men's and women's roles have resulted in a male-biased interpretation of the *Fürstengräber*, or princely graves, of the Late Hallstatt and early La Tène periods. Her paper evaluates a series of categories of grave goods on the basis of their combination in rich tumulus burials of the early Iron Age, tracing and critically evaluating what are seen as partly exclusive, partly overlapping sets of women's and men's grave goods in "First Order" or elite burials. She rightly points out that the lack of skeletal analysis is a serious problem in correctly identifying the rich graves as belonging to females or males. Arnold concludes with a discussion of several burials (Stuttgart-Bad Cannstatt, in southwestern Germany, and Vix, in Burgundy, France) which, due to their somewhat unusual combination of grave goods (spear points with women's hair ornaments at Stuttgart-Bad Cannstatt, exclusively feminine personal ornaments in an extraordinarily rich burial at Vix) thought to be exclusively associated with either men or women, have been variously attributed to men, women, or a third "transvestite warrior or priest" category. Arnold argues that grave goods such as weapons, thought to signify a (male) warrior occupation, may instead indicate rank. She attributes the introduction of the third gender category (in this case, high status males with feminine personal ornamentation) to a "reluctance to accord women significant social status," and argues for the simpler hypothesis that women in fact held positions of high status and power in early Iron Age society.

While this certainly appears to be a plausible interpretation for the Vix burial—that the "Princess" of Vix was in fact "deposed" by archaeologists unwilling to attribute such a rich burial to a female member of the elite—the paper leaves unexamined a series of intriguing questions raised by the burial evidence and its interpretation, and seems to conflate a set of issues pivotal for the further development of an engendered European prehistory. Will it always be a more parsimonious interpretation to assume two genders, in effect to examine the roles played by biological males and females rather than exploring what may in fact be a more complex set of social categories? Arnold suggests that indications of occupation and rank are easily conflated in burial evidence: what about indications of sex and gender or membership in other social categories? In the early Iron Age, as Arnold points out, elite burials throughout Central Europe, whether male or female, shared a rigidly-defined set of status markers, while lower-status burials were more heterogeneous. Weapons appear to play an ambiguous role among elite grave goods: they are found in all male high-status burials but are not necessarily absent in high-status female burials. An engendered approach to these high-status burials might move beyond the search for women among the upper echelons of early Iron Age society to examine the role that gender symbols (feminine ornamentation? weapons associated primarily with men?) may play in defining elite statuses. Arnold is certainly right in calling for more systematic physical anthropological work on these important burials, but the development of analytical frameworks for incorporating questions about gender into analyses of the accompanying symbols of the early Iron Age elite seems even more pressing. LEF

*mortuary analysis/Iron Age/Europe/France/Germany*

3. ARNOLD, KAREN, ROBERTA GILCHRIST, PAM GRAVES, AND SARAH TAYLOR 1988. Women and archaeology. *Archaeological Review from Cambridge* 7(1):2-8.

This article serves as the introduction to *ARC* volume 7(1), which takes "Women and Archaeology" as its theme. The authors (three editors and one contributor) include comments on each of the seven articles which follow, although their discussion ranges well beyond this. The authors divide the issues concerning women and archaeology into three broad and interconnected categories: the disciplinary conditions in which women work, the way women are portrayed in interpretations and presentations of the past, and issues of social theory. The article focuses primarily on this third category of theory and epistemology, delineating some of the intractable questions which need to be addressed in this area. Thus, the article poses numerous questions, such as "How far do we sustain the tyranny of sexual dichotomy (in the use of binary oppositions and gender essentialism)" p. 4? and "Why is it that people can appear to comply in their own subordination?"(p. 5). Answers are not attempted for the majority of these questions, and this emphasis on questions is in line with the authors' stated goals of provoking responses and debate (p. 7). One conclusion is that gender is a process of social negotiation, and hence, the agency of women should be central to any inquiry on the subject. They also predict that "gender archaeology" will open up new areas of inquiry and new scales of analysis, such as a greater concern with the household, the family, domestic labor, the preparation and consumption of food, and social interaction in general.

The theorizing and questions raised in this introduction set a high standard for the rest of the issue. Success in this aspect, however, is balanced by the fact that many of the important issues raised are simply dropped, and not explored further in either this work or those that follow. One such neglected issue is the possible differences between a feminist archaeology and a gender archaeology (terms which are used somewhat interchangeably throughout this article). The authors make the intriguing comment that feminist perspectives have applicability beyond issues of gender, but this point is never expanded upon. With this idea, as with many others, readers are left to draw their own conclusions. This might be the purpose of an introduction, and as such this article succeeds, though it also makes somewhat unsatisfying reading on its own. WDG

*sociopolitics of archaeology/epistemology/feminist critique*

4. ARSENAULT, DANIEL 1991. The representation of women in Moche iconography. In *The Archaeology of Gender: Proceedings of the Twenty-Second Annual Conference of the Archaeological Association of the University of Calgary,* edited by Dale Walde and Noreen D. Willows, 313-326. Archaeological Association, The University of Calgary, Calgary.

This study, which the author refers to as a contextual analysis, is specifically addressed toward Moche figures of women, discussing the attributes by which they are identified, their activities, and their position in relation to figures of men, gods, and animals. Arsenault aims to use female representation in art as a starting point for an analysis of gender relations in Moche society. In previous studies, researchers have concluded that the position of women in Moche society was inferior to that of men, but Arsenault suggests that the evidence needs to be re-evaluated.

## *A Gendered Past*

Images have been identified by iconologists as female in several ways. The presence of female genitalia, long braided hair, certain styles of clothing, and spindle whorls are all thought to indicate women, but these characteristics do not always occur together, and some have been shown to co-occur with male characteristics. Sometimes women are identified by the absence of attributes that are usually assumed to be male. Large figures associated with small ones are defined as mother and child. Couples involved in erotic activities are assumed to be heterosexual, and the ones with visible genitals support this assumption. Arsenault notes that the reliability of gender identification increases with the number of available criteria.

In his discussion of female activities, Arsenault follows Anne Marie Hocquenghem in dividing Moche cosmology into three worlds: the living, the ancestors, and the supernatural. Depictions of the world of the living include the images of mothers and children, weaving scenes, and food preparation. Religious scenes include women copulating with gods, wearing the paraphernalia of shamans, and performing burial activities. Skeleton-like figures are placed in the world of the ancestors. Some have penises but none have female genitals. Male skeletons are said to occupy central, active positions while female skeletons are in peripheral locations with children. Some scenes show skeletons involved in sexual activities with each other or with apparently living women. In the world of the supernatural, women appear in scenes with gods and monsters, or as supernatural characters themselves.

Arsenault makes several general observations. At any given period, female images are less numerous and less elaborate than male images. In the early phases, women only appear copulating or with children, and in the later phases, become involved in religious activities and supernatural scenes. The author concludes that the iconography presents a male standpoint, that it was primarily controlled by men with important religious and political statuses and used to promote their interests, but that at some point a minority of women gained access to the production of images and were able to present themselves in more active and important ways. However, it is not the interests of all women that were promoted, but only those of religious specialists such as shamans and priestesses who had allied themselves with the male religious elite.

The primary difficulty with Arsenault's argument is the projection of categories onto the past, for instance in identifying gender. Defining as female any adult carrying a child rests on a division of labor by gender that cannot be taken for granted. Similarly, it is stated that women are absent from battle scenes, but battling figures are called men because they carry weapons, so the interpretation of gender roles depends upon a previous assumption of those roles. The same problem arises in classifying scenes as religious or not. The suggestion that women become involved in religious (important) activities in the third iconographic phase depends upon child care and copulation being secular and unimportant. Without this assumption, all that can be said is that women are presented in a greater variety of activities through time.

An important point is that women may have different statuses and conflicting interests. One cannot assume that a change in representations of women indicates a change in the status of women as a whole. This valid point should be applied to males as well, but unfortunately, images created by a male religious elite are defined as "male standpoint" and those created by a female religious elite are said to emphasize sacredness at the expense of gender.

Another strength is the author's understanding that images can affect, as well as represent, beliefs and social relationships. But this leads to thorny interpretive questions which Arsenault sometimes handles unevenly. For instance, who made the images? For the earlier period it is said that men created the images because most of the images are of men. In the later period a minority of women controlled their own iconography. Why the later female figures are controlled by women and the earlier ones by men is unclear; one could as easily say that women in both periods were emphasizing different aspects of their experience. The connection between social groups, power, and pot designers needs to be more carefully thought out, perhaps in a broader contextual analysis that questions the place of iconography in Moche society as well as considering other evidence of gender relations. SF

*iconography/ceramic analysis/contextual archaeology/representation, theory of/Moche/Andes/South America*

## Annotated References

5. ARWILL-NORDBLADH, ELISABETH 1989. Oscar Montelius and the liberation of women: An example of archaeology, ideology and the early Swedish women's movement. In *Approaches to Swedish Prehistory: A Spectrum of Problems and Perspectives in Contemporary Research,* edited by Thomas B. Larsson and Hans Lundmark, 131-142. British Archaeological Reports International Series 500.

In this article Arwill-Nordbladh examines the connections between the early Women's Movement in Sweden (and more generally in Europe) and the works of 19th century social theorists. She places the struggle to obtain the right to vote and legal independence from the juridical and economic power of husbands or fathers in the context of social and economic changes in Swedish society, and discusses the prominant role of the well-educated middle class in this struggle. Into this context she places two works by Oscar Montelius, arguably the most influential Swedish archaeologist of all time and one who was widely read in other countries as well: "How long has woman been considered the property of man?", published in 1898 and "The women's issue in Sweden," published in 1906. In these articles Montelius discussed the evolution of the unequal power relations between the sexes in prehistory and history, drawing on the work of John Lubbock as well as relying on his own method of typological seriation to classify and link different ethnographically and historically documented marriage customs. He also described the future evolution of these relations as he foresaw them—a society in which men and women were equal. He claimed that women were the intellectual and emotional equals of men when not subjected to cultural influences that prevented their full development, and backed up his ideas of an equal society with evidence for the evolution of women's position based on archaeology and his views of cultural evolution. He called for equal educational opportunities for men and women, for the right for women to vote, for employment in the state and church to be opened to women, for equal pay for equal work and for the right for women to be elected to parliament.

Arwill-Nordbladh places Montelius' work in both a social and personal context (his wife was the president of the leading suffragette society in Sweden) and correctly stresses the influential role that archaeologists and social anthropologists played in the social, legal and intellectual debate on the "women's issue" of the period. Perhaps more importantly, she demonstrates, for those who have forgotten it, the intense intellectual and theoretical interest that the question of women's roles engendered in the late 19th and early 20th century. In our zeal to tackle the problem with fresh insights and new theoretical paradigms, we are apt to dismiss or forget that we are not the first generation of archaeologists and anthropologists to address the topic, nor the first to use the venue of archaeology to argue for political and social changes in our own society.

Arwill-Nordbladh documents an interesting and enlightening period in the history of archaeology, anthropology and the feminist movement, and provides a valuable reference for anyone interested in the history of gender research. KJ

*feminist critique/history of archaeology/Sweden/Scandinavia/Europe*


6. BAHN, PAUL G. 1986. No sex please, we're Aurignacians. *Rock Art Research* 3:99-105.

In this article, Bahn dispels the pseudo-scientific interpretation of certain Paleolithic carvings as representations of human vulvae. The history of this interpretation is explored for the block carvings of the Vezere Valley sites of southwest France, beginning with Breuil's work in the early part of this century and ending with more recent work. Breuil's original subjective inference of triangular shapes as representations of vulvae has been persistently recycled. Thus, an original *a priori* assumption has been elevated to explanation (i.e., tautology). Examples of alternative interpretations based on ethnographic analogy or inferences of similarity with other natural, animal, or human elements are discussed. However, these interpretations suffer similar problems in that they are unsubstantiated assumptions.

Bahn rightly points out the limitations of the sample size of representations in the Paleolithic record, the difficulty in using designs from one period of the Paleolithic to generalize about motifs throughout the entire Paleolithic, and the need for a more rigorous descriptive classification system. However, he does not explore the more pressing need for a systematic theory of representation and the testing of hypotheses using independent data sources. Bahn brings us to the level of description but goes no further. JDB

*Paleolithic/Europe/iconography/France/Breuil, Henri/rock art/representation, theory of/cave art*


7. BARRETT, JOHN C. 1989. Food, gender and metal: Questions of social reproduction. In *The Bronze Age-Iron Age Transition in Europe: Aspects of Continuity and Change in European Societies, c. 1200 to 500 BC,* edited by Marie Louise Stig Sorensen and Roger Thomas, 304-320. British Archaeological Reports International Series 483(ii).

Barrett evaluates transformations in the nature of social reproduction among the peoples inhabiting late Bronze Age communities in southern Britain during the mid-first millennium BC. He adopts a contextual interpretive perspective in this case study to examine how humans are themselves active agents in the construction and reproduction of their social systems. The purpose of his analysis is to break with the idea that cycles of material production, circulation through various types of exchange, and consumption are always driven by growing demands of consumption. Drawing on Giddens' structuration theory, he argues that these materialist cycles are better viewed as the products of "fields of discourse" between people which reproduce social relations and depend on the mobilization of symbols of domination. He proposes "The transformation of the products of one field of reproduction to the resources of another may always be a point of conflict because different authorities may be potentially reproduced by each field" (p. 309). The fields of discourse that structured gender relations among the populations inhabiting the Deverel-Rimbury communities of the chalk downland are Barrett's principle concern. It is implicit in Barrett's argument that the comprehension of gender relations in the past is predicated upon understanding the general process of social reproduction.

Barrett examines bronze working to evaluate if, and how, gendered divisions of labor in agricultural production and food preparation (set in two different fields of discourse) were dominated by the hegemony of a single authority. He situates the archaeological materials within specific fields of discourse pertaining to the cycles of agricultural production, human biological reproduction, and the transformation of agricultural products to food for human consumption. In doing this, Barrett argues that if a researcher separates each of these cycles for analysis, then materials composing the archaeological record cannot be given a single meaning, and that it is "meaningless" to combine agricultural products (i.e., grain), and food remains (i.e., bone), in a "false synthesis" of a community's economy (p. 310). Such synthesis prevents the understanding of material culture as the medium of social discourse and obscures our ability to perceive the code of the reproduction and transformation of historical knowledge which is preserved in the archaeological record.

Barrett conducts his analysis of metal working by isolating classes of artifacts, which he believes were initially circulated as symbols secondary to statuses reproduced by the discourse of age and gender. He assumes ornaments, personal tools, and weaponry are such items of material culture. Of these classes, weapons (i.e., swords) are most commonly found in late Bronze Age sites in southern Britain. Because the distribution of swords is heterogeneous, Barrett argues that they represent a material code through which rank was structured within the particular group that maintained their possession and used these artifacts as gifts or the essential symbolic element in ritual practices. Assuming swords "are the cultural resources controlled by the domination of another *field of discourse*," he examines other items, including axes, sickles, knives, awls, gouges, and leather cutting implements "which intervened in these other *fields*" (p. 315, emphasis original). Since all of these tools are bronze, Barrett suggests they may have been produced through the same relations of production that condition the manufacture of axes. Because axes and the tools of production would have been used in the transformation of natural resources and in the structuring of agricultural labor, Barrett further presumes that these tools, like swords, may have carried great symbolic value in these "other fields of discourse" underlying social reproduction. In his concluding comments, he tentatively links the symbolic meaning of tools of production with concepts of fertility (p. 317). Finally, he contends that the heterogeneous distribution of axes, including the deposition of large caches and the recovery of unfinished artifacts indicates that manufacture consumed much of the available supply of bronze. Some axes may have circulated as part of the local cycle of gift exchange (p. 315).

Given this framework of socially constructed meanings, symbols of domination, and human agency, Barrett suggests the delayed replacement of bronze by iron in southern Britain may simply be a function of the decline in the overall supply of bronze and the increase in knowledge of iron working, as opposed to some inherent value of iron itself. Thus he rejects the characterization of the transition from bronze to iron metallurgy as a political function of local elites attempting to fulfill their ritual and gift obligations. In support, he offers the observation that local supplies and the recycling of iron are similar in both the late Bronze and early Iron Ages in the region. Barrett also argues that because production is immediately social and therefore enters a field of discourse, artifacts and facilities associated with the production of artifacts commonly associated with high status do not themselves indicate a high status site.

This article is notable for its attempt to demonstrate how humans may be active agents in the transformation of their social relations. Barrett's bold application of Giddens' structuration theory for the interpretation of cultural assemblages is of interest to archaeologists for its conceptualization of artifacts, architecture, and settlement as material codes of discourse through which social relations were negotiated, reproduced, and transformed. He also challenges researchers to evaluate how gendered divisions of production and reproduction may become politically dominated by the hegemony of a solitary authority. Unfortunately, a number of methodological shortcomings cast doubt on both the validity of his interpretations and the appropriateness of his use of a contextual approach to operationalize structuration theory. Throughout this analysis, he relies on a poorly defined (and unreferenced) contextual approach for guiding archaeological interpretation, which results in his assuming that which he should be evaluating. Working from the premises "that any interest in the reproduction of (agrarian) society must commence with an understanding of the cycles of agricultural reproduction, human biological reproduction, and the transformation of agricultural products to food" and "archaeological materials can not have a single meaning" (p. 310), Barrett believes bronze axes — and by projection, all other bronze tools — pertain to more than just the field of discourse of production. He suggests these implements — like swords — also serve as symbols of fertility, which may have been treated as potential resources to secure the authority of political demands (see p. 317), without providing independent lines of evidence or the bridging arguments needed to support these interpretations. It should be noted that Barrett refutes the claims of objectivity made by many archaeologists who assume "the material conditions and the social system have a simultaneous existence prior to the actions of their human inhabitants" (p. 304). Barrett's methodology, however, imposes his own constructed meanings of archaeological materials on the past, thereby fulfilling his understanding of how the medium of discourse is reproduced and transformed. As a consequence, questions of social reproduction and the structure of gender relations in the past remain inadequately addressed. KFA

*postprocessualism/structuration theory/symbolism/contextual archaeology/metallurgy/Bronze Age/Great Britain/Europe*

8. BARRETT, JOHN C. 1988. Fields of discourse: Reconstituting a social archaeology. *Critique of Anthropology* 7(3):5-16.

    Barrett offers a reconsideration of the use of archaeological evidence, arguing that it should not be treated "as a *record of* past events and processes but as *evidence for* particular social practices" (p. 6). This represents a break both with functionalism and with approaches advocating an "archaeology of meaning." Based on Gidden's (1979, 1981) theory of structuration, he argues that social practices or the structuring of relationships should be the object of study: "Archaeology is the empirical examination of material evidence to discover how such practices were maintained within particular material conditions" (p. 9). Such a study of social practices requires heuristic devices which allow "us to think about the way time-space may have been occupied by such practices" (p. 11). Barrett defines one such device as the "field of discourse." "The *field* is an area in time-space occupied by virtue of the practice of a particular discourse.... and contain material conditions which contribute towards the structuring of practice. Archaeological evidence is the residue of these various material conditions" (ibid.). It has four analytical components: temporal frequency, spatial extent, cultural resources, and the transformations which take place in the latter as the field is reproduced. He sees the analytical strength of the field of discourse as threefold: "it is concerned with human relationships not material entities; time-space is fundamental to its definition; and it refuses single units of material residues fixed historical meaning" (ibid.).

    As an example, he considers his field of discourse approach in the context of an archaeology of gender. If gender is considered as structured through various types of discourse, then the archaeological study of gender does not depend upon methodological advancements to make visible gender activities in the archaeological record. Rather, "[i]t must be founded instead upon the critical realisation that gender relations and conflicts *are* historical forces" and "are always structured by control over certain human and material resources" (p. 13). EAB

*structuration theory/epistemology*

*References cited*
Giddens, A. 1979. *Central Problems in Social Theory*. MacMillan, London.

Giddens, A. 1981. *A Contemporary Critique of Historical Materialism*. MacMillan, London.

9. BARSTOW, ANN 1978. The uses of archaeology for women's history: James Mellaart's work on the Neolithic Goddess at Çatal Hüyük. *Feminist Studies* 4(3):7-17.

    Barstow argues that James Mellaart's work at Çatal Hüyük provides important evidence for a form of social organization in which women controlled most positions of authority and the traditional loci of male authority were absent or unvalued, and that this evidence has been systematically ignored by archaeologists. The materials at Çatal Hüyük are discussed, with emphasis on Mellaart's suggestions regarding the status of women at the site and their role in early religious practice. Barstow notes that she is not suggesting that matriarchies existed, but is describing a system where the relations between men and women need not be understood in terms of dominance and subordination. Despite this apparent equality, however, she suggests that women were responsible for the economic advances that made sedentism and food production possible, and for the creation of religion as well. She points out that "traditional" scholars have been slow to accept Mellaart's work, and argues that this is because most western religious thought is part of an ideology that oppresses women, embodied in western theologies that accept an equation between female power and the demonic. Barstow concludes that monotheistic western religions, by their "refusal to incorporate female spiritual experience...no longer speak to many women." She describes the Neolithic female/goddess representations as conveying "a sense of dignity and great strength," and describes her own feelings when seeing the Çatal Hüyük material for the first time. We cannot go back to the Goddess, she writes, but must create a new set of images and symbols from the autonomous experiences and values of women as an alternative to the male-dominated religions and cultural symbology of the western world.

Barstow's essay is premised on a series of assumptions regarding the role and status of women based on Mellaart's work. Unfortunately, many of the linking arguments necessary to support her inferences are missing, as is a discussion of possible alternatives to the interpretation offered. The notion that all women share a common set of experiences and values, implied and assumed by her argument, has been criticized by many feminist scholars as simplistic. Finally, Barstow's conclusions assume that agriculture, domestication of animals, weaving, and pottery making are activities exclusively associated with women — assumptions that other authors (e.g., #23) suggest are androcentric and ethnocentric when applied in other contexts. AWB

*Near East/Goddess/Neolithic/Mellaart, James/agriculture/agricultural origins/Çatal Hüyük/Turkey*

10. BENDER, BARBARA 1987. The roots of inequality. In *Domination and Resistance*, edited by Michael Rowlands, Christopher Tilley and Daniel Miller 83-95. Cambridge University Press, Cambridge.

Tracing the roots of social inequality to farming societies is ultimately a reification of artificial gender divisions in our own society, according to Bender. To understand the rise of social inequality we must look back further, to Upper Paleolithic societies.

Social complexity is associated with farming and husbandry in traditional approaches, Bender argues, because the labor returns required are often based on long-term investment rather than short-term gain. One generation thus "feeds" off a previous one, creating generational debts that may lead to senior/junior asymmetries. Asymmetries in foraging societies, however, are often seen not as marking "complexity" but "differentiation." Because seniors gain status due to their knowledge and experience, asymmetries are ephemeral since juniors may progress through the ranks to become senior in their turn. Bender points out, however, that all of the actors in this scenario are males—junior males advance to become high-status senior males. Half the population is ignored in such constructs. By "naturalizing" divisions seen in foraging societies in terms of familiar subsistence and technological strategies, we rationalize and legitimize distinctions within our own society rather than accounting for those in another.

Bender summarizes previous approaches to the Upper Paleolithic of southwest France and northwest Spain, concluding all are inadequate because each is premised on flawed "techno-environmental" paradigms. She points out that most of the "art" recovered from the Upper Paleolithic comes from only a few sites, and suggests that these sites may have been important in "naturalizing" an arbitrary division of labor, whereby men's control over social reproduction subsumes women's control over biological reproduction. Bender asserts that there is a "strong possibility" (p. 91) that these secret places were used to initiate young men, with the "capture" of depicted animals ultimtely linked to the "capture" of hunting as a male enterprise.

While both of Bender's main points are intriguing and worthy of note, they seem contradictory within the context of a single essay. Having argued that gender divisions are not natural but artificial, she then proceeds to uncritically project our own artificial constructs (male as hunter, male as agent of change wresting power from women) into Paleolithic Cantabria. While her interpretations of the Cantabrian data are a valuable exercise in structural-Marxist analysis, they depend upon assumptions regarding the universal roles of men and women rejected earlier in her own essay. AWB

*Paleolithic/Marxism/Spain/France*

11. BENDER, SUSAN J. 1991. Towards a history of women in northeastern U. S. archaeology. In *The Archaeology of Gender: Proceedings of the Twenty-Second Annual Conference of the Archaeological Association of the University of Calgary,* edited by Dale Walde and Noreen D. Willows, 211-216. Archaeological Association, The University of Calgary, Calgary.

Bender is interested in patterns in the professional development of women in archaeology in the Northeast. She begins with the thesis that "fieldwork has posed an historical barrier to women's professional advancement in archaeology" (p. 211). Within the frame of this idea, Bender then explores parallels in the careers of three prominent Northeastern women archaeologists: Mary Butler, Marian White, and Dena Dincauze. Their careers overlap to span a period from 1935 to the present.

First, Bender illustrates how fieldwork presented a barrier to women in the Northeast prior to the 1960s. The atmosphere of field research in the region excluded women not because they were physically unable (although the "expedition mentality" of fieldwork, which was believed to be difficult for women, was often cited as an excuse), but because the presence of women was felt by those in control to undermine the cooperative work atmosphere of all-male crews and to upset the status quo. Bad language, interest in sex, and a propensity for one male field director "to dig in his underwear" (p. 215) are among the factors cited by "informants" to have warranted against hiring women on field crews. Bender explores this milieu "not as a form of polemic, but as a means of coming to understand the context in which pioneering women archaeologists worked" (p. 213).

The author then notes a number of interesting parallels in the careers of the archaeologists examined. Butler, White, and Dincauze all attended undergraduate academic institutions in the Northeast known for educating women. This region historically supported women's higher education, and discrimination against women may have been lessened by the academic traditions that promoted women's equality. The three also undertook graduate work in the Northeast (White, in the Midwest proper, at the University of Michigan). All at some point in their careers gained support either from other professional women or from women's institutions. In addition, the three obtained necessary field training in other regions, due to barriers against for women in fieldwork in the Northeast. After overcoming this obstacle, each then went on to develop distinguished professional careers in Northeastern archaeology. Strikingly, each focused on "backyard archaeology," where fieldwork centered around an area near their families and homes.

Bender's analysis is short but very insightful and interesting. It is intriguing to compare the history of women in Northeastern archaeology with that of other regions. NSG-F

*United States, Northeast/history of archaeology/sociopolitics of archaeology*


12. BERTELSON, REIDAR, ARNVID LILLEHAMMER, AND JENNY-RITA NAESS (editors) 1987. *Were They All Men? An Examination of Sex Roles in Prehistoric Society.* Arkeologist Museum i Stavanger, Stavanger, Norway.

This volume is the result of a workshop held at Utstein Kloster, near Stavanger, Norway, in 1979. The workshop concentrated on the problems involved in identifying individuals in prehistory. As shown by the title of the volume (also the title of the workshop), it was directly concerned with feminism, androcentric bias in archaeology, and gender roles in prehistory. It is therefore one of the earliest recent efforts to address the topic of gender in and through archaeology, preceding expressions of interest in the topic in North America by at least five years. Although the original intent was to publish the papers presented, (the final versions of the papers were submitted for publication in 1980), it took almost six years to raise funds for publication. Three papers presented at the workshop were published elsewhere in the interim; eight others are published in this volume. Seven of the following eight are annotated in this bibliography.

Inger Haugen provides a short summary of aspects of the debate on gender in social anthropology and the utility of the household as an analytical concept in studying division of labor and redistribution. While the paper focuses on ethnographic analysis, the theory and methodology may be of interest to archaeologists. Synnøve Vinsrygg discusses the division of labor by sex in hunting and gathering societies, and Grete Lillehammer provides comments on Vinsrygg's paper. Gro Mandt discusses symbolic representations of women and of female fertility in Scandinavian Bronze Age rock art. Trond Løken correlates variables of the form and size of Norwegian Iron Age grave monuments with the grave goods and draws from this data

## Annotated References

evidence of gender-based differences in status and mortuary treatment. Liv Helga Dommasnes addresses problems similar to those Løken examines, but focuses more on the number and chronological and spatial distribution of male and female graves as evidence for variation in the roles and rank of women. Grete Lillehammer examines the theoretical underpinnings of mortuary analysis, and the place of the individual and of the society in mortuary ritual. Her article may be of interest to archaeologists, but while she treats the sex of the deceased as a variable in mortuary analysis, she does not address questions of gender. It is therefore the only work in the volume that was not annotated for inclusion in this bibliography. Finally, Anne Stalsberg examines grave finds of Scandinavian Viking ornaments from Russia as evidence of the presence and role of women in Viking settlements in the area.

Critical discussion of the articles is provided individually. It is worth reiterating that the work as a whole is important for its early attention to these issues. Had it been published and circulated as originally planned in 1980, it might well have engendered interest in the topic several years before Conkey and Spector's call to arms in 1984. KJ

*Scandinavia/Norway/individual in prehistory/division of labor/mortuary analysis/feminist critique/rock art/ iconography*

13. BIAGGI, CRISTINA 1986. The significance of the nudity, obesity and sexuality of the Maltese Goddess Figures. In *Archaeology and Fertility Cult in the Ancient Mediterranean: Papers presented at the First International Conference on Archaeology of the Ancient Mediterranean,* edited by A. Bonanno, 131-140. B.R. Grüner Publishing Co., Amsterdam.

This short paper, part of a conference volume on archaeology of the ancient Mediterranean, might be thought relevant to a list of publications on gender because it belongs to the school of "Great Goddess" interpretations of prehistoric religions in the Mediterranean and elsewhere in Europe. In this case, late Neolithic temple statues in Malta are interpreted as representing Great Goddess worship in a female-centered culture guided by priestesses.

The paper briefly examines characteristics of a group of 30 anthropomorphic sculptures found in Maltese temples dating from the late Neolithic (3000-2500 BC). The author begins with the assumption that the figures represent a local development on a universal theme of Great Goddess cults thought to originate in the Paleolithic. The Great Goddess hypothesis, based on the argument that a single universal philosophical idea dominated religious practices for tens of thousands of years, appears particularly weak in this specific context, since the figures, described as sharing a graceful, stylized obesity and a *lack* of sexual traits, are not clearly female and have in fact been argued by some to represent either male priests or eunuchs. Biaggi's interpretation of these sexless figures as representations of the Goddess rests on her assumption that obesity is associated with female fertility and that ochre, used to paint the figures, is "the color of the Goddess." Though she argues that there is a precedent for "sexless" goddess figurines in unspecified Paleolithic and early Neolithic female figures, she then goes on to describe the lack of sexual characteristics in the Late Neolithic Maltese figures as the result of "a process of evolution from figures whose power as sacred images lay in well defined sexual characteristics, to figures whose power lay in their opulence...The Maltese figures seem to embody cosmic power and overflowing fullness on a superhuman scale which is beyond dualism, beyond sex" (p. 137). Biaggi does not discuss why figures designed to transcend sex are to be usefully interpreted within the Great Goddess scheme. Generally, the paper underscores some of the difficulties of using the very general Great Goddess scenario unreservedly as a basis for interpreting local developments. LEF

*Goddess/figurines/Malta/Neolithic/Mediterranean/representation, theory of*

14. BINFORD, SALLY R. 1982. Are goddesses and matriarchies merely figments of feminist imagination? In *The Politics of Women's Spirituality: Essays on the Rise of Spiritual Power within the Feminist Movement,* edited by Charlene Spretnak, 541-549. Anchor Books, Garden City, New York.

This short paper, previously published in 1979 in both *Human Behavior* (May) and *Woman Spirit* 6(2), addresses four popular "Goddess" movement claims from an anthropological and archaeological (scientific) viewpoint. Binford's examination of the fourth claim ("Prehistoric art reveals the existence of the worship of the Mother Goddess and documents the former power of women") is the only one involving archaeological evidence. After sarcastically inquiring whether *Playboy's* art implies a matriarchal cultural system, Binford explains that "the method of assigning one's own meaning to certain symbols and then tracing them over broad geographic areas and through tens of thousands of years of cultural change is, to put it mildly, not a reliable means of reconstructing the past" (p. 547). A brief but outraged response by Merlin Stone states that Binford's "discussion about whether or not ancient Goddess worship existed...is much like inviting us into a discussion of whether or not World War II actually occurred" (p. 550). Stone goes on to state that Binford has chosen to "blind herself to the evidence of *seven thousand* years of artifacts...and the *three thousand* years of historical (i.e., written) material...as described by archaeologists" including "those listed in the *ten pages* of bibliography" of Stone's recent book. Another response by Charlene Spretnak, the volume editor, does not address the archaeological material except to charge Binford with "patriarchal attitudes...ignoring the decades of research by classicists and archaeologists" (p. 557). A counter-response by Binford discusses feminist politics and her view of "what a study of the past can teach us" without specific reference to archaeological data (p. 559).

These impassioned pieces would be most useful to assign for an undergraduate class, especially one dealing with representational art, or to better understand popular conceptions of archaeology or "cult" archaeology. SLD

*Europe/Paleolithic/Venus figurines/figurines/representation, theory of/Goddess/iconography*


15. BOARDMAN, JOHN 1991. The naked truth. *Oxford Journal of Archaeology* 10(1):119-121.

This short article summarizes the acrimonious debate concerning "the sex of the young person handling the peplos on the east frieze of the Parthenon" (p. 119). Boardman previously argued that the relief represents a girl, and that "the contours of her bottom" support his claim. In this article, after recapitulating the argument, he furthers his assertion by reference to the individual's clothing and the statement that "nudity for children...was quite acceptable in classical Greece" (p. 120). He ends by implying that the attack on his earlier work is based in the other author's prudish ethnocentrism.

Although Boardman admits that "appeal to the contours of her bottom...is not the type of argument that can be 'proved,'" in the next paragraph he argues that "the anatomical arguments...are the most objective" (p. 119). Regardless of the sex of the figure, or the validity of his other arguments, Boardman's ideas of the shape of a female vs. male buttock are probably rather subjective. This article (like many others in this bibliography) highlights the naive approach typically taken towards the representation of sex (or more accurately, gender) in the archaeological record, and the difficulties inhibiting an understanding of past gender roles. SLD

*Greece/Mediterranean/classical archaeology/representation, theory of/Parthenon*


16. BOLEN, KATHLEEN 1992. Prehistoric construction of mothering. In *Exploring Gender through Archaeology: Selected Papers from the 1991 Boone Conference,* edited by Cheryl Claassen, 49-62. Prehistory Press, Madison.

Contemporary western society views child-bearing and child-rearing, mothering, as limiting activities which hinder a woman's participation in wider society. Bolen challenges this view by breaking mothering into two components--biological and social. She suggests that the limiting social aspects of mothering are cultural constructions that have evolved fairly recently in western history.

Bolen suggests that mothering activities--parenting--cross-cut gender and age and do not require a bipolar gender construction. Ethnographic studies indicate that the social components of mothering are organized in a variety of ways and may have been so in the prehistoric past. Child-care activities are performed by siblings, grandparents, specialists, and fathers. Ways of organizing child-care activities which involve people other than the biological mother may have minimized social limitations.

This article does not provide ways to identify the organization of mothering activities in the prehistoric past. What it does do, however, is question current configurations of social relations as models to be used to interpret past societies. KMM

*ethnographic analogy/mothering/western society, contemporary/children/division of labor*


17. BOLEN, KATHLEEN M. 1991. Changing gender roles at the hunter-gatherer transition to farming. In *The Archaeology of Gender: Proceedings from the Twenty-Second Annual Conference of the Archaeological Association of the University of Calgary,* edited by Dale Walde and Noreen D. Willows, 400-405. Archaeological Association, The University of Calgary, Calgary.

In this paper, Bolen explores ideas about gender with reference to the development of food production in Central Europe. Her main point is that gender relations, in organizing social relationships, play a central and dynamic role in creating culture and bringing about cultural change. Bolen briefly summarizes archaeological manifestations of gender during the Linear Pottery period of central Europe. She draws on data from mortuary and domestic contexts, subsistence, and (indirectly) studies of prehistoric decision-making. Her analysis leads to a consideration of the division of labor, and she emphasizes the importance of women during the Mesolithic/Neolithic transition, especially in terms of their role in the development of agriculture. She does not, however, draw on concrete data from this region to detail the specific nature of these roles. Instead, this case is used as a launching point for a discussion of gender as a dynamic social process.

The strength of this paper lies in its self-conscious use of the term "gender," and its whole-hearted treatment of gender as a dynamic cultural construction. Bolen is careful to point out that gender conceptions are not coterminous with sex, and that concepts of "women" and "men" are not easily transported to cultural contexts beyond our own. The application of these abstract ideas about gender to the case of the Mesolithic/Neolithic transition is promising but quite vague; it is not yet fully developed or demonstrated in this short discussion. NSG-F

*Europe/Mesolithic/Neolithic/Linear Pottery period/gatherer-hunters/agriculture/agricultural origins/division of labor*


18. BOYE, L., B. DRAIBY, K. HVENEGAARD-LASSEN, AND V. ODEGAARD, translated by S. HOLTEN-DALL 1984. Towards an archaeology of women. *Archaeological Review from Cambridge* 3(1):82-85.

This short, polemical article considers why the study of women has not been taken up to a greater degree within the field of archaeology. The primary obstacle to this research is said to be our conception of women: "The concept of Woman which is held by our Capitalist, Bourgeois society is as obstructive to research as any other form of ethnocentrism" (p. 82), for it is the separation of production and reproduction under capitalism which has led to the equation of women with a devalued domestic sphere. The authors assert that women in the past have been involved in primary productive processes, and describe various androcentric interpretations which have deprived women of such recognition.

The authors also note that there has been growing interest of late in issues of gender and women's history, and wonder why archaeology in particular has lagged behind other disciplines. They suggest that "the fragmentary character of the archaeological source material may be the reason why historians, anthropologists and ethnographers are the ones who raised the question of women's position and role in prehistory, and not archaeologists" (p. 83). This work on women's issues and history is said to have taken two primary forms: the biological/physiological approach, on which the authors do not comment further, and the evolutionary approach, which seeks to document the origins of male dominance. This later approach, the search for "Womans Historic Defeat" [sic], is said to have begun with the work of Engels, whose origin theories are then summarized. The authors assert that Engels was so "deeply rooted in the norms of the Victorian Bourgeoisie" that he didn't see women as producers, and thus his linkage of fully developed patriarchy with private property needs to be reexamined (p. 84). In such a re-evaluation, the organization of production and reproduction should be approached as a coherent whole.

This article squeezes a great number of thought-provoking ideas into three pages. Unfortunately, the rhetoric, perhaps born of frustration and anger, does occasionally obstruct the arguments being advanced. The targets of their criticisms often appear over-simplified, and their critiques over-generalized. Thus, the authors focus on "Woman" as a universalist category which ignores sociocultural contexts, and portray the discipline of archaeology as a monolith of androcentrism (e.g., they seem to feel that the faulty reasoning equating rich female graves with high status husbands has gone unquestioned by all other archaeologists [p.83]). Even in 1984 there was a greater diversity of opinions within archaeology than they represent. However, the article does ask some important questions which are deserving of attention. WDG

*Marxism/capitalism/sociopolitics of archaeology/feminist critique/Victorian ideology*

19. BRASHLER, JANET G. 1991. When daddy was a shanty boy: The role of gender in the organization of the logging industry in highland West Virginia. *Historical Archaeology* 25:54-68.

Focusing on late nineteenth and early twentieth century logging camps in the Monongahela National Forest, Brashler examines the "relationship between gender, family organization, and economic and subsistence strategies in the context of industrialization in rural West Virginia" (p. 54). Logging camps are commonly assumed to have been occupied exclusively by men. Brashler shows that women and children were also present. Using oral history, documents, photographs, and surface survey, she concludes that in the early twentieth century there were at least three types of logging communities in the Monongahela: a mill town, a company family logging camp, and a series of small shanty camps. This differs from the typical model depicting only two types of communities: logging camps and mill towns. Brashler believes evidence is clear for the presence of women and children in addition to men at the mill town and logging camps studied, but she is not sure whether they were present in the shanty camps.

Brashler succeeds in making this article more than a simple addition of women to the logging camps. Rather, gender is a starting point from which to discuss the organization of logging camps and the differences between various types of logging communities. She also does a thorough job of detailing the research needed to better understand late nineteenth and early twentieth century logging communities. DLG

*historical archaeology/West Virginia/lUnited States, Southeast/logging camps/industrialization*

20. BRIDGES, PATRICIA S. 1989. Changes in activities with the shift to agriculture in the southeastern United States. *Current Anthropology* 30:385-394.

In this article Bridges employs data on bone morphology to explore changes in work loads and sexual division of labor during the transition from Archaic hunting and gathering (and horticulture) to Mississippian agriculture in the southeastern U.S. Bridges uses osteological samples from Middle/Late Archaic (6000-4000/4000-1000 BC) and Mature Mississippian (AD 1200-1500) sites in the Middle Tennessee River region of northwestern Alabama. She discusses recent research indicating that the adoption of large-scale agriculture involves greater exertion, evident in remodeling of the bone from increased strain. Bridges controls for age related and genetic differences between her samples. Measurements of long-bone lengths, diaphyseal diameters and circumferences, and computed axial tomography (CT) scanning were conducted to determine cross-sectional diaphyseal structure. This analysis resulted in the recognition of several patterns consistent with her two hypotheses: (1) overall, Mississippian agriculturists had thicker and stronger long bone diaphyses than Archaic people, indicating engagement in more strenuous activities, and (2) females apparently underwent more widespread diaphyseal remodeling than men, possibly indicating their greater role in agriculture and participation in more activities.

Bridges gives a well thought-out and supportable argument. She considers and controls for several other factors (such as disease, age and population genetics) that may affect her sample. Her logical arguments and their connection to a solid body of data are quite convincing. While the paper fulfills its goals, Bridges fails to consider the social implications of her argument. For instance, what effect could the changing role of women in agriculture have had on their social and political status? What does this study tell us about the role of women in the development of an agricultural way of life? While these questions are beyond the scope of the paper, they are not beyond its implications. JDB

*bone morphology/osteology/United States, Southeast/Alabama/Archaic period/Mississippian period/agriculture/agricultural origins/division of labor/gatherer-hunters*


21. BRIDGES, PATRICIA S. 1985. *Changes in Long Bone Structure with the Transition to Agriculture: Implications for Prehistoric Activities.* Ph.D. dissertation, Department of Anthropology, University of Michigan.

Assertions regarding changing divisions of labor are easier to make than assess. Rather than projecting historically observed divisions of labor into the past, Bridges uses these observations to frame a series of testable hypotheses regarding changes in long bone strength (resistance to compressive, bending, and torsional stresses) and cross-sectional shape across the shift from foraging to farming in the southeastern United States. These hypotheses are then assessed using skeletal series from Archaic and Mississippian populations from northwestern Alabama. Based on ethnohistoric descriptions, she predicted generally increased bone strength in the Mississippian period due to the rigors of habitual activities associated with agricultural economies, but also predicted that changes would be more marked for females, as women did the bulk of the agricultural labor, at least during the ethnohistoric period. Metric data and biomechanical calculations confirm her hypothesized changes, as well as suggesting intriguing changes in sexual dimorphism and bilateral asymmetries between the populations. While females showed overall greater increases in bone strength and mean diaphyseal dimensions for arms and legs combined, biomechanical estimates of leg strength increased disproportionately in males. Bridges suggests that this may be associated with greater demands placed on men by warfare or sport. Bridges' approach provides one example of the ways that multiple lines of evidence might be brought to bear in examining divisions of labor in past societies. AWB

*bone morphology/division of labor/osteology/United States, Southeast/Alabama/Archaic period/Mississippian period/agriculture/agricultural origins/gatherer-hunters*


22. BROMAN MORALES, VIVIAN, AND ROBERT J. BRAIDWOOD 1991. Shadows of doubt in identifying female images: A reply to Kehoe. *Antiquity* 65:914-915.

This is a brief reply to Kehoe's 1991 *Antiquity* article (#95), which questions whether a clay figurine recovered from the middle eastern Neolithic village of Sarab was indeed a female image. Broman Morales and Braidwood present a photograph of what does seem to be a figurine with breasts, commenting that if Kehoe had the final report from their project she might have reconsidered her statement. In addition they note that in the category of fragmentary images classified as breasts, ten "have, or did have, nipples clearly formed by a pellet of clay pressed onto the tip" (p. 914). Furthermore, they note that there are no holes for suspension in the figurine type illustrated, since Kehoe suggests that if the fragments were suspended from a string, the orientation of the figurine would be more phallic than feminine. Kehoe's brief comment on this reply, added to the end of the authors' remarks, states that the absence of a suspension device does render "other Sarab examples ambiguous compared to the best-preserved Dolní Vestonice carving and the Roman examples" (p. 915), but she still considers there to be great ambiguity in many figurines, including those from Sarab. SLD

*Iran/Neolithic/Venus figurines/figurines/Near East/Dolni Vestonice*

23. BRUHNS, KAREN OLSEN 1991. Sexual activities: Some thoughts on the sexual division of labor and archaeological interpretation. In *The Archaeology of Gender: Proceedings from the Twenty-Second Annual Conference of the Archaeological Association of the University of Calgary*, edited by Dale Walde and Noreen D. Willows, 420-429. Archaeological Association, The University of Calgary, Calgary.

Bruhns takes up the knotty problem of attributing gender to archaeological space, and discusses the shortcomings of simplistic associations between the distribution of particular items of material culture and of genders based on western preconceptions. A Minoan society reconstructed suspiciously like nineteenth century Europe serves as one example, but Bruhns is primarily concerned with such projections in the New World. She begins with a discussion of the metate, commonly characterized as a grinding slab on which women prepared corn meal. Bruhns notes that the metate was actually an all-purpose tool used by both genders, in a variety of different contexts, culinary and non-culinary. Simple assumptions regarding function of space based on the presence of a metate are meaningless, since metates had no single or simple function. Bruhns points out that this fact has been tacitly acknowledged by archaeologists finding metates in circumstances clearly outside domestic (hence women's) contexts, and thus reclassify the items as altars or thrones. Textile making is also commonly viewed as women's work, and Bruhns argues it cannot be simply attributed to one or another gender, but represents a complex task sequence in which various genders and age-groups participate. Bruhns adds that it is ethnocentric to presume women were the only Andean weavers, particularly since depictions of Moche weavers show figures she describes as male. Scenes of sexual activity show Moche women with long hair and distinctive dress, Bruhns states, and the absence of long hair and wrap dresses with pins means the figures must be male. It should be pointed out, however, that our culture is not unique in its possession of different representational tropes for scenes of sexual activity and industrial labor. But the larger point, that simplistic attributions of gender associations based on uncritical extensions of western sexual divisions of labor and space are unfounded and misleading, is clearly documented. Bruhns argues convincingly for the multidimensional roles of material culture, and for the complex interrelationship between gender roles, age roles, and the roles an artifact plays in daily life. AWB

*division of labor/representation, theory of/ethnographic analogy/Andes//Crete*


24. BRUMFIEL, ELIZABETH M. 1991. Weaving and cooking: Women's production in Aztec Mexico. In *Engendering Archaeology: Women and Prehistory*, edited by Joan M. Gero and Margaret W. Conkey, 224-251. Basil Blackwell, Cambridge, MA.

Brumfiel uses ethnohistoric documents as her starting point to discuss two important productive activities for women in Aztec Mexico: weaving and cooking. Although the documents indicate the productive activities in which women engaged, their utility is limited since they provide a static, oversimplified picture. Yet, as Brumfiel points out, household production was essential to population growth, agricultural intensification, and military success of the Aztec empire. To examine the role of women's labor in cloth production and food preparation, Brumfiel looks for archaeological evidence of these activities at three Late Postclassic communities with different levels of political organization in and around the Valley of Mexico, both before and after the Aztec conquest.

Brumfiel begins with weaving. Cloth played an important role outside the household, serving as tribute and used as a unit of currency in the market system. As clothing, it marked social status. Aztec rule should have increased the demand for cloth as tribute. Archaeological evidence for cloth production includes light spindle whorls for cotton and heavier ones for maguey. Contrary to Brumfiel's expectations, spindle whorl frequencies within the Valley of Mexico were lower after the Aztec conquest. Brumfiel explains this by arguing that cloth was more easily available through market exchange following Aztec conquest, and that female labor within the Valley of Mexico was redirected to intensive food production. Outside the Valley, cloth production increases dramatically, as predicted. Brumfiel then examines whether these increased demands on women's labor after Aztec dominance had any effect on how women organized cooking activities. The two artifacts examined are griddles, on which tortillas and special dried war provisions were made, and pots, in which sauces and atole were made. Ratios of pots to griddles in archaeological sites can therefore indicate not only what foods were being prepared, but can also be used to estimate the amount of time spent on food preparation. Pot foods are quick but not portable; griddle foods were more labor-intensive but highly portable. At the three sites under consideration, one shows little change from before to after Aztec rule, while the other two show clear decreases in the ratio of pots to griddles. Despite intensified tribute demands, at these two sites there seems to be a shift to more labor-intensive, but portable foods, which may reflect a more mobile labor force, with work carried out farther from home. This has interesting implications for change in household organization as well as for women's roles in such change. In contrast to ethnohistoric records, the archaeological evidence for women's production shows variability in both time and space.

Brumfiel avoids the common trap of imposing ethnohistoric evidence onto the past. The past Brumfiel depicts is dynamic. Although this article focuses on only two aspects of women's work, Brumfiel draws out their implications for other kinds of activities, as well as for household and state organization. This article illustrates how important domestic activities can be for understanding a broader social system (especially in looking at the effects of change on such a system). It is a bit sobering to reflect on whether such a study would have been possible without ethnohistoric documentation, however. The dynamics of the system would have been much less clear had Brumfiel not been able to attribute weaving and cooking to women. This may be daunting to archaeologists who lack ethnohistoric records, but this article still encourages careful examination of domestic production and its interrelationships with other aspects of the social and political system, where gender dynamics may be most accessible. TVZ

*Mexico/Aztecs/weaving/cooking/textiles/ceramic analysis/division of labor/subsistence/ethnohistory/ethnographic analogy*


25. BRUSH, KAREN A. 1988. Gender and mortuary analysis in Pagan Anglo-Saxon archaeology. *Archaeological Review from Cambridge* 7(1):76-89.

In this article, Brush examines the remains from the mixed cremation and inhumation cemetery at Spong Hill, Norfolk, England, to determine what can be learned of gender relations in fifth and sixth century pagan society. She argues that archaeologists often base their interpretations of the archaeological record on contemporary gender stereotypes, and that this is especially troublesome in mortuary analysis because of the "unhealthy dependence on grave goods to determine the sex of the deceased" and the fact that even the sexing of physical remains can be biased by preconceived ideas (p. 80). These admonitions are relevant for the inhumation burials at Spong Hill, where preservation was poor due to acidic soils.

In comparing the cremations and inhumations, Brush concludes that gender played a minor role in structuring the contents of the cremation burials but a major role in structuring those of the inhumations. She interprets this dichotomy as indicating that the act of cremation was seen as a gender- and sex-destroying process while inhumation preserved the individual's gender identity. A number of interpretations are put forth in order to explain the appearance, for a brief period, of the gender-marked inhumations within the larger cremation cemetery. These include the emergence of a social elite with external ties to other powerful groups, the coming of Christianity, and/or state formation. The disappearance of the inhumation ritual is explained by the acceptance of Christianity, and the removal of inhumation burials to a churchyard. Brush acknowledges in the conclusion that her interpretations are "interesting but speculative," and that more work in this area needs to be conducted.

Overall, Brush's article is a useful first step in the investigation of a very intriguing data set. She reaches reasonable conclusions, though the reasoning leading up to these interpretations seems a bit strained at times. For instance, the idea that the gender-preserving inhumations represent elite members of society is based on the premise that "among an elite group which held decision making powers for the community at large, gender is expected to be an important determinant of social role and power. Age and sex difference in such a group might be more rigidly defined in life than among less privileged individuals"(p. 85). However, it is not clear on what grounds this claim (that gender is a greater structuring element for elites than for commoners) is made. Also, it is not clear why, in this particular case, the vital gender of the elite should be carried into death. In similar fashion, many mortuary analyses assume too direct a link between the society as a whole and its mortuary practices. Most of Brush's interpretations are based on the premise that if the majority of the burials are not structured by gender (in their elements recoverable today), then the living society as a whole was not significantly structured by gender (pp. 76, 81). Assumptions must be made in constructing an archaeological interpretation; whenever possible, however, researchers should examine their hypotheses by other lines of evidence as well. This would be the best next step for the case at hand. WDG

*mortuary analysis/Anglo-Saxons/Great Britain/state formation*


26. BUCHANAN, KEITH 1963. The women of Angkor. *Eastern Horizon* 2(12):13-15.

Buchanan's essay in this popular magazine interprets the frequent use of the "feminine theme" in the bas-relief carvings at Angkor as reflecting features of Khmer society. In the Angkor carvings females are depicted as *devatas* (goddesses) and *apsaras* (dancing girls), and are viewed as indicative of the status of Khmer women. Khmer women, according to Buchanan had relatively high status which may have derived from an earlier matriarchal system; they held high administrative or commercial positions, and were celebrated for their wisdom in science and religion. The depiction of Khmer gods with goddesses and dancers in the Angkor carvings is suggested to be a direct reflection of the king's reality, i.e., a queen and numerous concubines/dancers. Succession to the throne was passed down also through the maternal side, he argues, and daughters of local nobility served as concubines to the king.

The carvings were executed over three centuries, during which time changes in styles of dress, ornamentation and hair were depicted. "These changes in feminine whims and...fashions" are not only distinctive but are an important basis for the subdivision by archaeologists of medieval Khmer history into its major art periods.

Although clearly intended for a general audience, this essay points to a rich body of data for research into questions of the meaning of female representational art in state-level societies and of the implications of gendered chronological periods. It also is an example of the uncritical interpretation of female representations, that is, as direct reflections of a past society. EAB

*Khmer/iconography/sculpture/Cambodia/Asia*


27. BUMSTED, M. PAMELA, JANE E. BOOKER, RAMON M. BARNES, THOMAS W. BOUTTON, GEORGE J. ARMELAGOS, JUAN CARLOS LERMAN, AND KLAUS BRENDEL 1990. Recognizing women in the archeological record. In *Powers of Observation: Alternative Views in Archaeology,* edited by Sarah M. Nelson and Alice B. Kehoe, 89-101. American Anthropological Association, Washington, D.C.

Bumsted et al. report on a stable carbon isotope analysis of bone from 51 adults from a prehistoric farming community in the midwestern United States. In an earlier study, these researchers found statistically significant differences between males and females in terms of carbon isotope composition of bone, although when the study was expanded, the results became less clear. They also found that, in samples from a population with a maize-based diet, carbon isotope ratios vary more among males than among females, although the average value is not much different between the sexes.

The researchers are interested in determining if and how diet differs by sex in this sample, as well as examining whether such differences relate to different nutritional levels. To explore these issues further, they analyze five female and four male skeletons for 13 chemical elements. They also analyze one bison and three antelope (all unsexable). They conclude that the only way to satisfactorily separate male human, female human, bison, and antelope into four discrete classes with a combination of carbon isotope values and elemental values. They point out, however, that not enough is known about male and female differences in bone chemistry to determine which differences are influenced by cultural dietary patterns and which reflect physiology. DLG

*stable isotope analysis/osteology/subsistence/mortuary analysis/agriculture/United States, Midwest*

# Annotated References

28. BURTT, FIONA 1987. "Man the Hunter": Gender bias in children's archaeology books. *Archaeological Review from Cambridge* 6(2):157-174.

This article examines 29 archaeology books written for children (listed in a separate bibliography at the end of the article) for evidence of gender bias. Potential uses of the past in legitimizing aspects of the present have been widely discussed in archaeology (Burtt cites Shanks and Tilley on the subject), but the greater susceptibility of children to such uses of the past deserves greater attention. Burtt notes that "children's archaeology books are, in effect, performing the classic ideological role of denying contradictions, naturalising the social order and representing sectional interests as universal" (p. 158). Burtt then goes on to document an astoundingly large number of examples from the children's books which illustrate how present gender inequalities are perpetuated.

Burtt documents many occurrences of sexist language (often prominent in the book title), and the marginalization of women in the accompanying illustrations. Messages of male=normal and female=deviant are projected to the children by the omission of women from the books' illustrations, such as in those depicting various stages of human evolution. Burtt claims that in her 29 book sample, "not one evolutionary table uses just females, mixed females and males, or even non-gender specific people"(p. 160). The omission of women from the illustrations and the over-emphasis on white males are not only gender-biased, but in some situations, demographically unreasonable. Burtt refers to one book in which a complete "stone age group" is pictured as consisting of thirteen men, one woman, and one child (p. 168). When women are pictured, they are usually placed within a domestic setting, in a subservient position in relation to the accompanying men (who are more often the topic of the accompanying text), and occasionally in the compromising position of a sexual object (pp. 160, 168). Burtt calculates actual percentages for a smaller set of seven books to support some of these assertions.

Another bias in these children's books can be found in the attribution of different values to female and male sex-linked activities. Hunting is generally glorified and gathering neglected (p. 167). Along with

the glorification of hunting, these books are said to naturalize aggression and violence as a positive factor of maleness (p. 169). Burtt is quite thorough in documenting gender bias in these books, and reminds us that they "will survive in print to be passively assimilated and added to children's mental store of 'facts'" (p. 165).

Although most of these books were written by non-archaeologists, Burtt argues that "they are valid archaeological texts and should be considered as such", and thereby subject to more vigorous critique by archaeologists (p. 172). Burtt also claims (citing Shanks and Tilley again) that simply correcting the biases is not enough; instead "the most unbiased way of presenting the past to children...would be to write a series of different interpretations, rather than looking for a unilinear past" (p. 172).

This article makes a number of important points and provides some noteworthy examples of gender bias in children's books. It's ironic, however, that after such a brilliant description of the problem, she only urges archaeologists to "examine more thoroughly" such works. She doesn't explicitly call for archaeologists to become more active in the production of archaeological books for children, either by writing or collaborating in the writing of new books. Her point on the susceptibility of children to gender bias (as the locus for the perpetuation of gender inequality) is well taken, and archaeologists should become more responsibly involved in education at all levels (on site, in museum exhibits, in the schools, and in the popular press). But her remedy of simply presenting children with different interpretations and letting them choose for themselves should be questioned. "Children do have critical faculties" (p. 172), but a goal of education is to further develop those critical faculties, and such abilities can only be learned through the critical comparison of competing ideas, not through the relativistic acceptance of a multitude of different interpretations.

This article is based on Burtt's 1987 undergraduate dissertation at Cambridge, and focuses primarily on English children's books. She notes that the McGraw-Hill Company and other American publishers drew up guidelines in 1974 for the use of non-sexist language and the equal treatment of both sexes in their books (a "recognition of inequality in textbooks [which] has yet to be officially realised by British publishers" [p. 171]). However, a similar study could profitably be made of American children's books dealing with archaeology and the past. For, although the biases are bound to be more subtle due to these guidelines, many may still be incorporated. WDG

*children's literature/education/discrimination/political uses of the past/gatherer-hunters*

29. CHABOT, NANCY JO 1988. The women of Jorvik. *Archaeological Review from Cambridge* 7(1):67-75.

This article is primarily a description of the Jorvik Viking Centre (J.V.C.) from the viewpoint of the visiting public. This innovative Heritage Centre in York, England, attempts to portray both archaeology and York's Viking past to the general public. Chabot wants to focus attention on centers such as the J.V.C. because their exhibits comprise one of the principal media for the presentation of archaeological interpretations to the British public (p. 67). However, she feels that along with such interpretations both gender bias and an inaccurate portrayal of archaeology are being conveyed.

Chabot describes the center in detail, including the ride in amusement-park style "time cars" through the reconstructed village. She also tries to uncover the messages put forth by the exhibit, with an eye towards how the past is used to naturalize or legitimate present sectional interests (after Leone, p. 73). She concludes that the Jorvik Viking Centre projects the equations: female=domestic, and Viking=men. She supports the latter point with the fact that the logo for the centre is a simplified Viking head, complete with mustache and helmet, and that two of the information panels discuss "Vikings" when it is clear that only males are meant. More convincingly, Chabot counts the depictions of females and males in the center, finding seven females and ten males depicted on the placards, and eight females and seventeen males depicted in the official guide. Within the exhibit itself, women figurines are marginalized, placed in the background, or within the houses. Also, all of the unexpected roles are given to men (the reconstruction includes one figurine placed on an outdoor toilet, and another which sits agonizing over a boil on his foot), while the women figurines are placed in more typical museum settings which attract much less attention.

The article ends with some considerations of the ideas conveyed to visitors to the J.V.C. about archaeological interpretations. Chabot claims that the artifacts are presented as proof for the reconstruction, as if archaeological interpretation were a straightforward, rather than a somewhat tenuous, affair. Chabot asserts that museum exhibits could avoid this misleading impression by either presenting alternative pasts constructed from the same data, or by including the visitor in the creation of the interpretations. Drawing on the writings of Shanks and Tilley, she envisions a museum where "the visitor creates the past along with the archaeologist...each visitor is just as much the active creator" (p. 74).

The gender imbalances described by Chabot do exist in the exhibit and should be corrected, but at times her critique seems to be stretching the issue. Her thoughts on the differing degrees of confidence within archaeological interpretations, and how this could possibly be conveyed to an audience to give a more accurate impression of the archaeological endeavor, are important. But her adoption of Shanks and Tilley's idea that the visitor take equal responsibility with the archaeologist for the archaeological reconstruction goes a step beyond simply illustrating the intricacies of archaeological interpretation. Undoubtedly this approach would create an interesting exhibit, and it should be attempted. However, it ignores the fact that, at some level, the public comes to such centers and museums to learn "informed views" on certain topics, and thus the "voice of the expert" can be banished only at the museum's peril. Chabot is right in looking for ways to enliven the visitor's experience and portray a more accurate picture of archaeological interpretation, but at the end of the trip the visitor will still want to know "the answer." And given the differing levels of interest, dedication, effort, training, goals, and ability among both museum visitors and professionals, such an answer should not be recreated each time by whoever happens to be present.

Throughout the paper, Chabot assumes a negative tone towards the Jorvik Viking Centre and its creators which is not explained. The phenomenal success of the center is hardly acknowledged (although she does mention that tourists stand in line for approximately four hours during high season for this fifteen minute ride). Chabot also does not give any consideration to what it is about this exhibit that makes it is so appealing to its visitors. Placing the J.V.C. within the larger context of the evolving nature of museums, and debates over how to balance entertainment with education, might have led to a more balanced perspective. Much as Disneyworld is said to have influenced the J.V.C., the J.V.C. is beginning to have an influence on more traditional museums (such as Canada's Museum of Civilization). The gender inequalities identified in the J.V.C. need to be addressed, but mixed in with that important point, this article has a hefty dose of the "skeptical graduate student visits a museum." WDG

*museums/Jorvik Viking Centre/Great Britain/education*

30. CHABOT, NANCY JO 1992. A man called Lucy: Self reflection in a museum exhibit. In *Writing the Past in the Present*, edited by Frederick Baker and Julian Thomas, 138-142. St. David's University College, Lampeter, England.

In this brief essay Chabot explores what she calls the onion analogy approach to critical self-reflection in archaeology: the interpretation of the past is the whole onion, and each layer of interpretation can be peeled away until only the core of the onion—the physical remains themselves—remain. She applies this approach to the British Museum's 1988 exhibit *Man's Fossil Relatives*. Chabot cites a series of gendered symbols, particularly the use of the terms "man" and "man's," as generic references to humans, and the use of male figures as hominid and early human exemplars, as choices "used to the advantage of a male-dominant perspective, one that can subordinate women or make them altogether invisible" (p. 139). Chabot describes two alternatives to this "mis-gendered" exhibit: (1) replace gendered symbols with gender-neutral or ambiguous symbols; or (2) challenge the male-dominated scenarios directly. She considers the paintings depicting life at Swanscombe, ca. 250,000 years ago, as a case in point. They depict men hunting or making tools, while women are shown nursing infants or performing tasks she describes as secondary in importance to those of men. It is somewhat confusing, however, that when women are portrayed as the exclusive users of hand axes Chabot views this not as a step forward but as further subordination of women through the reification of male-dominated divisions of labor. She argues instead that Swanscombe should be depicted through a series of alternative sets of paintings. In one set, for example, men's tasks or assumed tasks might assume prominence. In another, women's tasks or assumed tasks would be the focus. A final set might show task divisions assigned randomly or without respect to gender. All, she notes, are assumptions, and many more could be advanced. But by facing museum visitors with a series of alternative interpretations of archaeological data, she argues they can be made to choose those they find most appropriate and to confront their own assumptions. Chabot does not explain in what way choosing an interpretation they find comfortable would challenge existing stereotypes. AWB

*museums/political uses of the past/Great Britain/representation, theory of/Swanscombe*


31. CHENEY, SUSAN LAWRENCE 1991. Women and alcohol: Female influence on recreational patterns in the West 1880-1890. In *The Archaeology of Gender: Proceedings of the Twenty-Second Annual Conference of the Archaeological Association of the University of Calgary,* edited by Dale Walde and Noreen D. Willows, 479-489. Archaeological Association, The University of Calgary, Calgary.

Cheney combines historical documentation on "the drinking, smoking, and gambling typified by the cowboys" (p. 479) and women's ideal roles as homemakers, reformers, and "civilizers" with a comparison of the types of artifacts recovered from five very different types of frontier sites in rural, southern Alberta. Following an interesting summary of Victorian ideals for male and female behavior with a description of how they appear to have been played out by ranch families and workers on the Canadian Plains, Cheney predicts that there will be an inverse correlation between the number of artifacts that indicate female presence and those reflecting alcoholic consumption.

Two family farms, one ranch with two major occupation areas, a brothel in a small town, and an isolated North West Mounted Police post provide the data for the archaeological portion of Cheney's work. As Cheney explains, straight-forward comparison of artifact types is not very enlightening, partly because of differences in classification schemes used at the different sites. For instance, the artifacts from one family farm appear to include only two alcohol bottles, a much smaller percentage of the total artifact assemblage than found at the other sites. However, patent medicine bottles were not classified as alcohol at this site, as they were at others. Apparently, patent medicine may have constituted a major proportion of the alcohol consumed at some family farms.

Not surprisingly, both the brothel and the police outpost had the greatest quantities of "recreational artifacts," especially alcohol bottles. The pattern appears basically bimodal. Cheney's regression lines for female artifacts versus recreational artifacts at the six locales do not contribute much to her discussion. On the other hand, she does provide some perceptive insights into the variation in family life and women's roles from an era in which women are all too often stereotyped or ignored. SLD

*historical archaeology/Canada/Alberta/United States and Canada, Plains/division of labor/brothels/alcohol/ Victorian ideology*


32. CLAASSEN, CHERYL (editor) 1992. *Exploring Gender Through Archaeology: Selected Papers from the 1991 Boone Conference.* Prehistory Press, Madison.

Following on the heels of the Chacmool Conference volume (#176), this compilation of selected conference papers also includes transcripts from three workshops and syllabae from several courses concerning gender in prehistory. As with the other collected works listed here, these papers vary a great deal along theoretical and methodological lines, and have been annotated separately (see entries #16, 33, 83, 88, 93, 94, 116, 148, 172, 174).

# Annotated References

33. CLAASSEN, CHERYL 1992. Questioning gender: An introduction. In *Exploring Gender Through Archaeology: Selected Papers from the 1991 Boone Conference,* edited by Cheryl Claassen, 1-10. Prehistory Press, Madison.

This article is the introductory statement for *Exploring Gender Through Archaeology* (#32). It begins with a history of gender as a topic in archaeology, beginning with the publication of Conkey and Spector (#34), and continues by describing how the impetus for study and publication in gender increased following the 1988 Wedge Conference.

An archaeology of gender has been difficult to establish within the context of New Archaeology which de-emphasizes the importance of gender in understanding prehistory. Claassen also argues that it is difficult, if not impossible, to identify gender from material culture, spatial associations, or archaeological contexts of past societies. From this it follows that we are restricted to examination of sex and sex roles (except, perhaps, in situations where documentary evidence is available).

Claassen suggests that the reliance on sex to identify genders precludes the possibility of identifying gender independently of sex, and that this inability to separate gender from sex prevents us from understanding origins of stratification or hierarchy within egalitarian societies. We are also lacking in conceptual tools to measure blocked access to resources, a defining characteristic of hierarchical societies.

The article closes with a section introducing each of the papers in the volume. KMM

*epistemology/history of archaeology/processualism*


34. CLAASSEN, CHERYL P. (editor) 1992. Bibliography of archaeology and gender: Papers delivered at archaeology conferences 1964-1992. *Annotated Bibliographies for Anthropologists* 1(2).

This bibliography, comprised of abstracts of conference papers (written by the authors) or brief summaries (written by Claassen) is available on Microsoft Word format on both Mac and IBM compatible disks from Claassen, the editor for this computerized bibliography series. Many of the papers in Claassen's bibliography have been published, and the ones available at our press deadline are annotated more critically, and at greater length, in this bibliography. As any archaeologist who has attended a conference knows, abstracts do not always provide an accurate indication of whether or not a paper will prove interesting or useful. Nevertheless, this is an invaluable addition to the literature, especially for its summary of unpublished material, which states the authors' intents succintly and provides a quick overview of current work on gender in archaeology. Its electronic format makes it easy to search for keywords, authors, or phrases, although it is not indexed. Since it is available on disk, it should also be easy to update and expand this bibliography as the literature grows. SLD

*conference papers/bibliography/computer disk*


35. CLAASSEN, CHERYL P. 1991 Gender, shellfishing, and the Shell Mound Archaic. In *Engendering Archaeology: Women and Prehistory,* edited by Joan M. Gero and Margaret W. Conkey, 276-300. Basil Blackwell, Cambridge, MA.

In this article, Cheryl Claassen considers the relationship between gender and shellfishing in the Late Archaic and Early Woodland in southeastern North America. Unsatisfied with traditional ecological approaches to archaeology, she argues that the incorporation of gender into models of prehistory "provides nothing short of a revitalization movement for archaeology, offering new vigor to research undertakings." Most archaeological models of shellfish use have, according to Claassen, failed to incorporate gender, human choice, and cultural concerns such as activity scheduling, sex-roles, and symbolic meanings.

To make her case, Claassen presents a number of competing hypotheses which attempt to explain the abandonment of shell mound constructions at the transition from the Shell Mound Archaic to the Early Woodland period, at about 3000 BP. She discounts three traditional explanations which focus on overexploitation, environmental change, and human emigration. These factors are seen as potential contributors but unlikely causes for the change. Drawing on ethnographic evidence which shows shellfish collection was a task performed mostly by women and often children, Claassen proposes that the change was *caused* in some fashion by a change in women and children's labor allocation. She proposes four alternate hypotheses which more or less explicitly hinge on gender relations: (1) the starchy seed hypothesis; (2) the fishing hypothesis; (3) change in social unit collecting and/or consuming shellfish; and (4) ceremonial use of shells.

The starchy seed hypothesis is drawn from Smith's (1987) model for increasing starchy seed horticulture in the Early Woodland period. Starchy seeds provided a more efficient storable resource than shellfish, and could have presented a scheduling conflict in late summer and fall if collected by the same social unit. Claassen discounts this hypothesis because: (1) nut harvesting presented the same conflicts but nuts were exploited in both periods; (2) maize cultivators in later periods also collected molluscs; (3) Early Woodland folks could have solved the scheduling conflict by re-partitioning labor groups to collect both starchy seeds and molluscs; and (4) Early Woodland population growth would have required more food rather than less. The assumption of this hypothesis is that women (and children) were the social group normally collecting molluscs and starchy seeds, while men hunted or engaged in other activities.

The fishing hypothesis takes an alternative ethnographic analogue to shellfish collection. It assumes that men collected shellfish for fish bait. If this was the case, a change in male activities could have initiated the end of shell mounding. The currently available evidence does not suggest a reduction in fishing, but it could be the case that new fishing technologies were employed, reducing the need for bait. If this was the case, Claassen suggests we look for change in fish species composition in midden deposits. Alternately, she suggests that if cultigens indeed were first utilized in male ritual as proposed by Prentice (1986), perhaps an increase in cultigen use reduced the time spent in fishing and thus mollusc collection. This last possibility is, of course, countered by the evidence already presented for continuity of fishing through the transition, unless new technologies reduced the time demands of fishing.

Turning away from dietary hypotheses, Claassen next considers the possibility that changes in social organization led to the observed archaeological changes. Perhaps, she suggests, the Early Woodland witnessed a dispersal of social groups from a more centralized Late Archaic pattern. In this case, lower localized population densities would lead to lower shell mound accumulation rates and higher shell decomposition. Such a situation would lead to the near invisibility of Early Woodland shell mounding sites today. Claassen claims that there is insufficient evidence to evaluate this scenario and calls for more research.

Finally, Claassen offers her preferred hypothesis, for ceremonial and ideological change from the Late Archaic to the Early Woodland. Citing the evident symbolic importance of shells in Mesoamerican ideology and the dominant role of shells in burial ornamentation in the Eastern U.S. back to 6200 BP, she suggests that shell mounds may have been created for their symbolic importance as burial matrices and monuments. Claassen sees the change to the Early Woodland non-mounding pattern as a shift in ideological focus from shells to horticultural activities. This would fit with the occurrence of burials in the mounds and in the lack of habitation evidence at mound sites.

Claassen is to be commended for opening a new perspective to the study of shell mound builders and shellfish utilization as a whole. As gender provides a major axis for economic, social and ideological organization and orientation, it cannot be ignored in the quest for causation in archaeological (and social) transformations. Claassen's greatest contribution lies in the diversity of alternative hypotheses she brings to bear on the Archaic/Woodland transition and in her attempt to make gender a central issue in these hypotheses.

Despite its successes, this article falls short of its proclaimed goals on several counts. First, although Claassen discounts over-exploitation, optimal foraging, population pressure, and environmental change in favor of social organization and ideology, she fails to consider how these might be interconnected. For instance, the starchy seed hypothesis suggests a change in the optimal diet available to Early Woodland people. If shellfish were abandoned for starchy seeds, it should be demonstrable that starchy seeds do provide a more efficient, more nutritious, and/or more storable resource than shellfish, and that shellfish and starchy seeds do have conflicting harvesting schedules. It is an optimal foraging theorem that in such cases *all* effort will be spent exploiting the more efficient resource if the less efficient one does not offer anything critical and additional. It is possible that technological and informational developments at the beginning of the Early Woodland made starchy seeds a more efficient resource than molluscs and/or that some other resource was added or dropped from the diet which required nutritional compensation by dropping molluscs or adding starchy seeds to the diet.

## *Annotated References*

The other three hypotheses go equally unevaluated. Both the fishing hypothesis and the social dispersal hypothesis yield predictions testable in the archaeological record. In the first case, we should expect to find changes in the fishing paraphernalia as well as in species compositions (an ingenious idea raised but left unexplored in Claassen's analysis). In the second case, social dispersal should be evident in Early Woodland site distribution and site sizes. Claassen's ceremonialism hypothesis gets the most attention and seems to explain the inclusion of burials and the lack of habitation evidence near the Late Archaic mounds. It could also be that habitation during shellfishing season was less permanent and had less impact on the environment. Shell mound burials may include only those people who died during the shellfishing season. Other burial locations might have been used at other times of the year. This would be particularly likely if groups returned to the same shellfishing location year after year. No aspect of life is likely to be devoid of ideological significance, and Claassen is right to consider this in the Archaic-Woodland transition. The most important question raised by this hypothesis concerns the relationship between ideology and causality. The primary motivation for change may have been an ideological shift from shell symbolism to horticultural symbolism, but the shift in focus parallels a shift in dietary regimes, suggesting a tight correlation between ideology and economy. Did the horticultural Woodland period result from a capricious change in ideological preferences, or did ideology follow a pragmatic shift in subsistence focus?

Claassen makes a valuable contribution by presenting a series of alternative hypotheses for the explanation of the Shell Mound Archaic to Early Woodland transition. While I would argue she does not convincingly exclude any of them, the recognition of the potential role of gender in the hypotheses offers a new perspective which could, with the explicit testing of these alternative hypotheses lead to better explanations of the past and a "revitalization" of archaeology as Claassen proposes. JBF

*United States, Southeast /shell mounds/Archaic period/Early Woodland period/subsistence/division of labor/ gatherer-hunters/shellfishing*


36. CONKEY, MARGARET W. 1991. Does it make a difference? Feminist thinking and archaeologies of gender. In *The Archaeology of Gender: Proceedings of the Twenty-Second Annual Conference of the Archaeological Association of the University of Calgary,* edited by Dale Walde and Noreen D. Willows, 24-33. Archaeological Association, The University of Calgary, Calgary.

In this paper, Conkey addresses the question "What difference does it make to take a feminist perspective in archaeologies of gender?" By taking a feminist approach she does not mean archaeology should simply borrow and apply feminist theory and research, but rather engage with feminism to develop "a body of theory and the requisite conceptual frameworks for archaeological inquiry" (p. 24). She discusses some of the central concerns and goals of western feminism and feminist scholarship, which include: reclaiming women's experience as valid, theorizing this experience, and using this to develop a program of political action; examining gender relations; concern with how others and differences are represented; and a diminished interest in seeking cross-cultural generalizations as to what constitutes women's and men's experiences.

Feminist-theorizing offers a way of thinking which takes as its object of investigation "how to understand and (re-)constitute the self, gender, knowledge, social relations, and culture, without resorting to linear, teleological, hierarchical, holistic, or binary ways of thinking or being" (Flax 1987:622 cited on p. 25). Feminist thinking can offer archaeology: a body of theory and analysis that can help us think about gender relations (needed before we can analyze gender); scrutiny of western concepts and a critical self-positioning; placement of women at the center as subjects of inquiry while recognizing women as active agents in the gathering of knowledge; a strong commitment to theoretical knowledge; and the view that gender is not the only object/subject of knowledge (pp. 25-27). Taking on gender, however, does not guarantee a feminist archaeology, and Conkey discusses three factors which could inhibit the feminist transformation of archaeology: (1) adoption of a functionalist conception of gender; (2) considering gender as just another "variable" rather than as a central theoretical concept; and (3) marginalization of the scholarship of feminist archaeologists.

The implications of feminisms for archaeologies of gender include: a self-critical and reflexive stance; a variety both of interpretations and of readings; a commitment to empirical depth; the development of a richer, humanized archaeology and one tuned to understanding how differences are socially constructed and historically changing; central notion that there were people in prehistory; and gender as agency. Archaeology also has much to offer feminist scholarship, such as "a truly historical perspective on the social construction and changing nature and forms of 'difference'" (p. 29), and research on the "origins" question. Finally, Conkey argues that archaeology may be the field that can affect the feminist transformation in anthropology as a whole because it is better positioned both to empirically undermine the prevailing notions of women as an unchanging essence, and to redress the "'narrowness' to the concept of the human being (as) reflected in limited ways of understanding human behavior" (p. 30). EAB

*References cited*
Flax, J. 1987 Postmodernism and gender relations in feminist theory. *Signs* 12(4):621-643.

*epistemology/feminist critique*

37. CONKEY, MARGARET W. 1991. Contexts of action, contexts for power: Material culture and gender in the Magdalenian. In *Engendering Archaeology: Women and Prehistory*, edited by Joan M. Gero and Margaret W. Conkey, 57-92. Basil Blackwell, Cambridge, MA.

Conkey argues that if we are to introduce gender into studies of the Magdalenian we must devise models for (rather than models of) Upper Paleolithic society aimed at identifying contexts where gender categories might have been created. Her approach is less to attempt identification of genders in the past than to use gender as an analytical concept in its interpretation, treating gender as a major axis of social differentiation which may have come into play at particular sites and particular times. Conkey examines larger Magdalenian "aggregation" sites, outlining three "contexts of action" related to their occupation: (1) "beyond the households"; (2) "sequential hierarchies" (a term borrowed from Gregory Johnson's studies of scalar stress); and (3) "being connected." Gender categories may have come into play in such aggregation contexts, and aggregations may even have been premised in part on their existence. "Beyond the households" contexts represent occasional groupings beyond the minimal residential unit. Larger social groupings would require a renegotiation of social relations and a restructuring (at least temporarily) of social regulatory mechanisms, i.e., the creation of "sequential hierarchies." "Being connected" refers to social relations defined through long-distance exchange. In the case of the Magdalenian, these exchanges are marked archaeologically by different spatial and temporal patterning of portable art.

These arguments are applied to the remains from Cueto de la Mina, a Magdalenian rockshelter along the coast of Cantabrian Spain. Conkey's argument is at once informal yet demanding, and is based on a probabilistic appeal: given the material diversity and the variety of productive and manufacturing tasks they imply, some division of labor, and hence probably divisions by age and gender, must have been present. "This is not a material culture inventory," she argues, " that was monopolized by any one group or set of individuals; many different domains are represented and social differentiations, including sex-based differentiations had to have been 'at work'" (pp. 77-78). Conkey then imagines the social dynamics implicated by the material assemblage using what she describes as "stereotypic" divisions of labor. By imagining the social orders and tensions suggested by such gender roles, Conkey argues, we may generate more plausible social constructs for the interpretation of sites like Cueto de la Mina. Conkey does not elaborate on the linkage of gender categories and technological specialization, implicit in her assertion that material diversity demands social differentiation.

While Conkey argues that "finding" women in the past is not the point of her essay, it remains unclear how gender relations and roles can be systematically examined without associating particular genders with particular technologies— and in the absence of techniques for identifying genders in prehistory, referencing (either through acceptance or rejection) stereotypical gender categories. She suggests only that ongoing, more carefully controlled excavations at Magdalenian sites will permit "grounded structuralist inquiries into associations" (p. 82). Conkey's essay closes with an afterword discussing the conceptual baggage carried by many scholars in their travels to the Upper Paleolithic, concluding that we must redefine the Magdalenian as "a set of archaeological materials to be used in exploring some historically and contextually situated processes by which social lives (social formations) are constructed" (p. 86). Penetrating and thought-provoking, her essay offers new insights into the role gender may have played in Magdalenian society, but offers no means of assessing its role beyond plausibility. AWB

*division of labor/Cueto de la Mina/Paleolithic/Magdalenian/Spain*

38. CONKEY, MARGARET W. AND JOAN M. GERO 1991. Tensions, pluralities, and engendering archaeology: An introduction to women and prehistory. In *Engendering Archaeology: Women and prehistory*, edited by Joan M. Gero and Margaret W. Conkey, 3-30. Basil Blackwell, Cambridge, MA.

Conkey and Gero's introduction to *Engendering Archaeology* takes up feminist theory and its impact on archaeology. The three goals for the volume are: to continue exposing gender biases; to "find" women in prehistory; and to problematize underlying gender assumptions. Conkey and Gero call for the development of new conceptual frameworks that deal explicitly with gender relations. Using anthropological gender theory, they begin to build such a framework by rejecting biological determinism and recognizing gender as a culturally constituted and constituting process. Discovering past female and male activities is not a sufficient goal for an archaeology of gender. Instead, the variability in the structuring principles of gender and its intersection with other aspects of social life should be the focus. Such gender-based research, they contend, will turn archaeologists toward the social dynamics of the people under study, not just material culture. Because gender intersects with other cultural processes (e.g., economy, politics, craft specialization, state formation), gender-based research will study topics of traditional archaeological interest and perhaps, replace them. After discussing feminist theory and archaeology, Conkey and Gero review the chapters in the volume within this context.

Conkey and Gero make a wonderful effort to set up a framework to operationalize research on gender in archaeology. They provide frank discussion of the "tensions" involved in such an endeavor: how we are to contend with a rapidly evolving study, a wide range of research agendas, and the problematization of many analytical approaches. Their warning against dependence on ethnographic analogy which tends to collapse variability is of particular interest. They contend that the argument against engendering archaeology on methodological grounds is bunk: it results from reliance on activity attribution to gender in prehistory, an approach they reject. Their particular conceptual focus is innovative and well-argued. Their call for the incorporation of feminist and gender theory rather than a research program centered on identifying men and women in the past is timely. JDB

*epistemology/feminist critique*

39. CONKEY, MARGARET W. AND JANET D. SPECTOR 1984. Archaeology and the study of gender. *Advances in Archaeological Method and Theory* 7:1-38.

This article is a powerful and widely cited statement on gender and archaeology. Written at a time when virtually no work (in English) had appeared concerned explicitly with the study of gender in prehistory, it has influenced numerous studies in the eight years since its publication.

Conkey and Spector divide the article into two main sections. First, they discuss androcentric bias in anthropological and archaeological literature, arguing that most archaeological studies rely on ethnocentric, androcentric assumptions about gender, even while claiming that the application of gender to their research is not possible. They illustrate their argument with five well-known archaeological and ethnoarchaeological case studies, showing how work by Winters, Hill, Longacre, Deetz, and Yellen ignored possible ways of studying gender and pointing out the implicit (and untested) assumptions about gender roles in each of their studies. Conkey and Spector argue convincingly that "archaeologists, consciously or not, are propagating culturally particular ideas about gender in their interpretations and reconstructions of the past" (p. 2).

Second, they consider feminist contributions to the study of gender in anthropology and discuss ways to begin incorporating gender into archaeological research. Conkey and Spector emphasize the need for an anthropological theory of gender not unlike any other social dynamic; they feel strongly that gender must be incorporated into all anthropological studies, not marginalized to a "specialty" or appendix status. They focus on one specific analytical framework for an archaeological study of gender: task-differentiation analysis, as designed by Spector. Spector has used task-differentiation analysis only in cases where there are ethnographic or ethnohistoric sources, but the authors believe that similar analytical frameworks can, and must, be developed for archaeological cases without written records.

In the course of their discussion, Conkey and Spector review and synthesize a wide range of anthropological literature on gender. This article, with its extensive bibliography, is essential reading for anyone concerned with the anthropological study of gender, and especially so for those involved in the study of gender in prehistory. DLG

*epistemology/feminist critique/task differentiation approach*

40. CONKEY, MARGARET W. WITH SARAH H. WILLIAMS 1991. Original narratives: The political economy of gender in archaeology. In *Gender at the Crossroads of Knowledge: Feminist Anthropology in the Postmodern Era,* edited by Micaela di Leonardo, 102-139. University of California Press, Berkeley.

This is a critique of "origins research" in archaeology. Questions of origin are usually considered the most important of archaeological topics, and this allows them to structure the discipline, influence career success, reach the public, and make political statements. The authors argue that there are a number of characteristic features of origins research that should cause us to question its validity.

As narratives, stories about origins (of agriculture, hunting, art, and so on) use traditional narrative devices. One of these is the existence of "gaps" (such as those in the evolutionary sequence) each of which is critically important until filled, at which point another gap is created. A second common device is the "guarantee of continuity," which comes of using one set of analytical categories across millions of years and several species.

The archaeological issues that show up in public discourse are often origin questions, and frequently reflect current notions of gender, race, and class. Our tendency to isolate origins as separate from and knowable by the present masks the effect that the present context has on our knowledge of the past. Referring to DeLivre's discussion of ascending and descending anachronisms in Malagasy oral histories, the authors compare these to narratives of human evolution. They remark on the congruence between phenomena which are visible more remotely and those which are considered most easily inferred archaeologically, most causally important, and most male-oriented (lithic technology is an example). They further remark that in archaeology, control of origins is control of knowledge, since scholars who write about less than original phenomena have to first refer to the literature on origins.

One of the most problematic characteristics of origins research is its essentialism. To study the origin of "gender" it must first be understood as a unitary thing with universal, essential characteristics. This denies the importance of particular historical contexts and ignores the implications of feminist scholarship that gender roles and values are variable in space and time. Questioning the origin of gender asymmetry gives it an appearance of inevitability. Discussing narratives of human origins and the origins of art, the authors show how they assume and perpetuate current androcentric notions.

Rejecting origins research as an invalid approach, the authors suggest three alternative domains of inquiry. First are case studies of women in particular prehistoric contexts. Second is a theoretical consideration of the cultural construction of gender, which the authors suggest is necessarily postprocessual; postprocessualism they define as a collection of approaches including Marxism and feminism. Finally, the need to change existing paradigms is stressed. Conkey and Williams conclude that postprocessualism will be unable to do this without feminist archaeology, and that part of the process includes questioning traditional "objects of knowledge," of which origins research is a prime example.

This critical overview is valuable for an understanding of how we as archaeologists tell stories, and the kinds of stories we consider satisfying. It rightly urges a critical self-consciousness of the implications of our choice of questions and how archaeological narratives are affected by our present context. Most of the criticisms of particular arguments are keen and well-made; the tendency to draw "essential" qualities out of present phenomena and locate them in the past is especially applicable to research on a large and general scale.

Two limitations derive from the nature of the authors' undertaking. As a generalizing, occasionally polemic argument, it is woven out of many strands with varying objects, scopes and validity, including a number of arguments from worst cases. It is probably inappropriate to refer to the failure to find art among australopithecines as a "descending anachronism," since the term was coined to refer to a politically motivated manipulation of the past. Moreover, some points pertain strictly to origins research, while others pertain to any attempt to interpret the past or to any narrative. Some are not inevitable features but characteristics of unselfconscious research or simplistic universalizing models. It may not follow that all origins questions are inherently ideological in nature.

Secondly, many archaeologists would probably object to the way the authors define what we should study and how to go about it. Origins are not inherently universalizing (one can study the origin of agriculture in all cases, in the Americas, or in Mexico). Nor is the most particularist approach the least susceptible to political legitimation. For instance, considering the Spanish in Hispaniola and the British in India only in their respective cultural contexts masks and defuses the reality of European colonization. Finally, defining feminism as compatible only with postprocessualism implies that processual archaeologists cannot contribute to engendering the past, and allowing feminist archaeologists to ask only certain kinds of questions is at odds with the variety of views and theoretical approaches that the authors recognize as a hallmark of feminism. SF

*origins research/political uses of the past/feminist critique/hominids/Paleolithic Europe/postprocessualism/ revisionist theory*


41. CORDELL, LINDA S. 1991. Sisters of sun and spade, women archaeologists in the Southwest. In *The Archaeology of Gender: Proceedings of the Twenty-Second Annual Conference of the Archaeological Association of the University of Calgary*, edited by Dale Walde and Noreen D. Willows, 187-194. Archaeological Association, The University of Calgary, Calgary.

The Cordell paper was originally prepared for the Daughters of the Desert exhibit (Babcock and Parezo 1988). It consists of profiles of eight prominent women in Southwestern archaeology, including brief summaries of the archaeological careers of Anna Osler Shepard, Jean McWhirt Pinkley, Bertha Pauline Dutton, Florence Hawley Ellis, Marjorie Ferguson Lambert, Hannah Marie Wormington, Jane Holden Kelley, and Cynthia Irwin-Williams. All but Kelley and Irwin-Williams were born between 1900 and 1915, so these include the stories of some of the pioneer archaeologists in the Southwest. Cordell provides a brief biography for each woman, including birthplace, education, the kinds of jobs held in archaeology, publication record, and the importance of their work in Southwestern archaeology.

Cordell concludes that although their career trajectories were very different, a few common threads run through these women's lives. Most were Westerners, from small towns or ranches. Mentors played an important role in encouraging them to become archaeologists. They have been active in fieldwork for most of their lives, generally holding less prestigious and lower paying positions than their male counterparts, and their work has often been unrecognized and neglected in summary articles on Southwestern archaeology, general textbooks, and histories of archaeology. Another commonalty implicit in Cordell's profiles and summary is that only two of these women have held long-term academic jobs (although many of them have taught part time), which may have diminished their ability to influence their colleagues and later generations of students. The profiles of these women who have been important in Southwestern archaeology are both interesting and informative, although they are, of necessity, very brief. TVZ

*References cited*
Babcock, Barbara A. and Nancy Parezo 1988. *Daughters of the Desert: Women Anthropologists and the Native American Southwest, 1880-1980: An Illustrated Catalogue.* University of New Mexico Press, Albuquerque.

*United States, Southwest/United States, Western/history of archaeology/sociopolitics of archaeology*

42. CRABTREE, PAM J. 1991. Gender hierarchies and the sexual division of labor in the Natufian culture of the southern Levant. In *The Archaeology of Gender: Proceedings of the Twenty-Second Annual Conference of the Archaeological Association of the University of Calgary*, edited by Dale Walde and Noreen D. Willows, 384-391. Archaeological Association, The University of Calgary, Calgary.

Crabtree explores the possible role of women in the origins of agriculture by examining the role and position of women in the Natufian of the Levant (12,750-10,450 BP). In an explicitly gendered model of Natufian organization, Henry (1989) suggests that Natufian groups were matrilineal and matrilocal, since women needed to transmit the ownership of important nut and wild grain resources. Men specialized in hunting large ungulates and trade, while women and children gathered wild grains, nuts, and small game. He also suggests that the Natufians controlled population growth through female infanticide. Crabtree examines all of Henry's propositions and provides an alternative model of Natufian gender relations. She uses multiple lines of evidence, as does Henry, including decorative motifs, subsistence remains, mortuary data, and ethnographic analogy. Although Henry claims that design motifs are localized and thus indicate matrilocality, Crabtree challenges this on two fronts: first, that the designs are not in fact localized; second, that even if they were, ethnographic evidence shows that localized design styles also occur in patrilocal societies. Crabtree maintains that Henry's model of men hunting and women gathering owes more to faulty ethnographic analogy with the !Kung than to archaeological evidence. She provides a different model of the organization of labor involving cooperation between men and women, rather than a strict division of labor. The primary basis for her model is that grains, nuts, and other staples in the Natufian diet are extremely seasonal in availability and must be collected within a very short time. She suggests, therefore, that an ethnographic model from the Great Basin, where pine nut and rabbit exploitation were cooperative, would be a better model for Natufian labor organization.

Mortuary data does not indicate what tasks were performed by which gender since graves lack tools. Males, females, and children are all found with shell ornaments, which Crabtree interprets as meaning that the Natufians lacked a rigid division of labor by gender. While Henry interprets the underrepresentation of females in Natufian cemeteries as an indication of female infanticide, Crabtree argues that this difference may instead indicate an imbalance in favor of males in terms of social status and political power. If men and women cooperated in the exploitation of seasonal resources, Crabtree argues, then we must reconsider the view of women as the "inventors" of agriculture. Agriculture can be seen as the cause of great changes in the organization of labor, instead of the product of the gender division of labor, since the labor needs of agriculture and animal-raising are quite different from those of foraging. Domestication may have led to changes in the division of labor, resulting in the division of labor by gender.

This article raises interesting possibilities for future research. Crabtree brings forward important questions about Henry's model, and casts doubts on his interpretation of Natufian social organization. She shows that the same information can result in a very different interpretation of gender roles and relations. Her model of gender relations and its implications for the origins of plant domestication is thought-provoking. Although her discussion of decorative motifs and of critical resource seasonality does undermine Henry's model, the counter-model is not always better supported. Her ethnographic analogy, for example, is hardly stronger than that employed by Henry. Cooperative acquisition of critical, highly seasonal resources can be one component of a system where other tasks are gender specific. Nor does Crabtree's model necessarily preclude matrilineality or matrilocality. Although she argues against matrilineal organization, she seems reluctant to discuss alternatives. She discusses the gender hierarchies of the title only briefly, implying that burial in cemeteries might have been an indicator of relative status, but she never justifies this suggestion. It is also possible that the females were being buried elsewhere or in some other way that actually reflected high status. The mortuary data could conceivably even be used to argue more strongly against matrilineality, since cemeteries are often associated with the existence of corporate groups, such as clans. The preponderance of males in a cemetery could therefore be interpreted as an indication that males were more important in corporate groups, and in determining group membership, than females. Crabtree points out many of the weaknesses in Henry's model of gender relations, and although her counter-model has its own weaknesses, her discussion does raise new questions about gender roles and relations. TVZ

## Annotated References

*References cited*
Henry, Donald O. 1989. *From Foraging to Agriculture: The Levant at the End of the Ice Age.* University of Pennsylvania Press, Philadelphia.

*Near East/Natufian/agriculture/agricultural origins/trade/mortuary analysis/feminist critique/gatherer-hunters/division of labor/Neolithic/Levant/Israel*


43. DAMM, CHARLOTTE 1991. From burials to gender roles: Problems and potentials in postprocessual archaeology. In *The Archaeology of Gender: Proceedings of the Twenty-Second Annual Conference of the Archaeological Association of the University of Calgary,* edited by Dale Walde and Noreen D. Willows, 130-135. Archaeological Association, The University of Calgary, Calgary.

   This paper explores the possibilities for interpreting gender roles and relationships from mortuary evidence in the Danish Neolithic. Viewing material culture as an active part of society, not a passive reflection of it, Damm discusses the relationship between funeral ritual and the negotiation of social (including gender) organization. Because death changes the social status of the living, funerals are a context in which relationships are changed or reaffirmed. Material culture presents messages about, and is involved in, the transformation of those relationships.
   Damm presents evidence from burials of the late TRB megalithic tombs and Single Graves Culture. The TRB tombs contain piles of bones from mixed individuals and lack internal divisions. No association can be made between artifacts and individuals of a given gender. There are not enough people in the tombs to account for the whole of the population, suggesting that a subset, perhaps certain families or lineages, were given tomb burial. All that can be said about gender from this evidence is that it was not emphasized in the context of burials (this cannot be taken to mean that it was unimportant in other social contexts). What is important in this context is the distinction between presumably high status (tombed) and low status (absent) families or lineages; status is stressed at the expense of gender. Damm suggests that the relationships emphasized in burials are likely to be asymmetrical ones, especially contested ones needing legitimation.
   In the later Single Graves Culture, bones have not survived but in some cases they have left enough decomposed substance to identify burial position. Certain body orientations are associated with sets of grave goods. Comparison to similar graves with sexed skeletons in Germany aids in the identification of possible male and female graves, but even in Germany there are ambiguous cases (for example, most of the right-facing graves were male, but so were 15% of the left-facing ones). The problem of ambiguous graves raises many questions. Is body treatment or grave goods most likely to represent gender? What does a woman with a battle ax indicate about male and female roles? How would you recognize neutral genders? How are sex and gender related?
   The Single Graves Culture shows distinctions between men and women and between some men and others, but Damm contends that we cannot reliably interpret this difference as either equality or asymmetry. She suggests a possible interpretation that distinguishes senior men from junior men and women. Comparing the megalithic tombs with the Single Graves, she indicates a transition from status distinctions unrelated to gender to distinctions of gender and seniority, but what this means in terms of social relationships is unclear. Damm concludes by saying that in situations where the data on gender is absent or inconclusive, feminists have a responsibility to avoid neutrality and attempt to say something about gender relations while admitting the tenuous and hypothetical nature of their suggestions.
   Damm is one of the few archaeologists who talks theoretically about connections between gender relations and burials, instead of assuming the former to be a simple reflection of the latter. Working out that kind of theory is a large and difficult task, and she only begins it here, but it is good that someone recognizes the necessity of it. Moreover, she raises the important question of the relationship between sex and gender. Failing to differentiate these concepts and assuming that gender will show up in burials as a simple dichotomy isomorphic with sex is a potential pitfall in mortuary analyses that Damm successfully avoids. On the whole, this is a thoughtful article well aware of the difficulties involved in such analyses.
   Damm's assertion that burials will emphasize the asymmetrical relationship most in need of legiti-

mation allows her to interpret the megalithic tombs (though identifying asymmetrical social relationships by comparing data you have with data you do not is problematic), but gives her difficulties with the Single Graves, where difference, but not necessarily asymmtery, can be seen. This raises the knotty problem of how you can tell gender difference from gender inequality with mortuary data.

More could be said, or at least asked, about the Single Graves data. Under what social conditions might one expect distinctions between men and women to begin to be made simultaneously with distinctions between different groups of men? A pattern in which some men are set apart from other men who are associated with all women might in fact suggest a gender-related asymmetry (if, for instance, men attain seniority by becoming unlike women). Finally, her assertion that hypothesizing even in the absence of data is a social obligation is likely to irritate the empirically minded. SF

*postprocessualism/mortuary analysis/Denmark/Germany/Scandinavia/Neolithic*


44. DAMM, CHARLOTTE 1986. An appeal for women in archaeology. *Archaeological Review from Cambridge* 5:215-218.

Damm discusses sex ratios in English and Danish academia as well as the androcentrism apparent in European archaeological practice. The number of women entering graduate programs varies with the sociopolitical context of the degree sought. At Cambridge men far outnumber women in Ph.D. programs, whereas in Danish universities the reverse is true. Damm ties this to the impracticality of a Ph.D. in the Danish system. The M.A. level leads to field archaeological positions and is dominated by men. This situation has lead to the male domination of the discipline, despite a growing awareness of feminist issues by men. Damm attacks Randsborg (1986, #134) in particular as an example of androcentric bias in European archaeology. She points to uncritical ethnographic analogy and personally-based inferences as the major sources for androcentric bias. Damm calls for a remedial approach to gender through archaeology, stressing the investigation of men's and women's socioeconomic roles, the sexual division of labor, and reproductive roles. Womens' roles in these investigations are privileged due to their unique perception of power and gender roles.

While Damm's analysis of academic politics and her critique of Randsborg's article are timely and insightful, her portrayal of women as inherently better-suited to perceiving androcentrism and achieving interpretative "balance" is skewed. This is a question under examination in gender studies rather than a valid *a priori* assumption. The point of studying gender through the past is to become acquainted with its dynamic aspects. This includes gender ideology, and the perception of gender systems by both men and women. Thus, neither men nor women are inherently more appropriate as researchers or subjects of study. JDB

*sociopolitics of archaeology/discrimination/feminist critique/graduate training/Denmark/Great Britain*


45. DANZINGER, EVE 1991. Man and language in prehistory: Clues to gender conceptualization from semantic analysis. In *The Archaeology of Gender: Proceedings of the Twenty-Second Annual Conference of the Archaeological Association of the University of Calgary*, edited by Dale Walde and Noreen D. Willows, 309-312. Archaeological Association, The University of Calgary, Calgary.

Danzinger discusses a contemporary Mopan Mayan village where the valuation of women is inconsistent with the realities of gender relationships. Wives are forcibly controlled by their husbands in what they do, where they are allowed to go, and how they act, but women are not considered inferior, either by women or by men. There is a strong division of labor by gender, but women's work is not devalued. Both male and female informants report that men and women depend on each other's work and therefore respect each other. An ideology of equality is combined with an inequality of power.

Ideologically, Danzinger contends, it is seniority, not gender, that is considered "an axis of power." Even the relations between husband and wife are discussed in terms of the authority of seniors; a man's mother tells him how he must treat his wife.

## Annotated References

Believing that such a contradiction between ideology and behavior will not be reflected in the material remains of behavior, and so will elude archaeologists, Danzinger suggests linguistic studies as an alternative path to ideology. Semantic categories will reveal what is important in defining social categories. Using 2x2 matrices with columns of seniority and rows of gender, the author gives English and Mopan examples of names for various kin categories (siblings, parents and children, affines). For instance, English siblings are distinguished only by gender (brother/sister), regardless of seniority. Mopan siblings are distinguished by seniority first, senior siblings being secondarily distinguished by gender (older sister/older brother/younger sibling). From these analyses Danzinger claims that age always takes precedence over sex in defining Mopan social categories, and that this reflects the ideological situation she observed among them. She suggests that reconstructions of prehistoric languages will allow archaeologists to use similar semantic studies to gain access to prehistoric ideologies.

Danzinger's article is particularly valuable for considering the relationship between ideology and behavior with reference to gender, and for looking at the intersection of age and gender categories. The type of analysis that she suggests could potentially be useful wherever detailed linguistic evidence is available. There is some question, however, whether knowing the hierarchy of importance in distinguishing social categories necessarily gives access to an ideology of power. The linguistic analysis shows that seniority has precedence over gender in the definition of categories of kinship. The ethnographic evidence suggests that seniority has precedence over gender in the definition of power relationships. But these are not the same thing, and the former should not be considered a direct reflection of the latter. In the English sibling case, while gender takes semantic precedence, many informants may feel that power relations among siblings have as much to do with age as with sex. It also cannot be assumed that a single category (whether age, gender, wealth, or any other status) will be considered the axis of power; power may be conceived variously. SF

*semantics/ethnographic analogy/Maya/Mexico*

46. DEAGAN, KATHLEEN 1983. *Spanish St. Augustine: The Archaeology of a Colonial Creole Community.* Academic Press, New York.

This is not primarily a book about gender, but several of Deagan's chapters deal with gender relationships, and that particular strand is the subject of this review. Chapter Four, for instance, provides an introduction to the population of St. Augustine in the eighteenth century, which consisted of a European majority and minorities of Blacks and Indians. Intermarriage was predominantly between European men and Guale Indian women. Deagan asserts that the lack of Spanish-born women assured that most *criollo* families had some Indian ancestry.

Chapter Six, "The Mestizo Minority: Patterns of Intermarriage" suggests that Indian influence on Spanish culture should be apparent in female activities. *Mestizos* were generally poor and of lower status than *criollos*, and lived predominantly on the periphery of town. But it was possible to raise one's status by marrying up or by "criollization," distancing oneself from one's Indian past. Deagan expects to find Indian elements in women's spheres (cooking, sewing, childcare) which are not in public view. Male activities or socially visible areas (like architecture) should appear Hispanic. Evidence from a known *mestizo* site seems to support these expectations. Aboriginal cooking vessels are found in all households, but the *mestizo* house has the highest percentage. Tableware is European; aboriginal sherds cluster around the kitchen while Spanish majolica does not.

Using South's ceramic ratio, Deagan tries to determine whether the pattern observed at the *mestizo* house is a result of ethnicity (and therefore the presence of Indian or *mestizo* women) or income-based access to European goods. The details of this and related analyses are given in Chapter Ten. Deagan concludes that the presence and percentages of aboriginal ceramics show the adoption of aboriginal traits, the integration of aboriginal women, and restricted access to Hispanic wares. While favoring the primacy of ethnicity, she notes that the relative importance of these factors are difficult to assess until data from more *mestizo* households are available.

Deagan's work is particularly important for addressing gender, ethnicity, and economics in concert. One issue which should be explored further is how the boundaries between *criollo* and *mestizaje* are defined, maintained, and crossed. Given Deagan's statement that few *criollo* families did not have some Indian ancestry, it would be useful to broaden the focus to include *criollo* women and *mestizo* households of succeeding generations in which Indian women were not present.

The ceramic ratio seems to be a problematic tool for distinguishing income from ethnicity, since a high ratio could result from either a *mestizo* house with more aboriginal ceramics than the *criollo* neighbors, or an equal number of cooking pots but a lot fewer expensive European wares. Nor does this approach consider the possibility of differential use of ceramics in different households, since all aboriginal ware is defined as kitchen-related and only European goods are defined as tablewares. One can imagine, for instance, a poor Guale woman being content to use Guale pottery on her table (it would not be socially visible if she avoided serving it to company), and an equally poor *criollo* woman thinking aboriginal wares were inappropriate for table use. SF

*historical archaeology/ethnohistory/ceramic analysis/mestizaje/ethnicity/Florida/Guale/United States, Southeast*

47. DERRY, LINDA 1991. Daughters and sons-in-law of king cotton: Asymmetry in the structure and material culture of Cahawba, an antebellum Alabama town. In *The Archaeology of Gender: Proceedings of the Twenty-Second Annual Conference of the Archaeological Association of the University of Calgary*, edited by Dale Walde and Noreen D. Willows, 270-278. Archaeological Association, The University of Calgary, Calgary.

Derry begins with a brief critique of old-style Southern history where studies of antebellum social structure focused on status distinctions defined by wealth, ethnicity, or occupation. Recent Southern historians, however, are less inclined to define "class" and impose it on the past and are more interested in discerning what social categories and status distinctions were considered important by the people involved. Derry suggests that in this kind of research historians and archaeologists need each other; archaeologists can uncover the material remains of actual status categories, and historians can provide the documentary information to interpret what they mean.

Derry describes her ongoing project in antebellum Cahawba, Dallas County, Alabama. A wide variety of documents are being used to reveal patterns of kinship, economics, ethnicity, and so on. Using information gained in this way, Derry contradicts the thesis of a paper by William Barney, who used Dallas County census data and decided that kin ties were not particularly important because there seemed to be loose males in presumably economic relationships living in non-kin households. Derry points out that Barney's method of defining relationship by surnames led him to misclassify a wife's relatives (younger siblings, children from previous marriages) as unrelated. She goes on to show how the spatial patterning of Cahawba is in fact kin-based, houses and shops adjacent to each other often belonging to kin related through women.

Focusing on two constellations of intermarried families, she finds that the sons-in-law of important men frequently live near or go into business with their father-in-law. Many of her "action statements" (short historical narratives) concern the relationships between sisters, fathers and daughters, and male affines. She concludes that in Cahawba, and in the antebellum South as a whole, women were "social glue" uniting men in social and business relationships. She further contends that kinship was more important than wealth in structuring society, and that Cahawba people identified with their relatives more strongly than their class.

Having done the historical research, Derry presents plans for archaeological research in Cahawba to find out how the material culture signals the patterns and relationships that the documents have revealed.

On the whole, Derry aptly shows that kinship is an important consideration in the interpretation of social relationships and spatial patterning in antebellum Cahawba. The suggestion of matrilocality is particularly interesting, if difficult to evaluate from the evidence in the paper. It would take a statistical analysis of many different families to see if the pattern holds, but it would be worth pursuing. (Generalizing from a frontier town in Alabama to the South as a whole is, of course, another matter.)

The claim that kinship was of "premier importance in molding the structure of society" does not, however, necessarily follow from the information we are given. The clusters of related families described consist of rich people who marry other rich people. It is thus difficult to assess the importance of wealth versus kinship in the structure of society.

## Annotated References

The article suggests a relatively innocent view of the relationship between documentary and archaeological evidence and the ease with which they can be interpreted. Derry seems to expect material patterning in an archaeological site to reflect the truth of social patterning as seen in the documents. She recognizes that historians may have biases, but does not discuss the problem of biases in the historical record itself, or the possibility of contradictory but valid evidence from the archaeological record. SF

*historical archaeology/ethnicity/spatial analysis/Alabama/United States, Southeast*


48. DOBRES, MARCIA-ANNE 1988. Feminist archaeology and inquiries into gender relations: Some thoughts on universals, origin stories, and alternating paradigms. *Archaeological Review from Cambridge* 7(1):30-44.

Dobres defines what she sees as the two "significant feminist models" --one which asserts that "current scientific discourse is permeated by an androcentric paradigm" because of its explicitly objective approach, and the other which maintains that women contain a different or alternative voice. These two "models" are said to legitimate a hermeneutic approach to interpretation (p. 31).

Most current theorizing about social relations, and gender relations in particular, is claimed to be based on four underlying assumptions: that there exists a universal woman, a universal man, a universal domination/subordination dichotomy, and that "current situations are directly connected to a common beginning, and that if we can 'know' this past we can explain the present" (p. 32). Dobres turns to archaeological origin stories to demonstrate this point, and finds these four assumptions in both male- and female-centered theories of human origins. Both Man the Hunter and Woman the Gatherer models (and others such as Al-Hibri's theory on the origins of patriarchy) make these universalistic assumptions, and ignore historically-specific sociocultural contexts. Citing Ian Hodder, Dobres claims that reference to such universals and general laws denies people their freedom as well as their specificity and uniqueness. To assume such universals "defeats from the start the entire purpose of our inquiry" (p. 35).

Dobres next considers why origin stories have been so popular in the analysis of contemporary power structures. She focuses on the elements of continuity and tenacity in using the past as precedent. The importance of the past for the present obliges archaeologists to "at least recognise the various uses to which our stories are put in the present" (p. 38). She hopes that archaeologist can eliminate their need for origin stories, and their need for universals, by asking more contextual questions.

Dobres' final recommendation is that we abandon the search for "one UNIVERSAL paradigm" and instead adopt an epistemology "capable of accepting a degree of ambiguity between alternative (not 'competing') interpretations." She argues that such an accommodative approach is more in keeping with the feminist theories concerning a separate voice for women, and would lead to a more "embracing and tolerant science" (pp. 40-41).

This article insightfully attempts to find the common underlying assumptions shared by both male- and female-centered origin stories, and this is certainly a productive way to advance archaeological theory. However, the direction in which she then develops her theory is questionable. Her vilification of "universals" and embrace of "contextualism" is lopsided in that it doesn't acknowledge the dialectical relationship between generalities and specifics, both of which are always present and necessary. Also, her desired, more tolerant and embracing science would be productive to the degree that it incorporated new perspectives and a wider dialogue. But, at some level, there must be grounds for comparison. Scientific hypotheses and interpretations must compete and not simply constitute alternatives of equal likelihood, which would lead to an unwieldy relativism with no possibility for future development. This article usefully questions the implicit, universalist gender assumptions found in many contemporary theories. However, the brand of contextual archaeology offered in solution might not lead to a workable, or worthwhile, archaeology. WDG

*contextual archaeology/origins research/hermeneutics/postprocessualism/revisionist theory/feminist critique/ epistemology*

49. DOMMASNES, LIV HELGA 1991. Male/female roles and ranks in Late Iron Age Norway. In *Were They All Men? An Examination of Sex Roles in Prehistoric Society,* edited by Reidar Bertelson, Arnvid Lillehammer, and Jenny-Rita Naess, 65-77. Arkeologist Museum i Stavanger, Stavanger, Norway.

Dommasnes traces the role of and ranks available to women in Viking society through examination of burial data from four regions in Norway. Male graves are identified through the presence of weapons; female graves through the presence of oval brooches, a characteristic accessory of Viking women's dress in other areas of Scandinavia. Dommasnes obtains other evidence on the role of women in Viking society from the earliest codified laws (written down in the late eleventh century) and from early Icelandic sagas, while recognizing that the first codified laws of a recently Christianized and unified state and the literary traditions of a colonial society almost certainly are based on different traditions, agendas and social roles than the pre-Christian Viking society from which they sprang.

Accepting the historic evidence with these caveats, the author compares the burial data from the four regions and evaluates them in relation to the historical records. She notes that the ratio of male to female graves is everywhere greater than 1, and in most cases greater than 2. The ratio decreases everywhere in the 9th century and is lowest in coastal areas. All of the identified female graves are in areas of fertile soil, and most of them are from areas with evidence of settlement in earlier periods. A smaller percentage of the male graves are found in the oldest agricultural areas. Rich female graves are more common in areas with more imported European goods. She concludes that women's rank was based on their role as housewives and managers of farms, while high rank for men was associated with a larger range of economic activities, including warfare, piracy, and trade. In areas where such activities took men away from home for long periods of time, women took over a greater share of the agricultural tasks, obtaining higher status as a result. The beginnings of political unification in the ninth century and the warfare that accompanied this led to greater opportunities for women to obtain such status.

Dommasnes' article, along with the other articles in this volume, is to be praised for specifically examining the role of women in prehistory several years before the topic began to be widely addressed by American archaeologists (the papers were first presented at a workshop in 1979). The work is a solid contribution to the study of gender-based economic roles in prehistory. Given the importance that historic evidence plays in the development of her model of Iron Age gender roles, it could have been improved by a more critical comparison of possible similarities and differences in these economic roles in Late Iron Age and early Medieval societies. This is not to say that her conclusions on the roles of women in Late Iron Age society may not be correct, just that she does not pay sufficient attention to her own caveats on the effect of Christian traditions on the historic evidence on which she relies. Kitchen utensils are "only slightly more common in women's graves than in men's" (p. 74) and agricultural implements, especially sickles, are found most often in women's graves, but based on this she concludes that a division of labor similar to later Norwegian farming society, with "women responsible for indoor work, men for out-of-doors work, seems to be confirmed by the tool categories represented in male and female graves" (p. 75). While an interesting initial analysis, it would have benefited from more careful critique of the historic data and greater attention to changes occurring in the transition between Late Iron Age and Early Medieval society. KJ

*mortuary analysis/trade/Iron Age/Viking/Norway/Scandinavia/Europe*


50. DOMMASNES, LIV HELGA 1990. Feminist archaeology: Critique or theory building? In *Writing the Past in the Present,* edited by Frederick Baker and Julian Thomas, 24-31. St. David's University College, Lampeter, England.

Liv Helga Dommasnes discusses the role and character of a feminist archaeology, considering not only how to examine the past from a feminist viewpoint, but how to use the results of such an enterprise to change the present. She notes that there can be no logically valid inference from what was to what ought to be, and that there are serious fallacies in harnessing the past to the present through justifying ideologies. Instead, the past must be evaluated and used "to learn about our potential and avoid former mistakes" (p. 25).

# Annotated References

Dommasnes briefly describes the history of latter-day Scandinavian archaeology, concluding that much of the recent postprocessual critique was foreshadowed in Scandinavia by a group of humanistic archaeologists—mainly women—who were not caught up in the euphoria of the New Archaeology. But she sees certain problems with postprocessualist approaches as well. Whereas positivist approaches deny the full variability of human experience, which she sees as the proper object of anthropological inquiry, postprocessualist and poststructuralist archaeology leave the reader "with the impression that the only reality we can hope to grasp is the subjective one, the one that in phenomenological terminology is 'for me'" (p. 27). She argues for a middle path, based on two central assumptions: (1) that there is a reality independent of our perception of it; and (2) that even if our perceptions are colored by our own cultural constructs and context, these biases can be transcended and some kind of intersubjective, intercultural insight reached. "Without such assumptions," she writes, "archaeology as a scholarly discipline becomes meaningless, and no one except the individual practitioner needs to feel affected by its results" (p. 28).

Dommasnes argues for a feminist archaeology based on the feminist epistemological claim that men and women perceive the world in very different ways as the result of differing experiences and upbringing, and focusing on masculinity and femininity as both elements in the construction of society and as forces in historical process. She raises the question of how we might recognize men, women or children in the past, but provides no answers, merely asserting that by studying ideologies in the past these questions are soluble. She does not argue for a radically new approach, but simply contends that we need to incorporate gender perspectives in current constructs. The study of prehistoric ideologies, dialectics and power relations are central to such an endeavor, and she argues for a certain degree of epistemological pluralism, recognizing that while there may be one past out there, there remain many ways to perceive it.

Her arguments are concise but sometimes abbreviated, often making the linkages between points difficult to follow, and she occasionally uses terms in unusual ways, as when describing the testing of hypotheses as induction (i.e., based on reference to empirical observation, rather than reason alone), or in treatment of theoretical approaches (e.g., functionalism) as epistemologies.  AWB

*feminist critique/postprocessualism/epistemology/sociology of science/Scandinavia*


51. DOMMASNES, LIV HELGA AND ELSE JOHANSEN KLEPPE 1988. Women in archaeology in Norway. *Archaeological Review from Cambridge* 7(2):230-234.

Dommasnes and Kleppe provide descriptive summaries of the articles in the first five issues of *K.A.N.* (*Kvinner i arkeologi i Norge*), (Women in Archaeology in Norway), a biannual periodical which grew out of a seminar on "Archaeological feminist research and women in archaeological research" which was held in Norway in 1985. This journal is usually published in Scandinavian languages (although volumes three and five were also produced in English). More information about this journal can be found in *Nordic Archaeological Abstracts*, from which the summaries presented in this article were derived.

According to the summaries, the first few volumes of *K.A.N.* had a heavy emphasis on the sociopolitics of the discipline, and this concern continues into the later issues. There are also a number of historical articles, such as those focused on Hanna Rydh (born 1891), the first woman to obtain a doctorate in archaeology in Scandinavia. The fifth volume contains another historical piece which looks at the involvement of Hans Hildebrand and Oscar Montelius in the first Swedish feminist movement *Frerika-Bremer-forbundet*, although it is noted that this engagement was excluded from their archaeological work (as was Hanna Rydh's).

In addition to the summaries of *K.A.N.* articles, an address is given for subscriptions orders and membership in the society.

Given the amount of archaeological research and theoretical debate taking place in Scandinavia which is often (and unfortunately) neglected by the English-speaking world, it seems obvious that more and better translations and greater familiarity with the issues of interests on each side would be of benefit. This article plays a role in such an effort, and provides information that is not easily obtainable elsewhere. However, its brevity (each *K.A.N.* article is summarized in less than two or three sentences) and its lack of a critical component limits the utility of this review.

As a side note, the *Archaeological Review from Cambridge* seems to have misprinted one of the author's names in the title. The editors of the first four issues of *K.A.N.* were Liv Helga Dommasnes and Else Johansen Kleppe, and so it seems likely that the authors of this article are Kleppe and Liv Helga Dommasnes, not Commasnes as listed in *ARC*. WDG

*sociopolitics of archaeology/history of archaeology/Norway/Scandinavia*


52. DONLEY, LINDA W. 1982. House power: Swahili space and symbolic markers. In *Symbolic and Structural Archaeology*, edited by Ian Hodder, 63-73. Cambridge University Press, Cambridge.

DONLEY-REID, LINDA W. 1990. A structuring structure: The Swahili house. In *Domestic Architecture and the Use of Space*, edited by S. Kent, 114-126. Cambridge University Press, Cambridge.

These two articles are based on Donley-Reid's extensive ethnoarchaeological research in and around the town of Lamu, Kenya. Both articles (the second is something of an extension of the first) examine the structure, use, and symbolic meaning of the multi-story coral houses of the Swahili elite. Donley-Reid describes how material culture, such as porcelain plates and decorative wall niches, symbolically protect the inhabitants of the house from possible defilement from polluting activities such as birth, death, sexual intercourse and defecation. She also examines how rituals use the segmented interiors of the houses to reinforce the hierarchical social and symbolic order, such as one in which a new-born infant is carried to each room of the house and given a lengthy explanation of its uses and functions, for while the infant is too young to understand what is being said, the messages are not lost on the other participants in the ritual. Donley-Reid draws upon Giddens' theory of structuration to explore the reflexive relationships between people and their constructed environment - how culture can determine architectural form, and in return, how the ordered spaces and objects encourage the continuation of certain cultural elements. The second article goes further in using these theories in attempting to create a link between house style and ethnicity with which to challenge Mark Horton's interpretation of Swahili society as originally and essentially African in origin.

These articles are valuable correctives for Swahili archaeology in that, as Donley-Reid charges, other archaeologists working on the East African coast have not adequately utilized the contemporary society as a source for information and interpretations. Though neither article sets out to specifically address gender relations, the extreme patriarchy of the present-day system makes such issues relevant. Both articles detail the objectification of women in this society; women are considered to be impure and thus often decorated. This decoration (often beads or pendants made from porcelain sherds) not only protects and purifies, but is said to constitute a competitive display of male social status; men decorate the women so as not to be tainted themselves by association with worldly goods. In this society, the cultural ideal is for women never to leave the walls of the house in which they were born, and Donley-Reid reports living women who have experienced such an extreme degree of seclusion. How these gender relations are embedded within and perpetuated by the architecture and material culture is described only as a component of more inclusive interactions.

There are some problematic elements in these articles, such as the hypothesized link between ethnicity and sytle mentioned above. For one, Donley-Reid considers archaeology to be practically useless in the absence of supplemental information from historical documentation or ethographic observation in cases of apparent cultural continuity (1990:115), a stance which most prehistoric archaeologists must necessarily object to. For another, both papers, despite references to Giddens and Bourdieu, are noticeably devoid of social actors and lacking in a theory of agency. Swahili society may subjugate women in a number of ways, but Donley-Reid does not consider or look for the possibility of women actively contesting, challenging, or subverting such a social order. She similarly denies the potential for an active role to Swahili lower classes and slaves and to neighboring ethnic groups in exploring the origins of Swahili society, while at the same time reifying categories such as "African" and "Swahili" in using the present to interpret the past.

However, despite these particular criticisms, these two articles are in general quite successful. Both attempt to be explicit about the social theory utilized in their interpretation of the archaeological data, both point out the undeiable importance of ethonarchaeology, and both delineate the linkages between architecture, artifacts, and a cultural system. The 1982 article has been widely cited as a case study of a system in which gender relations and cultural meanings are reflected in and reinforced by the created environment; and though

I see more problems with the main arguments of the 1990 article, it is also an important contribution to an area deserving more published research. WDG

*architecture/spatial analysis/ethnoarchaeology/class/ethnicity/structuralism/trade/Swahili/Kenya/Africa*


53. DONLEY, LINDA W. 1987. Life in the Swahili town house reveals the symbolic meaning of spaces and artefact assemblages. *The African Archaeological Review*, 5:181-192.

DONLEY-REID, LINDA W. 1990. The power of Swahili porcelain, beads and pottery. In *Powers of Observation: Alternative Views in Archeology*, edited by Sarah M. Nelson and Alice B. Kehoe, 47-59. American Anthropological Association, Washington, D.C.

These two similar articles are based on Donley-Reid's ethnoarchaeological research in and around Lamu, Kenya (cf. the previous annotation). The information obtained from contemporary Swahili society is then used in the interpretation of remains recovered from excavations in three local eighteenth-century coral houses.

The first article is primarily concerned with ways in which the Swahili elite, or *waungwana*, keep their houses symbolically protected to ward off misfortune. The innermost room of the house, the *ndani*, is the site of many dangerous activities, such as sex, birth, and the washing of the dead. It is therefore ritually protected by numerous artifacts such as imported porcelain plates and mihrab-like niches. But the ritual activities of this room also leave physical traces which Donley-Reid was able to recover in her house excavations. For example, when a corpse is washed in this room prior to burial, a trench is dug to collect water from the ritual, which is treated as a symbolic grave by the women who are not allowed to leave the house to attend the burial in the cemetery. This trench was detectable in all three of her excavations, but such features have never been commented upon in other Swahili archaeological site reports, presumably because without the ethnographic detail the excavators did not know what to look for. Donley-Reid also recovered four still-born infant burials from the Lamu houses and five small pits with iron nails which she interprets as once having contained placentae based on present Swahili custom and the protective nature of iron in Swahili culture. This article also considers the protective capacities of other objects recovered archaeologically, such as porcelain, beads, and owl bones.

The second article also focuses more on material culture, and the symbolic use of objects for purification, such as porcelain plates used for protection from the evil eye. A successful aversion is thought to break the plate, and the resulting sherds are often worn as pendants or pressed into the clay walls of lower class houses. This article also examines how different colored beads work as "medicines," protecting the women who wear them at vulnerable times, such as during menstrual periods and after childbirth. Donley-Reid also outlines an ethnotaxonomy of local pottery and points out that incised decoration only occurs on pots which are used by women to prepare food for men (decoration to impede the possible transferral of pollutants).

Many researchers on style have noted the protective and cleansing functions which decoration may play in a culture. The strength of Donley-Reid's approach is that she has conducted the ethnoarchaeological research to determine both the symbolic meaning and the material correlates of certain behaviors, and then has looked for and found such traces in her excavations. These two articles give some consideration to the negotiation of gender roles between men and women, but Donley-Reid comes to the conclusion that "Swahili women are a muted group whose view of life has adjusted to a dominant male system" (1987:190). Yet since many of the protective functions of the decorative elements she identifies are not conscious to or acknowledged by the actors involved, it seems possible that at some level there is an alternative dialogue and resistance to the patriarchal social order.

Of particular interest in these articles are the introductions, in which Donley-Reid attempts to place her own work within a larger context, as the first female archaeologist to work on the East African coast. In an Islamic community where the house is a woman's private world, she admits that "As a woman, I found it easier to collect ethnographic information about the social or symbolic uses of objects within the Swahili household" (1990:49). Access may have been more difficult for the male researchers, but Donley-Reid primarily faults them for having treated Swahili culture as if it were extinct. The utility of her ethnoarchaeological work for the interpretation of archaeological remains affirms her position. Her archaeological excavations also differed from the other researchers on the East African coast, for whom, "an unstated goal...seems to have been to locate and excavate the earliest and/or largest buildings," which usually translated into a focus on mosques and chronologies (1990:48). Donley-Reid instead chose to focus on the symbolic meaning of the domestic architecture of later periods: "As a woman, I felt that exploring houses, a women's domain within the Swahili context, might yield new insights" (1987:183). The fact that Swahili men often spend the majority of their day relaxing at the mosque, while women spend the majority of their life within their home is paralleled by the different research designs adopted by male and female Euro-American archaeologists working in this area. In this regard, Donley-Reid's work shows the utility of the interaction of multiple interests and perspectives in archaeology. WDG

*household analysis/ethnoarchaeology/sociopolitics of archaeology/spatial analysis/Swahili/Kenya/Africa*


54. DUKE, PHILIP 1991. Recognizing gender in Plains hunting groups: Is it possible or even necessary? In *The Archaeology of Gender: Proceedings of the Twenty-Second Annual Conference of the Archaeological Association of the University of Calgary*, edited by Dale Walde and Noreen D. Willows, 280-283. Archaeological Association, The University of Calgary, Calgary.

In this self-described position paper, Duke examines the difficulties of recognizing and evaluating gender relations among prehistoric hunting and gathering peoples in the Great Plains of North America. Duke identifies three problems limiting gender-conscious archaeology in this region: (1) the identification and archaeological recognition of different gender categories; (2) the definition of relations between people of different genders; and (3) an assessment of the extent to which archaeological analysis is influenced by the ideological biases of the interpreters. In his examination of the first two problems, Duke highlights particular archaeological case studies that illustrate our inability to "recognize gender" in the archaeological record. In his brief consideration of ideological biases, Duke notes that archaeologists have traditionally devalued women in Plains societies, and that prehistoric Plains women continue to be characterized as domestic homemakers, pottery producers, or commodities of exchange. Although he welcomes recent revisionist studies, Duke expresses the concern that archaeologists may begin to overlook or minimize inequalities among these populations. In other words, archaeology runs the risk of once again using Native American histories to make political statements.

Given these considerations, Duke questions whether it is acceptable to attempt to "recognize gender" in every archaeological study. This does not imply that archaeologists should abandon gender studies, but simply acknowledges that gender issues are much more complex than archaeologists might otherwise wish to believe. He concludes that archaeologists should not be concerned that we cannot "recognize gender" in all prehistoric cases. Instead, this difficulty should be used as an opportunity to escape from "some of the strictures of ethnographic analogy" (p. 280) to make innovative and independent contributions to anthropological and historical understanding "in the areas of social roles and symbolism, if not in the development of gender hierarchies themselves" (p. 282).

This short paper successfully highlights many difficulties that archaeologists confront in the study of gender, especially with respect to the limitations of the archaeological record of prehistoric gatherer-hunters. His concern with the extent to which our analyses are influenced by our personal ideological biases is appropriate, and should "encourage archaeologists to question why interest in gender is recent, and to create models for the past which respond to the concerns generated by such reflection" (p. 280). Duke's call for archaeologists working with meager material records to be excused from necessarily having to "recognize gender" in favor of the opportunity to undertake other innovative research, however, reveals a facile understanding of the concept of gender. For example, even though Duke implies investigators must first be able to "recognize gender" in the material remains of the archaeological record before they can begin to evaluate gender relations, he appears confident that researchers will be able to address important new questions in the areas of social roles and symbolism. Duke does not acknowledge that social roles and symbolism may themselves be structured by gender relations.

Duke's argument also is disturbing because it limits our potential to understand the evolution of gender inequality. The conceptual limitations underlying Duke's central question highlight the continued need for archaeologists to develop a more comprehensive theory of gender free from an absolute dependency on the identification of specific gender categories in the surviving material residues of the past. KFA

*sociopolitics of archaeology/gatherer-hunters/symbolism/ethnographic analysis/epistemology/United States and Canada, Plains/North America*


55. EHRENBERG, MARGARET 1989. *Women in Prehistory*. University of Oklahoma Press, Norman.

Written for archaeologists who have not thought about gender and non-archaeologists who have, this book focuses on the roles and statuses of women in European prehistory, using evidence from documentary sources and ethnographic analogies as well as the archaeological evidence of burials, productive activities, settlements, and art. The author describes the problems inherent in these classes of evidence from the point of view of studying gender. The book then discusses selected topics from the Paleolithic through the Iron Age.

Ehrenberg's discussion of the Paleolithic uses the analogy of modern foragers to suggest a pattern of small groups, high mobility, and social equality. Claiming that women and men would have shared subsistence tasks when depending on gathered plants and scavenged meat, she expects dependence on large game hunting to bring about a division of labor by gender, referring to Zihlman's argument about hunting, risk, and child care. The author makes suggestions for the possible role of women in social developments stemming from long-term child care, and suggests that as major food providers women would have enjoyed status equal to that of men. Finally, she reviews archaeological evidence and interpretations of plant utilization, burials, and female figurines.

From the analogy of modern horticulturalists, Ehrenberg suggests that women had the primary role in the development of agriculture. Consequent on agriculture was sedentism, which allowed differential accumulation of goods, debt, and eventually social stratification. She outlines Neolithic European expansion and takes the form and size of longhouses to indicate matrilocal residence of monogamous families, changing to a patrilocal pattern after the advent of the plow. Plow agriculture, large scale herding, and the secondary products revolution are presented as a "take-over" of agriculture by men, with the consequent loss of status by women as they were increasingly relegated to secondary tasks.

In her discussion of the Bronze Age, Ehrenberg criticizes the interpretation of Minoan Crete as a matriarchy but affirms the participation of elite women in a variety of public activities. She presents evidence from three studies of burials in northwest Europe, evaluating their various implications for women's position. Emphasizing that the majority of burials do not have grave goods, she notes that whatever interpretations one makes probably apply only to elite women. Several other topics are briefly discussed, including a theory of trade and intermarriage between Scandinavia and Germany.

Evidence from the Iron Age includes images of women on Hallstatt vessels and Clarke's excavations at Glastonbury. Most of the chapter is concerned with the use of historical sources such as classical descriptions of European peoples. She lists the problems involved in using these sources, including their biases and political intent, but considers them valuable in spite of this. She presents the evidence in classical writings for women hunters, prophets, warriors, and rulers.

In the final chapter she points out that the relationship between production and status is not straightforward, but she contends that before the Bronze Age women were equal in status to men, and since then they have generally had a lower position with the exception of a few high status elite females.

Ehrenberg successfully brings together a large amount of data and a variety of interpretations in a way that would be particularly useful as an introduction for people unfamiliar with the literature. She succeeds in her effort to show that, even without new evidence, there is a lot of potential for using existing archaeological data to address gender questions. Problems in the book center around three issues. The first is the proposition that women's status is directly related to their productive activities, an idea which needs to be documented ethnographically rather than assumed. The logic behind it should also be questioned more closely. The classification of certain activities as "productive," for example, is problematic (to Ehrenberg, planting food is productive, but processing it is not), and so is the resulting value-laden interpretation of "non-productive" activities as "secondary roles." Assuming that women's status is unitary is another difficulty, and to her credit Ehrenberg explicitly avoids this in the discussions of the Bronze and Iron Ages.

A second issue is the use of ethnographic analogy. Ehrenberg is careful to qualify her analogies as hypothetical, but she does use them widely and adopts traditional sexual dichotomies such as the strict division of hunting and gathering, in spite of acknowledged exceptions and current critiques. Finally, the discussion of ethnohistoric sources would benefit from more specific suggestions as to how textual problems should be dealt with. Further suggestions for archaeological testing of questionable historic claims would also be useful. SF

*mortuary analysis/art/gatherer-hunters/trade/ethnographic analogy/division of labor/figurines/agriculture/ agricultural origins/Europe*

56. EISNER, WENDY R. 1991. The consequences of gender bias in mortuary analysis: A case study. In *The Archaeology of Gender: Proceedings of the Twenty-Second Annual Conference of the Archaeological Association of the University of Calgary*, edited by Dale Walde and Noreen D. Willows, 352-257. Archaeological Association, The University of Calgary, Calgary.

Eisner's study re-analyzes data from a Roman cemetery and concludes that current attitudes about gender shape our interpretation of mortuary data; we often interpret patterns as gender-related when they may indicate something else. She begins with a brief outline and critique of gender studies in archaeology. Most of this work has been limited to critiques of male bias, and more empirical work needs to be done to move gender into mainstream archaeology. We need gender studies which are not exclusively about women and not necessarily feminist. Gender must be combined with traditionally important topics if it is to have a more general effect on method and theory; otherwise, it will remain on the fringes. In addition, a change of perspective is needed in order to realize the influence our own cultural conceptions have on our archaeological interpretations. The issue of gender patterning in mortuary evidence is an example of such undue influence.

Because skeletons can be sexed, Eisner argues, we are inclined to think that patterns in graves have to do with gender, but this is not always the case. Sex is always a characteristic of burials, but gender roles and values, which are culturally constructed, may not be. Mistaking other patterns for gender can be avoided, she suggests, by doing statistical analyses of grave goods and then seeing what relationship they have to sex.

As an example, she uses data from the cemetery of a Roman military installation in Belgium. The excavators did not sex the skeletons biologically, but assigned them to male and female categories on the basis of goods, and they concluded that gender was an important determinant of mortuary patterning. Eisner notes the bias involved in deciding what objects should be "male" or "female." The specific criteria by which sex was determined are not given, but she infers three or four types of goods that seem to be used definitionally. Eisner takes these "male" and "female" goods and carries out several chi-square tests of the relationships between them. She concludes that while the male goods form a discrete category, the female category is invalid. Since the male goods are all military items, she suggests that the real distinction in the cemetery is between soldiers and civilians, not between men and women.

Eisner has a very different notion of what a gendered archaeology should be than do many authors of feminist critiques, who would object that gender cannot make an impact on general theory if it is divorced from feminism. Eisner argues for incorporation and change from within rather than radical overthrow.

The thesis of this paper, that if you start by assuming a simple gender-based distinction you will miss other important divisions in your data, is important and valid. Eisner is correct to distinguish between sex and gender, and her suggestion that rather than looking for gender right away we should look statistically for patterns and only then attempt to interpret them is a point that should be taken to heart.

Unfortunately, her tables do not test what she intends, and she shows some confusion in the text as to what she wants to compare. This statistical snarl makes it difficult to determine just what is the nature of these categories. Moreover, in the interpretive line, Eisner seems to assume that burials reflect social differences in a fairly direct way and that if gender is important it will show up as discrete male/female categories. Social roles like military and civilian are not necessarily ungendered. If sex should not be taken for gender, neither should gender be conceived as simple, dichotomized sex. SF

*mortuary analysis/Roman period/Belgium/Europe*

## Annotated References

57. ENGELSTAD, ERICKA 1991. Feminist theory and postprocessual archaeology. In *The Archaeology of Gender: Proceedings of the Twenty-Second Annual Conference of the Archaeological Association of the University of Calgary*, edited by Dale Walde and Noreen D. Willows, 116-120. Archaeology Association, The University of Calgary, Calgary.

    Engelstad presents a feminist critique of postprocessual archaeology, specifically those aspects which continue the androcentric bias found in processual archaeology. She begins with a discussion of feminism's main critique of science: the existence of a male bias in research methodology and theory. If this is the case then how, she asks, can it be possible to do good science? According to Harding (1986) there are several ways feminist theorists have approached this problem: by feminist empiricism, the feminist standpoint and feminist postmodernism. For some poststructuralists or postmodernists, it is the acceptance of the historically and socially contingent nature of theories that is viewed as providing limitless opportunities for analysis and theorizing, whereas others view this as having some extremely negative tendencies (e.g., relativism). One of the resulting problems she sees is that the practice of deciding between a plurality of meanings becomes a matter of power. Engelstad sees similar problems in postprocessual archaeology where prehistory and the archaeological record are considered metaphorically as a text. Her comments focus on the writings of Shanks and Tilley (1987a, 1987b) who "advocate the writing of many conflicting, politicized archaeologies" (p. 117). Again the problem is that "only power will be the deciding factor for which story is heard/read/written" (ibid.). Their unawareness she attributes to "the implied genderlessness of their analyses" (ibid.). Power is an essential aspect of Shanks and Tilley's view of human society, but they ignore its relations to the problems of gender. She critiques their inattention to gender as a structuring principle in society, and their coverage (one paragraph or less in each book) of feminist archaeology. Postprocessual archaeologists, she concludes, ignore the need for reflexivity in their own work and thinking, assume a singularly male readership and authorship, display a lack of understanding of themselves as gendered individuals and of gender as a structuring principle, and employ an unreflective use of value-laden dichotomies (e.g., public/private, nature/culture). Engelstad concludes that an androcentric postprocessual archaeology is not equally as valid as an anti-racist/sexist feminist archaeology. EAB

*References cited*
Harding, S. 1986. *The Science Question in Feminism*. Open University Press, Milton Keynes.

Shanks, M. and C. Tilley 1987a. *Reconstructing Archaeology: Theory and Practice*. Cambridge University Press, Cambridge.

Shanks, M. and C. Tilley 1987b. *Social Theory and Archaeology*. Polity Press, Cambridge.

*epistemology/feminist critique/sociopolitics of archaeology/processualism/postprocessualism*


58. ENGELSTAD, ERICKA 1991. Images of power and contradiction: Feminist theory and postprocessual archaeology. *Antiquity* 65:502-14

    Postprocessual archaeology is united in its criticism of positivist, functionalist, adaptationalist models ushered in by New Archaeology, which emphasizes objective hypothesis testing. Feminism is part of this movement in critiquing masculine bias in western "scientific" methods and theory and in questioning the concept of objectivity. Within feminist archaeology, however, there is some debate as to how science should be conducted. In this article, Engelstad explores this debate, comparing developments in feminism to other postprocessual movements.

    Engelstad identifies three major schools of feminist science: feminist empiricism, feminist standpoint, and feminist postmodernism. Feminist empiricism does not reject current methods or, presumably, theories of science, but asserts that science has been practiced inadequately. A feminist standpoint approach is related in that it does not reject methodology, but asserts that the feminist perspective is a superior and preferable standard for conducting science. Both contain empirical faults.

Feminist postmodernism shares a theoretical base with other postmodern schools in emphasizing that knowledge is historically and socially constituted. Divorcing the concept of knowledge from an absolute introduces problems of objectivity and relativism. A relativistic stance acknowledges a plurality of possible viewpoints which can be negotiated. Engelstad argues that this stance becomes a matter of power, the power to construct reality, which is rarely available to feminists and other minorities. She sees this approach as alienating many researchers who see reality as imposed upon their experiences. Two aspects of postmodernism, prehistory as text, and a concern for power as a critically important factor in social relations, are discussed as they relate to feminist archaeology. Engelstad indicates that literary criticism is construed as a male undertaking, and notes that discussions of power do not include gender as a stratifying element. She refers to a recent postprocessual archaeological textbook, *Reconstructing Archaeology* (Shanks and Tilley 1987) to make her points.

The author of this article concludes that postprocessual archaeology, if it continues in the direction that it is moving, does not contain a place for a feminist archaeology. A relativistic approach to conducting science may actually be detrimental to the establishment of a feminist archaeology. KMM

*References cited*
Shanks, M. and C. Tilley, 1987. *Reconstructing archaeology.* Cambridge University Press, Cambridge.

*postmodernism/epistemology/processualism/postprocessualism/feminist critique/sociology of science*


59. EYMAN, FRANCES 1968. The teshoa, a Shoshonean woman's knife: A study of American Indian chopper industries. *Pennsylvania Archaeologist* 34:9-52.

The *teshoa* is an artifact that is recorded ethnographically to have been used by Shoshone women prior to AD 1900. Eyman, in the article, discusses ethnographic accounts of *teshoa* use. She also systematically and thoroughly reviews its distribution and that of related artifact types in time and space at archaeological sites across mainly North America but also including South America and the Old World. Referred to by its Shoshone name, Eyman defines the *teshoa* as "a split or spall struck from a cobblestone. Its edge is thin and acute. The cutting edge is formed by the intersection of a split surface with the rind of a cobble" (p. 10). This artifact is believed by Eyman to be part of a larger "chopper complex" used by prehistoric women for thousands of years. She laments that these assemblages are often ignored or discarded by archaeologists.

The origins and cultural historical relationships between chopper industries is the primary focus of this paper. After reviewing the forms of and potential relationships between old world and new world chopper industries, Eyman concludes that the development of chopper industries in the New World postdated Paleo-Indian times and that "the chopper and the *teshoa* were Siberian reinventions less than 30,000 years in age" (p. 44). Some of the theoretical and informational content in her discussion is now dated; however, the central problem of understanding the development/evolution and use of these kinds of technologies remains of interest.

The article contains some useful ethnographic information, and complete distributional data known at the time of publication in 1968. Eyman recognizes the technological importance of a "simple" industry that today would be considered an "expedient" technological assemblage. She also notes the interesting contrast between these tools and bifacial forms which she posits represents the industries of people of different genders. This idea is one that has only recently been examined by archaeologists (see, for example, entries #65 and #148). Although a gender slant is secondary and not developed here, archaeologists interested in lithic technologies and how they may relate to gender will find Eyman's discussion useful. NSG-F

*lithic technology/United States, Western/Shoshone*

## Annotated References

60. FEINMAN, GARY M., LINDA M. NICHOLS, and WILLIAM D. MIDDLETON 1992. Archaeology in 1992: A perspective from the Society for American Archaeology Annual Meeting program. *American Antiquity* 57(3):448-458.

Feinman et al. consider data on presentations at the 1983, 1991 and 1992 annual meetings of the Society for American Archaeology to "examine the state of American archaeology" (p. 448). They explicitly discuss the changing role women play at the meetings and relative changes in gender in both number of presentations and topics considered. As with most such studies, the results can be interpreted either as showing encouraging trends toward equality or as confirming a continued failure to achieve that equality.

Participation by women rose from 25% of all papers in 1983 to 33% in 1992. Perhaps more significantly, the percentage of woman discussants, a position often viewed as prestigious and marking higher status, nearly tripled (from 8% in 1983 to 22% in 1992). This trend indicates an increase in perceived stature for women in the discipline, although the percentage of women discussants still lags somewhat behind the percentage of women giving papers. Since discussants are generally more senior scholars, it may be that the gap will close in coming years.

While Feinman et al. are wary of interpreting their data as confirming Gero's (#67, 68, 69) assertions that men are directed to higher status fieldwork projects while women are encouraged to conduct lower status laboratory analyses, they note a slight tendency for men to address questions of settlement and regional systems, while women more commonly deal with subsistence and production practices.

The authors acknowledge that there may be underlying sources of bias making some of the data not entirely comparable. Data from the 1991 and 1992 meetings, for instance, were drawn from codings prepared by the presenters themselves, while the 1983 data were coded by one of the study's authors. Overall, the data suggest that the climate for women in the discipline is warming, although they highlight the continuing gap between the number of women in the discipline and the number of women achieving high ranks and statuses within it. AWB

*sociopolitics of archaeology/conference papers/discrimination/Society for American Archaeology*


61. FLANNERY, KENT V. AND MARCUS C. WINTER 1976. Analyzing household activities. In *The Early Mesoamerican Village*, edited by Kent V. Flannery, 34-47. Academic Press, Orlando.

Flannery and Winter examine spatial associations within and between household clusters in Formative Oaxaca. Based on a limited sample of well-preserved house floors and features, they tentatively propose four categories of household activities: (1) universal household activities; (2) possibly specialized household activities, carried out at one or two houses in every village; (3) possible regional specializations, carried out at all houses in one area, but absent from houses in another; and (4) possibly unique specialization, perhaps restricted to certain wards or barrios at regional centers. While the relative numbers of male and female burials with various tool types are presented (e.g., pp. 38-39), for the most part these kinds of specialization are discussed in terms of "villagers" rather than one or another gender. They identify an intermediate level of analysis, between the level of feature and household or household cluster, where differential distributions of material may indicate men's and women's work areas. They note a tendency in at least some of the houses in their sample for men's activities to be associated with the left side of the house (divided along the midline from the entrance), while tools believed associated with women and women's tasks were more commonly found to the right. Tasks generally associated with men include flint chipping, hide working, shell working, land clearance, and various other kinds of manufacturing and extraction of resources. Women's tasks included various kinds of food preparation, spinning, sewing, etc..

Flannery and Winter do not demonstrate but instead assume that certain tools are associated with men's and women's tasks. While clear evidence for the gender associations of these tasks is not presented, neither are associations presented as empirically derived regularities but as tentative although empirically inspired hypotheses to be confirmed or refuted by later analysis of larger samples. In light of the comments of some other authors (cf. #23), it is intriguing that Flannery and Winter identify manos and metates with both men's and women's tasks, and implictly suggest that at least some of the chert reduction took place in women's areas. Given the small sample sizes and preliminary nature of the discussion, Flannery and Winter provide no clear answers to questions regarding the division of labor in Formative Oaxacan villages, but raise an important series of questions to be answered by subsequent research. AWB

*division of labor/household analysis/spatial analysis/Oaxaca/Mexico/Formative period*

62. FOOTE, CHERYL J. AND SANDRA K. SCHACKEL 1986. Indian women of New Mexico, 1535-1680. In *New Mexico Women: Intercultural Perspectives*, edited by Joan M. Jensen and Darlis A. Miller, 17-40. University of New Mexico Press, Albuquerque.

Foote and Schackel present a historical sketch of the changing lifeways of the Native American women who inhabited the region now known as New Mexico and Arizona between the time of their first direct contacts with Spaniards in 1535 through the outbreak of the Pueblo Revolt of 1680. This summary considers this period of stress, adjustment, and accommodation in terms of a process of cultural exchanges between the major Pueblo, Navajo, and Apache cultural groups, focusing on these women and the Spanish *conquistadors*, settlers, Colonial government officials, and Jesuit missionaries. The authors also review how the imposition of Spanish control over the region and the arrival of European material culture and technological organization amplified the frequency and impact of cultural interactions among the diverse Native American populations. Because the Spanish were in closest contact with the numerous Eastern Pueblo communities scattered primarily along the Rio Grande Valley, the authors focus most of their discussion on the exchanges between these populations.

Foote and Schackel use a wide range of ethnohistorical sources to provide a rich commentary on the activities, social roles, and interpersonal relationships in which Native American women were engaged. They identify the androcentric biases of the Spanish chroniclers, including their tendency to over-report women's domestic activities and under-report women's participation in religious observances relative to men. Nevertheless, Foote and Schackel also report references that pertain to women's primary responsibilities in house construction, wall replastering, and tending turkeys, as well as their involvement in fishing, rabbit hunting, warfare, and public ceremonies.

To increase the usefulness of their paper, the authors provide complete documentation for a long list of primary references supporting each of their major observations. Although Foote and Schackel repeatedly emphasize that this time was one of dynamic change, their summary does obscure the variability between different communities composing each of the major Pueblo, Navajo, and Apache culture groups. As a consequence of this single shortcoming in an otherwise excellent introductory text, readers unfamiliar with the extent of cultural diversity in the area may not refer to the primary references and may inadvertently employ a particular ethnohistorical observation in an inappropriate manner. KFA

*division of labor/ethnohistory/historical archaeology/Pueblo/Navajo/Apache/United States, Southwest*

63. FRATT, LEE 1991. A preliminary analysis of gender bias in the sixteenth and seventeenth century Spanish colonial documents of the American Southwest. In *The Archaeology of Gender: Proceedings of the Twenty-Second Annual Conference of the Archaeological Association of the University of Calgary*, edited by Dale Walde and Noreen D. Willows, 245-251. Archaeological Association, The University of Calgary, Calgary.

Fratt describes how documentary records left by a virtually all male cast of Spanish explorers, colonists, government officials, and missionaries in the North American Southwest has influenced models of culture contact and change and the archaeological interpretation of protohistoric Pueblo society. She notes

## Annotated References

that little attention has been devoted to identifying, evaluating, and compensating for gender bias in these texts. First, she examines gender biases in sixteenth and seventeenth century Spanish documents, and compares it to the kinds of gender bias represented in southwestern archaeological texts which were written almost exclusively by Anglo-American men. In this endeavor, Fratt draws upon the earlier analysis of Spanish gender bias by Foote and Schackel (#62), and the archaeological study of the protohistoric Zuñi village of Hawikuh in west-central New Mexico by Smith et al. (1966). Although she admits that she expected to find some fairly direct relationships between these ethnohistorical and archaeological texts, Fratt concludes "the links,...especially with regard to biases and assumptions about gender, social organization, social status, the activities of women and men, and culture change, are complex and convoluted" (p. 245). She suggests that the interplay between the nature of southwestern ethnographic research and the use of ethnographic analogy by archaeologists is a major factor underlying this complex relationship. Fratt asserts that gender bias introduced by the Spanish chroniclers and subsequently incorporated in interpretation by ethnographers using ethnohistoric texts may be altered and reinterpreted as a consequence of the ethnographers' gender biases. To understand the sources of gender bias in archaeological texts, therefore, Fratt argues researchers must consider two sets of biases: those held by the Spanish and those held by southwestern anthropologists.

Fratt's second topic traces changes in images of Pueblo women portrayed in a number of historical documents dating between AD 1581 and 1680, an interest which rises from current debate concerning the appropriateness of ethnographic analogy in archaeological interpretation. In her extended analysis and critique of Spanish colonial documents, Fratt operationalizes a feminist concern with "evaluating the status of women and formulating theories about changes in that status" (p. 247), proposing that chroniclers' assessments of the social position of Pueblo women may have changed as a consequence of their increasing knowledge of the language and culture of the Puebloan people. She contends this study will contribute to research addressing the differential impact of Spanish colonization on Native American women and men.

Fratt's analysis is based on a wide variety of ethnohistorical observations, documented in Foote and Schackel (#62) and other well-known secondary references. She divides the 100-year time span encompassed by her study into three periods: (1) early contacts (pre-AD 1580); (2) colonization (AD 1601-1610); and (3) escalating conflict between church and state officials (AD 1610-1680). Whereas Foote and Schackel argue that the status of Pueblo women did not appreciably change with contact, because of their continued economic contributions, Fratt concludes that there were substantive changes in women's status. Significantly, Fratt contends that even if "the status of Pueblo women within Pueblo society remained high despite Spanish contact and conquest, the changing image of Pueblo women from exotic object to suffering victim to political pawn that is conveyed by historical documents suggests their status within pre-Revolt Spanish society may have declined" (p. 250). To better understand these changes, Fratt calls for additional archaeological studies which explicitly address women's status, in addition to an examination of how their status and position within Spanish colonial society affected their status in Pueblo society. Given her assumption that the status of Pueblo women may be materially manifest, she suggests researchers examine changes in women's production of decorated ceramics, or their manufacture and use of corn grinding tools.

Fratt concisely addresses the issues that she raises. She provides an useful framework for assessing the relationship between the kinds of bias often present in early Spanish Colonial documents, ethnographic accounts, and archaeological interpretations. Fratt's analysis also builds on Foote and Shackel's study to reveal important new insights into the many ways Pueblo women's lives were modified both within their communities and in Spanish colonial society as the process of colonization evolved. In recognizing that Pueblo women were differentially affected by colonization, and that a Puebloan's status may be variably altered within several spheres of social interaction, Fratt establishes a preliminary outline for using ethnohistorical documents to help develop an archaeology of Pueblo Indian gender. Although Fratt emphasizes Pueblo women, her call for future research possesses the potential to contribute to our better understanding of how the activities, social roles, and interpersonal relationships of both Pueblo women and men changed through their first century of subjugation by the Spanish. KFA

*feminist critique/Pueblo/historical archaeology/New Mexico/United States, Southwest*

64. GERO, JOAN M. 1992 (in press). Feasts and females: Gender ideology and political meals in the Andes. *The Norwegian Archaeological Review*.

Gero begins this attempt to find women in the archaeological record and to understand the role gender played in one prehistoric political trajectory in the Andes with a discussion of the theoretical issues involved in "producing a feminist prehistory, specifically one that rejects a limited and limiting view of women as an unchanging essence and insists on seeing gender as historically constituted" (p. 1). Next, she describes the route she takes to this destination, which relies on "an explicitly evolutionary framework to understand change in gender systems" (p. 2) and archaeological and ethnohistoric analogies. The evolutionary changes are modeled on Gailey's (1987) Marxist inspired scenario for the transition from kin-based societies to class societies, and the analogies come from contemporaneous Recuay sites, Moche archaeology, and Inka ethnohistory.

Gero hypothesizes that the small, Early Intermediate Period (200 BC-AD 600) site of Queyash Alto in the north central highlands of Peru marks the location of political and ritual feasting by "an emerging ranked and recognized social authority, a prestigious *ayllu* (territory-holding kin-based group)" (p. 7). According to Gero, the recovery of copper *tupu* pins (clothes fasteners) and spindle whorls is evidence for prehistoric women in the ceremonial area of Queyash Alto. Given traditional Andean women's roles in food preparation and serving, iconographic evidence on pottery (including the portrayal of women who "hold cups and/or food and surround a larger, centrally placed and sometimes more elaborately dressed male" p. 11) and the presence of possible *chicha* (maize beer) vessels in the ceremonial portion of the site, Gero argues that women's roles in these feasts were "fundamental to the negotiation and reaffirmation of hierarchy and the subversion of kin relations," or "a structural fulcrum on which Andean political stratification was balanced" (p. 3).

Gero's model is plausible, and gender roles play a satisfyingly essential part of her processual model. It is appallingly difficult to link theory, including theory incorporating prehistoric gender relations, with a site's specifics, however, and the major weakness in her model lies in the unconvincing evidence for the various parts of her construct — for feasting, for *ayllus* (or ranked kin groups in general), for women's participation in feasting, and for the transition from kin-based to class societies at this particular point in Recuay history. In some cases, Gero is careful to point out the underlying assumptions of her ethnographic analogues, as with her description of weaving in the northern Andes and the association between spindle whorls and women proposed for Queyash Alto. In other cases, assumption is laid over assumption, as when the supposition that there were *ayllus* at Queyash Alto is followed by the surmise that the "high ranking women who resided at Queyash were *entitled* to participate in the elaborate ceremonialism, including perhaps the preparation of feasts, rather than the fact of their gender automatically requiring some ritual performance" (emphasis in original, p. 12).

In an area as full of ethnographic, historic, and archaeological variability as the Andes, there are myriad possibilities for social analogy. Given Gero's discussion, it is difficult to say if Early Intermediate Period Moche women and men are an appropriate analogue for the people at Queyash Alto. Furthermore, contrasting gender relations at Queyash Alto with those in Late Horizon Inka society at Cuzco leaves one wondering what happened in later periods in the Recuay area. The archaeological evidence for gender roles at Queyash Alto is rather tenuous for the role it plays in the model of Andean social evolution presented. Gero's model may not be far off the mark, but she will need stronger arguments and more rigorous testing, including an examination of alternative hypotheses, if this scenario is to withstand the criticism of Andean specialists. SLD

*References cited*
Gailey, Christine W. 1987. Evolutionary perspectives on gender hierarchy. In *Analyzing Gender*, edited by Beth B. Hess and Myra Ferree, 32-67. Newbury Park, Sage.

*state formation/subsistence/ceramic analysis/spatial analysis/class/Marxism/Peru/Inka/Moche/Recuay/ Queyash Alto*

## Annotated References

65. GERO, JOAN M. 1991. Genderlithics: Women's roles in stone tool production. In *Engendering Archaeology: Women and Prehistory*, edited by Joan M. Gero and Margaret W. Conkey, 163-193. Basil Blackwell, Cambridge, MA.

In this chapter, Gero turns her attention to the history and assumptions behind lithic analysis in archaeology. The production of stone tools is traditionally assumed to be a strictly male occupation. This position persists due to the narrow definition of tools as elaborated and/or finely retouched artifacts, ignoring both flake tools and the functional aspects of stone tools in general. The position is also enhanced by the exclusion of female archaeologists from knapping and experimental replication. This has reinforced a public image of Man-the-Toolmaker and androcentric interpretations of lithic tool production. Gero then focuses on the abilities of women as toolmakers. She posits that women were very active in most contexts studied by archaeologists. To perform their work, women needed ready access to tools; dependence on men for these tools or even raw materials would have been impractical. Reproductive roles or physical strength have little impact on stone tool manufacture and would not have particularly hampered women in this activity. Most importantly, the process of social valuation of lithic production probably often included women as active participants. Gero examines data from Huaricoto, a ritual and habitation center in highland Peru occupied during the preceramic, Initial, Early Horizon and Early Intermediate Periods (2000 BC-AD 600). She links gender to patterns in raw material utilization, tool preparation and contexts of preparation and use. Women controlled local materials and created expedient flake tools for domestic contexts whereas men controlled non-local materials which they used for more elaborate bifaces for ritual purposes. With time, domestic activity replaced ritual activity as womens' roles were concentrated in the household, while men were pulled into wider sociopolitical spheres (such as during state formation).

Gero deals a critical blow to the common assumption of Man-the-Toolmaker. She demonstrates that women could have made stone tools (there are no universal social, cultural or biological reasons why they shouldn't), and even identifies instances in the ethnographic literature of this occurrence. Her use of social value or "loading" in terms of tool morphology is interesting. She relates gender dynamics and tool production; reciprocal relations allow women to make more elaborate forms while hierarchical relations segregate tool production. However, she does not discuss this in greater depth in this paper. Consequently, she appears to make the traditional assumption of elaborate vs. expedient tools as male vs. female. In addition, in her example from Huaricoto, a simple "reading" of the patterns recognized is performed with the unqualified assumption that gender is the underlying cause. Gero notes but does not discuss the multiple lines of evidence needed to strengthen her argument. JDB

*lithic technology/division of labor/feminist critique/state formation/androcentrism/South America/Peru/Andes*

66. GERO, JOAN M. 1991. Gender divisions of labor in the construction of archaeological knowledge. In *The Archaeology of Gender: Proceedings of the Twenty-Second Annual Conference of the Archaeological Association of the University of Calgary*, edited by Dale Walde and Noreen D. Willows, 96-102. Archaeological Association, The University of Calgary, Calgary.

Gero contends that archaeological practice and knowledge is skewed by an ideological bias that systematically favors male practitioners and excludes female ones from preferred roles and status positions in the discipline. It is a sad commentary on the state of affairs, both in the archaeological community and American society at large, that in the 1990s an article such as Gero's has such a valid target: gender discrimination does indeed exist and sexual stereotyping can influence career choices. She attempts to demonstrate her argument for the existence of female subordination using numerical data gathered in the sub-fields of lithic studies, paleoethnobotany and paleozoology. For example, she finds that women represent approximately 20% of all archaeologists. A slightly higher percentage of women identify themselves as lithic analysts. Gero states that no women are engaged in modern flintknapping replications. Women, instead, tend to study informal, expedient technologies. Furthermore, Gero finds that among paleoethnobotanists, a significantly higher proportion are women (roughly 50%). Women are thus overrepreted in this specialty relative to their numbers in the field as a whole. She also suggests that men tend to dominate the more prestigious areas in paleoethnobotany, such as research on the origins of agriculture. In addition, women are also overrepresented in paleozoology. Men dominate the study of large mammals, especially as it pertains to big game hunting. She writes, "[w]omen are reaffirmed as secondary citizens, in the past for not being hunters, and in the present, as archaeologists for being outside the big-bone circle" (p. 100).

Gero points out the truism that scientific knowledge is a social construction, and hence is subject to all the bias and prejudices inherent in any form of dominant ideology (her so-called "constructivist analysis"). It may be demonstrably true, as Gero asserts, that "science is patriarchal and a profoundly male endeavor" (p. 97), yet, it seems an unwarranted assertion to denigrate all male contributions to archaeology as inherently biased and all female efforts as in some way good. She states: "Women's research, fundamentally and perhaps unconsciously feminist in its approach to the construction of knowledge constitutes a challenge to disciplinary frameworks, and if allowed to persist, necessarily presents a serious challenge to the categories, divisions, assumptions and meanings attached to knowledge" (p. 100). The effect is tarnished, however, when on the next page she asserts that "archaeology will continue to contain women's scholarship in a low-status, low technology, theoretically irrelevant position" (p. 101). This may come as a surprise to those women in archaeology who happen to hold prestigious positions (obtained of course through merit), or technology jobs on state-of-the-art applications, or who produce theoretical treatises on the cutting edge of the disciplinary limits.

Intellectual and social processes that produce discrimination, subjugation, segregation and injustice may be crippling to the people who experience them. The United States is full of groups who have been on the wrong end of asymmetrical power relationships. One result is the sort of discourse used by segments of the feminist community to stake out an extreme position, belittling any male contribution to the practice of science as biased and prejudiced, while at the same time exalting any contribution put forth by a woman, in order to draw society into debate for redress of their grievances. The discourse is not particularly pleasing or polite but the result is, at the very least, that one takes notice of the problem. It is equally true that Gero adopts such a polemical viewpoint in advancing her position as to alienate a portion of her audience that might otherwise agree with her. Such an approach may preclude a remedy to the situation she describes. MRF

*sociopolitics of archaeology/feminist critique/scientific explanation/lithic technologies/archaeobotany/faunal analysis/sociology of science*

67. GERO, JOAN M. 1988. Gender bias in archaeology: Here, then and now. In *Feminism within the Science and Health-Care Professions: Overcoming Resistance*, edited by Sue Rosser, 33-43. Pergamon Press, Oxford.

It would be difficult to state the main thesis of Gero's argument more succinctly than she herself has done:

> [A]rchaeologists have systematically misinterpreted and ignored the archaeological evidence for production by women in prehistory, and...female archaeologists today are similarly being denied access to productive processes in the archaeological enterprise (p. 33).

This article is essentially a recapitulation of earlier studies (discussed at greater length below; see #68, 69) using the same data in the same manner, and even recycling key phrases and titles as section headings. Gero argues that because women have been consistently undervalued and marginalized, both as researchers and subjects of research, women in archaeology have been relegated to an "analytic ghetto" (p. 43) by androcentric biases within both the discipline and its "state-controlled" source of funds, the National Science Foundation. While her conclusions can be critiqued (see below), it is worth noting that the trends she identifies are echoed by other researchers analyzing the same data (see John Yellen, #194) and more general data on the status of women in archaeology (Kramer and Stark, #100). AWB

*sociopolitics of archaeology/sociology of science/discrimination*

## Annotated References

68. GERO, JOAN M. 1985. Sociopolitics and the woman-at-home ideology. *American Antiquity* 50:342-350.

This article explores the interaction of archaeological practice and modern state society. Gero posits that archaeology is a function of state ideology, both constrained by and constraining the structural prerogatives of the state. The activities of archaeologists are controlled by the state in terms of presentist biases. Gero contends that archaeologists are "required" to make the past appear like the present. Archaeological interpretations thus support and maintain state-level society through ideological legitimation. Gero discusses androcentric bias in archaeological interpretations of division of labor, noting that this also structures the nature of professional roles in archaeology. Archaeologists who are mostly white males often interpret men in active roles and women in passive roles, and they themselves are often segregated, with men doing active field work and women doing passive laboratory work (the "woman-at-home" ideology). Gero uses data from three sources (*American Antiquity, Dissertation Abstracts International,* and *National Science Foundation Grants and Awards*) to support her contention. Bias is noted in the figures for males and females working in field and non-field oriented research in the period from 1960-1984 (with special emphasis on the periods of 1967-68 and 1979-80). While significant change is notable over this period, men dominated field-based research and women did more of the non-field research. Success rates for men and women in NSF granting also reveals bias. Women were more successful if they applied for non-field-based research funds (28%) than if they applied for field-based research funds (15%).

Gero's article is interesting from the standpoint of sociopolitical influences in archaeology, and provides a guideline for collection of data on gender issues in archaeology. However, little attention is given to sample statistics; portions of the sample are very limited and may lead to biased interpretations. Also, Gero makes unqualified statements concerning the sociopolitical embeddedness of archaeological praxis. Her conclusion that archaeological research simply reflects modern social ideology is not directly supported by the data she presents. JDB

*sociopolitics of archaeology/United States/discrimination/National Science Foundation/American Antiquity/ western society, contemporary*


69. GERO, JOAN M. 1983. Gender bias in archaeology: A cross-cultural perspective. In *The Sociopolitics of Archaeology*, edited by J. M. Gero, D. Lacy, and M. L. Blakey, 351-357. Research Report 23. Department of Anthropology, University of Massachusetts, Amherst.

Gero examines the status of women in American archaeology through three different avenues, focusing primarily on the representation of women in fieldwork versus labwork or analysis positions. First, she looks at *American Antiquity* reports of fieldwork projects in Mesoamerica in 1979 and 1980. Men outnumber women as project directors by a 5 to 1 margin. Second, she considers dissertations completed from 1978 to 1981, where men outnumber women two to one overall, and men were much more likely to do original fieldwork projects. Finally, she examines National Science Foundation grants and concludes that more grants go to men, at a ratio of 7.8 to 1. Men not only have a much higher success rate on grant applications, but are also more likely to receive funding for fieldwork. Even when women get grants, they receive less money. Gero compares these statistics with parallel information from South America. South American women are much better represented in publications than their North American counterparts. South American women also do as much fieldwork as men. Gero uses these data to show how the differential representation of women in U.S. archaeology is a cultural bias and has nothing to do with innate abilities. She also explains the seemingly paradoxical result that South American women seem to be working on an even footing with men. Finally, Gero points out that women in the U.S., over-represented in collections analysis, have an unparalleled opportunity to shape a new direction within archaeology, which is turning more towards the re-analysis of existing collections than to the excavation of ever decreasing numbers of archaeological sites.

This article is very similar to Gero's later articles (#67, #68), incorporating much of the same data. All three articles seek not only to demonstrate that women in American archaeology hold inferior positions, but also to explore some of the reasons for this difference. Along with the several other articles annotated in this volume by Stark and Kramer (#100), Stark (#163) and Yellen (#194), they provides a clear picture of how the position of women in archaeology has been changed in the last two decades. Where Gero's articles differ dramatically from the others, though, is in her cross-cultural comparison with South American archaeologists. TVZ

*sociopolitics of archaeology/discrimination/National Science Foundation/United States/South America*

70. GERO, JOAN M. AND MARGARET W. CONKEY (editors) 1991. *Engendering Archaeology: Women and Prehistory.* Basil Blackwell, Cambridge, MA.

The papers in *Engendering Archaeology* (annotated separately) are an outgrowth of a reserach conference held in April, 1988, at Wedge Plantation, South Carolina. The conference attempted to address what was seen as an absence of studies of women in prehistory and a dearth of researchers actively constructing models of gendered men and women in the prehistoric past (but see also Kehoe, #94). One of the papers in this volume, Rita Wright's "Women's Labor and Pottery Production in Prehistory," was not presented at the Wedge Conference, and papers by Doug Price on gender differences in bone chemistry and Prudence Rice on pottery production were presented at Wedge but are not included in the 1991 volume. Many of the Wedge papers were also presented in a 1989 Society for American Archaeology symposium. AWB

*Wedge Conference/conference papers/Society for American Archaeology*

## Annotated References

71. GERO, JOAN AND DOLORES ROOT 1990. Public presentations and private concerns: Archaeology in the pages of *National Geographic*. In *The Politics of the Past,* edited by P. Gathercole and D. Lowenthal, 19-37. Unwin Hyman, London.

    More than half of the *National Geographic* volumes published between 1900-1985 are examined in this survey of popular archaeology articles. For the most part, the authors focus on how the magazine's portrayal of archaeology reflects and legitimizes western (particularly male American) cultural values, including the democratic ideal, expansionism, and exploration and the thrill of discovery. Echoing Gero's (1985) examination of the sociopolitics of archaeology in the United States, the authors state that "The archaeology presented is also dominated by the actions and images of males, reiterating the sexual bias that makes exploration and discovery unambiguously man's work in a man's world" (p. 33). This would be a particularly appropriate article for an undergraduate class whose introduction to archaeology was through *National Geographic* and Indiana Jones. It would be interesting to examine how other popular magazines, such as *Smithsonian* or *Archaeology,* portray gender in archaeologists and in prehistory. SLD

*sociopolitics of archaeology/National Geographic/United States/western society, contemporary*

72. GIBB, JAMES G. AND JULIA A. KING 1991. Gender, activity areas, and homelots in the 17th-century Chesapeake region. *Historical Archaeology* 25(4):109-31.

    Gender relations of seventeenth century Chesapeake Bay colonists are the focus of this paper by James Gibb and Julia King. The authors address gender through the development of a task differentiation model based on historic documentation following Spector's (1983, #157) approach. According to their model, the division of labor on the Chesapeake frontier was organized around an ideal of domestic work versus commodity production, with the household as the main economic unit. Women were responsible for domestic tasks such as cooking and dairying while men produced tobacco. This model has definite spatial consequences for the division of labor since women's work takes place mainly on the homelot and men's work is carried out at a wider range of locales.

    Gibb and King examine spatial data from three seventeenth century homesteads in the Chesapeake region: the St. Johns site (18ST1-23), a large farmstead, and the Patuxent Point (18CV271) and Compton (18CV279) sites, two smaller adjacent farmsteads. Their analysis focuses on artifact distributions within middens, testing for statistical associations of specific kinds of materials between midden locales and architectural features. At two of the sites, Compton and Patuxent Point, "evidence of specialized spaces...is minimal, suggesting a great deal of overlap of women's and men's activities and little segregation and specialization of tasks on the homelot" (p. 125). At St. John's, however, middens were "most specialized" (p. 127). Gibb and King conclude that a division of labor organized around domestic versus commodity production was only present at the larger and more wealthy St. John's farmstead, which could afford to house more workers. At the other two sites, women did not have the resources to support a larger working household and were obligated to contribute to tobacco production. They suggest that such a system was not as efficient and did not increase household wealth.

    Two of the three sites analyzed do not conform to the expectations of the task differentiation model outlined. The authors explain this by presenting some provocative ideas relating the division of labor in colonial society to economic factors, namely available resources in terms of wealth. In this way, the authors begin to develop a theoretical framework for understanding how the division of labor may vary in different contexts. Their conclusions, however, are limited by problematic data. These are plow zone sites and it was impossible to control for different location uses through time. The authors were forced to treat occupations over roughly thirty year periods as single units for all of the sites. They also assume spatial segregation for gender specific activities even though the model predicts some spatial overlap. In spite of this, Gibb and King convincingly demonstrate the usefulness of the task differentiation approach for examining the division of labor archaeologically. NSG-F

*historical archaeology/division of labor/task differentiation approach/household analysis/spatial analysis/ dairying/United States, Northeast*

73. GIBBS, LIV 1987. Identifying gender representation in the archaeological record: A contextual study. In *The Archaeology of Contextual Meanings,* edited by Ian Hodder, 79-89. Cambridge University Press, Cambridge.

Gibbs suggests that material culture does not directly reflect gender, but has "social implications" which can be deduced if several different categories of data are compared. She looks at gender in Danish prehistory through burials and hoards, domestic contexts and artistic representations, concluding that there is evidence of changing gender relationships and gender tensions through time.

Noting the problems involved in assigning genders to burials by subjective interpretations of the gender of goods, the author begins by looking only at burials which have been biologically sexed. From these she asserts that there are in fact exclusive categories of male and female goods, and she uses this information to define the gender of unsexed burials, cremations, and those hoards that are collections of items similar to the sets of goods found in male and female burials. Hoards which are male-associated contain weapons or tools. Female-associated hoards contain jewelry and an occasional tool such as sickles. Male burials are always more numerous and have a greater variety of goods than female burials. Through time, this discrepancy in number increases; in the Late Bronze Age cremations, no female assemblages at all can be identified. Hoards seem to show an opposite trend. All of the early hoards are male-associated and all of the later ones are female-associated.

The author uses burials and hoards to make a connection between gender and agriculture. Sickles are found in male hoards and burials through the Early Bronze Age, and in female hoards (but never burials) in the Late Bronze Age. Gibbs suggests that women became increasingly involved in agriculture. Data on structures are reviewed and a trend toward greater complexity and elaboration is noted. The author argues that women may have been associated with the domestic sphere and that Late Bronze Age evidence of an increasing variety of economic activities within the house may indicate that more of these activities were being performed by women. Artistic evidence relevant to gender is scanty. Several figures dating to the Late Bronze Age have been found and most of them are of women. Rock carvings exist from the Bronze Age but cannot be dated more narrowly. Phallic figures are recognizably male but female representations are more difficult to identify.

Combining all of this evidence, Gibbs ventures an interpretation of gender relationships. In the early periods, men asserted their importance and their identity as warriors by burying weapons in hoards. As women became more involved in agriculture and therefore more economically productive, they began to assert the importance of their position. This led to tension between the genders. Men responded by burying women without female grave goods as a sign of male control, and by making rock carvings that rendered women invisible. Faced with this suppression, women asserted their identity by elaborating their realm--the home--and by ritually burying female goods in hoards.

This is an extremely ambitious paper that tries to deal with many strands of evidence over a long time span. The author is willing to take risks in order to tie these strands together in a coherent, intriguing, and socially plausible way. Inevitably, there are many places where her methods, logic, or assumptions are questionable, but the determination to use multiple lines of evidence is as admirable as it is unusual in gender studies.

Gibbs does not say clearly how she assigns gender to cremations, unsexed burials, and hoards, and some of the lists in her tables suggest that male and female artifacts are not so unambiguously separate as she suggests. The male goods seem to be a much more exclusive group than the female ones. She does not sufficiently consider the problem of what a hoard represents, how it might resemble a burial or not, whether it can be attributed to an individual, and how it is expected to serve as a locus for gender assertions. She assumes that the inability of an archaeologist to distinguish women in burials and art is not simply a matter of the ambiguity of interpretation, but is a deliberate attempt by prehistoric people to make women invisible.

Gibbs sometimes interprets the same pattern in opposite ways for men and women. Male visibility in graves is control, female visibility in hoards is protest; female invisibility is suppression, but male invisibility is not even an issue to be explained. This gives the impression of a prior text shaping interpretive calls. SF

*contextual analysis/mortuary analysis/architecture/division of labor/rock art/agriculture/spatial analysis/ Denmark/Scandinavia/Bronze Age*

# Annotated References

74. GILCHRIST, ROBERTA 1991. Women's archaeology? Political feminism, gender theory and historical revision. *Antiquity* 65:495-501.

In this article, Gilchrist discusses several different topics, all of which fall into the category "women's archaeology." Specifically, she looks at feminist political movements promoting equal professional opportunities for female archaeologists, gender theory and its application to archaeology, and revisionist works that attempt to draw attention to the role of women in the history of archaeology.

Gilchrist's discussion of political feminism is international in scope, and she argues that although political feminism has made some contributions to archaeological theory, it is mainly defined by political aims and, as such, cannot alone support an archaeological theory of gender. In her examination of gender theory, she emphasizes recognizing gender as a fundamental structuring principle in all archaeological studies and calls for the integration of gender into broader studies of social structure and social relations. Gilchrist views revisionist histories of archaeology as broadening our understanding of the discipline and its history, as well as contributing to a reevaluation of social norms which may in turn influence archaeology on a more theoretical level. She cautions, however, that these revisionist histories "must be accurate and convincing in addition to being thought-provoking" (p. 499). Finally, Gilchrist integrates her three lines of inquiry with a call for the application of "women's archaeology" to mainstream archaeological theory and practice. DLG

*epistemology/postprocessualism/revisionist theory/feminist critique/sociopolitics of archaeology*


75. GILCHRIST, ROBERTA 1988. The spatial archaeology of gender domains: A case study of medieval English nunneries. *Archaeological Review from Cambridge* 7(1):21-28.

Gilchrist proposes that the difficulty in establishing an archaeology of gender is due, in part, to the lack of a methodology appropriate to the recognition of gender, but feels that spatial analysis linked with cross-cultural studies which point out the important categories for analysis can help solve this problem. Her self-confessed goals for this paper are "to propose that gender domains are formulated by social organisations which initiate specialist divisions in labor, and that these gender domains can be examined using existing methods of archaeological spatial analysis" (p. 22).

This first goal relates to her arguments that discrete gender domains (domestic/private=female, powerful/public=male) are a result of "capitalist social relations." This argument is supported by her materialist definition of gender: "gender relations can be conceptualised as a dynamic between human reproduction and economic production" (p. 22). Spatial gender domains can then be linked with evolutionary models of social/sexual differentiation. Gilchrist begins with "kin corporate societies," and utilizes the arguments of "feminist phenomenologists" on the different ways women and men utilize space, and hence the different types of architectures each creates, in arguing that in these societies women had substantial power and control within the domestic domain (p. 23). It is only with the advent of state societies that the domestic domain becomes devalued and absolute.

The case study compares the plans of eight medieval English nunneries and eight monasteries with a modified form of Hillier and Hanson's syntactic approach. Four conclusions are presented concerning the spatial organization in each, involving primarily the greater accessibility of monasteries and the different arrangements of their elements. For instance, in nunneries the communal sleeping area was the most secluded, while in monasteries the most inaccessible area was the chapter house, where daily business was transacted. Gilchrist uses these conclusions to argue against "the idealised image proposed by contemporary feminists" (p. 26). For both medieval nuns and their secular counterparts, the enclosure and containment of women perpetuated their economic reliance on the patriarchal order, and so space can be seen as implicated in the perpetuation of a system of gender relations.

The conclusions presented in this paper are both interesting and suggestive, but this article is obviously only part of a larger work, for the case study itself fits onto a single page. Unfortunately, neither the syntactic methods nor their application are discussed. Thus the intriguing conclusions stand alone without any means to assess their validity.

The theory section leading up to the case study includes some valuable elements, including her discussion of Flannery and Winter's work on Oaxacan houses and Clarke's work at Iron Age Glastonbury, which serve as useful reminders that gender archaeology has been conducted in the past, although perhaps without as explicit a focus on gender relations. However, the theoretical buildup to the case study is in many places confusing (such as her assessment of earlier spatial approaches to gender). For example, Gilchrist advocates a "contextual" approach (p. 24), while elsewhere in the article she draws freely on cross cultural approaches. In particular, the theories of feminist phenomenologists as presented by Gilchrist seem dangerously close to the predefined application of ethnocentric ideas across cultural boundaries which a contextual approach is most emphatically against. More importantly, the article doesn't seem to achieve the two purposes which it sets out for itself. First, her unilinear approach to cultural evolution and the assumption that all state societies will have certain gender domains which are valued in specific ways are unconvincing. It is not explained why a devalued domestic domain associated with women is a necessary requisite for state organization. Second, her case study does demonstrate that archaeological spatial methods can be used to study gender domains in a medieval context. However, despite the fact that the article is meant to redress "the apparent absence of methodologies appropriate to the archaeological recognition of gender" (p. 21), her methods do not allow for the recognition of gender, but only for its analysis in light of other information. Thus, while the case study itself is worthy of attention, the theoretical buildup to it is less so, even though it constitutes the bulk of the article. WDG

*spatial analysis/contextual archaeology/medieval archaeology/architecture/Great Britain/Europe*

76. GIMBUTAS, MARIJA 1989. *The Language of the Goddess: Unearthing the Hidden Symbols of Western Civilization.* Thames and Hudson, London.

GIMBUTAS, MARIJA 1991. *The Civilization of the Goddess: The World of Old Europe.* Harper Collins Publishers, San Francisco.

These heavily-illustrated books, presented in a style somewhere between classroom text and coffee-table illustrated volume, elaborate a series of arguments about the characteristics of a female-centered "Old European" Neolithic cultural foundation of European civilization and its replacement by successive waves of invasion by a patriarchal proto-Indo-European society during the course of the Bronze Age. Gimbutas' arguments are interesting because they model a period of great social and economic change in terms of religious and social factors. One system of sacred figures and images is presumed to replace another, accompanied by profound social changes including the transformation of gender roles. Gimbutas is also the author of a series of influential scholarly papers on the timing and characteristics of the "Indo-Europeanization" of Europe (for example, Gimbutas 1977, 1979, 1980). These two books, expanding on the thesis of an earlier book not annotated (Gimbutas 1974), elaborate the religious and social aspects of the society preceding Indo-Europeanization, focusing on representations of the Great Goddess, the cult of the Goddess, and the role of women in a society modeled after a female-centered Pantheon.

*The Language of the Goddess* sets out to illustrate associations of images and motifs in the European Paleolithic and Neolithic. The book takes the form of an illustrated catalogue of Great Goddess imagery, divided into sections representing the four principle facets of the Goddess: "Life-Giving," "The Renewing and Eternal Earth," "Death and Regeneration," and "Energy and Unfolding." Within each section, chapters only a few pages long treat specific motifs, outlining their significance to "the language of the Goddess": for example, "Chevron and V as Bird-Goddess Symbols," "Zig-Zag and M Sign," and "Meander and Waterbirds." Three short concluding chapters ("The Place and Function of the Goddess," "Continuity and Transformation of the Goddess in the Indo-European and Christian Eras," and "The World View of the Culture of the Goddess") provide a brief discussion of Gimbutas' conception of the Goddess cult.

The general issues discussed in the concluding chapters of *The Language of the Goddess* are taken up at greater length in *The Civilization of the Goddess*. This more recent book is divided into 10 chapters, of which the first six provide a textbook-style region by region review of the European Neolithic. The discussion of each region is divided into short sections on chronology, villages and houses, cemeteries, "physical type of the population", economy, architecture, trade, and pottery. Extensive endnotes refer the reader to a broad literature. The final four chapters discuss "The Religion of the Goddess," "The Sacred Script," "Social Structure," and "The End of Old Europe: The Intrusion of Steppe Pastoralists from South Russia and the Transformation of Europe."

Gimbutas takes what she refers to as an "archaeomythological" approach to studies of the cult of the Goddess and associated social patterns. She claims that there are recurring associations between Goddess images (primarily female figurines and other representations of women) and a variety of other representations and symbols. On this basis she builds up a complex edifice of interpretations about the meaning of anthropomorphic and animal figures as well as abstract symbols based in the Paleolithic of western and southeastern Europe and extending into Neolithic and later times. In *The Language of the Goddess* the emphasis is on the iconic significance of both representational and abstract designs (i.e., a meander or "M" sign refers iconically to water, and emphasizes the life-giving properties of the Goddess). In *The Civilization of the Goddess* the chapter entitled "The Sacred Script" extends this premise, arguing that inscribed or painted signs on Neolithic pottery, figurines, and other objects form a set of core signs that make up a script showing some continuity of both semantic and phonetic values from Upper Paleolithic through historic times. In this view, the Paleolithic meander sign is incorporated into later scripts, but retains an association with water and perhaps even a phonetic value.

Gimbutas uses her interpretations of the specific meanings of representations and abstract symbols to reconstruct what she sees as the religion of the Goddess. From what she sees as an ancient emphasis on a feminine sacred principle, she goes on to propose an Old European social formation in which women enjoyed great prominence in religious and secular life. Gimbutas argues that interpretations of Old European social structure have been distorted by the assumption that early societies had to be like ours, or that matriarchy (as conceived of by nineteenth century scholars) must be the mirror image of patriarchy, with women ruling autocratically and by force. Instead, she suggests there was a "matristic" society, in which the "sexes are more or less on equal footing," without hierarchical ranking. She finds evidence for matriliny, women's prominence in social and economic roles, and for an economically egalitarian society in settlement evidence and mortuary remains. Supporting evidence also comes from myth, historic texts, and comparative linguistic data from what she terms "survivals" of Old European matriliny into Bronze Age and even historic times in the Aegean and among isolated groups elsewhere in Europe.

The gradual transformation of European society as a result of several waves of Indo-European invasion results in the replacement of this "matristic" and peace-loving civilization with a warlike patriarchal one. The ancient cult of the Goddess is, however, argued to have "gone underground," remaining buried in beliefs and fairy stories, and is said to be "now. . . reemerging from the forests and mountains, bringing us hope for the future, returning us to our most ancient human roots" (1989, p. 321).

Many of Gimbutas' specific arguments are not widely accepted, primarily because her treatment of evidence is selective rather than exhaustive and because she advances her own controversial interpretations without discussing alternative perspectives. A number of her general views on the religion and civilization of the Goddess are quite influential, however, at least in part because they reflect some very commonly held assumptions in studies of ancient art and religion.

The most important of these is the widely assumed association between representations of women, from Paleolithic "Venus" figurines to Neolithic female figures, and fertility. It is assumed that such "fertility cult figurines" indicate an emphasis on female reproductive capacity as a sacred principle. As in other "fertility cult" interpretations, Gimbutas' reliance on this principle leads to contradictions. The heart of Gimbutas' Great Goddess pantheon is an association between the female form, female fecundity, and concepts of life, death, and regeneration. In order to maintain the association with female form, she resorts to comparisons between the shape of the bucranium (bull's head and horns, associated with mortuary ritual in some Neolithic sites) and the uterus and fallopian tubes. Her insistence on direct reference to female anatomy is difficult to reconcile with her statement that the Goddess represents an androgynous sacred power, that female and male sexes were not "dichotomized" in the Neolithic, and that goddesses of regeneration may sometimes be portrayed with male genitalia. A number of scholars have pointed out the problems with assuming that representations of women must refer to sex, reproduction, or fertility, and Gimbutas' "archaeomythology" does not address these difficulties in any way.

A second common assumption is that symbols and representations can be compared between archaeological contexts widely separated in space and time, often without consideration of what may be transformations in the meaning of even historically related symbols. It is unlikely that an interpretation of ancient art that tries to explain representations from Upper Paleolithic and Neolithic contexts (a span of more than 25,000 years) in terms of a single belief system is going to get us very far. The failure to introduce theoretical perspectives for understanding social transformations also leads to confusion in Gimbutas' account of the "Indo-Europeanization" of Europe. Gimbutas wants us to imagine a (matristic) society fundamentally different from our own and discontinuous with a (patriarchal) later European prehistory and history, but then she interprets post-invasion evidence of matriliny as a survival. This is surely a weak concept for analyzing social transformations. In spite of what she admits are radical changes in religion and social structure, she sees an unbroken chain of matriliny associated with high status for women in a number of areas of Europe. These links between female-centered pantheons, matriliny, and women's status have been called into question by a number of scholars, and again, Gimbutas does not examine or counter these questions.

In these popular books, Gimbutas tells a story, sketching a set of bold ideas about early religion and society with broad strokes. It is clearly a story that she intends to be empowering to modern women. Because Gimbutas so consistently fails to address the questions raised by recent scholarship on gender in archaeology, however, the effect perpetuates and popularizes a set of myths about women and their roles in prehistoric societies. Although women's roles play a central part in Gimbutas' arguments, the *Goddess* books do nothing to bring us closer to a gendered European prehistory. LEF

*References cited*
Gimbutas, Marija 1977. The first wave of Eurasian steppe pastoralists into Copper Age Europe. *Journal of Indo-European Studies* 5:277-338.

Gimbutas, Marija 1979. The three waves of the Kurgan people into Old Europe. *Archives Suisses d'Anthropologie Générale* 43:113-17.

Gimbutas, Marija 1980. The Kurgan wave migration (c. 3400 - 3200 BC) into Europe and the following transformation of culture. *Journal of Near Eastern Studies* 8:273-315.

*fertility cults/Goddess/myth/iconography/religion/representation, theory of/trade/Venus figurines/Europe/ Neolithic/Paleolithic*


77. GRAHAM, ELIZABETH 1991. Women and gender in Maya prehistory. In *The Archaeology of Gender: Proceedings of the Twenty-Second Annual Conference of the Archaeological Association of the University of Calgary,* edited by Dale Walde and Noreen D. Willows, 470-478. Archaeological Association, The University of Calgary, Calgary.

In this article, Graham examines the activities of women in prehistoric Maya society, and identifies areas for future research. Her goal is a preliminary assessment of the potential of Mayan archaeology for developing a consciousness of an archaeology of gender. She points to the mechanistic and de-personalized approach of current theories as a significant impediment to discussion of specific behaviors within society.

Areas seen as possessing potential for engendered archaeological research include subsistence, specifically agriculture; physical remains of households, particularly kitchen areas; epigraphic remains; and burials. Ethnographic evidence suggests that kitchen gardens, primarily managed by women, may have been present in Maya prehistory, but have not received the attention that raised field mono-crop agriculture has. She suggests that examination of middens, representing primary deposition, for evidence of regular co-occurrence of materials, may be informative about gendered behaviors. Secondary deposition of artifacts incorporated into bricks will not exhibit these regular associations, although this would presumably not be a problem in short-term occupations. Related to this topic is the potential that kitchen organization has for informing us about gendered behaviors. The appearance of the *comol*, or griddle, at a time when other aspects of Maya society are changing suggests that these changes have impact on gendered behavior as well.

Epigraphic and mortuary research has had somewhat more success in establishing gendered research.

## *Annotated References*

Researchers have been able to identify several women of power from Maya glyphs; presumably future work will reveal more information about the roles of these women in society. Mortuary research has recovered the burials of several high status women who were buried in elaborate tombs.

Graham encourages archaeologists to begin moving away from theories and the attendant language which view Maya culture as a monolithic adaptive system, and towards flexible research programs which can recognize and cognize gendered, specifically women's, activities. Although not explicating what that science is, she cautions that science need not be cast aside for imagery, and notes that gendered activities result in material manifestations whose patterns can be detected and interpreted. However, she does not indicate an abandonment of the testing methodology which also appeared in New Archaeology with systems theory. KMM

*mortuary analysis/division of labor/spatial analysis/processualism/subsistence/ceramic analysis/Mexico/ Belize/Maya*


78. GRAUER, A. L. 1991. Life patterns of women from medieval York. In *The Archaeology of Gender: Proceedings of the Twenty-Second Annual Conference of the Archaeological Association of the University of Calgary,* edited by Dale Walde and Noreen D. Willows, 407-413. Archaeological Association, The University of Calgary, Calgary.

Grauer analyzes skeletal remains of more than 1,014 individuals collected from the excavation of the cemetery of St. Helen-on-the-Walls, York, England, to gain insights about medieval women, a research topic generally neglected. Specifically, she examines health and disease patterns of poor urban medieval women. Using paleodemographic analysis to assess mortality patterns and to detect the differential presence of stress between men and women, and paleopathological analysis to understand patterns of morbidity between the two sexes, she examine two expectations based on sixteenth century parish records which indicated a higher mortality rate for females. The first expectation was that female mortality would peak in early adulthood due to the presence of maternal stresses, and the second, that the overall health of the women would be affected by sanitation and crowded living conditions in combination with the former and would have resulted in iron-deficiency anemia and infection. The latter two would be indicated by skeletal lesions: porotic hyperostosis and periostitis, respectively.

The results of the paleodemographic analysis indicate mortality rates differed by sex with female mortality reaching a peak at the 25-35 age-group interval and male at the 35-45 age-group interval, and that males had a greater life expectancy than females. The former she interprets as consistent with Goldberg's (1986) argument that marriage during this period occurred at a relatively late age for women (mid-twenties), hence a delayed age of maternal stress. The delay in marriage resulted from opportunities for female employment in the cities, due to the shift from arable to pastoral land and from labor shortages caused by the plague. Evidence for the migration of women to the cities is indicated by a higher proportion of adult females (53.6%) in her sample. The explanation for the mortality pattern however does not explain the difference in life expectancy. The results of the paleopathology indicate that neither iron-deficiency anemia nor infection (in presence/absence and severity) were associated with sex. She does however find that her results question the assumption that women were consistently exposed to a greater number of stresses since the male skeletons did display a greater percentage (though not statistically significant) of periostitis than females. From this she suggests that the absence of pathological conditions in many of the female skeletons may indicate that women were unable to survive the episodes of stress in comparison to the male skeletons which displayed these conditions more frequently. This is taken as an indication that the men more successfully fought the disease allowing enough time for the skeletal tissue to be permanently scarred. She concludes that the health of men may have been superior to that of the women during the medieval period. EAB

*References cited*
Goldberg, P. 1986. Female labour, service and marriage in the late mediaeval urban north. *Northern History* 12:18-38.

*Great Britain/medieval archaeology/paleodemography/paleopathology/osteology*

79. GUILLÉN, ANN CYPHERS 1988. Thematic and contextual analyses of Chalcatzingo figurines. *Mexicon* 10:98-102.

Guillén reports contextual and thematic analyses of over 4,000 figurine fragments recovered from Middle Preclassic Cantera Phase (700-500 BC) deposits at Chalcatzingo, located in the central highlands of Mexico. Guillén contends that these artifacts, almost exclusively associated with habitation structures, attached patios, or adjacent trash dumps, provide new data on the structure of Chalcatzingo society and mechanisms of increased social differentiation (p. 99).

While previous investigators focused on the facial features and adornments of head fragments, Guillén's study emphasizes body forms. Guillén suggests that the bodily themes represented "closely reflect the immediate function" (p. 99) of these artifacts. She reports that 92% of all identifiable figurine bodies represent females; only 3% are identified as male, and 5% are classified as children. Guillén reports that there are a wide range of thematic distinctions within the category of female figurines. Her major categories, defined on the basis of physiological state, clothing, adornments, and activity include pregnant women in the first, second, and third trimesters, nonpregnant women (which she suggests may be adolescents, based on the small size of their breasts), women carrying or nursing children, women carrying ceramic vessels, and women costumed in ball game equipment (previously associated exclusively with males).

Based on the thematic classification of female figurine bodies, Guillén argues that the entire sequence of female transition rites (i.e., puberty, marriage, and pregnancy) may be represented. Citing ethnographic documentation that stresses women's importance in linking localized lineage groups in the Maya region, Guillén suggests that the identification of a sequence of female transition rites may, in turn, be the first archaeological evidence of formal age-grades or female sodalities in Mesoamerica. At this juncture, she also suggests that some female figurines may relate to curing ceremonies, noting that some of the figurines carry bundles like those used by Mandan and Iroquois female curers.

Noting that figurines were commonly deposited as mortuary offerings during the Early Preclassic period in central Mexico, Guillén suggests that the shift in figurine deposition to household contexts in the Middle Preclassic period may be related to regional population growth. Assuming that agricultural intensification necessarily accompanies this population increase (Boserup 1963), Guillén supposes that ranking would have soon followed, and that women were probably important "in the legitimation of differential social status" (p. 101). She also proposes that women at Chalcatzingo became more involved with domestic chores and less active in agricultural production in Middle Preclassic times (Ember 1983). Noting that female figurines are associated with food-processing areas, and citing ethnographic analogies regarding the allocation of food along kinship lines, age, and sex, Guillén concludes that Cantera phase figurines were probably primarily used by women, whose social roles were enhanced through the distribution of foodstuffs.

This article is noteworthy for its innovative attempt to use figurine body portions. Moreover, Guillén's suggestion that Chalcatzingo women played active roles in legitimizing increased status differentiation is intriguing. Her model of culture change between the Early and Middle Preclassic periods carries many implications that could be evaluated using available archaeological data. Guillén's short article, nevertheless, suffers from the fact that it attempts a more comprehensive distillation of her unpublished Ph.D. dissertation than the limitations of the publication space allow. As a consequence, too many interesting observations and ideas are packed into such a short text that the author is unable to adequately present the analytic methodology. Guillén does not specify the sizes of her thematic subsets or subsequent analytical categories. Her inference that figurines of nonpregnant women may be related to curing, marriage, or menarche rites is never justified, and figurine bodies classified as males and children are only briefly described (p. 99).

In general, Guillén neglects important theoretical questions concerning the relationships between thematic representations of age, social roles, and gender, and the ways archaeologists assign particular meanings to these artifacts. Her uncritical reliance on ethnographic analogy without warranting arguments for the numerous assumptions on which the venturesome interpretations are based, and her vitalistic portrayal of culture change, based on population growth as a prime mover, are also problematic. KFA

# Annotated References

*References cited*
Boserup, Esther 1963. *The Conditions of Agricultural Growth: The Economics of Agrarian Change.* Aldine, Chicago.

Ember, Carol R. 1983. The relative decline in women's contribution to agriculture with intensification. *American Anthropologist* 85:285-304.

*postprocessualism/processualism/epistemology/feminist critique/figurines/ethnographic analogy/Mexico*


80. HANDSMAN, RUSSELL G. 1991. Whose art was found at Lepenski Vir? Gender relations and power in archaeology. In *Engendering Archaeology: Women and Prehistory,* edited by Joan M. Gero and Margaret W. Conkey, 132-159. Basil Blackwell, Cambridge, MA.

An entertaining study playing on sources as diverse as Virginia Woolf and The Talking Heads, Handsman's reflections on the 1986 exhibition "The Art of Lepenski Vir" at a Southampton gallery sometimes tread the fine line between being theory-laden and theory-burdened. Throughout, Handsman discusses the questions he feels were raised unvoiced by the exhibit, attempting to dissect its political content and the ends of its organizers and excavators. Why, he asks, is this art now, and why was it art then? His responses betray a certain skepticism regarding the logic employed by both curators of art and of archaeology. It is art because the organizer of the exhibition selected objects based on their perceived artistic merit; archaeologists lack any other categorizations for such material, hence it is art. For Handsman, however, art is a lever of social inequality, a forum where power and social relations are contested. In this regard it is intriguing that his article is unique in *Engendering Archaeology* in having original artwork illustrating his points.

For Handsman, the central question whispered unvoiced at each step remains "whose art is this?," and the implicit answer supplied by the gallery and interpreters echoes everywhere—it belonged to and was created by men. Only a Marxian view informed by the structural oppositions prevalent in every sector of society and by a contextualist analysis situated in history can adequately imagine specific women's histories in the past (cf. p. 342), and understand their "true" relation to the art displayed. Handsman reconstructs the social relations and permutations at Lepenski Vir drawing on feminist, structural-Marxist, and contextualist theory to order the artifacts. He traces what he sees as "evidences and representations of ongoing yet discontinuous histories of social transformations in which an earlier Mesolithic cultural order, interlineage relations of equality and alliance, and an ideology of community began to be deconstructed" (p. 346). The most explicit examples of this process, he argues, are the monumental stone heads, which "represented the living and dead leaders of the dominant lineage in the Gorge. As such, this political art legitimated individuals even as their positions and power were being challenged" (p. 347, caption Fig. 12.8). A similarly contextual approach is necessary to address questions regarding gender, he argues, and hints at a number of patterns that could be interpreted as representing changes in gender relations and relations between age groups over time. How, he asks, "did the women of Lepenski Vir value themselves within the social communal relations they confronted? How were women and their values stereotyped, and how was their art appropriated?" (p. 353). Interpretations of the art, often including detailed arguments involving intergroup relations and even motivations, constitute the bulk of the essay. Archaeological data are not, however, presented to support these remarkably specific reconstructions.

Handsman's essay is at once challenging, thought-provoking and original. At the same time, it gives such primacy to *a priori* assumptions and constructs at the expense of the actual material remains from the site that the inhabitants speak with Handsman's voice, not their own. The reader is left wondering less whose art was found at Lepenski Vir than whose society is found in this article. AWB

*contextual archaeology/representation, theory of/museums/sculpture/Marxism/western society, contemporary/ Europe/Mesolithic/Lepenski Vir*

81. HASTORF, CHRISTINE A. 1991. Gender, space, and food in prehistory. In *Engendering Archaeology: Women and Prehistory*, edited by Joan M. Gero and Margaret W. Conkey, 132-159. Basil Blackwell, Cambridge, MA.

In this pilot study, Hastorf examines the proposition that the use and distribution of food may represent the development and maintenance of gender relations. She defines gender as socially constructed female and male categories, and contends that archaeological approaches linking food and culture remain underdeveloped because of the prevailing, unspoken assumption that women's activities, associated with plants and food processing, are of little importance in the study of "larger" issues of culture process.

To establish interpretable links between food systems and social relations, Hastorf examines general ethnological data on the relationships between food and gender in economics and politics. She describes how women's power often surrounds food distribution, and how this is shown by patterns of spatially discrete storage in societies in which women enjoy some degree of economic independence. In her review of anthropological approaches to gender in studies of the symbolism and meaning of food, Hastorf reports that where men have fairly clear control over social relations and moral codes, food and sex taboos tend to be absent. However, in cultures where this dominance is contested more openly between genders, taboos involving restrictions to specific foods are common. Hastorf concludes that "material aspects of gender relations *should* be present in archaeological assemblages" (p. 137, emphasis original).

Hastorf reports that contemporary Andean society is clearly gendered in domestic as well as cosmological realms, and stresses that this pattern is one of reciprocal dependence. Although central Andean women exercise power and influence in modern households, she notes that some archaeologists believe that women's status has diminished since the Inka conquest and subsequent subjugation by the Spanish. Hastorf asks whether archaeological data can be used to determine whether or not the social position of woman has, in fact, altered over time. She notes that the identification of gender from material patterns remains a major challenge for archaeological research, and contends that archaeological data must be linked to gender "before the meanings of the distributions can be considered or the tasks can be discussed in terms of control and interaction" (p. 133). Hastorf also states her concern "not so much with linking a gender with an activity, as much as gaining evidence of differential control in how the activities are performed" (p. 134).

Using distributions of archaeobotanical remains from residential and mortuary contexts in the prehispanic Sausa area in the central Andes, Hastorf provides two complementary approaches for examining changing social relations underlying prehistoric food and diet. The first, based on the proposition that the spatial distribution of food remains portrays aspects of social relations within the house, explores the roles of Sausa women and men during the pre-Inka Wanka II (AD 1300-1460) and post-Inka Wanka III (AD 1460-1532) phases. Noting a more restricted distribution of plant residues and an increased frequency of maize in the Wanka III compound in comparison to its Wanka II predecessor, Hastorf suggests that there may have been "an increased circumscription of female activities in the Inka phase of Sausa life" and a possible "intensification of female processing labor, representing an escalation of women's labor to support sociopolitical activities" (p. 148), which are dominated by men.

Hastorf's second approach considers how differential access to certain foods may signify different social positions for men and women. This portion of her analysis is based on stable carbon and nitrogen isotope delta values obtained from bone collagen samples from sexed human skeletons dating to the Wanka II (n=7) and Wanka III (n=21) phases. Hastorf reports that there is no evidence for differential consumption of plant foods between Wanka II females and males, but marked differences between the sexes in the Wanka III sample — the male diet was 1.5 ppm enriched in maize (p. 150). Higher mean delta values of nitrogen among males also suggests greater meat consumption. Hastorf concludes that while Sausa women were probably working harder to produce corn beer during the Wanka III phase, they apparently did not join in its political consumption.

Hastorf's paper is an excellent example of how anthropological theory and diverse ethnographic and archaeological data can address questions concerning the development and maintenance of gender relations through the study of boundedness and control over subsistence resources and space. The author takes great care in developing arguments linking artifacts, activity areas, and foodstuffs with gender labels, and she provides sufficient documentation on the archaeological context and structure of her data to allow the reader to critically evaluate the accuracy of her descriptive report and the appropriateness of her thought provoking interpretations. This is a significant contribution toward the development of an archaeological theory of gender. KFA

*processualism/subsistence/stable isotope analysis/archaeobotany/Sausa/Inka/Andes/Peru/South America*


82. HAUGEN, INGER 1987. Concentrating on women: Introduction to a debate in social anthropology. In *Were They All Men? An Examination of Sex Roles in Prehistoric Society,* edited by Reidar Bertelson, Arnvid Lillehammer, and Jenny-Rita Naess, 15-21. Arkeologist Museum i Stavanger, Stavanger, Norway.

Haugen's article traces one aspect of the debate on gender roles, specifically the role of women in social anthropology over the last two decades. She discusses the rising interest in the topic engendered by the women's movement and then focuses primarily on the structuralist argument of domestic vs. public spheres presented by Rosaldo in the early 1970s and the later criticism and rebuttal of the theory by Rosaldo and by others. She discusses problems ethnographers have faced in interpreting accounts given by male and female informants, and in assessing their own androcentric views or assumptions. Basing her argument largely on Rudie's work with Malay peasants, she suggests that the concept of household should be separated from that of family when addressing topics of economic contributions, division of labor, co-operation, redistribution, etc. This would allow the economic organization of the household to be reintegrated with other information on status and cultural values in order to better understand the role of women in society.

The short abstract accompanying the article suggests that it examines the debate in social anthropology within the framework of archaeology, or at least that it suggests ways in which the theoretical arguments of ethnology may be useful in interpreting the archaeological record. Indeed, recent archaeological work has focused on household organization, redistribution and economic cooperation. Unfortunately, the article does not address the theoretical or methodological problems of applying the work in social anthropology to archaeological data. The intent of the article appears to have been merely to alert readers to the existence of the debate in social anthropology. Given that social anthropology and archaeology are usually considerably more separate in European academica than in North America, this may well have been more useful to the original participants of the 1979 workshop in Norway from which this volume developed than to many North American archaeologists in the 1990s. If the reader is willing to attempt the unaided but necessary transition to archaeological data, the article provides a useful summary of some Scandinavian ethnology addressing the problems of household economics and redistribution. KJ

*household analysis/division of labor/Europe/Scandinavia/Norway*


83. HAYDEN, BRIAN 1992. Observing prehistoric women. In *Exploring Gender through Archaeology: Selected Papers from the 1991 Boone Conference,* edited by Cheryl Claassen, 33-48. Prehistory Press, Madison.

In this article, Hayden critiques the utility of several sources of information for inferring gendered behavior, status, or attitudes specifically for hunting and gathering societies. After establishing his research credentials to discuss gender issues, he discusses potential contributions of comparative ethnography, skeletal and mortuary studies, texts, art and mythology, physiological studies, and comparative zoology to an understanding gendered behavior in the past. He rightly notes that it is variation in gender behavior which will provide the most useful keys in understanding the origin of differences.

Comparative ethnography is considered to be a rich source for "generating conclusions about prehistoric gender-related behavior." He minimizes problems of androcentric bias in ethnographies, and feels that they may be reliably used to infer cross-cultural associations between women and certain types of activities, specifically childcare and gathering. His assertion that he doesn't understand why feminist scholars should object to theories which assign women to narrowly-defined devalued activities suggests a limited reading of gender literature.

Sexed skeletal populations may be examined for signs of gendered behavior which have left a record in the bones, while treatment of burials may yield information about gender roles and social organization. Texts seldom mention hunter/gatherers, and theory which reliably relates art and mythology to the structure of the society producing them is under-developed at this time.

Hayden suggests that studies whose comparability relies on implied genetic bases for inferred gendered behavior, physiological studies and comparative zoology are also a rich source of information about gendered behaviors in hunter/gatherer societies. He notes that sociobiological arguments are "considered to be politically incorrect by some students of gender," but does not address feminist disagreements with sociobiological arguments in detail.

Although the purpose of the paper is to discuss ways in which gendered behavior may be identified and explained, Hayden identifies the appropriate focus of study as the community, a genderless entity, rather than the gendered individuals who make up that community. He argues that to focus on individuals, or groups of individuals smaller than the community, is to invite subjective and particularistic explanations of behavior. He indicates that the proper scope of study should be the average behavior of the community. This emphasis would appear to be at odds with a focus on gendered behavior. In addition, his reliance on social patterns of extant hunter-gatherer groups for information about past social systems and sociobiological data promotes an argument for a traditional interpretation of gender roles in the prehistoric record, one that is currently questioned by feminist scholars working in a number of fields. KMM

*ethnographic analogy/sociobiology/gatherer-hunters/individual in prehistory/mortuary analysis/myth*


84. HAYDEN, BRIAN 1986. Old Europe: Sacred matriarchy or complementary opposition. In *Archaeology and Fertility Cult in the Ancient Mediterranean: Papers presented at the first International Conference on Archaeology of the Ancient Mediterranean*, edited by A. Bonanno, 17-30. B.R. Grüner Publishing Co, Amsterdam.

In this conference paper Hayden attempts a general critique of the Great Goddess/sacred matriarchy model of old European religion and society as presented by Marija Gimbutas. First, he addresses what Gimbutas argues is the symbolic dominance of the Great Goddess over male elements in the Old European pantheon, pointing out that motifs and designs associated by Gimbutas with the Goddess are so numerous and varied that "one wonders what is left." Hayden argues that some of these motifs, especially bulls, stags, rams, snakes, pillars, he-goats, and bucrania (bull's head and horns), are more logically associated with a masculine sacred force that he regards as complementary to the feminine. Other abstract symbols, including chevrons, meanders, and spirals, are suggested to represent general concepts not necessarily tied to specific deities or genders. A second point has to do with the omnipotence of Gimbutas' androgynous Goddess (incorporating the male principle, reproducing parthenogenetically). Based on his interpretations of symbols of a masculine sacred force and on broad comparisons to historically known pre-industrial religions, Hayden argues instead that a principle of sexual duality and complementarity might have prevailed in early religions. Finally, Hayden addresses the issue of matriarchal society in Old Europe, making two general points. First, he questions the notion of matriarchy on the grounds that a "female-dominated" society has not been known to exist in the ethnographic present. Second, he rejects the practice of inferring the relative social status of men and women from the predominance of male or female deities, arguing instead that one should make such inferences on the grounds of other archaeological evidence, including depictions of men's and women's activities that may reflect a sexual division of labor or differentiated gender roles.

While Hayden's point about the inappropriateness of inferring social structure from the characteristics of a sacred pantheon is well taken, he seems to miss the equally valid point that inferences about the structure of prehistoric religions may themselves be poorly grounded. He argues loosely from a comparative ethnological basis, and in places merely on grounds of "common sense," that certain images are likely to represent a masculine sacred force important in prehistoric religions from the Paleolithic through the Neolithic. He fails to adequately address the obvious pitfalls of assigning specific meanings to these symbols in the first place, and seems to ignore the dangers of tracing iconographic associations through archaeological contexts so far removed from one another in time and space. As a result, although Hayden criticizes Gimbutas for a lack of methodological rigor and excessive subjectivity, it is hard to see how his own scenario for Paleolithic and Neolithic religions avoids the same problems. LEF

*fertility cults/Mediterranean/Paleolithic/Neolithic/Gimbutas, Marija/Europe/Goddess/representation, theory of/iconography/matriarchy*


85. HODDER, IAN 1991. Gender representations and social reality. In *The Archaeology of Gender: Proceedings of the Twenty-Second Annual Conference of the Archaeological Association of the University of Calgary*, edited by Dale Walde and Noreen D. Willows, 11-16. Archaeological Association, The University of Calgary, Calgary.

Early and middle Neolithic complexes in central and southern Europe are characterized by the high visibility of female figures in art and of artifacts commonly associated with women. In the later Neolithic this pattern fades and is replaced by an increasing emphasis on men and what are seen as masculine activities. Hodder turns to these data to explore the role of gender in a specific prehistoric system and the role that gender plays in illuminating problems of meaning, representation and power.

Hodder candidly discusses changes in his own interpretations of these patterns, revealing his initial assumptions and misconceptions. He concludes that his belief that there was insufficient evidence to choose between very different kinds of interpretations was actually based on male bias. He was, he states, simply frustrated because he believed that the relations of production were the actual loci of power, and he saw no way to go beyond the "light, insubstantial symbols to the deeper-voiced resources and powers which lay behind them" (p. 13). He had been "trying to do the impossible" because representations of power may be disjunct from the actual powers themselves. His male biases had led him to two errors: (1) thinking that there were simple relationships between the relations of production and gender domination (untrue because both cultural values and systems of representation intervene); and (2) that more general, positivist theories of representational systems and gender could be applied in different societies, which is incorrect because "representational systems involving gender are constructed historically and specifically" (p. 14).

Hodder shifts abruptly from south central to western European Neolithic cultures, explaining that he lacks the space to actually address the problems framed in the previous pages. Instead, he briefly illustrates his approach with reference to the SOM culture in the Paris basin. His aim is to outline an approach that is "historical and hermeneutic while remaining reflexively critical" (p. 15).

> ...A critical hermeneutic approach is necessary if we want to show how gender relations are experienced and given meaning, how they are used to define personhood and how they are involved in subtle ways in multidimensional relations of power. (p. 15)

An annotation is hardly the proper venue to consider the strengths and weaknesses of Hodder's conception of contextualism, but two logical inconsistencies within the context of this article are worth mentioning. First, while Hodder explicitly rejects positivist and general theories of representation and gender, arguing that both are constructed within a specific historical and cultural context, he nevertheless takes the theoretical apparatus developed in south-central Europe and applies it directly to rather different cultures in the Paris basin. He does so despite his earlier statement that the same data or patterns can have very different meanings in different societies. Second, the ability of latter-day archaeologists to understand the precise nuances of meaning constructed specifically and historically some thousands of years and kilometers away (cf. "by planting the dead in the ground society was renewed and regenerated", p. 14) suggests an uncritical, cross-cultural universality that Hodder takes pains to reject earlier in the essay. Alternatively, it suggests that meanings are not teased from the archaeological record but projected into it, and that they inform us of the specific historical context of present archaeological theory rather than the meanings of past representational systems.

The article is quite short, and given the more substantive discussions of these issues provided elsewhere by Hodder (see #86, 87) at least some of the inconsistencies may reflect the contribution's brevity. AWB

*postprocessualism/contextual archaeology/representation, theory of/France/Europe/Neolithic*

86. HODDER, IAN 1987. Contextual archaeology: An interpretation of Çatal Hüyük and a discussion of the origins of agriculture. *Institute of Archaeology Bulletin* 24:43-56.

In this article, Hodder attempts to demonstrate the methodology and value of contextual archaeology through a reanalysis of Mellaart's data from and interpretations of Çatal Hüyük and a consideration of the significance of this analysis for a theory of the development of agriculture. Before introducing the data, however, he directs some caveats at the reader: interpreting meaning of archaeological data is a difficult undertaking and it is difficult to know what meaning or meanings are correct. Relying on cross-cultural, universal meanings of material symbols is fraught with difficulty since it is not easy to know a cross-cultural universal when you see one. Contextual archaeology assesses cross-cultural universals critically, "involving an evaluation of the relationship between a past context and a present context" (p. 43). Hodder admits that in order to undertake this evaluation, contextualism relies on exceptionally good data, with "a richly networked symbolic system" (p. 43). With the reader thus forewarned of potential pitfalls, he turns to the wealth of material culture documented from Çatal Hüyük.

Hodder first "deconstructs" two previous interpretations of the data: that there is a spatial separation between ritual and secular rooms at the site (he argues that all rooms functioned as living areas) and that the wall reliefs of human figures are representations of the Mother Goddess. He then analyzes Mellart's original description and interpretation of the data in terms of three sets of structural oppositions: (1) male:female; (2) wild:domestic; and (3) inside:outside. Based upon the associations of representational figurines, wall sculptures, paintings, etc., he argues that female figures or symbols are associated with the wild and with death through their association with certain predators (leopards) and scavengers (vultures, foxes and weasels), and that men are associated with the wild through an association with aurochs and hunting. Death is associated with the inside of houses through wall paintings and through burials beneath platforms in the houses. Furthermore, there is a separation between the southern part of the houses with the hearth and oven (domestic), and the northern part with the platforms, wall decoration and burials (wild/death).

Based on the traces he draws through the richly networked material culture of Çatal Hüyük, Hodder concludes that the main dimensions of meaning at the site involve these three oppositions and that negotiation of these oppositions would have taken place in the relationships between men and women. He suggests that the productive efforts of women were denied (pottery and the hearth area in houses were undecorated, and there is little agricultural symbolism) while their reproductive potential was made dangerous. "The dependence of society on women is incorporated, transformed and denied" (p. 52).

He further maintains that the manipulation of this network of symbolic associations and symbolic value was critical for the development of agriculture. Fear of the wild led to the need to control it and "to tame the world within us" (p. 52), a taming that appears to be intimately linked to relations between men and women.

> It is not only psychological problems which are involved in the taming process. The 'wild within us' incorporates social divisions within society, as the Çatal Hüyük evidence suggests. The moment of reproduction is itself linked to death. It has been easiest to discuss such fears in relation to male-female strategies. Yet, because of the association of the fundamental sexual pairing with danger and death, it is conceivable that many of the social relationships based on reproductive links, or on the circulation of men and women, were similarly imbued with avoidance, danger, fear and death. The taming of the wild is thus intimately connected to the ability to change society and also to control it. (pp. 52-53)

In later periods and at Hacilar, where the temporal span immediately follows that at Çatal Hüyük, the importance of the wild-domestic opposition appears to have lessened.

> The domestication of the natural world, perhaps partly born of a desire to arrest internal fears, implies an erosion of the central importance of the wild in the symbolic constitution of social life. But this 'culturing' process was long, emotive and difficult and the violence in the imagery of Çatal Hüyük marks its passage. The two-sided nature of female sexuality was always to remain, but its centrality declined as hunting and the wild declined. Figurines, hunting and images of the wild gradually disappear together. (p. 55)

Hodder traces interesting associations between different material symbols that occur at Çatal Hüyük. While it is wise to take seriously his initial caveats on the dangers inherent in using cross-cultural universals (which his structural oppositions are, if not on exactly the same level of analysis as linear signs=male), he does much to explore the richness of the data set. Hodder admits in his conclusions that there are holes in the data from the site and suggests that it is really this insight into the role of psychological fears and the desire "to domesticate the wild within us and within society" (p. 55) that constitutes the main contribution of this article.

There are, however, several aspects of this psychological taming process that Hodder has ignored. If female sexuality was made dangerous and female contributions to prodution and reproduction were transformed and denied, who was the active agent? If women were linked with the wild and death, and fear of the wild (in society as well as in nature) and a desire to control it were driving forces in the development of agriculture and domestication, who was doing the domesticating, and thus the controlling? Were the "negotiations between men and women within the domestic context" (p. 52) that are seen in the material symbols at Çatal Hüyük negotiations between both the sexes or a manifesto of one? Was the fear of female sexuality felt by both sexes or only one? Hodder does not specifically address the question of the gender of the painters, sculptors and domesticators at Çatal Hüyük, a striking ommission in an article that deals with the negotiation and construction of gender relations through paintings, sculpture and the development of agriculture. His tacit assumptions on this issue seem to have more to do with symbolic manipulation in our own culture than in the Neolithic society of Çatal Hüyük. KJ

*agricultural origins/contextual archaeology/Çatal Hüyük/Neolithic/Near East/Turkey*


87. HODDER, IAN 1983. Burials, houses, women and men in the European Neolithic. In *Ideology, Power, and Prehistory*, edited by Daniel Miller and Christopher Tilley, 51-68. Cambridge University Press, Cambridge.

Hodder critiques processual archaeologists' approaches that attempt to relate megaliths to general principles such as marking territorial boundaries and/or the emergence of economic and social tensions without considering the megaliths' variability and historical context. He suggests that a major shortcoming of these processual approaches has been the removal of megaliths and Neolithic burials from the domain of the ideological.

Hodder attempts to systematically compare central and northwestern European megaliths and long houses in the fifth and fourth millennia BC. He claims that this exercise reveals eight essential similarities, including: (1) construction; (2) ratios of length to width; (3 5) location, orientation and elaboration of entrances; (6) internal organization; (7) internal decoration; and (8) associated lateral ditches. Given these substantive similarities, Hodder suggests that burial tombs represent a symbolic transformation of earlier and contemporary houses. To examine the significance of this association, he claims it is necessary to assess the symbolic and social context of long houses in central Europe and argues that "the type of house and pottery symbolism identified in the central European early and middle Neolithic is appropriate in a social context where primary social strategies revolve around male-female relationships, which are themselves linked to competition between lineages for control of labor" (p. 53).

Using ethnoarchaeological studies of acephalous lineage groups from East Africa, Hodder formulates a specific hypothesis that "in small-scale lineage-based societies in which the major concern is to increase labor power, the control of women by men, and the negotiation of position by women will become the dominant feature of social relations and will often involve cultural elaboration of the domestic sphere" (p. 61). He notes that this hypothesis incorporates two fundamental relationships: the link between domestic symbolic complexity and male-female negotiation of social position, and the tie between male-female relationships and reproduction.

Noting the widespread relationship between elaboration of the Baringo domestic context and the position of women, Hodder suggests that the type of organization found in central European long houses with controlled access is linked to social strategies of control and seclusion. He contends that "The preparation and provision of food in the domestic context, for adults and offspring, has great symbolic potential in any society concerned with the reproduction and expansion of its labor power and with the control over its reproductive and productive potential" (p. 62). The specific form of the European houses, therefore, is related to "marking out" and naturalizing women's social position, and the importance of lineages when labor was the key variable in the productive system. Hodder proposes that when land was scarcer than labor at the end of the fourth millennia BC, emphasis changed from the domestic context to the mediating properties of the supernatural realm, as expressed in the tombs by control over the lineage. Competition between descent lines for control over offspring would reduce women's ability to negotiate social positions, since they would no longer be at the focus of competing claims. With the devaluation of women in the domestic context, houses become smaller and less ornate. Simultaneously, women's domestic position is emphasized by the separate ritual context of increasingly elaborate communal megalithic tombs, as lineage groups appropriate female reproduction in an attempt to resolve claims to reproductive and productive resources.

This article's relevance lies in Hodder's emphasis that processual approaches to megalithic tombs "are not so much wrong as limited" (p. 64), and its early use of gender relations in explaining culture change. He effectively illustrates how a careful application of a contextual approach that incorporates evaluations of meaning and social context with existing theories provides a framework for examining how collective monumental burials acted as territorial markers and legitimized increasingly restricted access to critical resources. Although Hodder only considers the significance of houses, mound shapes, decoration, and orientation, he suggests that researchers use ceramic data to determine whether or not women were removed from pottery production and its symbolic complex, to provide an independent test of his hypothesized trend toward increasing male dominance and control. KFA

*postprocessualism/contextual archaeology/architecture/megaliths/mortuary analysis/Neolithic/Europe/Africa*


88. HOLLIMON, SANDRA E. 1992. Health consequences of sexual division of labor among prehistoric Native Americans: The Chumash of California and the Arikara of the North Plains. In *Exploring Gender in Archaeology: Selected Papers from the 1991 Boone Conference,* edited by Cheryl Claassen, 81-88. Prehistory Press, Madison.

Hollimon's paper compares evidence for differences in overall health between skeletal populations from the Chumash (see also #89) of California and the Arikara of the American Plains, focusing on sexual differences that may reflect divisions of labor. Hollimon examines demography, the incidence of degenerative joint disease, dental decay, enamel hypoplasia, infectious disease, and trauma. Many of the differences observed may reflect individual age rather than division of labor. Overall, the Chumash tended to live longer, and Hollimon attributes many of the conditions observed among the Chumash to their greater lifespan. Arikara males, who tended to live longer than Arikara females (average age of death was 35 for males, 28 for females), also tended to exhibit greater evidence for degenerative joint diseases and dental decay. Her essay presents rather a mixed view of health among both groups. Chumash males and females enjoyed relatively equal health, while the differences between Arikara males and females were more pronounced. One of the more sensitive indicators of gender distinctions (since it reflects pre-adult nutrition, and hence is not compromised by different ages at death) is enamel hypoplasia. Incidence of hypoplastic defects suggests that women among the Chumash and males among the Arikara were in poorer health or had access to lower-quality foodstuffs than their counterparts of the opposite sex. It is not clear, however, whether differences in health in pre-adults would would necessarily be indicative of differences in access to high-quality foods in older age groups. A third gender, the berdache, is also present in both Arikara and Chumash society, although not recognized in either sample. Hollimon discusses the difficulties of identifying berdaches in burial contexts.

Hollimon describes her paper as demonstrating "that there were specific health consequences associated with the divisions of labor practiced by the Chumash...and the Arikaras" (p. 86). It should be noted, however, that her data are equivocal at best. The skeletal evidence does not actually provide evidence for interpreting the division of labor. Instead, Hollimon attributes observed skeletal differences to divisions of labor observed and described ethnohistorically. AWB

*division of labor/skeletal remains/mortuary analysis/California/Chumash/United States and Canada, Plains/ Arikara/subsistence/paleopathology*


89. HOLLIMON, SANDRA E. 1991. Health consequences of divisions of labor among the Chumash Indians of southern California. In *The Archaeology of Gender: Proceedings of the Twenty-Second Annual Conference of the Archaeological Association of the University of Calgary*, edited by Dale Walde and Noreen D. Willows, 462-469. Archaeological Association, The University of Calgary, Calgary.

In framing her study, Hollimon is careful to emphasize that the term "the division of labor" does not refer to an inflexible, static aspect of social organization (p. 462). She recognizes that the division of labor by biological sex is only one way to organize labor, and that other variables, such as age and class, may simultaneously structure labor. Hollimon states that her purpose is to provide an example of how an analysis of divisions of labor can be used to study prehistoric gender, and to consider the consequences of a social division of labor (p. 462).

Hollimon examines skeletal remains from over 800 human burials dating between 3500 BC-AD 1804, associated artifacts, and ethnohistoric evidence for Chumash labor organization. Biological sex and health (reflected by the incidence of nutritional stress or physical injury) are specified, and then the artifact assemblage is used to arbitrarily assign "gender" categories to specific artifact types from general patterns manifest in cross-cultural gatherer-hunter ethnographies. Hollimon, however, makes it clear that this a heuristic device, which allows her to assess the degree to which her idealized model for "a sexual division of labor was reflected in a mortuary context" (p. 463). Lastly, Hollimon divides Chumash prehistory into three periods: Early (3500 - 1200 BC); Middle (1200 BC - AD 1150); and Late (AD 1150 to 1804).

Following a series of chi-square tests on burial and artifact associations by time period, Hollimon concludes that the "gender" of a given artifact is a poor predictor of the sex of a particular burial (p. 464). Chumash ethnographic data suggests that it is more likely that goods buried with an individual signify something about the people who interred the deceased, rather than simply reflecting the deseased's previous economic activities. Hollimon adds that an osteological examination provides greater insight into the economic activities and health of prehistoric Chumash men and women in different time periods. The frequency of degenerative joint disease (arthritis), dental caries and other dental pathologies, porotic hyperostosis, infectious diseases, and interpersonal violence present some interesting contrasts. Based on dental data alone, females appear to have been more nutritionally compromised and/or under greater disease stress than males throughout the prehistoric sequence. Hollimon thinks this means that females had less access to prime resources than males, or that females had comparable access, but with greater energetic demands from pregnancy and lactation. Patterns of activity-induced pathology indicate a temporal decrease in the degree of labor differentiation by sex. In the Early and Middle periods, males and females display roughly equal infectious disease rates, but the extent and severity of infections tends to be greater among males. In contrast, in the Late period, females were twice as likely to contract infectious disease, and the severity of their illness was much greater. Female incidence of traumatic injuries may also have been higher at this time. In light of paleoclimatological and archaeological data showing environmental deterioration, a shift to marine resources, and population aggregation (all in the Late period), Hollimon suggests that women were disproportionately and adversely affected.

Hollimon's ambitious study of the health consequences of the divisions of labor among prehistoric Chumash women and men constitutes an important contribution for the development of an archaeology of gender. The first part of her analysis warns us about the dangers of assuming that biological sex can be determined from "gendered" artifact types. The second part effectively illustrates how a division of labor may be dynamic, and how men and women may respond differently to environmental changes. Her skeletal analysis identifies a number of intriguing patterns which should inspire further inquiry.

The most visible shortcoming is Hollimon's failure to provide adequate descriptive statistics in support to her arguments on the health consequences of prehistoric Chumash divisions of labor. More importantly, although less visibly, Hollimon's interpretive discussion underscores the difficulty in examining the structure of prehistoric gender systems. Although Hollimon describes a third Chumash gender category (the berdache), she states that it is currently impossible to identify the berdache in mortuary contexts. Hollimon proceeds to impose biological sex on socially constructed gender categories. Following the introduction, children, whose skeletal remains are nondiagnostic for biological sex, are excluded from consideration.

Hollimon's difficulty in operationalizing her evaluation of prehistoric Chumash gender is underscored by her failure to define what gender entails with respect to the social division of labor. Nevertheless, her recognition that other variables such as age and social status may also condition social divisions of labor points to potentially productive avenues of study. By drawing on existing archaeological theory concerning the evaluation of social status, and including the dimension of age into her analysis, Hollimon can build on this already impressive baseline study to provide a more informed framework for an archaeological theory of gender. KFA

*division of labor/subsistence/mortuary analysis/osteology/gatherer-hunters/Chumash/California/United States, Western*

90. JACKSON, THOMAS L. 1991. Pounding acorn: Women's production as social and economic focus. In *Engendering Archaeology: Women and Prehistory*, edited by Joan M. Gero and Margaret W. Conkey, 301-325. Basil Blackwell, Cambridge, MA.

Jackson discusses women's labor as related to acorn procurement and processing, examining historical, ethnographic, and archaeological data for late prehistoric and early historic cultures in the western Sierra Nevada region of California. He argues that women's acorn gathering and processing structures inter- and intra-community social and economic relations, as well as subsistence and settlement. One goal is "to demonstrate the considerable value of conjoining a theoretical perspective that engenders the past with an empirical data base in contemporary archaeology" (p. 303). The first part of Jackson's article reviews Western Mono ethnohistoric literature related to acorns, bedrock processing features and implements, and the construction and use of granaries. All competent family members, regardless of age or gender, were involved in acorn collection, but only women processed acorns and constructed, maintained, and used bedrock milling and storage facilities.

Next, Jackson evaluates acorn processing in ethnohistory and archaeology. Noting that archaeological interpretations of bedrock mortars are poorly developed, Jackson contends that researchers have failed to consider the possibility that women made these facilities. Since gender is a fundamental element of culture expressed in the archaeological record, Jackson argues that the distribution of bedrock mortars constitutes a map of the organizational and logistical strategies that women used in these subsistence practices. Adopting a perspective which views women as active, vital participants, Jackson also evaluates patterns of intra-site spatial organization, the relationship between production and reproduction, and social relations of property and production. He also considers the cognitive implications of the development and elaboration of a productive technology that is fixed in place.

Jackson concludes that because the organization of women's acorn production was a fundamental in structuring Western Mono culture, it was also fundamental to other Native American cultures with similar subsistence bases (pp. 320-321). Bedrock processing facilities represent significant investments in long-term productivity. Since the construction, maintenance, and use of bedrock mortars and above ground granaries restricted mobility, Jackson suggests that when these technologies were implemented around AD 1000, the way in which the natural environment was perceived and used was irrevocably altered. Lastly he suggests (based on ethnographic analogy), that although prehistoric Sierra Nevada women controlled the means and the products of their labor, these products, at least in part, were used by men who controlled inter-group exchange.

This revisionist attempt gives full credit to women's active, innovative roles in the evolution of human societies, and Jackson provides a compelling examination of the multi-level implications of the shift from mobile milling stones to bedrock mortar acorn processing technologies. His discussion of how these new technologies, presumably incorporated into cultural repertoires by women changed their relationship to their environment is of particular interest. Jackson's failure to use ethnohistorical information to contribute further to the study of gendered relations of production is disappointing and narrows the utility of this particular analysis. Nevertheless, this points to innovative methodologies that archaeologists can use to examine the structural bases of prehistoric human social relations. KFA

*division of labor/subsistence/Mono/California/United States, Western*

91. JENSEN, JOAN M. AND DARLIS A. MILLER 1986. Appendix A: Early Woman in New Mexico. In *New Mexico Women: Intercultural Perspectives*, edited by Joan M. Jensen and Darlis A. Miller, 377-385. University of New Mexico Press, Albuquerque.

This brief essay provides a historical sketch of the lifeways of Native American women inhabiting the territory now known as New Mexico between 12,000 BC and AD 1540, as reconstructed by ethnologists and archaeologists in a variety of well known texts. Unfortunately, several of these articles are now badly outdated. The authors' reliance on these references is largely a consequence of the fact that they are not anthropological archaeologists but historians. Their lack of familiarity with the archaeological literature, in combination with their reliance on obsolescent arguments about the origins of corn agriculture in the northern Southwest, results in several errors and oversimplifications.

Although the authors may be guilty of uncritically accepting traditional archaeological reconstructions of gender divisions of labor, they cast prehistoric Native American women in active economic and social roles in the development of indigenous cultures. Significantly, their characterization of these women's dynamic roles effectively complements the roles of prehistoric male counterparts. Native American women are portrayed as contributing significantly to development of new technologies, not merely quietly gathering foodstuffs, processing hides, or nurturing children. Jensen and Miller's article is useful in that it includes women in New Mexico prehistory, illustrating that past lifeways can be presented with a more balanced gender perspective. KFA

*subsistence/division of labor/agriculture/Pueblo Indians/New Mexico/United States, Southwest*

92. JONES, SIAN AND SHARON PAY 1990. The legacy of Eve. In *The Politics of the Past*, edited by P. Gathercole and D. Lowenthal, 160-171. Unwin Hyman, London.

This brief essay on the construction and communication of archaeological knowledge springs from a explicitly feminist perspective. Jones and Pay contend that the public arena in which women's past is most depreciated is the museum — both in displays and in collections. After a brief look at several museum displays in which the authors believe women have been significantly omitted or devalued (including the Jorvik Viking Centre in Great Britain, also critiqued in Chabot, #29), Jones and Pay move on to the basis of this devaluation--"the marginalization, if not exclusion, of women's experience" (p. 163). They argue that in order to understand women's experience in the past, new feminist theories and methodologies must be developed.

In the following pages, they touch on topics as diverse as oral history, gender bias in language and in the practice of archaeology, feminist historiography, and some of the approaches to gender in archaeology described elsewhere in this bibliography. In the final section, Jones and Pay list some of the new approaches towards the portrayal of women that "female museum professionals" and "women curators" have implemented, admitting, however, that "little attempt has been made to challenge the existing male framework or to reassess collection strategies" (p. 167). They conclude that "existing structures and disciplinary divisions within museums need to be changed radically" (p. 169).

Jones and Pay are forthright about their political perspective (and this paper is most appropriate in a book titled *The Politics of the Past*), but their assertion that women (and only women?) are or should be concerned with gender representation is somewhat disturbing. The connections between museum policies and archaeology and theory are not well developed, and their examples of related feminist works ramble a bit. They do present some interesting examples of exhibit changes influenced or proposed by the British group WHAM! (Women, Heritage and Museums). This is nevertheless an important look at what becomes of archaeological data and how biases can be played out in the public arena. SLD

*sociopolitics of archaeology/museums/feminist critique/Great Britain/Europe/Jorvik Viking Centre/WHAM!*

93. JOYCE, ROSEMARY 1992. Images of gender and labor organization in Classic Maya society. In *Exploring Gender Through Archaeology: Selected Papers from the 1991 Boone Conference,* edited by Cheryl Claassen, 63-70. Prehistory Press, Madison.

In this succinct paper, Joyce looks at how Maya gender (as opposed to sex) is represented in Classic period stone sculpture, ceramics, and figurines. Following a brief but useful working definition of gender and a cogent description of her data, she examines the complementary male and female elite and commoner gender roles portrayed, and compares these roles with those described in this area in the sixteenth century by Diego de Landa. Women's participation in feasting and in household and temple rituals is emphasized, since there is a notable discrepancy between Landa's account describing few or no women in most public rituals, and the archaeological (sculptural) representations of elite women (identified by costume and the accompanying gendered glyphs) participating in these events. Women shown in presumably less privileged media, such as on ceramics or as figurines, on the other hand, are not seen acting in rituals, as men are, but are commonly portrayed at productive efforts, such as weaving, grinding corn, or preparing food.

Joyce suggests that the depiction of women in elite ritual where they are commonly shown holding ceramic bowls or cloth bundles is ideologically linked to lower status women's production. Both "imply sequences of production which transformed natural raw materials into culturally defined forms" (p. 66). She goes on to argue that "the emphasis on complementary gender categories is a crucial part of the construction of elite claims to totalizing power" (p. 63), and that a well-known instance of "female gender identity, expressed in costume...associated with male sexual identity, may represent an attempt by male Maya elites to subsume in themselves the totality of social differentiation" (p. 68). Interestingly, this figure's costume combines elements from male *and* female costumes.

This is an insightful look at gender relations in a complex social context. As Claassen notes in her introduction to the Boone volume, the historical and social framework provided by Maya texts (including writing on the monumental sculpture itself) gives archaeologists more information on gender than is available in many prehistoric contexts (p. 5). This may be one reason why Joyce can so clearly separate gender and sex. In this respect, studies on Maya gender are comparable to studies done in some other archaic states (cf. Pollock 1991, #131), or in historical archaeology. It is fortunate that this additional information is available, because as Joyce shows, gender, as well as class, plays an important role in political ideology and economy.

Joyce's description of the complementary nature of gender in Maya ideology, and how this may be manipulated and represented by the elite, is clearly and convincingly described. When the ruler wears elements of female costume, representing the totality of genders, can this be seen as an alternate gender? Does this occur in other contexts and is this seen elsewhere in Mesoamerica? Whether or not elite women's roles in public ritual (as shown on monumental sculpture) were seen as the equivalent of lower class women's production (as portrayed by the smaller and more portable media) is not quite so clear. Joyce argues that the cloth bundles that women are shown holding "recall the role of weaver," while the "ceramic vessels held in a similar fashion may relate women to food production" (p. 68), but it is also possible that elite women merely served in subsidiary roles in some rituals, such as holding the blood-letting dishes for men. Perhaps further research will clarify this. Although this article is an excellent introduction to Maya gender, it is clear that an entire book (profusely illustrated with the images Joyce describes) could be written on the subject. Such a work would be invaluable for any archaeologist attempting to understand Maya social and political organization, as well as for anyone interested in the variations of gender relations in complex societies. SLD

*Maya/figurines/representation, theory of/ethnohistory/religion/class/ceramic analysis/sculpture/Mexico/ Belize/Guatemala*

## Annotated References

94. KEHOE, ALICE 1992. The muted class: Unshackling tradition. In *Exploring Gender through Archaeology: Selected Papers from the 1991 Boone Conference*, edited by Cheryl Claassen, 23-32. Prehistory Press, Madison.

    Kehoe examines the roles and forms of domination in academic discourse. She calls for an "outsider" or revisionist approach, challenging accepted ideas and relations of power rather than trying to achieve acceptance within them. Muted groups—not only women, but any who dissent from the dominant mode of discourse—are marginalized through attributes including gender, caste and class into subordination to the dominant class of propertied western European men. Kehoe sees the political economy of domination equally active within scholastic circles, as academics jealously guard the intellectual capital of their ideas against the interests of others. Importantly, she sees these relations reflected not only in the actions of the dominant class, but in those who would achieve dominance through a critique of the existing power relations. The rise of certain traditions of the gender in archaeology movement are seen as attempts to create "cones of dependence" and citation cliques serving to control discussion and reproduce asymmetries of power and influence within the canon. For Kehoe, the important characteristics of feminist consciousness are an acceptance of alternative discourses and a rejection of hierarchies of dominance. "From the perspective of an outsider," she writes, "who dominates—white upper-class male or white upper-class female—is beside the point" (p. 27). She argues instead for a "praxis of research and stimulating discussion" that acknowledges reflexive and even contradictory subjectivities:

> As scholars, we must resist control by favored schools of research,
> their mapped-out modes of discourse and quoting circles, as earnestly as we
> seek to uncover field data. Pure science is a virgin mother: either a miracle
> unlikely to be met in our lives, or a chimera. (p. 28)

    Kehoe's article is illustrated by a remarkable drawing by Henri Breuil showing a gendered vision of the Paleolithic, where women are busily making stone tools and repairing spears. Since l'Abbe Breuil is often held up as a prime example of the unreflexive and androcentrically-blindered male archaeology that has hindered attempts to see gendered men and women in prehistory, the iconoclastic effect of the illustration is considerable. AWB

*sociology of science/discrimination/sociopolitics of archaeology/political uses of the past/class*

95. KEHOE, ALICE B. 1991. No possible, probable shadow of doubt. *Antiquity* 65:129-131.

    Although Kehoe states that "This note is not a contribution to feminist archaeology or the archaeology of gender" (p. 130), she does question traditional interpretations of gender representations by pointing out that some of "the Upper Palaeolithic carvings routinely identified as breasts" may also be interpreted as male genitalia. In fact, if the holes in some of these items are for suspension, as Kehoe suggests (using some carvings from Dolní Vestonice as examples), their orientation definitely implies "Mars rather than Venus"(p. 129). Kehoe adds that similar objects, such as a clay figurine at the Neolithic village of Sarab (Iran) may be similarly misidentified. Broman Morales and Braidwood assert that this figure is undeniably female in a later issue of *Antiquity* (#22). SLD

*Venus figurines/figurines/representation, theory of/Iran/Neolithic/Paleolithic/Europe/Near East*

96. KEHOE, ALICE B. 1991. The weaver's wraith. In *The Archaeology of Gender: Proceedings of the Twenty-Second Annual Conference of the Archaeological Association of the University of Calgary*, edited by Dale Walde and Noreen D. Willows, 430-435. Archaeological Association, The University of Calgary, Calgary.

In this short article, Kehoe calls for greater attention to the paradigms within which the syntagms of archaeological data are interpreted. She claims that in general, archaeological interpretations are distorted by paradigms that overemphasize hunting technology, i.e., paradigms based on androcentric biases and nineteenth century preconceptions of "savages." She argues specifically that the analogies used in interpreting data from Magdalenian sites have led researchers to ignore the role of non-lithic technologies in these societies. Taking Canadian Indian groups as an analogical base for interpretations of Magdalenian society, Kehoe argues that gender roles in the contemporary and prehistoric societies would have been broadly similar. She postulates that Magdalenian women may have been responsible for technologies involving pliable and perishable materials that are un- or under-represented in the archaeological record, and that the manufacture of lines would have been an important example of such "women's work" (p. 433). She argues further that other textiles such as baskets, mats and perhaps even cloth could have been produced using Magdalenian technology, and ends with the tacit suggestion that common Magdalenian tools could have functioned in textile manufacture.

While Kehoe's general caveat—that we ought not ignore the possible role of textile manufacture and other "invisible" technologies in Magdalenian society (or any other prehistoric society, for that matter)—is well taken, the picture of Magdalenian gender roles she draws is overly broad for the narrow basis of environmental similarity on which it rests. She relies on Brown's conclusions on the restrictions child care places on tasks allotted to women (Brown 1970) for theoretical support for the division of labor in both the Canadian and the European Paleolithic societies. She does not consider either the actual proportion of women involved in caring for young children, the extent to which child care restricts women's activities, or the availability of alternative caretakers, which have been addressed in many responses to Brown's seminal article. The problem of the extent to which Magdalenian artifacts may reflect textile production is an interesting one. The assumption that such technologies would have been the domain of women is unwarranted given the abbreviated analogical argument presented here. KJ

*References cited*
Brown, Judith 1970. A note on the sexual division of labor by sex. *American Anthropologist* 72(5):1074-1078.

*textiles/division of labor/ethnographic analogy/gatherer-hunters/Paleolithic/Europe/Magdalenian*


97. KEHOE, ALICE B. 1990. Points and lines. In *Powers of Observation: Alternative Views in Archeology*, edited by Sarah M. Nelson and Alice B. Kehoe, 23-37. American Anthropological Association, Washington, D.C.

Kehoe argues that the meaning of archaeological data is constructed within the relatively narrow confines of established social convention, and that interpretations going against convention are given little credence. She sets the foundational paradigm of prehistoric archaeology firmly within evolutionary frameworks both confirming and legitimizing the exploitation of non-western peoples, largely through the identification of "less evolved" humans with those of the non-western world. From this perspective, Kehoe suggests that interpretations of Paleolithic artifacts as bone "points" reflects less the functional uses of these items than ethnocentric and even racist presuppositions concerning the brutishness of paleolithic, and thus by extension non-western, life.

The widespread identification of chipped stone artifacts as "projectile point" is not a value-free estimation of function, but instead "smacks of Men-Brutes of the forest" (p. 26), particularly since a great many such items are apparently not projectiles but are probably knives. Kehoe suggests that it is just such images, maintained through the interpretation of multiple function or functionally non-specific items as "points," that have disadvantaged arguments for agriculture in Archaic and Mesolithic contexts.

## Annotated References

Turning to the Paleolithic, Kehoe argues that artifacts commonly called bone points may better be described as netting needles. Analysis of Franco-Cantabrian cave art by Julius Lips and Kurt Lindner suggests the widespread use of snares and nets, and Kehoe suggests that the significance of these "bone points" lies in the creation of lines (hence the "points and lines" of the title) for nets, snares, mats, etc., rather than as actual points. She compares Magdalenian artifacts from Pekarna, Czechoslovakia to modern Ingalik toolkits, and argues for functional equivalence between many of the awls and needles of the Ingalik assemblages with formally similar types in the Pekarna assemblage. The systematic interpretation of such items as points is seen as reflecting androcentric biases and the presumed subordination of women.

Importantly, Kehoe goes a step beyond this argument. She points out that while this represents a systematic undervaluing of roles viewed as women's and artifacts associated with women's tasks, this tells us little about the actual gender associations of the artifacts themselves. Showing that a class of artifacts has been misidentified due to androcentric biases operating against tasks associated with women in western culture says much about our own society, but in no way assures that these artifacts had similar gender associations in Paleolithic contexts. Ancillary evidence can strongly support analogical inferences regarding the function of an artifact, but the chain of reasoning linking an artifact to one or another gender is longer and less secure. AWB

*epistemology/ethnographic analogy/division of labor/Paleolithic/Czechoslovakia/Europe*


98. KELLEY, JANE H. AND WARREN HILL 1991. Relationships between graduate training and placement in Canadian archaeology. In *The Archaeology of Gender: Proceedings of the Twenty-Second Annual Conference of the Archaeological Association of the University of Calgary*, edited by Dale Walde and Noreen D. Willows, 195-200. Archaeological Association, The University of Calgary, Calgary.

Kelley and Hill examine the demographics of Canadian graduate programs in archaeology from 1966 to 1990, focusing on gender issues. They are especially concerned with the representation of women in professional jobs compared to graduate programs.

After a brief discussion of general graduate programs and jobs in Canadian archaeology, they study the relationship between training and professional placement at the University of Calgary. They find more women than men have withdrawn from the Calgary graduate program over the years, and more men than women doctorates hold permanent academic positions. It should be noted, however, that the number of female doctorates is extremely small. The authors also find a greater number of men than women had children during the time they were in the program. Although a greater number of women than men with M.A. degrees from Calgary went on to pursue Ph.D. degrees, either at Calgary or elsewhere, women are not represented in the job market in the proportion in which they are in graduate training programs. Kelley and Hill discuss their findings in light of overall trends in the academic job market, and call on universities to make training programs more flexible so as to minimize the discrepancy between training and placement. DLG

*Canada/sociopolitics of archaeology/graduate training/discrimination*


99. KORNFELD, MARCEL AND JULIE FRANCIS 1991. A preliminary historical outline of northwestern High Plains gender systems. In *The Archaeology of Gender: Proceedings of the Twenty-Second Annual Conference of the Archaeological Association of the University of Calgary*, edited by Dale Walde and Noreen D. Willows, 444-451. Archaeological Association, The University of Calgary, Calgary.

Kornfeld and Francis outline how gender may have changed through the course of Plains prehistory. They begin by noting that few studies have addressed the topic of gender in Plains archaeology, and that little is known about the nature of gender relations through time. They criticize Thomas' Monitor Valley study, where it is argued that women are "invisible" because the kinds of artifacts recovered (e.g., projectile points) were most probably used exclusively by men. Instead, they argue, the notion of invisibility is inherently faulty and cannot possibly be 'true.' Simply, if women were not present at a particluar location, this does not make them 'invisible,' it simply demonstrates the nature of the gender system. That is, if women (or men) were not in place A, they must have been in place B, and this tells us something about the organization of gender systems. (p. 446)

The authors then summarize Plains prehistory and highlight possible associated gender systems. They posit that prehistoric gender relations were shaped by settlement and subsistence concerns ("modes of production" [p. 445]). The authors argue that during Paleoindian times gender roles were fluid where residential mobility was high. Fluidity offered "adaptive advantages during times of resource stress" (p. 447). As increasingly logistical strategies were adopted by Archaic peoples, gender roles became more complex. During the later prehistoric periods, communal bison hunting, developing social interactions, exchange, and horticultural practices were associated with the growth of social inequalities, including gender inequality. Gender roles became increasingly rigid as horticulture gained importance. Finally, the Protohistoric Period, which witnessed the introduction of new forms of production, was characterized by the exploitation of women's labor.

Kornfeld and Francis lay out a preliminary framework for gender research that can be tested and developed in the future. This paper is brief, and only a sketch of how gender systems relate to larger economic strategies is presented here. A less condensed version would be valuable. As the authors point out, "except for the Protohistoric Period, gender systems during any portion of prehistory are of interest because they are virtually unknown" (p. 448). Their work is a welcome first step towards a larger understanding of gender in prehistory on the Plains and beyond. NSG-F

*gender dynamics/division of labor/Archaic period//Paleoindian period/United States and Canada, Plains/ United States, Western*


100. KRAMER, CAROL AND MIRIAM STARK 1988. The status of women in archaeology. *Anthropology Newsletter* 29(9):1,11-12.

This brief articles summarizes the results of a survey of the status of women in archaeology. In many respects similar to Gero's (#67) study of National Science Foundation (NSF) funding, their survey finds that women are generally less likely to receive graduate funding; less likely to complete degree programs; less likely to find jobs, particularly at major universities, after completing their degrees; and less able to obtain research funding if they succeed in finding a position. While the ratio of women to men in most of the programs surveyed was roughly 50/50, attrition rates were higher for women. In the period 1976-1981, women submitted only 36% of the accepted dissertations. More disturbingly, the figure was somewhat lower (33%) at major universities. A similar pattern is reflected in the composition of faculty— the proportion of women on the faculty was lower for major universities than for all programs surveyed. Women were also less likely to receive research funding than their male colleagues. While women represent half of the graduate population, only a third of the NSF predoctoral grants were awarded to women.

The authors note a systematic bias against women at all stages of their professional careers, but do not identify the source or form of the bias. It is not altogether clear whether outright androcentrism and discrimination are at work, or if the biases are more subtle. Their data suggest, for example, that women are more likely to pursue careers in Old World archaeology. Perhaps as a result, women generally submit proposals for longer (median 16.5 months for women, 12 months for men) and slightly more costly (mean $93,778 for women, $91,790 for men) projects, and compete for a smaller number of job openings, particularly at major universities. Such data are intriguing, especially in light of Gero's (#67) documentation of gender distinctions in research roles.

Kramer and Stark's survey indicates that women continue to face significant obstacles to professional advancement in archaeology. Their data are particularly troubling in that major universities (i.e., universities that produce the majority of doctorates in archaeology) may be a more hostile climate for women than smaller schools, and that the majority of students entering the job market are trained in programs reproducing institutional barriers to the advacement of women. AWB

*discrimination/graduate training/sociopolitics of archaeology/National Science Foundation*

101. LARSEN, MARY ANN 1991. Determining the function of a "Men's House." In *The Archaeology of Gender: Proceedings of the Twenty-Second Annual Conference of the Archaeological Association of the University of Calgary*, edited by Dale Walde and Noreen D. Willows, 165-175. Archaeological Association, The University of Calgary, Calgary.

In this article, Mary Ann Larsen challenges the common stereotype in Alaskan archaeology which equates large communal structures (*kasigit*) with men's houses. This stereotype is based, she claims, on an uncritical reading of the ethnographic record and on untested ethnographic analogy. She finds three basic types of *kasigit* in the ethnographic record of Alaska: an interior form, of temporary construction; a southern (Bering Sea) coastal form, of semisubterranean and permanent construction; and a north coastal form, also at least semi-permanent. Only the second type can be considered a "men's house" as it was used as a men's dormitory, as well as a workshop, ceremonial center, and single-sex sweatbath. Both women and men were reported to use the other two *kasigit* types. In the interior, structures were used for multiple village social and ceremonial gatherings, while the north coastal type was used for storage of whaling equipment, as a workshop, and for ceremonial functions.

Larsen uses this ethnographic information to inform interpretation of a large oval, semisubterranean structure dating back about 3000 years, discovered at the site of Onion Portage in the interior of northwest Alaska. She establishes structural and functional analogues from the three ethnographic types and compares expected patterns of construction and artifact/waste distribution. The Onion Portage structure failed to fit the predictions from any of the analogues, and appears to have been used exclusively as a workshop area (based on refuse from lithic tool production), and lacks any evidence of ceremonial activity. Larsen concludes that the Onion Portage structure cannot be considered a *kasigit* in any ethnographically reported sense, and she casts serious doubt on its interpretation as a "men's house."

This article provides an important critique of the Alaskan "men's house" stereotype. While this term appears to be appropriate to some degree for the Bering Sea Eskimo *kasigit*, it cannot be applied uniformly to all Alaskan communal structures, either ethnographically or archaeologically. In addition to this important critique, Larsen offers a reasonable method for evaluating the function of archaeological features with ethnographic analogy. Testing is the critical step in applying ethnographic analogy successfully, and Larsen effectively employs such a program in demonstrating the *inapplicability* of any available specific analogies to the prehistoric structure.

There are, however, three points of difference I would like to take with Larsen's philosophy and procedure. The first concerns her emphasis on what she calls an "ethno-analogical approach" grounded in her "belief that, at least in a loose sense, all prehistoric archaeological interpretation is analogical in nature by virtue of our drawing our hypotheses from ethnographic data." Although I recognize the relevance of the ethnographic record as a source for archaeological hypothesis formation, I strongly disagree that it is the only legitimate source for hypotheses. If such were the case it would prevent us from ever properly explaining archaeological patterning produced by groups operating according to different social and environmental constraints than those available for ethnographic observation over the past few hundred years. It certainly would inhibit our attempts to understand evolutionary implications of the Paleolithic, and it assumes that all expected individual and cultural variability has been ethnographically reported. A more fruitful approach attempts to explain patterning (technically different than "interpreting" pattern) through the development and testing of theoretical models derived in part from ethnographic insights and in part from a flexible intuition which challenges stigmatized assumptions and asks how else a given pattern might have been generated. The problems with ethnographic analogies lie not only in the typical failure to test them, but also in their potential to bias our approach to prehistory. Larsen's philosophical point is well taken, but she needs to consider the critical role that imagination (coupled with rigorous testing procedures) plays in our field.

Related to this concern, I question Larsen's choice of the "modern" *kasigit* from the north and west coasts and adjacent interior region for her analogies. While it is clear that they form a logical group given their geographic proximity to Onion Portage, the separation of approximately 3000 years between the archaeological and ethnographic examples makes me wonder why any direct parallels would be expected. A more effective analogical comparison might attempt to account for and control for changes by contextualizing the Onion Portage structure in a larger cultural framework and accounting for at least minimal cultural changes in the intervening 3000 years. I realize that the current state of archaeological knowledge may prevent a full contextualization along these lines, but I find it unthinkable that the function of a structure could be understood in isolation from its integration into a larger cultural complex.

Finally, this study suffers from the type of detail given to the analogical test cases. Comparisons were based in part on material features like number of entrances and type of construction. Using these kinds of categories to identify parallels in function must be spurious if such elements are determined more by changing environmental constraints and cultural traditions. Larsen's use of test implications based on refuse disposal and manufacturing debris directly related to function is more promising, but what this study needs desperately is a theoretical framework from which the author could generate more thorough and integrated hypotheses about similar or different site and structure functions. While I would never suggest that Larsen should have single handedly produced a theory of Northwestern Alaskan prehistoric social organization, cultural adaptation, and spatial organization in a single article such as this, her difficulty in contextualizing the Onion Portage structure and providing a compelling analysis of its function seems to reflect a lack of such theory to draw upon.

In sum, Larsen's critique of the "men's house" interpretation is extremely valuable and her methodological approach successful but limited. If we hope to gain a more complete understanding of social dynamics, including those of gender, in the prehistoric archaeological record, we need to begin developing contextualized models of cultural organization and interaction. JBF

*architecture/spatial analysis/Arctic/Subarctic/Athabaskan/Yupik/Eskimo/Alaska*


102. LATTA, MARTHA A. 1991. The captive bride syndrome: Iroquoian behavior or archaeological myth? In *The Archaeology of Gender: Proceedings of the Twenty-Second Annual Conference of the Archaeological Association of the University of Calgary*, edited by Dale Walde and Noreen D. Willows, 17-23. Archaeological Association, The University of Calgary, Calgary.

Latta discusses the archaeological problem of historic Iroquoian sites on which there are always a limited number of sherds from different Iroquoian groups. Disputing the common interpretation that these indicate the movement of women ("captive brides"), the author contends that the sherds are an accidental result of contact between groups in a time of increasing trade and warfare.

After briefly reviewing previous work on Iroquoian ceramics, Latta warns against simplistic models and states that the foreign types have no discernible pattern of distribution, but are evenly spread over all sites and site contexts. She discusses three kinds of models that have been used in attempts to explain the phenomenon: movement of pots, social changes reflected in ceramic changes, and the movement of women potters.

The first category suggests trade of pots with their contents rather than trade of pots directly. Under the second category, which does not actually address the foreign sherd problem, Latta cites her previous work suggesting that a simplification of ceramic styles might indicate a decline of the matrilineage. Under the third category, she reviews arguments for intermarriage, captive brides, and feast or trade visits exposing potters to foreign styles. Another suggestion has considered movements of refugees from one group to another, but Latta notes that this would result in a different pattern of sherd distribution.

Stating that the "captive bride" remains the most popular explanation, the author turns to ethnohistoric evidence to evaluate it. She finds that all references to captive wives are of Algonquian women captured by Iroquoian groups. This would not result in foreign Iroquoian sherds. While there are a few references to Huron women captured by the Iroquois or vice-versa, these apparently result in the death of the woman, not her marriage. Latta further notes, with reference to trade and feast visits, that women do not appear to make long trips away from home, while men commonly do so.

Proceeding to her own interpretation, the author describes a type of small, squat vessel with constricted neck and small handles that appears at initial European contact. She suggests that these pots were tied into canoes and used as cooking and chamber pots during voyages (documents indicate that ceramics were used for these purposes). Likely to break during travel, these pots might have been replaced by foreign vessels, and sherds from the broken ones saved as curiosities in the host village. The increase in trade which is documented for the sixteenth century thus would have resulted in more accidents and higher frequencies of foreign sherds on sites. What has been interpreted as the movement of women in this case would not involve women at all.

This paper presents a good example of the usefulness of ethnohistoric sources for pricking holes in archaeological constructs, and the hazards of ignoring such sources when they exist. The argument from vessel types, however, is made questionable from Latta's own description of the squat pots as too small to cook anything but single servings of pottage, so narrow-necked that it would be difficult to reach the contents, and so small and thin that they would be likely to burn easily if used for cooking. These are not promising characteristics for a mess kit. Furthermore, it should be specified whether the foreign rim sherds did indeed come from such small, constricted vessels.

Apart from the question of vessel types, the basic idea that increasing contact might result in unintentional scatters of foreign sherds is an interesting suggestion. What is needed is stronger evidence to support it over ideas like the exchange of pots with or without contents, or simply intermarriage. Latta disputes the existence of captive wives but does not address the possibility of willing ones. SF

*ceramic production/historical archaeology/ethnohistory/trade/Iroquois/United States, Northeast*


103. LØKEN, TROND 1987. The correlation between the shape of grave monuments and sex in the Iron Age, based on material from Østfold and Vestfold. In *Were they all men? An Examination of Sex Roles in Prehistoric Society*, edited by Reidar Bertelson, Arnvid Lillehammer, and Jenny-Rita Naess, 65-77. Arkeologist Museum i Stavanger, Stavanger, Norway.

Løken presents an analysis of Iron Age mortuary data from southeastern Norway in which the shape, size and construction material of grave monuments is correlated with the presence of artifacts associated with one sex. The analysis is based partly on previously published material and partly on original research. In the absence of identified osteological material, burials were classified as male or female based on the presence of certain artifacts (weapons/ornaments). Where the correlations of these artifacts with others (different types of tools and vessels) were sufficiently strong, these were used to categorize the latter artifact types as male or female. The type of grave monument (cairn versus round barrow versus long barrow), monument diameter and height, and mortuary treatment (cremation versus inhumation) were then compared for male and female graves in the Early and Late Iron Age. The analysis reveals interesting differences in the correlation of sex, mortuary treatment, and monument type in the two periods. These include an increased correlation of male burials with inhumation, a change the author suggests may be due to increasing male contact with Christian burial customs, and the correlation of long barrows, which may be symbolically linked to houses, with female burials.

While it may seem to be based largely on twentieth century preconceptions of Iron Age gender roles, the initial classification of weapons as male artifacts and certain types of ornaments as female artifacts stems from archaeological and historical data from other periods. The rest of the correlations and associations discussed are carefully examined, and although some of the interpretations are speculative, they are cautious and well thought-out. KJ

*Scandinavia/Norway/Iron Age/mortuary analysis/Christianization*


104. LOTH, HEINRICH 1987. *Women in Ancient Africa*. Lawrence Hill and Company, Westport, Connecticut.

Although this book is copiously and beautifully illustrated with drawings and photographs of art from archaeological contexts, the text unfortunately relies only on historic and ethnographic accounts to portray women's roles and status in ancient Africa. SLD

*figurines/sculpture/ethnohistory/ethnographic analogy/Africa*

105. LOWELL, JULIE C. 1991. Reflections of sex roles in the archaeological record: Insights from Hopi and Zuni ethnographic data. In *The Archaeology of Gender: Proceedings of the Twenty-Second Annual Conference of the Archaeological Association of the University of Calgary*, edited by Dale Walde and Noreen D. Willows, 452-461. Archaeological Association, The University of Calgary, Calgary.

Lowell uses ethnographic records from the Western Pueblos (Hopi and Zuni) to examine the social use of space. She looks at four different spaces and examines how each was used by men and women. The four areas she considers are the dwelling, the kiva, the village, and the area outside the village. The dwelling is the only one of these spaces where female activities predominate. Groups of matrilineally related women own dwellings, and perform food preparation, food storage, cooking, serving, and craft production within them. While female activities are focused on natal households, male activities are dispersed among natal households, marital households, and kiva groups. Kivas are a site for male activities, primarily religious in nature, although among the Hopi craft manufacture also takes place in kivas. Women rarely participate in kiva ceremonies.

Lowell says less about the use of space at the level of the entire village, except to state that ceremonies and government are largely the domain of men. Work parties are drawn from village men, while women feed the workers and prepare village-wide feasts. Areas outside the village are primarily used by men. Although women own fields, men produce crops, hunt, tend livestock, procure raw materials, and trade.

The use of space in the ethnographic record has implications for interpreting the archaeological record. Lowell also asserts that archaeology, unlike ethnography, can provide information about how the use of space changes. In Puebloan archaeological sites, Lowell concludes that food-related features and artifacts in dwellings were primarily made and used by women, while tools related to hunting, warfare, and possibly agriculture were made and used by men. Kivas were probably male-dominated prehistorically as well as historically, and features and tools found within them were probably the results of male activities. Fields, if they can be identified archaeologically, were probably the province of men, at least in late prehistory. Earlier, says Lowell, it is unclear whether men or women were farming. Overall, then, male activities were more varied and spatially dispersed than female activities, so female activities which took place primarily in villages may be more visible archaeologically.

Lowell's approach to the Western Pueblo ethnography is similar to Spector's (1983, #157) use of Hidatsa ethnography. Many of the spatial patterns Lowell observes are surprisingly similar to those documented among the Hidatsa by Spector. Comparison with patrilineal or patrilocal groups might be illuminating.

Lowell's study is limited by the nature of the ethnographic data. Her discussion of different spaces and gendered use is interesting, but contains some significant gaps. Her discussion of dwellings and kivas is the most detailed; treatment of other areas is much thinner. The use of public village spaces for domestic functions or details of the use of such space during public ceremonies is neglected, as is the use of communal spaces for such activities as animal butchering, plant processing, pottery manufacture, visiting and information exchange, or children's play. One wonders if the use of exterior, public village spaces is simply missing from ethnographies. Also, water carrying is shown as a female activity within the dwelling, but there is no indication from where water is brought. The locations of water sources could have interesting implications for how women used space outside the dwelling.

Lowell asserts that this kind of ethnographic analogy can help Southwestern archaeologists assign certain areas, tools, and activities to genders, and provide an examination of how activities, particularly female ones, change. She does not address how to avoid simply projecting ethnographic patterns onto the archaeological record. Overzealous application might obscure activity changes. If dwellings are assumed to be women's primary activity locus, it may be difficult to see places or times in which men used dwellings more, or in which women used outside spaces more.

This study, and others like it, are perhaps most useful in allowing us to model the effects of different kinds of changes on the division of labor. Rather than trying to impose the ethnography on the past, we can use this information to pose questions and derive expectations about the patterns we might find in the past. For example, Lowell implies that although males did the bulk of the agricultural work ethnographically, females may have done more agricultural labor in prehistory. We can then ask how an increase in women's involvement in agriculture might change their activity patterns, and those of men, and look for archaeological correlates of the different possible patterns. Overall, Lowell's article is quite useful since she synthesizes a great deal of ethnographic data and enables us to clearly see the different spatial patterning in male and female activities. In contrast to the common assumption that women are "invisible" in the archaeological record, she shows that in the Southwest, at least, women may be far more visible than men. Her broader goal of looking at changes in activities through time will probably be harder to achieve, but she has given us one tool with which to approach the question. TVZ

*ethnohistory/agriculture/spatial analysis/division of labor/United States, Southwest/United States and Canada, Plains/Zuni/Hopi/Pueblo/Hidatsa*


106. MANDT, GRO 1987. Female symbolism in rock art. In *Were They All Men? An Examination of Sex Roles in Prehistoric Society,* edited by Reidar Bertelson, Arnvid Lillehammer and Jenny-Rita Naess, 65-77. Arkeologist Museum i Stavanger, Stavanger, Norway.

Mandt's expressed goal in this work is to "chercher la femme" in Scandinavian rock art, i.e. to identify symbols "representing women, female characteristics or both, or ideas associated with these" (p. 36). She briefly addresses interpretations of Paleolithic rock art, then describes two broad stylistic traditions of Scandinavian rock art. The "hunting" rock art is dominated by motifs identified as game animals and by male and female figures with marked sexual organs and is believed to date to the Neolithic. "Agrarian" rock art has motifs depicting plowing, cattle, warfare, boats and carts, as well as footprints, rare handprints, and geometrical designs. Phallic men are common, and women are usually identified by hair style, the lack of an erect penis, and by pairings with phallic males in scenes of coitus. The agrarian style is believed to date to the Bronze Age, ca. 1800-500 BC.

Mandt focuses her analysis on the agrarian rock art. She notes that male figures are common and female figures are rare, and that due to the agricultural scenes and the predominance of phallic males, motifs have often been interpreted as symbolizing fertility. Since "archetypal myths suggest that women often play a dominant part in cults and rites connected with agriculture," and that "a strong element of female symbolism among the 'agrarian' rock pictures" (p. 40) would therefore be expected, Mandt's problem becomes explaining the lack of female figures.

She notes that objects associated with females, such as ornaments, are common in hoards and votive deposits in the Late Bronze Age, and concludes from this that the deposits were offerings to a female deity representing fertility. She rejects the possibility that rock art was associated with a different, male deity, and proceeds to examine the motifs common in the rock art for associations with women or female fertility. She traces many such associations between particular motifs (e.g., boats, carts, trees, snakes and spirals) and female fertility or a female fertility goddess. Most of the associations she explores originate in Greek, Roman or Egyptian mythology, European folk lore, or "occur in most religions, in popular traditions all over the world, in 'primitive' metaphysics and mysticism, in iconographic representations and in popular art" (p. 48). Moving somewhat closer to home, she also cites Tacitus' description, ca. 500 to 1500 years later, of the transportation of a Germanic fertility goddess in a wagon as evidence of the association of a fertility goddess and carts. She concludes:

> It seemed relevant to regard a variety of motifs as symbols of fertility, rebirth and immortality connected with the female element of religion, either in the shape of a goddess or as supernatural powers of a feminine kind....votive-deposits and rock art may probably represent different aspects of religion. Further, the phallic men may be considered mates and worshippers of the goddess, showing their exultant ability to make her pregnant, and thus in turn fertilize the earth.... (p. 51)

While Mandt has many interesting observations on the gender attribution of prehistoric behavior that is often presumed to be associated with religious activities (i.e., hoards and rock art), she does not rigorously examine the context or spatial associations of the motifs, nor detail her logic for assuming that fertility symbolism should naturally be associated with one gender. Her work relies to a great extent on myths and symbolic associations that exist in the minds of twentieth century Europeans. There is no evidence for its existence in the minds of their prehistoric forebears. The uncritical use of comparative material from periods and areas widely separated from the Scandinavian Bronze Age, the unquestioning assumption that specific symbolic associations are universal, or nearly so, and leaps of faith and logic remove this article from the most speculative anthropological studies of prehistoric gender symbolism and place it closer to the body of literature that attempts to rewrite our own myths and reform our own symbolism to answer specific political, social and spiritual goals. If such is Mandt's intent, this article's success is better evaluated elsewhere. KJ

*rock art/fertility cults/religion/myth/gatherer-hunters/iconography/Goddess/Scandinavia/Bronze Age/ Neolithic*

107. MANDT, GRO 1986. Searching for female deities in the religious manifestation of the Scandinavian Bronze Age. In *Words and Objects,* edited by G. Steinsland, 111-126. Norwegian University Press, Norway.

This article is a slightly expanded and reworked version of the paper above, although, due to delays in publication, the earlier version was actually published a year after this one. There is no significant difference in the argument or conclusions of the two articles, although it is worth noting that the underlying assumptions of the argument are more clearly presented in this version. The research is presented here less as an archaeological work than as a comparative study of myth; it is at least, in the terms of the subtitle to this volume, a rather one-sided dialogue. It is perhaps more just to let scholars of the history of religion and comparative religion evaluate its utility in their disciplines than to assess it for its archaeological argument alone. KJ

*rock art/religion/Goddess/fertility cults/myth/Scandinavia/Bronze Age*

108. MARSHALL, YVONNE 1985. Who made the Lapita pots? A case study in gender archaeology. *The Journal of the Polynesian Society* 94(3):205-233.

Marshall sets out to answer the title question by constructing an ethnographic model of gender and pottery production. She is interested in how labor is divided, and in what situations men or women tend to make pots. Since there is almost no ethnographic documentation for pottery making in the Pacific, she extends her ethnographic comparison to New Guinea, looking at contexts in which pots were made by males, females, or both. She provides an extensive appendix of sources on New Guinea pottery. Using these data she makes a number of generalizations concerning gender and pottery production. Female pottery production is strongly associated with island or coastal locations. Female potters primarily make domestic vessels with restricted portions of the vessel decorated. They often emphasize perfection of form and use a simple tool kit. Women do not gain status from their skill as potters or control local and inland trade, whereas men control the extensive maritime trade network in which pottery is an important trade item. In contrast, male and dual gender production is found usually found inland, produces either domestic or ritual pottery, often with extensive and complex decoration, and specializes in the elaboration of decoration. In shared pottery production systems, women often make vessels and men decorate them, primarily for ceremonial purposes. Male and shared potteries are not associated with extensive trade.

Marshall tests these generalizations against meager ethnographic data from the islands of Fiji, Vanuatu, and New Caledonia, which all have female ceramic production. Her model seems to hold up, although the ethnographic sources are not always complete. She then applies the model to prehistoric Lapita pottery, found largely in coastal locations, primarily domestic in function, with repetitive decoration often limited to the neck. Lapita pots were clearly important in oceanic trade. Obviously these characteristics are all most similar to the ethnographic cases in which women made the pottery, and Marshall concludes that women made Lapita pots. She also discusses why Lapita pottery became less and less complex until it disappeared, concluding that as trade networks broke down, pottery became less important and was supplanted by other cooking methods. Female artistic expression in the Pacific was transferred to the medium of bark cloth.

Marshall summarizes an impressive amount of ethnographic data, and her comparison does contain several similarities which point to women as the Lapita potters. This article is frustrating, however, because

## *Annotated References*

Marshall consistently fails to discuss the implications of her ethnographic model for gender dynamics, despite numerous opportunities. Since Marshall is interested in the division of labor only as it applies to pottery production, the relationship between pottery production and other activities remains obscure. The complementary relationship between pottery production and long-distance trade is highlighted, but it would be helpful to know what other kinds of activities people are engaged in, and whether any other kinds of items are produced for trade. In the inland potteries, men make much of the pottery, but it is not clear what women do. Marshall states that the shared potteries produce primarily ceremonial wares, begging the question of who produces domestic pottery, or what is substituted for it. In addition, the patterns derived from the ethnographic record are static and devoid of any kind of explanation. Marshall has compiled a trait list without drawing the links among the traits. Why should there be a relation between geographic setting and who makes pottery? Or between gender and style of decoration?

The consequences of potters' gender for broader gender relations is only implied. Coastal, female pottery production seems to be necessarily linked to male maritime trade, both ethnographically and archaeologically, and this holds certain implications for the relative status of men and women, as well as for the ways in which changes in pottery production, trade, or some other activity might differentially impact men and women. At the very end, Marshall does address the consequences of change, although the causes of the decline in trade are not clarified. It is clear that changes in trade and pottery production must have had profound impacts on the division of labor and gender roles, yet the information presented is insufficient to allow Marshall to investigate gender relations or the effects of change. TVZ

*ceramic analysis/ceramic production/trade/division of labor/ethnographic analogy/Pacific/Polynesia/New Guinea/Lapita*


109. MATHEWS, ZENA PEARLSTONE 1980. Seneca figurines: A case of misplaced modesty. In *Studies on Iroquoian Culture*, edited by Nancy Bonvillain, 71-86. Occasional Publications in Northeastern Anthropology 6. Franklin Pierce College, Ridge, NH.

This paper is a good example of a study concerning gender in archaeology carried out prior to the current plethora of works on the subject. Mathews examines Euro-centric and androcentric biases (without using these loaded terms) in functional explanations applied to Iroquois figurines, and suggests some alternative explanations for a sample of figurines based on their archaeological context and the ethnohistoric record. Thirty-one Seneca figurines (most made of antler or bone) from eight protohistoric sites in New York that date from 1550 to 1675 comprise Mathews' sample.

As Mathews reviews, earlier explanations for these figurines often attribute them to Jesuit influences, particularly since many seemed to be females in "modest" or "chaste" positions — reminiscent of a "chaste virginal protectress" (p. 72). In her more detailed analysis of the sexual attributes, poses, and hand gestures associated with a sample of well-provenienced Seneca figurines, she found that only seven possessed clear female attributes (breasts, vulvae, or hair in a tress as typical for Iroquois women). Out of the fourteen figurines with what she calls the "hand on chest/hand to abdomen" gesture, only two are unequivocally female. Furthermore, two of the figurines in this pose appear to be wearing a mask or headdress, which was a male (ceremonial) prerogative in historic times.

After discussing some stylistic differences which appear to be related to chronology, Mathews brings up the fact that when these figurines have been found in Seneca burials, they are always associated with infants or children or adolescents. Next, she reviews Iroquois ethnographic and ethnohistoric literature for information on figurines, especially as related to children. Interestingly, in these societies, human figurines appear to have been mainly associated with witchcraft or power, and thus could not be assumed to be children's toys. Accordingly, Mathews concludes that it is more likely that these figurines served to protect children's souls than as virginal images related to Jesuits beliefs.

Although Mathews does not address gender *per se*, this is a well-written and well-reasoned article that puts a problematic class of (gendered) artifacts into a rich cultural context. Although archaeologists in other areas may not have the wealth of ethnohistoric and ethnographic background available to Iroquois specialists, this article deserves wider circulation among those interested in figurines, their gender and their related functions and meanings. SLD

*mortuary analysis/figurines/iconography/historical archaeology/representation, theory of/United States, Northeast/New York/Seneca/Iroquois*

110. MAURER, BILL 1991. Feminist challenges to archaeology: Avoiding an epistemology of the "other." In *The Archaeology of Gender: Proceedings of the Twenty-Second Annual Conference of the Archaeological Association of the University of Calgary*, edited by Dale Walde and Noreen D. Willows, 414-419. Archaeological Association, The University of Calgary, Calgary.

This paper outlines some of the contributions gender studies and archaeology can make to each other, and examines previous studies which incorporate the two disciplines. Maurer identifies three areas in gender studies to which archaeology can contribute: the origins of gender and the formation of sex-based hierarchies; the spatial dimensions of gender; and material culture aspects of gender relationships. Maurer agrees with Conkey and Spector's (1984) argument that the main value of feminist gender studies for archaeology is its focus on people. Such a focus can "help in the archaeological effort to reintegrate the agents in prehistory and to obtain a more holistic view of past cultures" (p. 415).

He identifies two types of previous studies incorporating archaeology and gender studies: the task differentiation approach of Conkey and Spector (1984) and Spector (1983) [see annotations #s 39, 157], and the contextual approach of symbolic and structural archaeologists (e.g., Hodder 1982, 1983) and of those conducting activity area analyses. The strength of the task differentiation approach is in developing models of the interrelationships between gender and material culture; its weakness, however, results from the exhaustive cataloging of tasks required before any conclusions can be made and its reliance on ethnoarchaeological data. The contextual approach can serve to elucidate the symbolic and structural relationships between material culture and gender, but yet runs the risk of observer-bias and universalist assumptions about the roles and activities of males and females. That is, the contextual approach creates "an archaeological 'other' imbued with characteristics defined by us and, thus, a part of us" (p. 417). The main problem confronting the development of an archaeology of gender is not just the creation of an archaeological other but one further imbued with traits of the Western "other"--Woman. His tentative suggestion for overcoming this hurdle is to investigate "the internal relationships within the distorted Western opposition between subjectivity and objectivity" (ibid.). This will create new research in gender in archaeology tied both to the material aspects of gender and "to a self-reflexive anthropological critical practice, interested in the recognition of differently constituted subjects and individual notions of the self and selfhood" (ibid.). EAB

*References cited*
Hodder, Ian (editor) 1982. *Symbolic and Structural Archaeology*. Cambridge University Press, Cambridge.

Hodder, Ian 1983. Burials, houses, women and men in the European Mesolithic. In *Ideology, Power and Prehistory*, edited by D. Miller and C. Tilley, 51-68. Cambridge University Press, Cambridge.

*gender studies/task differentiation approach/contextual archaeology/epistemology/feminist critique*

111. MCCAFFERTY, SHARISSE D. AND GEOFFREY G. MCCAFFERTY 1988. Powerful women and the myth of male dominance in Aztec society. *Archaeological Review from Cambridge* 7(1):45-59.

This article takes a "Marxist-feminist" perspective in searching for "alternative strategies of female resistance," in the belief that (contrary to some gender relations studies) there is never a complete monopoly over the sources of power, authority, and prestige. McCafferty and McCafferty summarize the work of other researchers who have looked at female participation in Aztec society, and fault them primarily for their uncritical acceptance of the ethnohistoric sources and the androcentric biases contained therein. They assert that "Aztec gender relationships were based more on dialectical oppositions than on hierarchy"(p. 47). In support of this proposition they attempt to identify powerful women in Aztec society.

The main avenues of social mobility in Aztec society were participation in trade, in the priesthood, and in warfare, and the role of women in each of these is discussed. The most important of these for female power was the priesthood, and a number of female deities and their roles are discussed. The complementary (rather than hierarchical) nature of gender relations in the society is emphasized. "Males did not dominate women, although the resources of power which they controlled may have been more 'important', at least under an androcentric Western definition of cultural relevance."(p. 52). Within Aztec society, the authors argue that "the actual distribution of power was separated by the unambiguous distinctions of gender identity"(p. 55), and thus terms like domination or subordination don't apply. These conclusions on the role of women in Aztec society are backed up by twelve illustrations from various Codices, which are considered to be less biased than the written accounts.

Among the positive elements in this article is the authors' treatment of the work of other researchers, in that they prefer to "use this opportunity to construct rather than deconstruct" (p. 47). Such an attitude is necessary for an archaeology of gender to move away from playing simply a corrective role in response to androcentric bias and towards the creation of positive contributions. The article and the collected illustrations also provide useful specific details on the life of women in Aztec society.

However, on the more negative side, their conclusion that power did not cross gender lines seems counter-intuitive for a working social system, and seems to be based on insufficient data. The conclusions are supported by the documentation of powerful women's roles in all three avenues of social mobility, though the arguments seem a bit contrived. For example, since women are generally believed not to have taken part in ritual battles, McCafferty and McCafferty document what they consider to be the "structural equivalents" of combat, such as ceremonies in which the women engaged in mock battles with spindles and whorls or the exaltation of mothers who are considered warriors having taken their children as captives (p. 52). However, structural or symbolic equivalency need not imply that equivalent social power and prestige were derived from these metaphors and mock battles. Moreover, in an article searching for "alternative strategies of female resistance," it seems strange that something as powerful as motherhood and childbirth is given value only as a metaphor for warfare. The authors are correct in cautioning against androcentric Western definitions of what is important or relevant within a culture (p. 52), and in their critical approach to the ethnohistoric sources. However, their view of an Aztec society full of powerful women and discrete gender classes, and devoid of any gender inequality, is not supported by the evidence presented. WDG

*ethnohistory/religion/mothering/trade/feminist critique/Marxism/Aztec/Mexico*

112. MCEWAN, BONNIE G. 1991. The archaeology of women in the Spanish New World. *Historical Archaeology* 25(4):33-41.

McEwan responds to the need for studies of gender in the archaeology of colonial period Spanish America in this article. Relying on ethnohistorical documents relating to the social, economic and domestic roles of Spanish, Native American and African women in Spanish colonial society, she proposes a number of archaeological correlates to "expose" women in the material record. Spanish women are most "visible" in the domestic aspects of high status homes; Native American women are most "visible" in the domestic and economic spheres of lower status homes; and African women are most obvious in the material remains of slavery and servitude. Data from sites in Florida and the Caribbean serve to illustrate her hypotheses.

While this is an interesting and useful attempt to examine the role of women in Spanish colonial society, McEwan fails to address two problems. First, the reliance on strict interpretations of ethnohistorical material to provide archaeological correlates both biases her approach toward the Spanish perspective and obscures the complex variability that no doubt characterized gender relations at the juncture of Spanish, indigenous and African cultures. Secondly, the article lacks the theoretical strength needed to approach this complex problem. Anthropological considerations of gender theory are ignored and McEwan chooses to focus only on women and not on the dynamics of gender relations. While resolving these problems is beyond the scope of McEwan's paper, the article would greatly benefit from just such an exercise. JDB

*historical archaeology/ethnicity/class/slavery/ethnohistory/Spanish Colonial period/Florida/Caribbean/ United States, Southeast*


113. MCGHEE, ROBERT 1977. Ivory for the Sea Woman: The symbolic attributes of a prehistoric technology. *Canadian Journal of Archaeology* 1:141-148.

    This article represents an early attempt to apply a structuralist approach to an archaeological problem. Focusing on the Thule culture of the North American Arctic (dating roughly from AD 1000 to 1600), McGhee compiles data from five archaeological sites and notes a general pattern in the kinds of raw materials used to manufacture certain kinds of artifacts. Barbless and single barb points similar to those used in caribou hunting by historic Inuit peoples are made from antler, while sea mammal harpoon heads tend to be made from ivory and sea mammal bone. In addition, much of the ivory in Thule assemblages is associated with items used by women in historic Inuit cultures. McGhee suggests that this dichotomy cannot be understood as functional in origin, but is a product of prehistoric belief systems tied to gender. McGhee then uses ethnographic data on Inuit beliefs to argue that ivory is symbolically associated with sea mammals, women, birds, sea ice, and winter. Antler, on the other hand, is associated with land mammals (especially caribou), men, land, and summer. He concludes that this set of oppositions may have applied to prehistoric Thule culture as well as the historic Inuit, and that these oppositions explain the antler/ivory-sea mammal bone dichotomy in Thule technologies.

    McGhee's analysis and the idea that patterns of raw materials in prehistoric assemblages may be linked to gender ideologies hold unrealized potential for the study of gender in archaeology. He does not, however, present an argument against a functional explanation of raw material patterning. For example, this dichotomy may be related to settlement patterns or timing in the manufacture of technological items (i.e., certain types of raw materials might be available at specific times). Furthermore, McGhee assumes a rigid division of labor and static gender ideologies in order to explain technology. He assumes that gender ideologies characterizing historic Inuit peoples also apply to prehistoric Thule cultures. In spite of this, McGhee's presentation relating ideology and technology is noteworthy. It is an impressive early attempt to link gender ideology with the archaeological record. NSG-F

*structuralism/Arctic/Inuit/Thule/Canada*


114. MEYERS, CAROL 1988. *Discovering Eve: Ancient Israelite Women in Context.* Oxford University Press, New York.

    This innovative study examines the status of women in a Mediterranean Iron Age tribal society. The author challenges conventional interpretations of the role of Israelite women in pre-state society as subservient, and uses Biblical texts, archaeological data, and comparative ethnology to argue that their status was comparable to that of men in the same society. Her study shows that translators have allowed values of contemporary society to influence the fidelity of translations of Hebrew texts in a way that devalues the position of women. This is not a trivial point, as Biblical texts are part of the Judao-Christian tradition which has had a significant impact on religious and political attitudes in the Western world.

    Chapter 1 establishes the relevance of this study to feminist scholars engaged in examining origins of contemporary social attitudes, to Biblical scholars and archaeologists, and to anthropologists who work with tribal societies. It also addresses the nature of the sources. The Biblical texts were composed over a 1000 year period and were recorded at a later date by male members of an elite sector of state-level society. This privileged view of the society has also influenced the nature of the texts and must be taken into account in exegesis. Archaeological data consist of excavation and survey of both urban and rural sites in the region. Cross-cultural material from ethnographic studies of tribal societies are also consulted.

## Annotated References

Chapter 2 provides background for specific issues addressed in the study. Meyers introduces some of the topics of major importance in gender studies and discusses the nature of debate among feminist scholars in a clear and readable fashion. Through a discussion of patriarchy as it is understood by feminist scholars, she contrasts patriarchy with patrilineality, power with authority, and private with public domains of power. She also discusses some of the problems inherent in cross-cultural studies which assess women's status.

In Chapter 3, cultural and ecological data are presented to establish early Israelite communities as pioneer farmers in the relatively unsettled upland regions of Palestine. A map of the region, a more detailed discussion of the climate as it structured the agricultural cycle, and a cultural chronology would have facilitated this discussion.

Chapters 4 and 5 present a re-translation of several key verses in Genesis, whose rendering by other translators has been used to justify subservience of women to men. Using her expertise as a Biblical scholar, Meyer makes an argument that these verses (Gen. 2-3,3:16), when translated accurately and considered in context, do not indicate that women in tribal Israelite society were in any way considered inferior to men. It is a fascinating example of a projection of the values of contemporary society onto a reading of the past.

The Israelite woman's role in the household is considered in some detail in Chapter 6. Meyer uses excavation data and data from ethnographic tribal societies to examine aspects of economy, child-rearing, and religion. She suggests that Israelite women's activities devolved primarily around house and children. The textual evidence indicates, however, that unlike contemporary society, this was not considered devalued work, nor were women subordinate to men.

In her final chapter Meyer argues that patrilineality and patrilocality was a response to variable ecological conditions. High inheritance value was placed on land improved through terracing and planting of orchards and groves. Equal emphasis was placed on detailed knowledge of local ecological conditions to manage crops on land. This knowledge, which was controlled by men who customarily did major agricultural work, was of little use when transferred to another area. Women's knowledge of running a household was more transferable; patrilocality was, therefore, the cultural norm. However, a patrilineal system should not be seen as one that necessarily suppresses women. Meyer sees men's and women's roles in tribal Israelite society as complementary. However, with the introduction of Greco-Roman philosophies stressing dualistic world views, and the decreased importance of the household as the economic unit of production, women's status is state society began to decline, although Meyers argues that the status of many men declined as well. KMM

*biblical archaeology/historical archaeology/Iron Age/Palestine/Israel/Near East/Mediterranean*


115. MILLER, VIRGINIA E. 1988. The role of gender in Precolumbian art and architecture: An Introduction. In *The Role of Gender in Precolumbian Art and Architecture,* edited by Virginia E. Miller, vii-xviii. University Press of America, Lanham, MD.

Miller's introduction to *The Role of Gender in Precolumbian Art and Architecture* provides an overview of recent treatments of gender, both in art history in general and in the iconography and architecture of the Americas in particular. She briefly examines both the social roles of women as revealed by documentary, architectural and icnographic evidence and the role of gender in precolumbian representational techniques. Miller describes changes in the interpretation of precolumbian art, noting that scholars have incresingly recognized that many of the figures presumed to be male actually represent women— as deities, rulers and individuals. She suggests that in the absence of primary or secondary female sexual characteristics representations are assumed to be male is an intriguing idea, as it parallels marked/unmarked linguistic categories. The remainder of the essay introduces the individual contributions (several of which are annotated separately in this volume). AWB

*architecture/iconography/representation, theory of/ethnohistory/Mexico/South America*

116. MITCHELL, CHRISTI 1992. Activating women in Arikara ceramic production. In *Exploring Gender Through Archaeology: Selected Papers from the 1991 Boone Conference,* edited by Cheryl Claassen, 89-94. Prehistory Press, Madison.

As explicitly stated, this brief paper emerges from "Feminist Archaeology." It is basically a piece of revisionist archaeology or historical revisionism which attempts to:

> adopt a feminist perspective and apply it to James Deetz's 1965 monograph, *The Dynamics of Social Change in Arikara Ceramics,* in hopes of demonstrating how, by asking engendered questions, our reconstructions of past social organizations are forced to change. Also...how the androcentric biases and assumptions prevalent in his work have limited and formed his reconstruction of the past. (p. 89)

Mitchell's critique of androcentric bias in Deetz's work is problematic in many respects. First of all, she states that "By focusing on trade, Deetz creates a world in which the actions of men change the society, while those of women, who are almost unmentioned, are directionless. Their ceramics passively reflect the changes brought about by the men's actions" (p. 90). While acknowledging that "many of the examples of androcentrism in Deetz's study are a result of the androcentric bias found in the primary sources he uses," Mitchell "does not relieve Deetz of blame, for he chose to accept these sources as objective and valid, while at the same time he chose to cite selectively his assumptions regarding the roles and activities of women and men while ignoring other potentially important information" (p. 91).

Mitchell goes on to criticize Deetz for not emphasizing possible roles women may have played in trade (after having stated that it is androcentric to focus on trade at all), for not emphasizing women's roles in "food producing economic activities or the processes of ceramic manufacture (in terms of spatial and temporal dimensions)" (p. 91), and for using population estimates from primary sources that base village population on the number of men per village. Mitchell also states that when Deetz does cite accounts including active women, they are only used as "an indicator of matrilocality" (p. 91), and furthermore, she argues, even "Deetz's assumption that the Arikara women were uniquely responsible for ceramic production can be questioned" (p. 91).

Following some other critiques of Deetz's methods (not concerned with gender), Mitchell goes on to consider some "possible alternative readings of the information presented in the Arikara ceramic assemblage, scenarios that activate the Arikara women" (p. 92). Instead of attributing the diminished association of stylistic attributes to a change in residence patterns, as Deetz did, Mitchell suggests that "new ideas and contacts influenced and broke down the old culture that was perhaps carefully symbolized on the ceramics" and that "the potters (be they male or female) may have taken an active role in communicating and sharing strategies between the groups in contact with each other or simply expressing pervasive change through their decorative art" or that "a more individualistic oriented consciousness inspired by the materialistic concepts that were being introduced by traders" occurred (p. 92). In conclusion, Mitchell critiques Deetz's search for "a single cause and effect sequence of change," suggesting that "a veritable multitude of interrelated forces were at work" (p. 93).

First of all, it is not obvious that an emphasis on trade as a factor in cultural change is inherently androcentric, any more than an emphasis on ceramics or agriculture (in the Plains or eastern North America) is inherently gynocentric. And although Deetz may indeed be guilty of accepting some of the androcentric biases of the primary sources, I do not think this means he "tacitly supports passages by Tabeau that describe women as 'slaves' and 'property,'" as Mitchell charges (p. 91). Furthermore, every author writing about a specific topic must cite selectively while ignoring other information. Mitchell herself does this by ignoring all of the recent ethnohistoric work on the Arikara (such as Rogers 1990) and other studies on gender in Native American groups on the Plains (such as the papers in Albers and Medicine 1983). And although it is true that "the sources never preclude men from participation" in ceramic manufacture (p. 91), it can be argued that it would be androcentric *not* to assume women were the potters at the Medicine Crow Site, given the fact that all the ethnohistoric evidence attributes ceramic manufacture to women (for a similar argument concerning women and agriculture, see Watson and Kennedy 1991, #180). By attributing ceramic manufacture specifically to women, and focusing on the role that matrilocal relationships play in society, Deetz, on the contrary, appears to be considerably less androcentric than most of his contemporaries or some recent authors.

## *Annotated References*

In short, many of the accusations of androcentrism in Deetz's work are inappropriate. Obviously, the degree of androcentrism in a particular work is a subjective matter. Luckily, there is no single feminist standpoint (in archaeology or in feminism in general) that declares what is and what is not androcentric. Readers should judge the two works themselves, however, and see whose explanations they find more carefully reasoned and researched. As a final note, I would like to add that Mitchell's title is somewhat unfortunate for this topic, since it implies that Arikara women are passive and need an archaeologist to activate them. SLD

*References cited*
Albers, Patricia and Beatrice Medicine 1983. *The Hidden Half: Studies of Plains Indian Women.* University Press of America, New York.

Deetz, James 1965. The dynamics of change in Arikara ceramics. *Illinois Studies in Anthropology* 4. University of Illinois Press, Urbana.

Rogers, J. Daniel 1990. *Objects of Change: The Archaeology and History of Arikara Contact with Europeans.* Smithsonian Institution Press, Washington, D.C.

*ethnohistory/ceramic production/trade/feminist critique/ceramic analysis/Deetz, James/Arikara/United States and Canada, Plains*


117. MULLER, VIANA 1985 Origins of class and gender hierarchy in northwest Europe. *Dialectical Anthropology* 10:93-105.

In this article, Viana Muller traces the evolution of northwest European class and gender inequality "from kin-based to civil societies." In the case of the Germanic tribes, she argues that the transformation was brought about through the establishment of male military retinues independent of the clan networks. These military retinues arose to capture slaves for trade with the Romans. Previously, warfare was clan-based, focused on defense or the capture of new land, and had, according to Tacitus and Caesar, included women and men alike. As the new military bands of men were cut loose from traditional extended kin-groups, they no longer had to heed reciprocal responsibility, and women lost equal status. The military chief became a patron to the men, rewarding their service with gifts, making them his dependents, and the women became dependents of their husbands, forced to do the bulk of the family's productive labor. In the following centuries, this prototype expanded to encompass the land/labor system as a whole with elite manor "patrons" overseeing a retinue of "client" laborers dependent on the lord for protection and resources in bad years in return for labor. The loss of the kin-based units is evident in records of "allods" or free peasants who owned their land as a family unit instead of a clan. Finally, between AD 300 and 700, the emergence of soldier-colonies established for criminals, foreigners, and "unfree men" marks the existence of institutional class inequality.

Muller argues that the development of the family based "allodial unit," established as a patron/client system in miniature with the husband as "lord" and the wife and servants as dependents, replaced the communal equality of the kin-based system. Following Karen Sacks (1979), this new structure is believed to have cut women off from their "sister" networks and from communal rights to the land they worked. Instead, women provided the family labor which allowed men to supply the labor for elite patrons as part of the elite/peasant, patron/client relationship. A nested hierarchy yielded and reinforced multiple class and gender hierarchies. Interestingly, among the Salian Franks and the Welch, women appear to have retained equal rights in production and reproduction as evidenced by their inheritance and divorce stipulations.

This is an interesting account, but it was unclear how much of this was supported by documentary evidence and how much was conjectural. The only archaeology cited was used to demonstrate some form of social inequality in the Late Bronze Age of Western Europe. This model is consistent with others that consider the effects of hierarchy on gender inequality (cf. Gailey 1985), and its emphasis on patron/client relationships is a useful way to envision the developing dominance-subordinance relations in both class and gender. Muller's demonstration of the fundamental interrelatedness of class hierarchy and gender hierarchy is impressive, but I wish that more had been done to develop a picture of the preceding kin-based system of relationships. We are asked to accept, on faith, that gender equality existed in the germanic tribes before the Roman contact period. I am particularly distressed at Muller's apparently uncritical acceptance of Karen Sacks' "sister" concept of gender equality in kin-based cultural systems. This article would benefit from more explicit attention to sources of data and the explicit linkages between data and the model developed. JBF

*References cited*
Gailey, Christine 1985. The state of the state in anthropology. *Dialectical Anthropology* 9:65-91.

Sacks, Karen 1979. *Sisters and wives*. Greenwood Press, Westport, Connecticut.

*state formation/class/trade/ethnohistory/Roman period/Europe/Bronze Age/Iron Age*


118. MURRAY, M.A. 1934. Female fertility figures. *Journal of the Royal Anthropological Institute* 64:93-100, plus plates VIII-XII.

Murray argues that female fertility figurines can be divided into three main types: (1) the Universal Mother or Isis type; (2) the Divine Woman or Ishtar type; and (3) the Personified Yoni or Baubo type. The first, representing motherhood either directly through representations of mother-and-child or indirectly through an emphasis on secondary sexual characteristics, especially breasts, is described as equally worshipped by men, women and children "at all times and in all religions" (p. 94). The second, representing an ideal woman and generally characterized by perfection rather than exaggeration of form, is felt to represent woman as object of desire and is associated exclusively with male veneration. They are "limited in their appeal, for they appeal to men only and leave a woman unmoved, and are nothing to a child" (p. 94). The final form is essentially a representation of female genitalia, usually viewed from the front with thighs widespread, and secondary sexual characteristics underplayed or even absent. "The front view is essential, the genitalia must be exaggerated in size and somewhat distorted in position, and the attitude of the figure may be such as to show the pudenda in a specially marked manner" (p. 94). Intriguingly, Murray argues that this final form is commonly found in houses or graves and is associated with women. She argues that this final class of figure was for the use of women only. Murray examines one group of representations belonging to this final class, the *Sheila-na-gig* figures peculiar to the British Isles, in some detail. In closing she suggests the possible function of the figures as representations designed for women and by women to stimulate their sexual desire, and notes that she suggests this psychological explanation "for so much of the published work on female psychology is founded on the masculine ideas of what a woman should feel or be" (p. 99).

Certainly numerous criticisms could be made of Murray's analysis. The arguments are not entirely compelling, and range freely over time and space in choosing illustrative material and evidence. Given her premise, that these figurines fit into a series of universal niches based on religious sentiment, this is not surprising. While she phrases her study in terms of universals, it focuses only on Mediterranean and European figures. It is nevertheless a remarkable work for its time, going beyond typological concerns to examine the context and function of these artifacts and suggest interpretations based not on men's projections of the psychology of women but on the opinions of a woman belonging to the same tradition as the creators of many of the artifacts. Nor does she draw artificial boundaries between modern Self and ancient Other—she sees the use of the Baubo figure continuing into modern times, and notes that they were considered so significant that Baubo figures in the form of the *Sheila-na-gig* were generally affixed to Christian churches in prominent and highly visible locations. AWB

*iconography/sculpture/fertility cults/representation, theory of/figurines/Europe/Mediterranean*

## *Annotated References*

119. NELSON, MARGARET C. AND DEBORAH L. CROOKS 1991. Dual anthropology career couples: Different strategies and different success rates. In *The Archaeology of Gender: Proceedings of the Twenty-Second Annual Conference of the Archaeological Association of the University of Calgary,* edited by Dale Walde and Noreen D. Willows, 220-225. Archaeological Association, The University of Calgary, Calgary.

Nelson and Crooks conducted a study of dual career couples, where both partners are anthropologists, to determine positions held, career goals obtained and the number employed in separate or shared positions by the same institution. They received 40 responses (19 men, 21 women) from 21 couples out of 76 couples who were sent questionnaires. Most, but not all of the couples, were in academic positions. Based upon their responses, they identify the following trends:

Women are less likely to hold permanent academic positions than their partners, especially if the women received their degrees substantially after their partners. (There were no cases where the reverse was true.)

Women are less likely to have obtained their original career goals (in most cases stated as an academic appointment) and more likely to have changed their goals.

Departments are reluctant to hire both partners in either dual or shared positions because of overt or covert anti-nepotism rules and concerns regarding the autonomy or potential bloc voting of the two individuals.

The authors conclude that dual career couples in anthropology face barriers to achieving career goals and that women face the greatest barriers. Unfortunately, while these conclusions might reflect aspects of the complicated reality of academic hiring, the limited data set does not fully support any of their conclusions. The sample size is small and none of their observations are statistically significant. The data are not presented clearly and there are confusing mistakes/typographical errors that make them difficult to assess (e.g., it is unclear whether the number of individuals who changed career goals is fifteen or five). To their credit, the authors note that their conclusions are tentative and require follow-up. They do not, however, note that the numbers are not statistically significant and do not adequately support their conclusions. The goals of the study are laudable and the topic is of interest to an increasing number of anthropologists and institutions. A larger sample size, a more rigorous format for presenting their data, and some attention to statistical technique would have improved this study and should be included in follow-up research. KJ

*discrimination/sociopolitics of archaeology/United States*

120. NELSON, SARAH M. 1991. The "Goddess Temple" and the status of women at Niuheliang, China. In *The Archaeology of Gender: Proceedings of the Twenty-Second Annual Conference of the Archaeological Association of the University of Calgary,* edited by Dale Walde and Noreen D. Willows, 302-308. Archaeological Association, The University of Calgary, Calgary.

Nelson's paper focuses on the meaning of the life-sized female statues from the site of Niuheliang in northeastern China, posing questions as to what can be inferred about women's status and the relationship between goddess worship and the role of women in the socially stratified Hongshan culture. The site dates to 3500-3000 BC and yielded the remains of a platform and an irregularly shaped building which contained the statues (interpreted as a ceremonial center), a group of high-status burials and jade ornaments.

Following Sanday's use of origin myths as "scripts" for interpreting male/female relationships, and the general correlation between the presence of female origin myths and high status for women, Nelson considers the Niuheliang statues as a script from which to hypothesize about female power, status and autonomy in Hongshan culture. She examines two independent lines of evidence for support: skeletal evidence and "continuous threads in Chinese culture which could be followed back to women of power" (p. 303). The latter consists of mortuary evidence from the richly accompanied tomb of Fu Hao of the Shang dynasty (sixteenth to tenth centuries BC). According to the oracle bones, Fu Hao was a woman of importance, possibly the king's consort or a leader of armies. Nelson interprets this evidence as indicative of the autonomy and power of upper class women during this dynasty. Evidence which ties this to the Niuheliang comes in the form of bronze mirrors in the style of this site's region, which she views as strengthening "the possibility of a persistent tradition of female power" (p. 304). Skeletal evidence comes from six burial clusters at the site, but only brief information (e.g., position of the skeleton, associated artifacts, grave/tomb form and size) for a sample of the burials is presented.

Nelson concurs with the original designation of this site as a ceremonial center, and sees evidence of a highly complex culture in the complexities of the site and in the creation at Niuheliang of the mythical pig-dragon animal.

As Nelson herself states, in order to test hypotheses about gender meanings at this site it is necessary to know the sex of the skeletons. However, even if all of the skeletons are female it is difficult to agree with her proposed conclusion that the "women were the priestesses and perhaps secular rulers as well as the goddess" (p. 308). More systematic mortuary analysis is required before such a conclusion would be supported. At this stage, it would have been interesting for her to offer an analysis of the unsexed mortuary remains for evidence of gender differences expected within the context of a complex society such as the one represented in part at Niuheliang. This could then be later compared with a reanalysis of the data which includes the sex of the skeletons. This could provide important insights into approaching gender through archaeological mortuary remains. It is also difficult to assess the relevance of the Shang data to the interpretation of female status/power during this earlier period; the chronological and sociopolitical differences seem to be of too great a magnitude to be useful to answering her questions. Finally, a twist on her approach of viewing the female statues as a script would be to use these as a potential source of data for answering questions on female status/power in pre-state complex societies. EAB

*mortuary analysis/sculpture/myth/class/Hongshan culture/Shang dynasty/China/Asia*


121. NELSON, SARAH H. 1991. Women archaeologists in Asia and the Pacific. In *The Archaeology of Gender: Proceedings of the Twenty-Second Annual Conference of the Archaeological Association of the University of Calgary*, edited by Dale Wilde and Noreen D. Willows, 217-219. Archaeological Association, The University of Calgary, Calgary.

Nelson compiles data on U.S. and Canadian women archaeologists working in Asia and the Pacific, and offers several observations concerning gender issues and the structure of archaeological practice in North America. Using membership/conference participant lists current as of 1989, she identified 31 North American archaeologists working in the Asia/Pacific region, with the following distribution: 0 women and 6 men in the Pacific, 4 women and 8 men in East Asia, and 4 women and 9 men in Southeast Asia. She lists several problems archaeologists face in working in this region which she believes help to explain both the small numbers of archaeologists and the underrepresentation of women. These include: (1) greater costs, and she cites the recent finding of Kramer and Stark (#160) that women have not been particularly successful in receiving large grants; (2) new language, often with an unfamiliar writing system, which may require several years training to acquire; (3) potential unwelcome atmosphere for American archaeologists by Asian/Pacific archaeologists; and (4) cultural differences which often include the attitude in Asian countries that archaeology is not appropriate for women.

She explores these data further to determine if this small group who, given the difficulties of working in Asia, might be characterized as "very energetic, dedicated and hard-working" are sought out by "elite" universities (using Hurlbert's [1976] definition). Five of the eight women are listed in AAA Guide to Departments of Anthropology 1989, with none at elite departments and only one in a Ph.D. granting department. Of the 17 men, four are at elite institutions, seven in the next two rankings of universities, and 12 at either unranked institutions or unlisted. Based on these findings, she offers an hypothesis concerning the marginalization of North American women archaeologists who work in the Asia/Pacific region. Briefly, she posits that the Asia/Pacific region is seen as a marginal area, and the women who work in this area are marginalized further because of few colleagues and few opportunities to publish in "mainstream" journals. In comparison, the men who work in this area are viewed as having access to an unusual data source, and thus are sought out by elite universities.

## *Annotated References*

Nelson's analysis of these limited available data indicate some interesting complexities in gender bias in the practice of archaeology. Her hypothesis certainly warrants further testing, although the part postulating further marginalization of women because of limited opportunities to publish in mainstream journals seems equally applicable to the men who work in this region. EAB

*References cited*
Hurlbert, B. 1976. Status and exchange in the profession of anthropology. *American Anthropologist* 78:272-284.

*sociopolitics of archaeology/discrimination/United States/Canada/Asia/Pacific*


122. NELSON, SARAH M. 1990. Diversity of Upper Paleolithic "Venus" figurines and archaeological mythology. In *Powers of Observation: Alternative Views in Archaeology*, edited by Sarah M. Nelson and Alice B. Kehoe, 11-22. American Anthropological Association, Washington, D.C.

This article examines why, for so long, all Upper Paleolithic "Venus" figurines have been assumed to be the same. Nelson looks at how these figurines are commonly portrayed, concluding that they are usually described as quite similar, although they vary greatly in all respects other than sex. Variability in body shapes is ignored and breasts, buttocks, and pregnancy are constantly emphasized. The function most commonly ascribed to them is "fertility." Nelson analyzes some of the hidden assumptions in figurine descriptions: that they were made by and for men, that nakedness is erotic, and that breasts denote sexuality. All of these assumptions are firmly rooted in our own cultural stereotypes about gender. Alternative explanations for the function of these figurines include ancestor images, clan-mother representations, or priestly paraphernalia.

Rather than trying to support an alternative explanation for the functions of these figurines, like Rice (#138), Nelson explores why they are described in such stereotyped ways. This article is particularly useful for emphasizing the cultural baggage that archaeologists bring to the study of figurines. It would be very useful to learn more about how figurines, and representations in general, operate ethnographically. Without exploring the kinds of functions figurines can perform, our ability to get at the meanings of prehistoric figurines is hampered. TVZ

*representation, theory of/figurines/Venus figurines/fertility cults/Europe/western society, contemporary/ Paleolithic*


123. NILES, SUSAN 1988. Pachamama, Pachatata: Gender and sacred space in Amantani. In *The Role of Gender in Precolumbian Art and Architecture*, edited by Virginia E. Miller, 135-146. University Press of America, Lanham, MD.

Niles examines the role of gender in spatial patterning and religious architecture at Amantaní, an island in Lake Titicaca. The island is dominated by two mountain peaks, called Pachamama (Earth Mother) and Pachatata (Earth Father) respectively, separated by a low saddle. Each has a temple at the summit. While Niles does not suggest the age or cultural affiliation of the shrine on Pachamama, she suggests that Pachatata may be associated with the Pucara style of the Early Intermediate Period (ca. 500 BC to AD 400) or the Tiahuanaco Style of the Early Intermediate Period and Middle Horizon. She describes the roles of the shrines in controlling agricultural production, and based on the presence of similar patterns and calendrical dates for festivals concludes that there is a pattern of paired male-female deities (or perhaps Janus-like deities representing both genders) in the Andean highlands. She attempts to isolate several characteristics of associated ritual, and points to patterns in religious architecture that she sees as tied to gender dualisms. She notes in passing that the distinction observed elsewhere in the Andes between circular and square constructions may correspond to female and male patterns, respectively. AWB

*architecture/religion/spatial analysis//South America/Andes/Amantaní*

124. O'BRIEN, PATRICIA J. 1990. Evidence for the antiquity of gender roles in the central Plains tradition. In *Powers of Observation: Alternative Views in Archeology,* edited by Sarah M. Nelson and Alice B. Kehoe, 61-72. American Anthropological Association, Washington, D.C.

Patricia O'Brien eloquently states "our ability to identify female and male behavior from the archaeological record is a product of both our recovery techniques and our research questions, and of our unstated assumptions *per se*" (p. 61). In order to circumvent these problems, O'Brien draws on historic Pawnee ideology to elucidate gender from patterns recovered archaeologically. She focuses on two Central Plains sites, the C. C. Witt site and the Holidome site.

O'Brien first reviews elements of Pawnee cosmology that she believes are significant for interpreting the archaeological record. Most important to her arguments are beliefs concerning the deities Morning Star and Evening Star. In addition, a variety of dualities pervade Pawnee beliefs, including male/female, night/day, and west/east. O'Brien links these concepts to archaeological finds. For example, she suggests that human sacrifice associated with the Morning Star ritual may be represented at the C. C. Witt mound, where an adolescent female was buried together with thirty-two projectile points. At an earth lodge at the C. C. Witt site, spatial distributions of certain types of artifacts dovetail with expectations of use by men and women in eastern and western sectors of the lodge. The spatial layout of the lodge itself and faunal remains within it provide additional links to Pawnee cosmology. At the Holidome site, artifacts historically associated with Pawnee women's activities are found associated with lithic debitage, suggesting that women both made and used stone tools at this site.

O'Brien suggests that Pawnee cosmology and gender ideologies were present as early as AD 1300 in the Central Plains. Although some of her conclusions are suggestive, rather than definitive, this article is important because it attempts to examine the role cosmology (including gender) plays in shaping the archaeological record, a role often overlooked by archaeologists. NSG-F

*spatial analysis/mortuary analysis/lithic technology/ethnohistory/religion/United States and Canada, Plains*


125. ORPHANIDES, ANDREAS G. 1988. A critique of suggested interpretations of prehistoric anthropomorphic figurines. *Journal of Business and Society* 1:164-171.

In this short article, Andreas Orphanides effectively critiques several interpretations used to explain the significance of prehistoric anthropomorphic figurines world-wide. She argues that no single function is likely to account for all of these figurines, and is especially critical of "Mother Goddess" interpretations, for which she finds no supporting evidence. Orphanides also reviews interpretations of figurines as toys or dolls, as concubines or servants in the afterlife (in mortuary contexts), as mourners, initiation figures, or as "sorcerer's agents" for sympathetic magic. In each case, Orphanides finds insufficient evidence and a lack of any critical theoretical or methodological framework. She sums up her critique of Ucko's (1968) multiple interpretive framework with a particularly insightful statement applicable to all archaeological uses of ethnographic analogy:

> Ucko's methodological line is welcome (that being a recognition of the likely heterogeneity of figurine functions); his approach, however, lacks a detailed hypothesis and test implications, whereas the ethnohistoric analogies he extensively uses do not lie within acceptable geographical and chronological margins. The value of ethnohistoric analogy as a useful tool in archaeology cannot be underestimated but its misuse (and abuse) may provide solutions to particular problems which lie far away from the truth.

Although by no means a necessary pitfall of an archaeology of gender, many attempts suffer from this problem. As Orphanides suggests, the theoretical linkages and methodological practices which will enable archaeologists to transcend the ethnographic record in explorations of past gender systems need to be developed. JBF

*figurines/ethnographic analogy/Goddess*

## Annotated References

126. OYUELA-CAYCEDO, AUGUSTO 1991. Ideology and structure of gender spaces: The case of the Kaggaba Indians. In *The Archaeology of Gender: Proceedings of the Twenty-Second Annual Conference of the Archaeological Association of the University of Calgary*, edited by Dale Walde and Noreen D. Willows, 327-335. Archaeological Association, The University of Calgary, Calgary.

This article describes the ways that gender oppositions and inequalities of rank are reflected and recreated in the spatial organization of the Kaggaba Indians of Colombia. The author presents the division of space on the level of household, village, and valley system as an opposition of the male, pure, sacred pole and the female, polluted, profane pole. He stresses the role of priestly authority in maintaining balance in a universe of oppositions.

Oyuela-Caycedo shows that sacred knowledge, the cultural value that inequality is based upon and understood in terms of, is the same in the oppression of women by men, non-priests by priests, and low status lineages by high status ones. The linkage between gender inequality and other inequalities is further demonstrated in the distinction between highland and lowland areas. Gendered space is more strongly marked (via separate male and female dwellings) in the highlands, the sacred extreme of the valley world, where there are more religious hamlets and high-ranking priests. He also suggests that this pattern persists because gender inequality is used to justify and preserve rank inequality. The author offers an adaptive explanation for gender separation of houses, suggesting that the colonization of the highlands, which are agriculturally poor, was the last chance to ease population growth through migration. After this it was necessary to limit population, and the sexual separation of houses was adopted as a kind of birth control, enforced by an ideology that sex with women prevented men from attaining sacred knowledge.

Discussing the cultural history of the area, the author concludes that there has been a shift in authority from the sixteenth century chiefdoms where political power was sanctified by religion to the modern situation where religious power is sanctified by gender. He also outlines the historical background of the current symbolic organization of space, pointing out that various elements of the system have different histories and time depth. Stress is laid upon the ways that spatial organization has varied within an overarching ideology of mediated oppositions.

The author does an admirable job of discussing different dimensions of inequality in terms of each other and showing how they connect on the cosmological map. It is particularly interesting, for scholars concerned with the nature of gender inequality, that he does not view gender and rank as separate realms, but as different manifestations of a single currency of inequality, which is the differential access to sacred knowledge. The adaptive argument, however, is both extraneous to the main thesis and weak (there is no reason to suppose that separate houses reduce population growth unless you assume that people can have sex only in houses). Conceptually, the most important problem in this article has to do with gender separation and inequality. This is a society in which spatial segregation is associated with actual inequalities of both rank and gender. But although Oyuela-Caycedo questions the inequality of rank, he questions gender separation, rather than gender inequality, the latter being stated but unexplored. Gender separation is said to preserve inequalities of rank and the position of priests, and to be upheld itself by an ideology of female pollution and the restriction of sacred knowledge to men. Thus, rank needs justification and gender inequality provides it; gender inequality is not considered to need justification of its own. SF

*spatial analysis/religion/ethnohistory/ethnographic analogy/Colombia/South America/Kaggaba*

127. PIRIE, VICTORIA 1985. Women, heritage and museums. *Archaeological Review from Cambridge* 4:117-118.

In this short letter Pirie discusses the role of women in museums and the treatment of gender in museum exhibits. She notes a lack of women employees in museums. Pirie relies upon general statistics for archaeologists and provides little information which directly pertains to museum employment practices. However, she does provide some insight into the role of museums in portraying gender, particularly women. Object orientation, the passive portrayal of women's roles, and the pervasive androcentrism within archaeology are discussed in the context of museum studies. Museum exhibits, like archaeological interpretation, often uncritically incorporate these elements which perpetuate the subordination of women. Women, Heritage and Museums (WHAM!), an organization which seeks to redress these problems, promotes a positive image for women and a change in museum agendas, attitudes and practices. JDB

*museums/sociopolitics of archaeology/discrimination/WHAM!*

128. POHL, MARY DELAND 1991. Women, animal rearing, and social status: The case of the Formative Period Maya of Central America. In *The Archaeology of Gender: Proceedings of the Twenty-Second Annual Conference of the Archaeological Association of the University of Calgary*, edited by Dale Walde and Noreen D. Willows, 392-399. Archaeological Association, The University of Calgary, Calgary.

In this article, Pohl examines the relationship between gender and political transformation in the Lowland Maya Formative Period. Based on ethnographic, ethnohistoric, and iconographic data, she argues that women were the primary caretakers of both children and animals (primarily dog and deer), and that they were also the primary producers of textiles from the Formative through the "ethnographic" period. She then demonstrates the increased importance of dog and deer meat at Formative elite centers, based upon changing frequencies of dog and deer MNI relative to the total faunal collections. Linking these two lines of evidence, Pohl suggests that women, through their roles as animal caretakers, played a critical role in Formative society. As demand for meat and laborers increased, women would have had important control as child rearers/ socializers and as meat and textile producers. They would have had a certain amount of economic leverage, but these same responsibilities would have prevented them from full control over their own production. Instead, it is argued, men who were free of the nearly constant demands of child and animal rearing were able to appropriate these products for political purposes. As tribute demands increased, it is posited, women raised more children and animals, further increasing their collective importance and limiting their free time and status.

This is a compelling analysis as far as it goes. Pohl makes a reasonable case with the data available and does a better job than most at showing how a gender division of labor could have been manipulated in, and crucial to, social transformation. Despite its strengths, there are a few areas where this paper could be further developed. First, I would like to know more about women's and men's economic roles in the preceding periods to better understand the significance of the Formative in changing gender relationships and the "institutionalization of gender subordination." To clarify the dynamics of the gender division of labor through the Formative analysis of men's roles as well as those of women would be helpful. I also found myself wondering whether gender dynamics were the same or different in the elite class. Pohl cites evidence that on occasion women ruled political centers in Classic times, but she dismisses these cases as exceptions. But it might in fact be the case that different gender divisions of labor and subsequent gender statuses emerged in the different "classes." Although not described as such, the women in Pohl's study constitute tribute producers and most logically would have developed into "working class" producers in the Classic Period.

Although not critical to the analysis presented, I think that Pohl overstates the parallels between children and domestic animals. She speaks of "domesticating children" and "socializing animals." The critical similarities are in the *dependencies* of both small children and domestic animals on the regular attention of a caretaker. Although humans *are* indeed animals, there are fundamental differences in the time and care commitments needed for human offspring and animals. It might be interesting to consider how women came to be the caretakers of domestic animals in the transition to food producers from food gatherers. It might relate to patterns of childcare which were most conducive to the addition of domestic animals. But again this could only be developed with attention to men's activities as well as women's. Finally, in regard to the specific archaeological methods used, there is a potential problem in Pohl's assumption that an increase in MNI of deer and dog *relative to the other fauna present* represents an increase in the importance of these animals as resources. It could be that the other fauna decrease as a consequence of increased importance of plant resources such as maize and beans, and that deer and dog were not affected for other reasons. Nevertheless, I think it likely that the emergence of deer and dog as the most significant meat source in the Formative supports Pohl's analysis. What is critical and missing is an analysis of the importance of non-meat resources and who procured and who controlled them, in order to better understand the changing social dynamics.

Pohl offers an interesting case study with implications for the development of a "gendered" theory of political evolution, inequality and division of labor. While my critique offers areas that would be interesting to pursue further, this article focuses well on one facet in the Formative transition which has been understudied. The arguments are strong and the data well applied. It remains to be seen if subsequent research will strengthen, refine, or challenge these findings. JBF

*figurines/subsistence/division of labor/state formation/ethnographic analogy/ehnohistory/spatial analysis/ Maya/Mexico/Belize/Guatemala/Formative period*

129. POHL, MARY AND LAWRENCE H. FELDMAN 1982. The traditional role of women and animals in Lowland Maya economy. In *Maya Subsistence: Essays in Memory of Dennis E. Puleston*, edited by Kent V. Flannery, 295-311. Academic Press, New York.

Pohl and Feldman use this chapter to present ethnohistoric and archaeological information concerning the role of Mayan women in providing animals for religious and economic purposes during the Late Classic through Colonial periods. The deer and peccaries sacrificed in Maya agricultural ritual were often raised by women, as were turkeys and dogs used in other rituals. Women frequently provided fowl, dogs, and pigs for tribute in food and for trade. Women also produced cloth and kept bees. The political power of women was located in the economic control provided by these activities. Even following the economic reorganization accompanying the Spanish conquest, many women maintained economic independence from men.

Pohl and Feldman's discussion provides insight into the religious ritual and economy of the Maya. They demonstrate that women did play a significant economic role in Maya society. This role may have allowed a certain degree of independence for women. However, their data say little about the importance of women's roles in Maya economics. No information is provided on how Maya men and women interacted in ritual and economic contexts. In addition, their reading of ethnohistoric and archaeological information is somewhat eclectic; the ideas presented would be difficult to test archaeologically. JDB

*subsistence/division of labor/ethnographic analogy/ethnohistory/trade/Classic period/Colonial period/ Mexico/Belize/Guatemala/Maya*

130. POLLAK, JANET 1991. Excavating Auel: The gender roles of Earth's children. In *The Archaeology of Gender: Proceedings of the Twenty-Second Annual Conference of the Archaeological Association of the University of Calgary*, edited by Dale Walde and Noreen D. Willows, 297-300. Archaeological Association, The University of Calgary, Calgary.

In this short article Pollock sets out to examine gender roles assigned to fictional Neanderthal and Cro-Magnon groups in Jean Auel's popular novels set in a European prehistoric past. Much of the paper simply provides a synopsis of the life of Ayla, the main character in the Auel novels, and describes features of the division of labor and general attitudes about sex, women, and men among Auel's "Clan people" (Neanderthals) and "Others" (Cro-Magnon). She follows this with a short analytical section in which the author's voice is represented primarily by a series of questions and "What If's," and Jean Auel's responses appear as lengthy quotes out of a letter written to Pollock.

The paper touches briefly on a number of interesting questions ranging from common assumptions about a universal sexual division of labor to questions about the character of Neanderthal cultural and information-storage systems. Auel's fictional account features rigid, stereotypical gender relations among Neanderthals governed by a static, sex-differentiated memory. Cro-Magnon behavior is presented as more flexible, with high status for women based on a mystical concern with female fertility. Pollock points out that this contrast rests on interpretations of Upper Paleolithic female figurines as symbols of fertility or "Venuses." She suggests a series of problems with the fertility-symbol interpretation of these figures, focusing on the wide range of gender ideologies that might conceivably be represented. Unfortunately, this discussion is not based on an understanding of the relevant literature on Paleolithic representations, and is largely limited to a series of rather vague suggestions without supporting discussion: "What if the Venuses represent women's interests independent of men? What if some Upper Paleolithic women shared few interests that are defined as women's interests by Western heterosexual feminists?" (p. 299). The result is a jumble of speculations about what may be conflicting gender ideologies both among feminist and non-feminist archaeologists and among women in the Paleolithic past.

What remains unclear in Pollock's paper is whether Auel's novels are to be admired and emulated for adopting a speculative "What If" approach and for raising questions that archaeological research might address, or whether the books are to be dismissed because they reflect "the gender biases of 12 years ago." Are archaeologists, according to Pollock, to learn from Auel or to educate her in critical approaches to "the site reports and syntheses of the mostly male prehistorians" (p. 299)? LEF

*fiction/Auel, Jean/Venus figurines/Europe/Paleolithic*


131. POLLOCK, SUSAN 1991. Women in a men's world: Images of Sumerian women. In *Engendering Archaeology: Women and prehistory*, edited by Joan M. Gero and Margaret W. Conkey, 329-365. Basil Blackwell, Cambridge, MA.

Pollock uses documentary references, mortuary data and cylinder seal representations to study the economic, political and social roles of women in ancient Sumerian and Akkadian Mesopotamia (Early Dynastic and Sargonic Periods). It is evident from the early texts that women occupied important positions (such as queens and priestesses), had control over lands, and participated greatly in the labor pool. Mortuary data from the royal cemetery at Ur indicate sex distinctive marking among higher statuses, while lower status females were not as visible as elite females. Some elite females also appear to have controlled the lives of subordinates of both sexes. Seals in elite burials also pattern by sex: males were represented in conflict scenes, and females were shown in banquet scenes. The banquet scene seals, with representations of both males and females, were apparently of lesser importance since few impressions from these seals have been found. These representations imply that both men and women participated in some rituals, and that there were exclusive male rituals. In general, there are few representations of women, and those that exist appear to suggest passive activities (compared to active male roles). This contradicts the documentary and burial evidence, and suggests to Pollock that women are portrayed through the eyes and actions of men.

Pollock introduces the economic, social and political lives of Sumerian women. Her textual evidence, mortuary data and iconographic representations are carefully analyzed and coherently integrated. She skillfully reveals the opportunities open to women in political and economic positions in both secular and religious spheres. Her work is also insightful for its treatment of class relations as they cross-cut gender. However, her ideas concerning a gender ideology of active vs. passive role portrayal for men and women, and the representations as products of male activity, require further verification. The active/passive dichotomy may be more a projection of our own gender relations than a Sumerian pattern. JDB

*mortuary analysis/iconography/class/Near East/Sumer/Akkad/Mesopotamia/Iraq*


132. POMEROY, SARAH B. 1991. The study of women in antiquity: Past, present, and future. *American Journal of Philology* 112(2):263-68.

Pomeroy surveys the state of the study of women in Classics, touching on past developments, current trends, and prospects for future research. The author conducted an informal analysis of the literature by examining a total of forty-five journals found in two libraries. Twenty-three journals included at least one article relevant to the study of women. Pomeroy reasons, "[t]his little survey confirmed my sense that the study of women has, indeed, become part, albeit a very small part, of the mainstream of Classical Studies" (p. 264). Some specific gaps in knowledge result from the current failure of some researchers to recognize the difference between men's ideas about women and women's historical accounts of themselves. Thus some scholars rely solely on male sources in historical analyses of the role of women. In addition, Pomeroy laments a predominance of scholars employing literary rather than historical approaches to the study of women in antiquity. She calls for a more integrated (and anthropological) approach examining gender as well as "class, age, ethnicity, regional specificity, historical period, and change over time" (p. 266). Future prospects include increasing attention to women's everyday lives, and Pomeroy notes that "archaeologists, and to a lesser extent, art historians will be able to make a substantial contribution to the field" (p. 266). Some interesting ideas on advancing women's studies and equity in the field are put forth towards the end of this paper. Pomeroy cites a colleague who suggests that evaluation reviews of articles and books consider whether the topic of women is at all addressed by the work. Whether or not scholars appropriately reference women authors should also be consciously included as an evaluation criterion. As Pomeroy puts it, "we must take care lest they become a 'muted group'"(p. 267). She also notes that the numbers of publications by women in classics increased following a system of "anonymous refereeing." She concludes by briefly critiquing some recent books focusing on women in Classical Studies. NSG-F

*classical archaeology/ethnicity/feminist critique*

133. PURSER, MARGARET 1991. "Several Paradise ladies are visiting in town": Gender strategies in the early industrial west. *Historical Archaeology* 25(4):6-16.

Purser discusses the importance of gender for reconstructing past social process, then recounts two case studies that examine gender using both historical and archaeological data from the western United States. The fluidity of settlement composition in western mining towns challenges the traditional analytical units of "household" and "family," so Purser focuses on differences in gender specific behavioral patterns. Using data from local newspaper accounts of men's and women's visits to other settlements, Purser analyzes mobility patterns and the significance of the kinds of visits recorded. Men's visits centered on public establishments—the courthouse, taverns, and commercial stores— while women visited exclusively in private homes. In one case, the Grass Flats, Nevada, settlement, women's visits crosscut environmental and productive zones, serving an important economic function by helping to forge and maintain social relations that could be called upon at need. In the less fluid and more prosperous community of Paradise Valley, California, the patterns show a somewhat different focus, with long-term visits usually centered on the East Coast or Europe.

Purser makes a number of valuable points, not least of which is to again emphasize that studies of *gender* in the past are not the same as studies of *women*. Some of Purser's statements, such as that there is no need for finding ways of "digging up" gender, or of associating gender groups with material correlates (p. 6), must nevertheless be regarded with skepticism. These statements reflect the availability of historical documents for charting gender dynamics, which frees the analyst from the evidential constraints affecting many archaeologists. It would not be possible to conduct such a study given currently available methodologies for identifying and systematically studying gender from the material record alone. Purser's study is most worthwhile, however, as an example of the incorporation of gender-informed theory into a research program and of an anthropological approach to the early history of the western United States. AWB

*historical archaeology/nineteenth century/United States, Western*

134. RANDSBORG, KLAVS 1986. Women in prehistory: The Danish example. *Acta Archaeologica* 55:143-154.

This article is essentially an unaltered version of a previously unpublished lecture delivered by Randsborg to the University of Copenhagen in 1975, the one-hundredth anniversary of the admittance of women to the University. As such, it is clearly a groundbreaking work in the study of gender in prehistory; it is unfortunate that this paper was not published until more than a decade after it was written.

Randsborg studies the changing roles and statuses of women in Denmark from the Mesolithic through the Viking period. He first discusses broad theoretical issues involved in the study of women in the archaeological record, then focuses specifically on Danish prehistory. In the general theoretical section, Randsborg focuses on the importance of ethnographic analogy for understanding pre-industrial societies, and also briefly discusses the difficulties of inferring living statuses from mortuary data. Randsborg then considers the changing role of women in Danish prehistory. Most of his interpretations are based on skeletal data

and grave goods associated with sexed burials. He argues that prior to the development of social stratification, beginning with the Neolithic Single Grave period, women and men had equal social status, but with the development of stratified societies, women's work became restricted to household activities, and their status was no longer equal to that of men.

Some of Randsborg's conclusions may be questioned in light of the 17 years of research on gender in prehistory since he wrote this paper. In many cases, the data he used could also support alternative conclusions, but his work remains a pioneering example of a creative study of gendered archaeology using multiple lines of archaeological and anthropological evidence. As such, it should be of interest even to those not directly concerned with Danish prehistory. DLG

*mortuary analysis/ethnographic analogy/Denmark/Scadinavia/Neolithic/Mesolithic/Viking*

135. REED, LINDA J. 1991. Women in the Subarctic: Was gathering a viable economic activity? In *The Archaeology of Gender: Proceedings of the Twenty-Second Annual Conference of the Archaeological Association of the University of Calgary*, edited by Dale Walde and Noreen D. Willows, 292-296. Archaeological Association, The University of Calgary, Calgary.

This article considers the role of plant gathering in subarctic Athabascan economies from prehistory to modern times. Though not clearly stated, the focus is on ethnohistoric and historic documentation as well as the author's own ethnographic fieldwork. No archaeological information was included. According to Reed, too little consideration has been given to the role of plant resources in traditional subarctic hunter-

## Annotated References

gatherer societies. The focus on protein and fat requirements, she claims, obscures the important role of plant resources in balanced nutrition, and the role of plant products in technology has been underexamined. In archaeological contexts, this can be linked to the perishability of many of these products, but Reed is correct to point out this bias in subsequent reconstructions of traditional lifeways. Plant foods and plant products, in Reed's view, contributed fundamentally to traditional Athabascan life. Turning to the post-European contact period, Reed explains how Europeans came to depend on trade with Athabascans for gathered vegetable foods to balance a meat-rich diet. This relationship increased the significance of plant gathering and provided native groups access to valued European goods. It is unclear how significant the trade in plant goods was compared to that of furs themselves, or of meat products, and it would be useful to know more along these lines to better evaluate the trade economy. Finally, Reed provides information on modern subsistence plant use. She describes the collection of berries for consumption and their importance in inter-village social engagements such as potlatches, and she explains how various plant products are used as construction materials in summer fish camps, as medicine, and for the production of basketry for the tourist market.

There are several useful ideas and pieces of information in this article. Reed is correct to point to an overemphasis on meat and animals in descriptions of traditional subsistence practices. This is most likely due to a combination of factors including the near invisibility of plant remains archaeologically, androcentric assumptions on the part of investigators, and traditions of biased ethnohistoric reporting (by men) of men and their most visible roles as hunters and trappers. It would be interesting to know whether the fur trade actually increased the gender division of labor in Athabascan society by providing incentives for men to spend more time trapping and hunting or whether it led to a reduction in gender division of labor, as women could tend trap lines as well as men. The modern observations made by Reed provide information both on the traditional knowledge and uses of plant products and of possible material correlates to certain plant uses, such as the underground storage of berries in birch baskets and construction of drying racks and smoke houses at fish camps which could be identified archaeologically. The traditional knowledge and uses could be further explored to better understand the dynamic and complicated system of cultural adaptation, and although archaeology is never mentioned and can not be considered a significant motivation for this study, it nevertheless can benefit from some of the "ethnoarchaeological" information presented.

Despite these valuable points, the article has several distracting flaws. It is discouragingly short and poorly organized, and hasty preparation may be ultimately responsible for many of the more serious problems. The stated purpose of the article was to explore the "economic importance of wild plant products in the subarctic [by focusing] on the traditional roles of women as gatherers." I failed to gain an understanding either of the "importance" of wild plant resources or of the role of women in the changing economies. If "importance" is to be meaningful, either qualitatively or quantitatively, it must be measurable. Importance might be measured in relation to hunted and trapped resources, in relation to per capita time spent gathering relative to other activities, or in the relative value placed on gathering. In any case, the importance of gathering cannot be assessed without reference to the larger economic system. In addition, while Reed observed women engaged in the various activities described in the modern examples, the assumption of women = gatherers went unchallenged. If we are to re-assess traditional and false stereotypes of gender-specific realms of behavior, we must consider gender divisions of labor more critically. As Reed states in the beginning of her article, "the traditional survival strategy was to maintain both a flexible social organization and a cyclical pattern of resource usage." In the demanding subarctic environment, what could be less adaptive than a rigid gender division of labor? Finally, the modern study must be understood as a seasonal study, based on "two field seasons... encompassing eight months of research," presumably carried out during two summer seasons. This limits the overall significance of the study where much more could be said about the use of wild plants and about the dynamics of the cultural system itself with year-round observation. These limitations aside, this paper is a start to what will hopefully be an informative examination of wild plant resource use in the subarctic interior. JBF

*subsistence/division of labor/gatherer-hunters/ethnographic analogy/fur trade/subarctic/Athabascan*

136. RENFREW, COLIN 1986. The prehistoric Maltese achievement and its interpretation. In *Archaeology and Fertility Cult in the Ancient Mediterranean: Papers presented at the First International Conference on Archaeology of the Ancient Mediterranean,* edited by A. Bonanno, 118-130. B.R. Grüner Publishing Co, Amsterdam.

In this paper Renfrew addresses himself to the participants of an international conference on the archaeology of the ancient Mediterranean. He focused his discussion on what he referred to as a series of myths inherited by archaeologists working on Malta. These include the "myth of the Minoan connection," partly resulting from simultaneous archaeological discoveries on Malta and Crete, the simplistic notion of relatedness between "megalithic" monuments on Malta and those in north-western and western Europe, and the myth of a universal Great Earth Mother. Renfrew's very constructive treatment of these issues does not reject any of these notions out of hand, but points out that they have rarely, if ever, been presented and rigorously examined as hypotheses rather than accepted truths.

This paper is relevant to this list of references on gender in archaeology in that it presents a coherent critique of the controversial Great Earth Mother scenario for early Mediterranean religions. The most general point of the article is a discussion of the limitations of existing interpretive frameworks for understanding early religious systems. Renfrew begins with a reminder that symbols have meanings which are arbitrarily ascribed and therefore cannot be directly "read" by the archaeologist. Symbols must be analyzed within their own context. The relevant context for studies of early religion is divided in this paper into three levels or kinds. First, Renfrew suggests that analysis should begin at a very clearly-defined and fairly restricted *spatial* and *temporal* scale, moving to comparisons far removed in time or space only from the basis of a sound analysis of local phenomena. Second, since he is interested in the ways in which religious organization may reflect social organization, Renfrew places the analysis of early religions and iconography in a *social* context, or in the context of at least a general idea of the structure of society. On this basis, he questions the facile analogies frequently made between female figurines or sculptures in far-flung archaeological contexts, pointing out that similarities of form can arise for a number of reasons, not necessarily through any direct historical connection. Finally, he stresses the general importance of recognizing that internal dynamics may fundamentally transform religious systems and iconography without the necessity of resorting to explanations involving external influences. Renfrew concludes that the necessary information about the contextual background of early Maltese religion is not yet in place, and that progress in understanding the related iconography will only take place if archaeologists reject the old interpretations of a universal Great Mother and critically reexamine the concept of "fertility cult."

Renfrew's emphasis on addressing "fertility cult" and the Great Earth Mother as hypotheses, and his examination of some underlying theoretical issues, are extremely welcome in a field which has been dominated by discussion of specific interpretations rather than basic interpretive frameworks. Especially, his discussion of the importance of defining the context and scale relevant to a particular analysis seems a particularly apt criticism of existing literature on fertility cults in the ancient Mediterranean, which are characterized by broad comparisons between, for example, female figurines of the Paleolithic and Neolithic. LEF

*iconography/religion/fertility cults/Goddess/megaliths/Malta/Crete/Mediterranean*


137. REYNOLDS, NICHOLAS 1988. The rape of the Anglo-Saxon women. *Antiquity* 62:715-718.

HAWKES, SONIA CHADWICK AND CALVIN WELLS 1975. Crime and punishment in an Anglo-Saxon cemetery? *Antiquity* 49:118-122.

These articles represent on the one hand a bold interpretation of the significance of two burials at the Anglo-Saxon cemetery at Worthy Park, Kingsworthy, and on the other, a skeptical response pointing out problems with the original reconstruction. Hawkes and Wells note that Anglo-Saxon burials are commonly buried supine or slightly flexed, and usually include remains of clothing fasteners or jewelry. Two burials at Worthy Park differ markedly from this pattern, buried prone, and with no identifiable clothing, fasteners or jewelry. Analysis of one of the individuals from these graves, a woman aged about 16 years, revealed a cavity in the popliteal area of the left femur and a distinctive exostosis on the right femur projecting about 60 mm medially from the proximal end of the linea aspera. Both skeletal features are interpreted as representing mechanical trauma from rape. Using literary data as analogical evidence, they view this burial as that of a young woman impregnated during rape, who then concealed her shame and was later killed "for the tarnish she had brought upom her family's honor" when her pregnancy became apparent. She was buried naked and in a position that "in some way reflects her punishment" (1975:122).

Reynolds dismisses these interpretations as "phoney" (1988:716). He argues that post-mortem movement of burials is common, particularly when inhumations are placed in coffins rather than covered directly with soil. The position of the bodies may mark nothing more than postmortem formation processes, and the lesions observed on one of the skeletons are as likely to result from horseback riding as rape. He further rejects the documentary evidence presented by Hawkes and Wells as unsystematic and in many cases not directly relevant to the case at hand. And yet Reynolds' concern is less with the accuracy of the reconstruction than with the way it was reached, lest "archaeology can remain as the laughingstock of historians" (1988:718). He describes the interpretations of Hawkes and Wells as "pseudo-ethnography," and indeed some of the graves are described in ways that suggest the authors emphasized interpretation over description (one burial, for instance, is described as lying in a "quiescent, or at least acquiescent, posture" [Hawkes and Wells 1975:119]). The sketchiness of the available evidence makes it difficult to determine whose reconstruction is correct, but Reynolds' plea for adequately recording detailed information about burials is certainly appropriate, and his interpretation requires a less active imagination. This exchange highlights the difficulties of addressing questions of gender relations and fine-scale reconstruction of behavior without detailed and explicit methodological frameworks guiding interpretation, and without fine-scale excavation methods and records as well. AWB

*mortuary analysis/ethnographic analogy/rape/paleopathology/osteology/Anglo-Saxons/Great Britain*


138. RICE, PATRICIA C. 1981. Prehistoric Venuses: Symbols of motherhood or womanhood? *Journal of Anthropological Research* 37(4): 402-414.

Rice examines the widespread belief that Upper Paleolithic "Venus figurines," dating from 27,000 to 20,000 BP represent fertility, and presents an alternative suggestion: these figures represent womanhood in general. She looks at 188 figurines, and has four observers record five body attributes on the figurines which correspond to age and reproductive status. She concludes that the majority of the figurines do not depict pregnant women, but portray a range of ages: pre-reproductive (23%), pregnant (17%), reproductive age but not pregnant (38%), and post-reproductive (22%). Rice compares these categories to age categories known from Paleolithic skeletal evidence and contemporary hunter-gatherers, then uses age pyramids to assign ages to the figurine groupings and to estimate the proportion of women in a population pregnant at any given time. For hunter-gatherers in general, 23% are pre-reproductive (ages 10-14), 17% are pregnant (ages 15-35), 41% are not pregnant (ages 15-35) and 19% are post-reproductive (over 35). Rice concludes that the similarity between these two age profiles indicates that the "Venuses" represent the full life span of women. Since such a small proportion of the figurines portray pregnant women, it is unlikely that they represent fertility. They may represent women's roles as providers of food, caretakers of children, as the core of the social group, or as sacred and mystical beings.

Rice shows clearly that the Upper Paleolithic Venus figurines are not all the same, and provides some of the reasons why people have been predisposed to assume that they represent fertility. Unfortunately, her alternative explanation for the figurines also suffers from many weaknesses. She has a fairly large sample, but they come from all over Europe, cover a time span of 7000 years, and are often from poor archaeological contexts. Although Rice treats this as a single sample, it should be clear that there is no reason to believe that these figurines signify the same thing in different places at different times. The method used to categorize the figurines does not assign them to unequivocal age categories. From the table illustrating the rating method, it appears that the four people rating the figurines often disagreed. Percentages of figurines in each reproductive category may have been quite different with different observers. Studies of modern hunter-gatherers since 1977 have not only produced more detailed demographic data, but have cast doubt on the utility of using modern populations as analogues for past ones. Rice's assumption that age at menarche was between 10 and 12 is surprisingly early, as is her estimate of 15 as the average age at first birth. If these ages or the age at the end of childbearing change, the proportions of women in each reproductive category change, and might not match the figurine proportions. Finally, in the last section, the discussion of the figurines' possible meanings is poorly supported. However, this article does open up avenues for research, not only into the meaning of the Upper Paleolithic figurines, but into the meanings and functions of figurines in general. TVZ

*figurines/Venus figurines/mothering/ethnographic analogy/gatherer-hunters/paleodemography/Paleolithic/ Europe*

139. RICE, PATRICIA C. AND ANN L. PATERSON 1988. Anthropomorphs in cave art: An empirical assessment. *American Anthropologist* 90:664-674.

This article presents a statistical study of anthropomorphic Upper Paleolithic cave art from southern France and Northern Spain. Patricia Rice and Ann Paterson examine how human representations are spatially related to one another, to the animal representations, and to the human and faunal remains in the caves, and examine the activities represented by the sex-marked figures. Of 116 figures thought to be anthropomorphic, 67 could be attributed sex ("gender"). Of these, Rice and Paterson find the males (78% of the "gendered" representations) to be more likely to be engaged in some active behavior and portrayed alone or near representations of animal prey. Females (only 22% of the sexable figures) appear most often in groups and as inactive. Additionally, they find that male and female figures are always kept apart from one another, a discovery which might indicate differential use of caves and cave areas by men and women. "Females are...never painted or rendered as stick figures, are always engraved, are never masked or hybrids, are always inactive, and are never near rare animal species.... Males... can be painted or engraved, and may be rendered as stick figures. Males are often portrayed as masked or hybrids, are either active or passive, and are unexpectedly found near rare species."

This is an interesting data set and the patterns reported are intriguing. Yet there is potential for misinterpretation given that the sample is drawn from 32 caves distributed over hundreds of square kilometers and presumably spanning tens of thousands of years. The fact that most of the caves yielded only one or two anthropomorphic figures each adds to this concern. An additional bias might lie in those "anthropomorphs" for which no sex/gender was given. The drastic underrepresentation of females reported would be rectified if all or some of these "ungendered" figures were in fact intended to represent females. This is an intriguing notion because it would suggest a category of representations (and perhaps a social category of persons or status of activities) for which sexual characterization was unimportant. It might be the case that women were only sexually marked in those representations where their status as sexual females was important. In other activities, they may have been characterized as androgynous. It may also be the case that females are just more difficult to identify in these figures. Males on the other hand might have more often been "sex-marked" both in symbolically sexual and non-sexual contexts because of the ease of sexual attribution (attached genitalia). Again it may simply be easier to recognize male genitalia in this art, leading to higher recognition of "male" figures. It is not clear if the activities and postures identified for the "gendered" anthropomorphs fit those of the "ungendered" ones. Such a comparison might provide a means of attributing sex/gender to these unmarked figures or might lead to the identification of a third social category of activities or social identity.

One confusion in this analysis lies in the use of the term "gender." Gender, as a culturally constructed system of sexual identity, is not the same as biological/reproductive sex. Sex attribution of these figures is presumably made on the basis of depicted reproductive organs. The goal of a sex/gender analysis is to determine how the cultural gender categories are built up from and draped over biological sex. Assuming they are isomorphic from the start prevents the identification of different cultural patterns which could critically change our understandings of gender dynamics. Illustrations of the figures being discussed would be valuable as well.

Although there are several problems in the nature of this data base, and biases in the analysis, this study is valuable for its systematic approach to Upper Paleolithic art, for its explicit attempt to identify gender so far back into the past where little data exist to address the topic, and for its controversial findings. There are bound to be challenges to the conclusions of an active/passive gender dichotomy in the Upper Paleolithic, and it can only be hoped that such challenges promote additional research.  JBF

*representation, theory of/cave art/rock art/France/Spain/Europe/Paleolithic*


140. RICE, PRUDENCE M. 1991. Women and prehistoric pottery production. In *The Archaeology of Gender: Proceedings of the Twenty-Second Annual Conference of the Archaeological Association of the University of Calgary*, edited by Dale Walde and Noreen D. Willows, 436-443. Archaeological Association, The University of Calgary, Calgary.

This paper reviews a selection of the ethnographic and archaeological literature on women in pottery production. Rice focuses on several topics which include: (1) The sexual division of pottery production in which she discusses findings from Murdock and Provost's (1973) cross-cultural analysis. (2) Hypotheses on the origins of pottery, and its association with either males or females. In neither the case of the first production of clay objects nor of the first pottery does she find any reason for these or any activities from which they may have developed to be the exclusive practice of or use by males or females. (3) The invention of the potter's wheel—by males or females, and whether its use involved a transition from females to males as potters, or from males without to males with the wheel; its diffusion; and the time-depth for areas where men are the exclusive users of the potters wheel. Rice rejects Foster's (1959) explanation that the correlation between males and the potter's wheel is due to greater physical strength in men, and explores several alternative explanations including compatibility of motor patterns, the tendency for males to have more external contacts and innovations introduced to them, and traditional avoidance of certain tools or activities. (4) Prehistoric pottery production—identifying its location and understanding its organization. Using ethnographic examples she critiques the craft production organization models used by archaeologists, which associate women with domestic production and men with workshops, as overly simplified and biased because they are based upon western capitalist notions of production. Also in relation to gender in production, she raises the question as to the possibility that the concept of specialization is biased and rooted in western capitalist ideas of economic efficiency. (5) The relationship between ceramic and cultural changes (including modern developments), and the implications for women's roles. For example, she cites the case where in areas of the Philippines an emphasis on a cash economy involving men resulted in women as the primary pottery producers.
This paper provides a useful overview of many questions and assumptions made regarding women and pottery production. Rice is unable to present more fully developed critiques in this brief format, but does point out important areas of research and model-building warranting an explicit consideration of gender. EAB

*References cited*
Foster, G. 1959. The potter's wheel: An analysis of idea and artifact in invention. *Southwestern Journal of Anthropology* 15:99-119.

Murdock, G. and C. Provost 1973. Factors in the division of labor by sex: A cross-cultural analysis. *Ethnology* 12:203-225.

*ceramic analysis/ceramic production/division of labor/ethnographic analogy*


141. RIDGWAY, BRUNILDE SISMONDO 1987. Ancient Greek women and art: The material evidence. *American Journal of Archaeology* 91:399-409.

Ridgway uses a "a sample group of extant monuments that can be demonstrably connected with women in various ways" (p. 399) from Greece from the ninth century BC through the Hellenistic period (ending at 31 BC) to examine women's roles as patrons of art and architecture. She notes that classical literature is filled with sources describing women in antiquity, but adds that these sources suffer biases not inherent in material culture—thus her focus on "women as sponsors of architectural projects...and dedicators of statues and other offerings" (p. 399). Ridgway's description of dedicatory inscriptions, such as the one done by Nikandre of Naxos around 650 BC, in which Nikandre describes herself as "excellent among others," following with the names of her father, brother, and husband (in that order) are interesting examples of this kind of evidence from the early period following the Greek Dark Ages (p. 400).

Ridgway concludes that although it is clear that women, especially queens, played an important role in the public sphere during the Hellenistic period (which she notes is well supported by the literary evidence), she was surprised at "the relative importance of women--as sponsors and as 'users' of *objets d'art*--in the early phases," (p. 409) from the eighth to fifth centuries BC, which suggests "a greater role of women in public life than hitherto acknowledged." She closes with some suggestions for future work that would flesh out an understanding of the temporal and geographical differences of ancient Greek women's roles and status and how common women could be approached through the archaeological record.

Ridgway's study of Greek monuments is based upon inscriptions and items selected from a nine-century span, and her caution in making inferences about women's changing roles in this period is laudable. Her descriptions of art and architecture and a tantalizing bit of their social context are authoritative and thorough without being overly pedantic. It is interesting that this article was written before the recent burst of interest in gender in archaeology. It seems to have been inspired by a different strain of feminist scholarship. Some anthropologically oriented readers may feel the work suffers from the absence of an explicit theoretical framework or goal (other than a compensatory discovery of women in the archaeological record), but this article is certainly not alone in its goal of putting women into history. SLD

*architecture/sculpture/classical archaeology/Hellenistic period/Greece/Mediterranean*

142. ROBB, JOHN 1992. Gender, ideology and social inequality in prehistoric Italy. Paper presented at the symposium "Social Dynamics of the Prehistoric Central Mediterranean," Annual Meeting of the Society for American Archaeology, Pittsburgh.

Unlike numerous other articles that have dealt with gender inequality, Robb's paper attempts to delimit a very clear theoretical framework from which to interpret gender, ideological systems, and structures of inequality. Although one may argue with the premises of some of his initial propositions, such as his notion of ideology as "a specific group of foregrounded symbols, usually established through ritual and concerned with defining value" (p 2), Robb nonetheless develops a specific orientation for interpreting gender relations in the archaeological record with a special emphasis on identifying how gender inequality may be manifested. The question of how gender ideology originates and permeates most cultures, and the means whereby symbolic manipulation occurs, is analyzed and defined through a structural analysis. He then attempts to apply his analysis to a data set from Italy.

It is Robb's premise that a series of iconographic representations present in the Italian archaeological record from the Late Neolithic period through the Bronze Age can be made understandable if interpreted as manifestations of gender ideology. He suggests images associated with daggers, oxen, plows, stags, hunting and weapons, which have a long and varied history in the region (p. 4), can be rendered intelligible through employing a structural analysis, while assuming a dominant male ideology. The symbols taken from different contexts over a long period of time may be seen as contributing toward a unified whole whose central organizing principle revolves around the legitimation and institutionalization of male dominance. Robb suggests that from the Late Neolithic into the Bronze Age, unequal distributions of prestige characterized gender relations. This contributed to what he calls "an internal conflict model" (p. 8). The iconography of this model is used to demonstrate the inegalitarian character of gender ideologies. Males are opposed structurally to subservient females, or others, who would not have access to structures of power. These symbols are means for defining male and females statuses and identities.

The author recognizes that several problems exist in trying to operationalize these ideas archaeologically. Associating symbolic materials with individuals entails inferring statuses (or lack thereof). Detailing the specific how and why gender inequalities came into being, and were perpetuated through time and space, are also difficult to address. Nonetheless, Robb presents a number of insightful propositions with which to begin grappling with the notions of ideology, gender and power relations in the archaeological record. MRF

*structuralism/iconography/rock art/Neolithic/Copper Age/Bronze Age/Italy/Mediterranean*


143. ROHRLICH, RUBY 1980. State formation in Sumer and the subjugation of women. *Feminist Studies* (6)1:76-102.

Essentially a reinterpretation of Morgan and Engel's theories of the rise of private property and social complexity, Rohrlich's essay argues that previous explanations for the origins of the state are inadequate because they fail to give primacy to the rise of patriarchy as a crucial factor in early state formation. Drawing on Mellaart's work at Çatal Hüyük and its interpretation by Ann Barstow (#9), she argues that pre-Ubaid social forms were characterized by "egalitarian relations between women and men, which were central to the democratic process" (pp. 83-84). Increasing militarism and economic stratification forced women into secondary roles, and Rohrlich traces what she sees as changes in the place of women as rulers, goddesses, priestesses, scribes, warriors, entrepeneurs, prostitutes and slaves over the course of Sumerian civilization. For each, she argues, women had high status in early periods, declining over time as patriarchal forces tightened their grip on society. Rohrlich suggests that resistance to accepting the notion of an earlier, matriarchal period (what she calls "the omission or distortion of data dissonant with the ideology of universal female subordination") reflects a rejection by "traditional scholars" of any past social arrangements where women had higher—or even equal—status.

Rohrlich's argument is an intriguing one, but is largely based upon a series of social changes suggested less by the data than by grand social theories of the nineteenth century. Some arguments seem rather forced. She argues that pursuits such as writing, farming, medicine, etc. (all highly valued and with generally positive associations) were probably dominated by women since the patron deities are female, yet the aspect of Inanna as war goddess (an apparently negative association) is an example of "making the victim the criminal, attributing to women the causes of intercity discord." Rohrlich's main thesis, that the changing role of women in Sumerian society may be crucial to understanding the social transformations leading to the emergence of state-level polities, is valuable. The specifics of her argument, however, are subject to challenge on both empirical and logical grounds. AWB

*state formation/matriarchy/slavery/religion/class/Marxism/Sumer/Turkey/Near East*


144. ROHRLICH-LEAVITT, RUBY 1978. Women in transition: Crete and Sumer. In *Becoming Visible: Women in European History,* edited by R. Bridenthal and C. Koonz, 36-59. Houghton Mifflin, Boston.

In this article, Rohrlich-Leavitt attempts to prove that "Minoan Crete, the first European civilization, was a matriarchy" (p. 38). She uses archaeological evidence to illustrate women's status and roles and many other aspects of social and political organization through several periods, beginning with Crete's "Anatolian Antecedents" at Çatal Hüyük, then moving on to Neolithic and Minoan Crete. Next Rohrlich-Leavitt contrasts Crete with contemporary Sumer, focusing on women as seen through religious art and artifacts. She concludes that "a comparison of the archaeological data shows that Minoan arts and crafts reached heights not attained by any other Bronze Age civilization, in a society that left the artists, and the people as a whole, relatively free to be creative and innovative" (p. 58). In Sumer, on the other hand, "male domination was more and more reflected in religion" (p. 55), "women were pushed out of political decision making...deprived of education and ousted from lucrative and prestigious professions...segregated from the kinship group...[and] made totally dependent on the male heads of the patrilineal family" (p. 57). This difference is reflected in Sumerian art, which "became more and more stereotyped and static as private property, political centralization, and militarism became increasingly dominant" (p. 57).

Although Rohrlich-Leavitt never explicitly states it in this article, it is clear that she is working from an early Marxist theoretical framework in which the origins of private property and state-level organization emerge hand in hand with the subjugation of women. Unfortunately, for this is a widely published and well-read book, Rohrlich-Leavitt makes several objectionable leaps of logic from the archaeological record to her reconstruction of prehistoric life. For instance, she states that "Women's social preeminence at Çatal Hüyük is clear...the clan was unmistakably matrilineal and matrilocal" (pp. 39-40). This is based entirely upon the premise that small platforms belonging to men were "often moved about [in the house], but the much larger main platform, which belonged to the woman, never changed its place" (p. 40). Furthermore, children were buried with women or under the platforms, never with men, and females were more common than males in representational art. Is this proof of matrilineality, let alone social preeminence? At Minoan Crete, Rohrlich-Leavitt states unequivocally "the artifacts provide clear evidence that the status of women in this relatively rich and free society was very high" (p. 46). The only evidence she offers to indicate that Crete fulfills her model of this prehistoric egalitarian society is that women were "the most frequently portrayed in the arts and crafts" (p. 46), particularly in religious contexts.

It is undeniable that androcentric biases have caused many archaeologists working in this area to overlook or de-emphasize women's roles and status in both public and private spheres (for a recent revision see Pollock, #131), but it also seems clear that Rohrlich-Leavitt's reconstructions are unconstrained by the archaeological data or any linking arguments. This work may have been a valiant and well-meaning (but dangerously naive) attempt for the time it was published (1978), but it has little to recommend it today. A Marxist model may be appropriate for examining state origins and female oppression, but inspiration for building these models and testing them must be sought elsewhere. SLD

*architecture/iconography/religion/class/Neolithic/Bronze Age/Sumer/Crete/Turkey/Near East/Mediterranean*


145. ROOSEVELT, ANNA C. 1988. Interpreting certain female images in prehistoric art. In *The Role of Gender in Precolumbian Art and Architecture,* edited by Virginia E. Miller, 1-29. University Press of America, Lanham, MD.

Roosevelt uses collections of figurines in the Museum of the American Indian from many areas and time periods (including Formative period central Mexico, Formative Maya sites on the Gulf Coast, the central Andes, and late prehistoric Amazonia) in this general overview of the prehistoric occurrence of female figurines expressing sexual themes traditionally related to fertility. Following a general introduction to studies of prehistoric art and iconography and a description of the figurines from the various areas (accompanied by photographs), Roosevelt argues that the "context, style, and iconography of the figurines suggest that they belonged to a woman's domestic cult of female sexuality and fertility" (p. 13). Since the figurines "are most common in household refuse in domestic activity areas associated with female activities...(and) very rare in the contexts associated with high ritual and men's activities of the type from which women are traditionally excluded," Roosevelt suggests that "the figurines were more likely related more narrowly to concerns over female fertility, rather than to crop fertility...it seems plausible that women made and used them to enhance their reproductive success through a kind of sympathetic magic" (p. 15).

Although Roosevelt does acknowledge that it is unlikely that there is a single functional explanation behind all of these figurines, she argues that the prehistoric cultures that produced them have "striking sociopolitical, economic, and demographic commonalities that may help to explain the occurrence of this type of female iconography" (p. 1). All of the societies with the figurines she describes were emerging chiefdoms or early states, and Roosevelt suggests that the figurines reflect the "populationist" ideology of a period of economic and demographic growth. She goes on to predict that women in these societies should have a higher birth rate, which is archaeologically visible (thus a possible test of her hypothesis), as opposed to women in earlier horticultural or hunting and gathering societies or later complex state societies. In these more or less politically complex contexts, she points out, this type of figurine is not so prevalent.

Roosevelt tackles several big issues concerning prehistoric gender, iconography, and figurine function in this paper, and unfortunately does not have the room to do them all justice. The idea that certain figurine iconography is correlated with emergent chiefdoms and states is interesting, but it is argued on such a broad scale that it would be difficult to test. Furthermore, the fact that people and labor are in demand in these societies, and that there was a high birth rate, does not prove that the figurines played a role in female reproductive ritual. Roosevelt's hypothesis also presumes an iconographic and functional unity among the figurines described. Although these figures undeniably share certain sexual characteristics, their placement in a single analytic group is unconvincing. Roosevelt's explanation of the intriguing exceptions, including the Paleolithic "Venus figurines," is not compelling enough to make the pattern hold.

On the other hand, Roosevelt does look at these old data in an innovative manner, linking iconography and sex and gender with archaeology's traditional processual concerns, such as population growth, political evolution, and agricultural intensification. Some of the figurines she describes may very well have been used in the manner she suggests. A more detailed or contextual examination of the female figurine iconography and sociopolitics of one of the areas she describes may prove more enlightening. SLD

*chiefdom formation/state formation/figurines/paleodemography/fertility cults/Formative period/Mexico/Peru/ Brazil/Amazonia*


146. RUSSELL, PAMELA 1991. Men only? The myths about European Palaeolithic artists. In *The Archaeology of Gender: Proceedings of the Twenty-Second Annual Conference of the Archaeological Association of the University of Calgary*, edited by Dale Walde and Noreen D. Willows, 346-351. Archaeological Association, The University of Calgary, Calgary.

This short contribution examines the question of who were Paleolithic artists. Russell argues that interpretations of Paleolithic art to date focus primarily on hunting, mysticism, and belief systems that have traditionally been seen by prehistorians as the domain of men. Women, by implication, are excluded from an important area of Paleolithic culture. She then presents a scattering of ethnographic and archaeological evidence aimed at discrediting what she sees as a series of myths about Paleolithic art that appear to confirm these traditional interpretations. The myths that she tries to counter include: art is a male pursuit in ethnographically known hunter-gatherer groups such as the Australian Aborigines, cave art in the Upper Paleolithic is likely to have had ritual significance because they occur in locations difficult of access, and cave art deals directly with hunting because animals are commonly depicted. Russell tries to argue that the common interpretation that the cave art had a religious or mystical function is an unwarranted assumption, and that art in the Paleolithic could have played many roles, including practical, non-magical ones such as teaching and various kinds of notation. Engraved objects are often found in near-hearth contexts in open-air sites; Russell concludes from this that art may have been produced in distinctly non-magical social contexts, and was in some cases not "hidden" in deep caves but was visible and available to all members of social groups.

While Russell's emphasis on the multiple functions that depictions and signs may have had in Paleolithic cultures is certainly welcome, it is not clear that removing the assumption of magical context from interpretations of Paleolithic art necessarily makes it either more or less likely that women would have played a part in producing the images. Russell suggests that women may, for example, have played a role in using mobile art (or "early writing surfaces") to teach children, keep accounts, and record time, among other purposes. These suggestions about women's roles in Paleolithic social groups are lightly made and may be perfectly plausible, but they underscore a problem with the approach taken here: a traditional absence of consideration of the roles women may have played in producing Paleolithic art should not be replaced by equally traditional, unexamined notions about women's roles in hunter-gatherer societies. LEF

*cave art/rock art/iconography/gatherer-hunters/ethnographic analogy/Paleolithic/Europe*


147. SAMSON, ROSS 1988. Superwomen, wonderwomen, great women, and real women. *Archaeological Review from Cambridge* 7(1):60-66.

This article explores the possibility that due to the tension between active politics and social analysis in feminism (a characteristic also found in Marxism), "a rhetorical use of past conditions will develop which is not necessarily commensurate with the analytical development of a theory of gender relations" (p. 60). Samson does not condemn the rhetorical use of the past in present political struggles, but does warn that it might lead to the production of "a very uncritical history," such as some attempts to write the history of great women, as alluded to in his title.

Samson identifies three rhetorical uses of the past that could be used in arguments supporting women's rights: that women have always suffered, that women have always struggled, and that "women were once, in a golden past, the complete equals of men." His paper focuses on the attempt to create this golden past through the writing of great women histories. The search for women's original dominance is claimed to be flawed from the very beginning, because of humans' evolutionary trajectory: "In view of the ubiquitous dominance of males among primates, such a thesis concerned with 'Woman's Historic Defeat' must also take into consideration how the development of 'humanity' reversed women's role, before male dominance was reasserted"(p. 61). Creating and focusing on great women in the past can lead to an apologetic approach which "may be even more harmful to present political aspirations" given its underlying assumptions (p. 62). Samson then attempts to illustrate this by examining two 'great women' of the early medieval period.

Samson's two examples are Queen Brunhilde and "Aud the Deep-Minded." Both of these women (the latter is actually a goddess) are claimed to have achieved power only in the context of being widows, thus achieving legal independence, i.e., they became men. Samson anticipates criticism of this position and states: "one might jump at such a claim [that Brunhilde wielded power as an honorary male] and say that I have naturalised male political dominance by marginalising the atypical situations of powerful women. This is quite untrue and if argued would reveal how much more work on gender relations is needed, and how uncritical the great women syndrome can be. Early medieval women, whether slaves or queens, had no legal existence"(p. 64). Samson argues that critical historical analyses of the exploitation of women leads to better rhetorical arguments than an over-reliance on superwomen.

There is much in this article with which I disagreed. Many of the statements come across as controversial, and are rarely supported. As quoted above, Samson comes close to a biological determinism for male dominance in humans. He also makes a number of sweeping generalizations such as "The history of great women...reveals how other structures of power, under circumstances beyond the control of the female historical actress, give her temporary authority not generally accorded her sex." (p. 65). In describing what he sees as an analogous situation to "great women history," Samson states that "Among American historians, apologists are embarrassingly active in the study of slavery," although the citation accompanying this assertion is a "personal communication," i.e., the sweeping characterization of American historians is only second-hand. In the same paragraph, Samson goes on to proclaim that "the history of slavery has few political overtones in European circles for there is little self-recognition among any classes or social groups in the slaves of the past" (p. 63). This statement denies the status "European" to the many long-time citizens of African or Afro-Caribbean descent of Britain and other countries. These loose statements are perhaps indicative of the fact that although the *Archaeological Review from Cambridge* often includes cutting edge articles and notable authors, it is still a student-run journal. This might explain why one of this article's primary sources, a book by Barbara Crawford, is cited, discussed, and quoted (pp. 62-63), but is missing from the bibliography.

Among the positive aspects of Samson's article, the tension between political action and social analysis is an important topic and deserves more attention than it has so far received in our discipline. Also, the point is well made that if we do find exploitation in the past, it should be faced with open eyes, and not rationalized or explained away (although a greater attempt could have been made to find resisting and unconsenting voices). In any case, while Samson's conclusions are perhaps too focused on and constrained by medieval history, the issues raised by him are serious and deserve attention. WDG

*political uses of the past/feminist critique/medieval archaeology/individual in prehistory/revisionist theory/ Europe*

148. SASSAMAN, KENNETH E. 1992. Gender and technology at the Archaic-Woodland "transition." In *Exploring Gender through Archaeology: Selected Papers from the 1991 Boone Conference*, edited by Cheryl Claasen, 71-79. Prehistory Press, Madison.

This article deals with gender in relation to ceramic and lithic technologies across the Archaic-Woodland transition in the southeastern United States. In the first, more elaborate, section of the paper,

## Annotated References

Sassaman explores the role of gender as a central variable influencing the introduction and spread of early ceramics in the Southeast. In the second section of the paper, the author considers how notions of lithic technologies for the Archaic versus Woodland are influenced by how archaeologists identify sites and assemblages for these periods.

Sassaman begins with the idea that "gender is the primary social variable in the labor process in forager or hunter-gatherer societies" (p. 71). He then builds an argument linking the development and spread of pottery production by women to a gain in status as shellfishing became more prominent in some areas during Archaic times. Sassaman believes that pottery and "direct-heat cooking," which would have been a technological advantage for women, spread when "women...were able to assert authority over the production, distribution, and consumption of a key food resource, in this case shellfish" (p. 73). He also introduces men's involvement in long-distance exchange of steatite vessels as a second variable influencing the cultural acceptance of ceramic technologies. He argues that in those areas where such networks were most active, resistance to the introduction of ceramics was greatest, due to men's control and profit from the flow of steatite bowls. This scenario for the adoption of ceramic technologies in the Southeast centers on the pattern of a coastal distribution of early ceramics and its staggered development across the Eastern Woodlands.

Sassaman then shifts gears and addresses lithic technologies across the Archaic-Woodland interface. He points out that while Archaic sites are generally identified on the basis of diagnostic stone tools (namely hafted bifaces), Woodland sites are identified through diagnostic ceramic assemblages. Changes in lithic technologies often believed to be associated with these periods may thus be "partly shaped by a shift in focus from men's roles to women's roles in stone tool production and use" (p. 75). Sassaman's general conclusion is that archaeologists need to bring gender and the sexual division of labor into the analysis of lithic technology, especially for understanding tool use and design, and for elucidating how formal and expedient tool assemblages may be complementary.

Sassaman presents an intriguing perspective on technology across the Archaic-Woodland transition. In order to develop his argument, a number of key assumptions are made. First, he assumes a static division of labor where women were responsible for shellfishing and ceramic production, while men participated in long distance trade. He also assumes that women's status was directly related to their autonomy over the labor process and contributions to subsistence. These fundamental assumptions are not without problems. Although much of the ethnohistoric literature for the area suggests a division of labor along these lines, Sassaman excludes possibilities for differences in the past, for varying contexts, or for the evolution of gender relations into the form we believe they took in later prehistoric and protohistoric times. Such an approach assumes a division of labor, rather than targeting it as a research question. Only recently have researchers questioned an exclusively male role in lithic production; a similar critical examination of gender in relation to North American ceramic production, shellfishing, exchange networks, gathering, hunting, and a variety of other topics would also prove invaluable. In addition, Sassaman's theoretical link that women's status is tied to their degree of economic autonomy (oriented around shellfishing) is, in fact, a wide-open question. Feminist anthropologists have questioned why and how gender inequalities vary cross-culturally, and the economic foundations of women's status are not yet adequately demonstrated. Sassaman does not do justice to this debated topic. In all fairness, his analysis is groundbreaking and hence preliminary. In attempting to examine questions of culture change, however, he essentially puts the cart in front of the horse by not addressing these fundamental premises.

Despite these problems, Sassaman can be credited with presenting a refreshingly original perspective on prehistoric technologies from a social slant, while also recognizing biases inherent in archaeological approaches to technology. This approach, which consciously uses gender as a starting point for addressing questions of technological change, provides much food for thought for research. Sassaman's work sheds new light on technological studies . NSG-F

*ceramic production/lithic technology/shellfishing/division of labor/Archaic period/Early Woodland period/ United States, Southeast*

149. SCOTT, ELIZABETH M. 1991. A feminist approach to historical archaeology: eighteenth century fur trade society at Michilimackinac. *Historical Archaeology* 25(4):42-53.

Placing herself within a framework of feminist and historical materialist theory, Scott attempts to look at gender roles through archaeological evidence of subsistence activities, but concludes that the interpretation of women's activities from these remains is problematic.

Scott focuses on subsistence, stating that social, economic, and symbolic information can be gleaned from the archaeological remains of both foodstuffs and food-related activities. She points out that gender, race, ethnicity, and socioeconomic position are connected and must be considered together. She then outlines the history of the fur-trading community of Michilimackinac in northern Michigan, a diverse collection of British, French Canadian, métis, African-American and Native American people. Noting the potential biases of documents written primarily by upper class British men, Scott suggests that the affect of these biases on interpretation may be reduced by using them as sources for making an activity-differentiation framework (citing Spector 1983). She first reads the documents for information on the division of subsistence labor by gender, ethnicity, and other categories. Then she reads them for associations of specific foods and artifacts with particular genders within each social group.

The documents indicate several differences in the subsistence activities of socioeconomic classes. Fewer ethnic differences are reported, since Europeans learned Native American ways of procuring and preparing local resources, and the fact that most imported goods came from Britain tends to mask other ethnic differences. The Native American division of gender tasks is described in some detail, but since they did not live inside the fort where all excavation has so far been done, this information is not of much archaeological benefit. The few references to gendered European tasks have men hunting, fishing, and farming, and women (but also soldiers) cooking. French Canadian women are also said to direct maple sugaring operations.

Scott looks at archaeological evidence from three households, none of which are recorded as housing women and one of which is recorded as a bachelor home. Hunting and fishing equipment in these houses she attributes to male activities, and basket remains to either male or female activities. Evidence for food preparation presents a problem, however. If women are usually the cooks but there are no women recorded as living in a house, how can you know whether the men cooked for themselves or had female servants or mistresses?

Scott concludes that with current information it is impossible to identify women's activities from subsistence remains; extending this further, she asserts that you cannot discuss gender using evidence of activities. She suggests that clothing and ornaments are probably a more fruitful route toward the study of gender in historical archaeology.

This is primarily a methodological paper with a useful compilation of documentary information and some good suggestions for how ethnic, socioeconomic, and gender differences may be masked or revealed by historical and archaeological evidence. Scott is probably correct in deciding that focusing solely on subsistence activities is not the best way to get at gender relationships, particularly in a frontier situation where many households are likely to be womanless. She would benefit from broadening her scope to include other types of evidence, which might allow her to broaden her archaeological research questions to encompass more than the presence or absence of women. SF

*historical archaeology/subsistence/ethnicity/class/division of labor/fur trade/Michigan/United States, Midwest*


150. SCOTT, ELIZABETH M. 1991. Gender in complex colonial societies: The material goods of everyday life in a late eighteenth century fur trading community. In *The Archaeology of Gender: Proceedings of the Twenty-Second Annual Conference of the Archaeological Association of the University of Calgary*, edited by Dale Walde and Noreen D. Willows, 490-495. Archaeological Association, The University of Calgary, Calgary.

This article attempts to approach gender through evidence of clothing and ornamentation, as the author suggests at the end of her article "A Feminist Approach to Historical Archaeology." The author stresses the interconnectedness of gender, ethnicity, and socioeconomics, and the usefulness of combining feminist and historical materialist approaches. Referring to her earlier work, she states that evidence from

activities can indicate whether men lived in a house, but not whether women lived there. Evidence from clothing and ornaments, however, may make women visible.

Scott uses merchandise account ledgers and estate inventories to show how many clothing items are specified by gender, economic status ("common" and "fine" items), and ethnicity ("Indian shoes"). Accessories such as ribbons, buckles, and belts are listed as well as sewing notions such as thimbles, needles, and scissors. Many of these items are common on archaeological sites, and Scott suggests that they may be used to identify genders or ethnic groups in much the same way that pottery types have been used to identify wealth distinctions.

Scott concludes that until historical archaeologists use such evidence to identify the presence of women and men in archaeological sites, they will be unable to assign genders to activities. The call to engender the archaeological remains of clothing points out a potentially useful and currently underused body of data. However, one might also wish to see in this article some formulation of questions beyond the assignment of tasks to genders, questions which deal with social relationships and are informed by the bodies of theory that Scott espouses. SF

*historical archaeology/ethnicity/fur trade/Michigan/United States, Midwest*

151. SEIFERT, DONNA J. 1991. Introduction: Gender in Historical Archaeology. *Historical Archaeology* 25(4):1-4.

This is the introduction to an issue of *Historical Archaeology* devoted entirely to gender. Seifert, the volume editor, emphasizes the need for archaeological studies of gender to go beyond adding women to the historical record to understanding gender as a central structuring principle in past and present social relations.

This volume complements recent collections of studies of gender in prehistory such as Gero and Conkey's *Engendering Archaeology*. Seifert briefly discusses each of the nine articles in the volume, which are reviewed separately in this bibliography. DLG

*historical archaeology/United States*


152. SEIFERT, DONNA J. 1991. Within site of the White House: The archaeology of working women. *Historical Archaeology* 25(4):82-108.

According to the abstract, "The relationship between consumer behavior, household composition, and household function in turn-of-the-century Washington, D.C., is elucidated by understanding women's work" (p. 82). To prove this point, Seifert focuses on archaeological and historical records for three households (two working class families and a brothel) in an area known as Hooker's Division just east of the White House. After describing the history of this neighborhood, especially in relation to women's roles and economic opportunities in the late nineteenth and early twentieth centuries, Seifert compares these artifact assemblages, adding comparable data from two other working class households elsewhere in Washington to enlarge her sample. First, artifacts are grouped into categories such as architecture, kitchen, furniture, clothing, personal (including pencils, keys, coins, jewelry, eyeglass parts), tobacco, and activities (tools, toys, lighting glass) as outlined by South (1977). Bar charts comparing category percentages for the four families and the brothel show some interesting differences as well as similarities. For instance, the brothel had a much higher percentage of clothing items (largely buttons, from both male and female clothing), personal items, tobacco pipes, and lighting glass. Furthermore, large amounts of beef bones were found in the brothel, but not in the working class houses.

Some of the reasons behind the different artifacts patterns are fairly obvious. The higher levels of lighting glass (from lamps, fixtures, and outside lights) found in the brothel, for instance, relate to its late-night business hours. The relatively high quantities of buttons, personal items, pipes, and beef bone is attributed to both the commercial function of the brothel and the economic position of the women who lived there. As Seifert points out, the inhabitants of these "female boarding houses" were able to afford (and may indeed needed to have) more elaborate dress than other "working women." Although beefsteaks may have been served to customers at the brothel, from the quantities found, Seifert argues that women living in these houses enjoyed a better diet than did other women in the neighborhood.

Seifert skillfully combines historical sources (including census records, contemporaneous newspaper articles, city directories, insurance maps, interviews and general works on women and economics for the period) with the archaeological data, using each to complement the other. Evidence on class, race, and gender relations all make this an interesting look at some neglected areas in United States history—women's roles in the family homes and in an unarguably gendered business. By associating individual and family names with specific households and their archaeological evidence, Seifert adds another very human dimension to this social history. SLD

*References cited*
South, Stanley 1977. *Method and Theory in Historical Archaeology*. Academic Press, New York.

*historical archaeology/faunal analysis/brothels/class/subsistence/Washington, D.C./United States*


153. SEMPOWSKI, MARTHA L. 1986. Differential mortuary treatment of Seneca women: Some social inferences. *Archaeology of Eastern North America* 14:35-44.

This paper presents "preliminary results of an analysis of mortuary practices at six Seneca sites occupied during the period of initial contact-1565-1687 AD" (p. 36), and considers the implications for women's status in traditional Iroquois societies. A brief review of the extensive ethnohistoric literature on Iroquois women serves as an introduction. The burial data are taken largely from excavation notes curated at the Rochester Museum of Arts and Sciences in New York. According to Sempowski, "fairly secure sex identification by the excavator provided the first criterion for selection of the burials to be studied" (p. 36). Grave goods from 179 "male" and 175 "female" inhumations are examined in order to ascertain "differences in the way adult males and females were treated at death at these sites" (p. 36). First, Sempowski examines the diversity of artifact types found with female vs. male burials, and finds that in general, males had a greater diversity of artifact types preserved with them. This pattern does not appear to change in the time period represented by the six sites.

Next, artifacts are also grouped into four categories: (1) foods or food related containers, (2) ornamental objects, 3) tools and weapons, and 4) ceremonial objects. Percentages of male and female burials with these categories at the six sites are presented in a series of bar charts. Females consistently have higher percentages of objects only in the first category (foods or food related containers), largely due to the higher percentage of indigenous pottery found with female burials. There are no significant differences in percentages of ornamental objects found with males vs. females, although perforated animal teeth are exclusively associated with males. Males were far more frequently buried with tools and weapons, and many items in this category (such as flakers, points, scrapers, scissors, whetstones, and guns "were almost exclusively associated with males...Only grinding stones and iron axes occurred more frequently with females" (p. 41). Males also have consistently higher percentages of ceremonial objects (especially pipes and mineral pigments) buried with them, although females did tend to have more rattles. Interestingly, ornamental objects did not appear to be sex exclusive (see Whelan, #183, for a similar analysis involving ornaments associated with Native American burials). Sempowski concludes that "this study does not appear to support the belief or contention that women held a position of elevated status relative to that of men in traditional Seneca society" (p. 41).

Sempowski's study addresses a classic anthropological and ethnohistoric case with archaeological data well before the popularization of "gender archaeology." The major problem inherent in her analysis lies in the "fairly secure sex identification" performed by the excavators decades ago. Was the assignment of sex based on skeletal evidence or was it influenced by the grave goods found with the biological remains? Is it still possible to check the original sex assignments? Sempowski does not address this potential bias which may dramatically alter or invalidate her conclusions, although she does state that future analyses will be more detailed. If the original assignment of sex to these Seneca women and men *is* correct, Sempowski has outlined some interesting mortuary evidence for protohistoric and prehistoric gender roles in the northeastern U.S. that will bear deeper scrutiny. SLD

*mortuary analysis/ethnohistory/Seneca/United States, Northeast*


154. SMALL, DAVID B. 1991. Initial study of the structure of women's seclusion in the archaeological past. In *The Archaeology of Gender: Proceedings of the Twenty-Second Annual Conference of the Archaeological Association of the University of Calgary,* edited by Dale Walde and Noreen D. Willows, 336-342. Archaeological Association, The University of Calgary, Calgary.

This short paper advocates a structuralist approach to the archaeology of women's seclusion (as in harems or purdah, not menstrual seclusion) in complex societies. First of all, Small recaps Hodder's (1984) suggestions about female seclusion in Europe in the Neolithic and outlines some of the steps needed to understand how "this over-arching structure operates in different communities." Next, he offers some preliminary observations from ethnographic work that may be useful to archaeologists. He contrasts houseplans from Tunis, which illustrate a traditional Islamic "women, family, trusted associates" vs. "outsiders" architectural pattern, with the use of house space in Hindu communities with a tradition of purdah, and then goes on to look at predicted differences between small and large Moslem communities. Finally, he compares houseplans in two sixteenth and seventeenth century Ottoman communities (Ankara and Kayseri). In Kayseri, the political situation "should have put substantially more emphasis on the negotiation of male honor" (p. 341), and Small sees this reflected in differences in floorplans and the elaboration of the thresholds.

Although structuralist language and arguments can be difficult for those uninitiated in their use, Small presents some ideas that should be of interest to anyone working in an area with a history of female seclusion. As he clearly points out, our ethnographic understanding of this complex set of ideologies and behaviors (and corresponding symbols and material remains) needs further development before it can be applied archaeologically. This could indeed "be a very important branch of the study of past gender relations" (p. 341), but as Small impresses upon the reader, the cultural context of seclusion plays an all- important role in its expression. SLD

*References cited*
Hodder, Ian 1984. Burials, houses, women and men in the European Neolithic. In *Ideology, Power and Prehistory*, edited by Daniel Miller and Christopher Tilley, 51-68. Cambridge University Press, Cambridge.

*structuralism/contextual archaeology/architecture/spatial analysis/Tunis/Africa*


155. SMITH, BRUCE D. 1992. Reconciling the gender-credit critique and the floodplain weed theory of plant domestication. Paper presented at the 57th Annual Meeting of the Society for American Archaeology, Pittsburgh.

SMITH, BRUCE D. 1993 (in preparation). Reconciling the gender-credit critique and the floodplain weed theory of plant domestication. In *Archaeology of Eastern North America*, edited by James Stoltman.

In these papers, Smith responds to Watson and Kennedy (#180), who criticize some of his earlier work for not acknowledging women's roles in the evolution of agriculture in the prehistoric eastern United States. Smith takes this opportunity to argue that his construct and Watson and Kennedy's "should be viewed in terms of their considerable areas of commonalty and compatibility," detailing four main areas in which their models differ. First of all, Smith argues that domestication occurred *independently* in the eastern U.S., beginning with the cultivation of *Cucurbita* gourds in the Middle Archaic period. Watson and Kennedy imply that *Cucurbita* was introduced to this area. In a tongue-in-cheek postprocessual footnote to the SAA paper (this section was omitted from the published version), complete with binary oppositions and the politically charged language of empowerment and resistance, Smith suggests that by making the eastern U.S. a secondary center (a passive recipient of crops from Mesoamerica, presumably introduced by male traders), Watson and Kennedy have themselves made their "gender-credit" model ethnocentric and androcentric.

Smith's second section addresses the concept of gender-credit itself, arguing that his (and many other) gender-neutral approaches are not intrinsically androcentric, but operate on a different scale of analysis not mutually exclusive with a gender-credit approach. He goes on to suggest that the political rhetoric typical of "newly emerging approaches in archaeology" may in fact obscure productive research involving gender roles.

The next point of contention is the issue of human (in this case female) intentionality in the process of plant domestication. Watson and Kennedy argue that Smith's coevolutionary model "downplays stress, drive, intention, or innovation of any sort" and state that "it may turn out to be the case that some if not all of the species initially domesticated would have required special, self-conscious, and deliberate treatment to convert them to garden crops" (1991:267). Smith acknowledges that human intentionality is downplayed in his earlier models, and responds with "an important and necessary change in emphasis," highlighting the role women probably played in storing and planting seed stock. He disagrees, however, that all of the indigenous crops required "directed self conscious scrutiny and selection" to produce the morphological changes seen in the archaeological record, arguing that many of the altered characteristics are not visible to the naked eye. Smith's final point addresses differing opinions on the time span when these crops became economically important. He argues that the fact these plants played a minor role in subsistence for a long time does not diminish women's accomplishments in producing them. Smith concludes by reiterating the changes that could be made in both their model and his, applauding Watson and Kennedy for "illuminating the potential rich variety of interesting research problems involving issues of gender" in the Archaic period, and suggesting a few gender-related questions for future research in this area.

Many of Smith's criticisms are valid, although neither the indigenous domestication of *Cucurbita* nor the timing of the increased use of native crops are critical parts of Watson and Kennedy's general argument. Most readers will probably find his discussion of gender-neutral models vs. Watson and Kennedy's gender-credit model (which Smith characterizes as "the no neutral zone rule") the most interesting section of this paper. Smith raises some important theoretical questions—for example, "Must archaeologists attempt to assign gender credit, male or female, in all situations of past innovation in order to avoid the gender bias label?" The discussion of intentionality (a battle zone between some processual and postprocessual archaeologists) is also well thought out. Many readers will find the post-processual footnote the most entertaining part of the paper, although some may feel Smith is adding insult to injury by mimicking their rhetoric. SLD

*agriculture/agricultural origins/postprocessual/processual/Watson. P.J./Kennedy, M.C./Archaic period/ United States, Southeast*

156. SPECTOR, JANET D. 1991. What this awl means: Toward a feminist archaeology. In *Engendering Archaeology: Women and Prehistory*, edited by Joan M. Gero and Margaret W. Conkey, 388-406. Basil Blackwell, Cambridge, MA.

Spector uses this paper for a personal exposition of her research over the last twenty years. Using feminist theory she attempts to build a non-androcentric framework for archaeological investigation (the "task differentiation" approach). This framework utilizes ethnographic and ethnohistoric data to find relationships between gender specific tasks and their material and non-material correlates which are then related to archaeological sites (a modification of the direct historical approach). Specifically, this is applied to the Dakota Indians (Wahpeton) of Minnesota at the Little Rapids site (ca. AD 1840). While this approach yields a significant amount of data on gender roles, Spector finds the results sterile and generic. To delve deeper into the social life of these people, she creates a fictional account involving a bone awl handle found during excavation. This exercise allows her to explore the insights made during her conventional research in a more lively context. She compares her story to the lifeless accounts produced by traditional archaeologists, and points out that the differences in emphasis yield wholly different viewpoints, such as whether we should focus on the European trade goods themselves, or how they were employed and valued.

Spector's story is an interesting exercise but is difficult to treat in a straightforward manner. The goals of scientific narrative and fictional narrative, such as this, are different. Spector fails to clarify what she considers to be archaeology's goals. Is it a scientific means of discovery or a humanistic means of subjective exploration? Clearly, if she wishes archaeologists to use fictional narrative, it must be the latter. The value of fiction cannot be denied. It adds to the interest and aesthetics of archaeological interpretation. However, it should not exceed its role as an additive. There is no means of assessing the degree of certainty we can place in any fictional story, but this is a primary function of scientific narrative. Fictional narrative cannot facilitate scientific inquiry or hypothesis testing and thus a strict fictional approach (which Spector never truly espouses) compromises one aspect of discovery. Lastly, Spector recognizes that her story requires "scientific footnoting" to explain the insights revealed in the story. Thus, scientific narrative cannot (and should not) be avoided. JDB

*historical archaeology/ethnohistory/task differentiation approach/division of labor/fiction//Minnesota/ Dakota/United States and Canada, Plains*

157. SPECTOR, JANET D. 1983. Male/female task differentiation among the Hidatsa: Toward the development of an archaeological approach to the study of gender. In *The Hidden Half: Studies of Plains Indian Women*, edited by Patricia Albers and Beatrice Medicine, 77-99. University Press of America, Washington D.C.

In this widely cited paper, Spector looks at male/female task differentiation revealed in ethnographic accounts from the Great Plains Hidatsa. Her goals are to see how views of stability and change alter by explicitly considering gender, and to look at what can be learned about gender through archaeology. Spector analyzes gender specific activities, their location in space, scheduling, and the materials used and produced using two ethnographies from the early part of the century. She acknowledges the limitations of this material, including the lack of chronological control, attention to material culture, and details considering the division of labor.

Spector concludes that the lives of Hidatsa men and women were quite separate and distinct. Women tended to work with related women in their matrilineal household at tasks involving food, wood, and water collection, hide processing, and building of structures and facilities. Their work took place in the lodges, villages, and nearby gardens, while men spent some time in lodges but much more time outside the village. Men worked in groups that were divided on the basis of age, rather than household-based. It appears that most women's tasks had to be done daily, whereas men had few daily activities but were often gone for long periods. Spector provides detailed tables displaying this information. This information has implications concerning which locations tend to be multifunctional as opposed to specialized. It also implies that spaces used by women tend to have more stationary facilities than those used by men. Spector cautions against interpreting this differentiation of tasks by gender as an example of female exclusion, pointing out that both men and women were excluded from each other's activities. This pattern may also be interpreted as gender autonomy, with gender differentiated access to information. Spector points out that we still need more information on ethnographic task differentiation before attempting to explain archaeological patterns. She also suggests that changes in population, technology, trade patterns, etc., may have very different impacts on women and men.

This paper may not accomplish its original goal of aiding archaeologists in interpreting prehistoric gender roles and relations, but it raises a number of interesting and illuminating points. Even with ethnographic data that are admittedly inadequate, Spector manages to pull out a lot of the variation in female and male tasks, examining tasks performed and their temporal, spatial, and social characteristics. Spector's focus on the spatial dimension, which stresses that spaces can be used by different genders in very different ways is of particular use to archaeologists. This has interesting implications for the visibility of males and females in the archaeological record, as well as underlining the importance of excavating areas outside of dwellings. It is disappointing that there has been little follow-up to this article, although several recent articles annotated in this volume do use Spector's methods as a starting point for their own analyses. WDG

*ethnoarchaeology/task differentiation approach/ethnographic analogy/spatial analysis/division of labor/ Hidatsa/United States and Canada, Plains*


158. SPECTOR, JANET D. AND MARY K. WHELAN 1989. Incorporating gender into archaeology courses. In *Gender and Anthropology: Critical Reviews for Research and Teaching*, edited by Sandra Morgen, 65-94. American Anthropological Association, Washington, D.C.

Spector and Whelan provide a thoughtful discussion of issues concerning bringing gender into the classroom. They target three broad topics for examination. First, they present a concise critique of androcentric and ethnocentric biases found in the field. The authors argue that gender roles are often stereotyped according to notions of gender of our own culture, that different valuing of the roles of men versus women is pervasive, and that these ideas are commonly exposed to students in archaeology courses. "The persistence of these stereotypes in archaeology says more about our own culture than about those we attempt to describe and understand" (p. 67), they state. Their argument is strongly illustrated by reference to textbooks by Campbell (1985), Fagan (1986), Jolly and Plog (1986), and Jurmain *et al.* (1987). They also point out the importance of language use in the classroom, and that simply replacing androcentric terms (such as "Man") with gender neutral language is not a real solution in that studies become "genderless" and hence hollow, or supposedly neutral images are associated with specific genders by students. Instead, they advocate using "neutral language, illustrations, and discussions...to problematize the notion of gender" (p. 78). Second, in order to deal with gender, Spector and Whelan argue that key concepts first need to be specified and methods developed. They proceed to draw a distinction between sex (a biological given) and gender (a "culturally determined and *variable*" [p. 69] phenomenon), and then define a variety of related terms, including gender role, gender identity, gender attribution, and gender ideology. Finally, the authors launch into a discussion of two critical lines of inquiry for anthropological archaeology: (1) the evolution of gender, and (2) the development of gender inequalities. Both processes are believed to be central in that " [r]ecognizing the emergence of gender difference and stratification as evolutionary processes to be explained rather than assumed as universal establishes a new vantage point for revising current understandings of world prehistory in general. Ultimately, we may discover...that bringing gender into the center of analysis demands major revisions in the way prehistory is understood" (p. 75). They suggest focusing on people's activities to elucidate processes of culture change. Drawing on work of Draper and others, the authors then present an analysis of changes in gender roles, and gender ideologies and inequalities associated with increasingly sedentary lifestyles among !Kung people.

Appended at the end of the article are three fully developed classroom exercises that can be directly employed or built upon in teaching. Also provided is a short annotated bibliography of feminist works in archaeology. It is heartening that since publication of this article only a few years ago, the numbers of relevant archaeological sources has virtually skyrocketed. A second, unannotated bibliography lists ethnohistoric/ethnographic sources on gender relations. Overall, this article is extremely useful. Spector and Whelan's work successfully facilitates a critical awareness in teaching and in archaeological research. NSG-F

*References cited*
Campbell, Bernard G. 1985. *Humankind Emerging*. 4th edition. Little, Brown, Boston.

Fagan, Brian 1986. *People of the Earth*. 5th edition. Little, Brown, Boston.

Jolly, Clifford and Fred Plog 1986. *Physical Anthropology and Archaeology*. 3rd edition. Knopf, New York.

Jurmain, Robert, Harry Nelson, and William A. Turnbaugh 1987. *Understanding Physical Anthropology and Archeology*. 3rd edition. West Publishing, St. Paul, Minnesota.

*feminist critique/text books/education/Western society, contemporary*


159. SPENCER-WOOD, SUZANNE M. 1992. A feminist program for nonsexist archaeology. In *Quandaries and Quests: Visions of Archaeology's Future*, edited by Luanne Wandsnider, 98-114. Center for Archaeological Investigations Occasional Paper No. 20. Southern Illinois University, Carbondale.

Suzanne Spencer-Wood proposes a "feminist paradigm" for archaeology that would correct the androcentrism inherent in other common archaeological approaches. She begins by identifying the problem of androcentric bias in typical archaeological research. This includes an emphasis on male activities as primary, the presentation of the past as ungendered, and the equation of women with passivity, lower status, and a universalized biological identity. These biases are not only problematic for inhibiting accurate understandings of the past, but have direct feedback into the way we understand women and men in modern society and "support the oppression of women in the present." Spencer-Wood identifies feminism as the best theoretical perspective from which to rectify the problem of androcentrism. According to her, "[f]eminism is a theoretical perspective for understanding the ways gender, as a fundamental cultural construct, structures all aspects of culture and conditions the behavior of all members of society, including men and children, as well as women." She contrasts this with the study of gender from a nonfeminist position, which would merely add women to male-centered models, and ultimately support these androcentrisms.

Spencer-Wood examines processual, postprocessual, and critical archaeologies and concludes that they are all essentially androcentric or have supported androcentrism by excluding gender and a feminist standpoint from a central role in analysis and interpretation. Instead, she proposes "a feminist paradigm for developing nonsexist constructions of the past... combin[ing] empiricism, feminist standpoint theory and some aspects of feminist postmodernism, *while rejecting relativism"* [emphasis added]. She believes that a feminist position is necessary to see through sexist androcentrism but also that data constrain interpretation. She claims "[t]he greater validity of feminist interpretations and critiques results from their use of widely accepted empirical methodology to identify and correct androcentric biases that are easily recognized within conventional standards." Also, instead of accepting gender as a "universal unitary social category," this "paradigm" would "research the relationships between gender norms and ideals and the flexibility in the actual operation of gender systems."

In order to implement the "feminist theoretical standpoint," Spencer-Wood argues we need to begin asking feminist research questions and to try to learn how women and men are "powerful agents of culture change, who construct their own gender ideologies, behaviors, and relationships." In addition, it is necessary to bring about "changes in standard ethnographic practices of research, publishing, teaching, and tenure."

Spencer-Wood makes a powerful and convincing argument through this article. Her combination of explicit definition and strong argumentation set this article in the company of Alison Wylie's publications as seminal in the rapidly developing literature on gender and feminist archaeology. However, serious problems with several of the positions taken in the article must be addressed. In preface, I should state that I think each of these issues is problematic only when taken to logical extremes. My first concern focuses on Spencer-Wood's commitment to "feminist standpoint theory." While I agree that humans inevitably bring a subjective bias to research, I disagree that the standpoint approach is *the* way to see beyond it. Indeed, taking a "new" or "different" standpoint or perspective on an issue offers no guarantee of increasing objectivity. It is often useful to challenge our preconceived assumptions by taking different perspectives and I would argue this is a good way to identify contentious assumptions to be examined more closely. But it is the explicit evaluation of these subjective biases with empirical methodology that is our only hope for more objectively focusing on issues of interest. Assuming that one is capable of taking or incorporating different standpoints, the standpoint method is useful for identifying critical bias, but is *not* the solution to the problem, only a technique for identifying it. I would adamantly disagree with any position that claimed that only certain people or groups of people are capable of taking certain standpoints.

My second concern relates to Spencer-Wood's opposition of feminist theory and "androcentric" theory. I disagree with the conclusion that what is not "feminist" is therefore androcentrically sexist. This opposition denies the theoretical possibility of a gynocentric standpoint or sexism which could be equally debilitating in the attempt to interpret the past (or the present).

While I do not accept some aspects of Spencer-Wood's position, this article provides one of the strongest justifications in print for the legitimate and critical role that an explicitly feminist archaeology can bring to the field to correct misinterpretations of the past and rectify social injustice in the present. JBF

*feminist standpoint theory/epistemology/processualism/postprocessualism/revisionist theory/postmodernism*


160. SPENCER-WOOD, SUZANNE M. 1991. Toward a feminist historical archaeology of the construction of gender. In *The Archaeology of Gender: Proceedings of the Twenty-Second Annual Conference of the Archaeological Association of the University of Calgary,* edited by Dale Walde and Noreen D. Willows, 234-244. Archaeological Association, The University of Calgary, Calgary.

Spencer-Wood offers a historical outline and critique of gender research in historical archaeology. Her thesis is that much of the work that has been done has simply added women to existing, androcentric models of the past, and that a true feminist approach must change the models as well.

The author summarizes the growth of gender research as a trend from monolithic male/female categories to greater awareness of the diversity of gender roles across class and ethnic groups. Historical archaeologists commonly make three mistakes: some ignore gender and use male generalizations, some look only at female roles which are currently undervalued and assume that they have always been undervalued, and some look at a wide variety of roles but assume that anything a woman did had low value because a woman did it.

Much of the article focuses on the public (male)/private (female) dichotomy which is commonly assumed by historical archaeologists. The author claims that the public/domestic model projects the low status of housework onto the past and that Marxist models of production and reproduction do this in a more sophisticated way, reifying the subordinate position of women. The model misrepresents the reality of gender roles by ignoring women who worked outside the home. It also ignores employment such as piecework, day nurseries, and boarding housekeeping which were usually done by women and combine the categories of work and home. When historical archaeologists look at women in the public sphere they tend to view them as exceptions or consider them from a male point of view (calling brothels, for instance, a "sporting subculture").

Gender research, according to Spencer-Wood, is of three kinds. Supplemental research merely adds women to sexist models. Polyvocal research, which presents both male and female historical accounts, also reifies androcentric views by treating the accounts as equally valid and not pointing out the biases in the male view. Feminist approaches to history research women's viewpoints to produce more accurate models of the past, focusing on women's power and their own positive views about their roles. As an example the author discusses the nineteenth century "Cult of Domesticity" and contemporary alternatives to it, including her own work on the Domestic Reform movement. Domestic Reformers accepted the public/domestic split but used it to extend the domestic realm to areas like nursing and elementary school teaching, and to win suffrage by claiming the moral superiority of women.

There are many pertinent points in this critique, particularly as concerns the need to make new models and to change not only the subjects of our history but also our viewpoints and assumptions. The suggestion that we might learn how to alter our models of history by reading new historical sources (such as women's diaries and letters) and reading old histories in more self-consciously critical ways is certainly valid.

The article's weakness lies in its exclusive acceptance of positive and empowering views of women. In Spencer-Wood's view, documents written by women are free of sexist bias, which is inherent in male ones. Gender ideologies are more complicated than this. Gender inequality, for instance, can be accepted and viewed positively and still be inequality. The example of Domestic Reform is a good one; the author recognizes the movement as empowering to women, but does not see that it also upheld ideas of natural capacities, inherent differences in ability, and appropriate spheres for men and women, concepts which postponed ideological equality. Similarly, the critique of Marxist theories leaves one wondering how the historical fact of female oppression can be studied or explained without being labeled "reification." SF

*feminist critique/historical archaeology/brothels/Marxism/Victorian ideology/United States*

161. STALSBERG, ANNE 1987 The interpretation of women's objects of Scandinavian origin from the Viking period found in Russia. In *Were They All Men? An Examination of Sex Roles in Prehistoric Society,* edited by Reider Bertelsen, Arnvid Lillehammer, and Jenny-Rita Naess, 89-100. Arkeologisk Museum i Stavanger, Stavanger, Norway.

This article explores Scandinavian interaction in "Old Russia" during the Viking Period (AD 800-1050). Anne Stalsberg attempts to revise previous interpretations by focusing on the involvement of women in this interaction. The article falls into two roughly equal parts. In the first, Stalsberg presents burial evidence to argue that free Scandinavian women ventured into "Old Russia" along with Scandinavian men, and in the second part, she considers the implications of these data for different models of interaction: agricultural expansion and settlement, pirating, conquest, mercenary employment, or trade.

The identification of Scandinavian women in the archaeological record requires attribution of both sex/gender and ethnicity to archaeological materials and human remains. Stalsberg uses material clearly identifiable as Scandinavian to attribute ethnicity to burials. The materials used include: women and men's brooches, swords, scabbard chapes, shield bosses, strap mounts and buckles, Thor's hammer rings, runic inscriptions, and "a few unique items." In addition, "graves with a boat and with sword or spearhead intentionally damaged or vertically thrust into the ground under the grave" are considered Scandinavian. Having compiled data on the occurrences of these Scandinavian materials in burials around Eastern Europe, Stalsberg finds 99 Scandinavian burials, of which 37 are women, 32 are men, 21 are male/female couples, 1 is a child and 8 are unidentifiable. Women's graves span the entire two hundred and fifty year period and include valuable silver items indicating free-person status with access to prestige items.

Next, Stalsberg looks at burial distributions and assemblages to test the five models of Scandinavian/Old Russian interaction listed above. She finds two distribution patterns dividing the lands adjacent to the Gulf of Finland from the interior territories accessible only by portage. In the coastal region, Scandinavian graves are found mixed with "native" graves in the same mounds and Scandinavian burial mounds are found intermixed with "native" burial mounds. The general pattern is one of a scattered distribution. In contrast, Scandinavian graves in the interior are "concentrated in centres of some importance." Stalsberg suggests that agricultural settlement or piracy could explain the coastal pattern, though she doubts that women would have participated in piracy. She thinks that the concentration of burials in elite centers and the vulnerability of portage escape routes argues against such models in the interior. Mercenary and trading relationships are posited for interaction in the interior. Trading is suggested in the interior by the inclusion of weights and scales in some Scandinavian (and other) burials. Conquest is ruled out entirely for both regions because of the low proportion of Scandinavian burials compared to "native" burials (maximum 10.2%) and because of the apparently peaceful interactions in both areas.

Finally, Stalsberg briefly examines reasons for the disappearance of Scandinavian influence around AD 1050. Rejecting assimilation into Slavic society as an explanation, she offers three alternatives: (1) the material could have changed under Christian influence with the Viking Period materials losing currency; (2) the nature of contacts could have changed; or (3) the Scandinavians finished their mercenary or trading jobs and went home.

Stalsberg's article is not without flaws. One major problem lies in her assumption that graves without obvious Scandinavian materials belong to native "Old Russian" individuals. She does this in order to avoid giving a "false ratio" of Scandinavian to native graves due to the "more conspicuous" nature of the Scandinavian graves. Stalsberg may simply replace one false ratio with another. Unless native Russian graves are ethnically marked in some way and can be directly compared to Scandinavian ones, ratios remain suspect. There is a possibility that some Scandinavians (for instance, lower status individuals) were buried with less ethnically specific and durable material objects. If this were the case, it would dramatically change Stalsberg's conclusion that the Scandinavian presence was small in proportion to the native population. A major component in Stalsberg's argument are the assumptions that Scandinavian culture was patriarchal and that women would not have been fighters or pirates. Perhaps she has documentation or strong archaeological evidence of this from other studies, but no supporting evidence is provided and there is cross-cultural evidence that in some contexts women have been warriors and directly involved in aggressive military campaigns (see #117).

Stalsberg also fails to consider the possibility that male warriors or traders might have taken native wives and adorned them with Scandinavian goods or that native Russians might have wished to identify with Scandinavians and thus adopted Scandinavian costume. Ethnicity is not a fixed social categorization, and ethnic identities can be reoriented for political, economic, and ideological reasons. To resolve these problems, more work is needed to identify the nature of interactions and the status and power differentials involved. Were the Scandinavians better marked because they had higher status or access to more valuable objects? Were the native elite actually exploiting the Scandinavian art and raw materials for their own purposes? Were the Scandinavians actually trading these materials to the native elites?

Also probematic are the implicit assumptions about social meaning and the symbolic nature of costume. Stalsberg writes, "can we be sure of the ethnic identification [of Scandinavian women based on the occurrence of a pair of Scandinavian oval brooches]? Other ethnic groups can adopt an alien brooch and use it on their costume, but it is less likely that a woman would adopt an alien costume as this would be loaded with too many social signals." While Stalsberg is undoubtedly correct that the use of a costume composed of several independent parts is likely to signal the marking of an identity, it is precisely the manipulation of social signals that might be the intended purpose of the costume. Such assumptions need to be considered in a more theoretical context. Finally, Stalsberg never explains how women's and men's graves were distinguished. Hopefully these attributions were based on biological morphology rather than grave associations, but the lack of clarification on this point is troubling. JBF

*ethnicity/trade/mortuary analysis/Viking/Russia/Scandinavia/Europe*


162. STANLEY, AUTUMN 1981. Daughters of Isis, daughters of Demeter: When women sowed and reaped. *Women's Studies International Quarterly* 43:289-304.

Also published in *Women, Technology and Innovation,* edited by Joan Rothschild (1982, Pergamon Press, New York), this article attempts to show that "Evidence from anthropology, archaeology, mythology and primate ethology indicates women were the main gatherers, processors, and storers of plant food...and thus the most logical ones to have invented the tools and methods involved in this work" (p. 289). Its arguments are similar to, although less anthropologically sophisticated than, Watson and Kennedy's (#180) work. Although archaeological data such as agricultural tools, food processing implements, and crops (mainly from the Middle East) are included, no archaeological evidence linking these artifacts or tasks with gender is presented. SLD

*agricultural origins/agriculture/myth/Near East*

*Annotated References*

163. STARK, MIRIAM 1991. A perspective on women's status in American archaeology. In *The Archaeology of Gender: Proceedings of the Twenty-Second Annual Conference of the Archaeological Association of the University of Calgary*, edited by Dale Walde and Noreen D. Willows, 187-194. Archaeological Association, The University of Calgary, Calgary.

This is a follow-up to Kramer and Stark's (#100) article on the status of women in American archaeology, and repeats much of the information presented there, as well as presenting newer and more detailed data. Stark considers a number of indicators of women's status relative to men within archaeology, including the number of doctorates granted from 1976-1986; the number and nature of National Science Foundation, National Geographic, and National Endowment for the Humanities grants awarded to men and women; the percentages of women in academic jobs at different levels; the number of women who were single authors in *American Antiquity*; and the representation of women in nonacademic archaeological jobs. As Stark says, this information can be viewed optimistically or pessimistically since it reflects improvement in women's status as well as pervasive, systemic gender discrimination. Women are still underrepresented in academic positions, especially at the full professor level, and tend to be disproportionately concentrated in part-time and adjunct positions. Women are also underrepresented in non-academic positions. Senior female archaeologists apply for grants significantly less often than their male colleagues. On the other hand, men and women now have more nearly comparable success in getting grants, in contrast to the statistics presented by Gero in 1983 (#69). The proportion of women receiving doctorates in archaeology is slightly higher than the national norm across academic fields. The number of women in academic positions has increased significantly in the last 10 years, and the proportion of single authors in American Antiquity who are women is actually higher than the proportion of women in anthropology departments. Non-academic positions have also seen an increase in the number of women, although many of these are still part-time or seasonal positions. Stark closes by briefly discussing what may be some of the underlying causes for the continued imbalance. She considers the effects of social pressures on women, the difficulties of combining families and fieldwork, and discusses continuing bias at the institutional level, in hiring, in networking, and in the structure of graduate programs.

It is particularly interesting to consider this article in the light of many other articles that cover the same ground, including Gero (#67, 68, 69), Kramer and Stark (#100), and Yellen (#194). An article on the status of women in archaeology has appeared at least once every two or three years since the early 1980s, which allows us to gauge change over the last two decades, since some of the data date to the 1970s. As Stark points out, some changes have been positive, while others have been disappointingly slow. TVZ

*sociopolitics of archaeology/discrimination/National Science Foundation/National Endowment for the Humanities/National Geographic Society*

164. STIG SØRENSON, MARIE LOUISE 1991. The construction of gender through appearance. In *The Archaeology of Gender: Proceedings of the Twenty-Second Annual Conference of the Archaeological Association of the University of Calgary*, edited by Dale Walde and Noreen D. Willows, 121-129. Archaeological Association, The University of Calgary, Calgary.

Beginning with a theoretical discussion of gender as a social construct, the nature of material culture, and the relation between these concepts, Stig Sørenson argues that feminist theories viewing gender as a social construct may be fruitfully combined with postprocessual archaeological theories that emphasize the active and negotiated nature of material culture. A wealth of well-preserved mortuary evidence from Bronze Age Denmark is used to "demonstrate the social importance of dress" and "how meanings can be transformed over time and how different levels of meanings can be superimposed upon each other" (p. 122). Following a general description of mortuary customs, Stig Sørenson focuses on successive levels of analysis of cloth, clothing, and costume, in turn. At each level, she examines the potential for visual communication, the symbolization of gender, social importance, and the variations found between sexes and through time. It is only with complete costumes, she argues, that a "readable gender dress code appears. It is at this level that the differences in women's clothing merge into a female category vis-a-vis a male one" (p. 125). Interestingly, there appears to be a single male costume but two female costumes. The different female costumes "were not related to seasonality, regionality or absolute age (of the individual)" (Hvass 1981, parentheses added), and she cites current interpretations which focus on differences in social roles (Kristiansen 1974) and marital status (Eskildsen and Lomborg 1976). Finally, Stig Sørenson states that "certain elements show clear gender categorisation, some give a more ambiguous message about difference, and others appear non-gendered. The categorisation of gender did not permeate all aspects of dress" (p. 127). After discussing the feasibility of recognizing the negotiation of gender categories through these material remains, she offers some alternative suggestions for "the meaning of gender differences as it emerges from the costumes...as belonging contextually to that particular society."

Although it is not entirely clear if gender (as a social construct) is always isomorphic with biological sex in Bronze Age Denmark, Stig Sørenson is commendably cautious in applying "meaning" and seeing "negotiation" in the material culture she describes. For instance, in regard to costume, she states that "Their difference is not apparently associated with values such as superiority, suppression, or 'secondary' statuses. Such an evaluation of appearance may have existed, but is [not] accessible for outsiders. An alternative interpretation, which suggests that appearance was not concerned with asymmetry, is possible." ["not" in brackets added, since "not" appears to fit both grammatically, in relation to "but", and in the context of her argument — this is a rather unfortunate typographical error; (p. 127)]. It is hard to believe that this fascinating material (no pun intended) was "until recently marginalised" as Stig Sørenson states in her endnote on sources. SLD

*References cited*
Eskildsen, L. and E. Lomborg 1976. Giftetanker. *Skalk* 5:18-26.

Hvass, L. 1981. *Egtvedpigen*. Sesam, Viborg.

Kristiansen, K. 1974. Glerupfundet. *Hikvin* 1:7-39.

*mortuary analysis/textiles/costume/postprocessualism/Denmark/Scandinavia/Europe/Bronze Age*


165. STIG SØRENSON, MARIE-LOUISE 1988. Is there a feminist contribution to archaeology? *Archaeological Review from Cambridge* 7(1):9-20.

In looking for the possible feminist contribution to archaeology, Sørenson notes first how feminist theory and concerns have been marginalized within archaeology, and takes as her example the *Archaeological Review from Cambridge* which she helped create, and which was meant to be an alternative voice dealing with controversial issues. In her eyes, the primary contribution of feminist theories is not its focus on women, or on the relations between men and women, but the critical, self-reflective nature of theory production which it encourages.

Sørenson begins by pointing out that while women have not been totally ignored by earlier generations of archaeologists, they have been stereotypically presented in their interpretations. She discusses early writers who looked at gender relations, such as Montelius and Engels, and urges that their ethnocentric and androcentric elements be viewed in light of their times, thus enabling constructive critiques. The same view is taken of present knowledge production, with the warning that: "There is no necessary bond of solidarity between women of different generations, since our social experiences separate us as much as our sex may unite us. We therefore have to be aware of the danger of sentimentalizing the women in our own subject and of misconstructing the history of our disciplinary development. We are too easily prevented from accepting our own social embeddedness."(p. 12). The excesses of feminist theory in archaeology, works which merely turn the tables and present women as the active and driving force of history to the complete exclusion of men, are attributed to a lack of "self-reflectiveness." Thus, not even a more balanced inclusion of women and men in the study of the past is sufficient, for it is "not sufficient for museum designers to start to show women as active participants in history or to up-grade or challenge the values associated with domestic work, if we have not understood why those changes were needed." (p. 15). For this we need theory-building, although Sørenson warns that this should not be allowed to create a split between practical and academic archaeology. Feminist contributions to archaeology affect not only our methodologies and theories concerning the past, but also the involvement of women in the profession in the present. Sørenson concludes with four reasons for why there should be a feminist contribution in archaeology: (1) a fuller history can be written by incorporating multiple perspectives; (2) gender relations are an integral part of any social theory, and such theory and its use must be made more explicit within archaeology; (3) gender and its categorization are potential bases for power relations, important because "all discourses require that humans exercise some form of power over each other"(p. 17); and (4) archaeology is presently being used to legitimate a particular gender mythology, and a feminist archaeology could challenge this usage. Sørenson ends her article by turning her title around and asking what hopefully will be the more fruitful question as gender issues become mainstreamed: What is the archaeological contribution to feminist theory?

Sørenson's article is an interesting contribution, in both its ideas and in their expressions. Many of the ideas advanced, such as her rejection of female solidarity due to a more basic cultural and temporal embeddedness, seem uncustomary. This relativistic tendency is reinforced by the dismissal of evolutionary approaches in favor of a more contextual approach to archaeology. Although it shouldn't be used, as she does, as grounds for the rejection of evolutionary approaches, Sørenson does make the important political point that "women's rights and roles in the present do not need legitimation through the past"(p. 13). In urging the adoption of critical theory, she doesn't sufficiently explain why this is the one bias-free platform which can expose all others and see itself at the same time. Self-reflectiveness can improve any approach, regardless of the social theory to which it is attached. However, it can't solve all problems or banish all biases and subjectivity, though it can drastically improve the quality of our archaeology. WDG

*epistemology/feminist critique/sociopolitics of archaeology/contextual archaeology/history of archaeology*

166. STIG-SØRENSON, MARIE LOUISE 1987. Material order and cultural classification: The role of bronze objects in the transition from Bronze Age to Iron Age in Scandinavia. In *The Archaeology of Contextual Meanings,* edited by Ian Hodder, 90-101. Cambridge University Press, Cambridge.

Working broadly within a theoretical approach that views material culture as texts that communicate complex social and/or individual meanings, Stig Sørenson argues that bronze artifacts were both more active and more isolated in the role they played in Late Bronze Age society than is usually presumed. They are more active because "[they] participated in creating, evolving, and transforming their own context, and the changes within the objects are therefore not merely adaptations to changes within other structures of society...." (p. 94), and are more isolated because they have an internal logic that is not shared by other aspects of material culture. She describes this logic in terms of three structural oppositions: (1) external:internal (or foreign:local); (2) unique:standardized; and (3) male:female. She takes the structuralist stance that these oppositions are general and are not specific to Bronze Age Scandinavia, but emphasizes that their meaning and importance are based upon particular historical context.

Stig Sørensen discusses bronzes from periods V and VI in relation to these oppositions: bronzes that are locally produced vs. exotic, highly standardized vs. unique or unusual, and associated with males vs. females. The correlations she observes—e.g., weapons (male artifacts) are more likely to be unique and/or exotic whereas ornaments (female artifacts) are highly standardized and locally produced—are intriguing, but she spends a relatively small proportion of her argument exploring possible explanations for this, noting only:

> There is therefore no basis for assuming that women held richer positions than men in the
> late Bronze Age. Rather, it can be suggested that women and men were associated with
> two different universes of material objects which partly involved different ritual activities.
> (p. 100)

Her primary interest is not in the gender distinctions that can be seen in the bronzes, nor, for that matter, in any one of the structural oppositions she examines, but in tracing the ways in which these oppositions structured and formed the material culture, and how material culture in turn reproduced these structures. If the reader accepts the assumptions of structuralist argument, her analysis of the important structuring principals of this material corpus is thoughtful and well argued.

But despite the promise of the title and abstract, the explanation for the collapse of this system of structured oppositions and the drastic decrease in the use of bronze that occurs with the transition to the Iron Age is neither well developed nor theoretically consistant with the remainder of the article. Social and economic changes occuring at the transition from the Bronze Age to the Iron Age are first dismissed as an explanation for the changes in material culture and then immediately accepted as playing a central role.

> The dramatic change in the material culture at the end of period VI is, however, not prima-
> rily related to [differences between the economy and social structures of the Bronze Age
> and Iron Age] and is here suggested to be the result rather of the inability of the bronzes and
> their ascribed meanings/functions to adapt conceptually and functionally to a transformation

of the economic basis and in particular to changes in organization and relations of production. (pg. 101)

This difficultly in settling on an explanatory paradigm—the primacy of widespread structural principles that give material systems an internal dynamic of their own vs. the ruling force of the economic base to which material systems adapt or fail to adapt vs. the contextual specificity of the individual historic case—weakens the article and leaves the reader feeling slightly schizophrenic. In her conclusions Stig Sørensen tries to explain an important archaeological transition with too many theoretical approaches and fails to do justice to either theories or data. KJ

*metallurgy/structuralism/contextual archaeology/Scandinavia/Bronze Age/Iron Age*

167. STINE, LINDA FRANCE 1992. Social differentiation down on the farm. In *Exploring Gender Trough Archaeology: Selected Papers from the 1991 Boone Conference*, edited by Cheryl Claasen, 103-110. Prehistory Press, Madison.

Stine argues that social differentiation cannot be adequately understood in terms of one variable, but is defined by the interaction of several variables, such as race, gender, class, and status. Drawing on interviews, documents, architecture, and investigation of sub-surface features, she examines the material correlates of social differentiation in two early twentieth century households in a small community in North Carolina. Although one family is Euro-American and one family is African-American, similarity in economic stratum and status appears to have heavily influenced the materials found in each household.

Economic concerns seem to have been the major factor structuring material inventories, architecture, and gender roles of the two households. Ceramics from the two areas were indistinguishable and the houses were "almost mirror images." Public architecture also reflected differential access to economic resources; the Afro-American school was substantially smaller than the Euro-American one.

Economic concerns seem also to have impinged on gender roles within these two households. Public institutions, such as the local high school, supported the ideology of a proper sphere for women's labor being inside the home. Men's proper sphere was outside the home. Tenant farm families, however, often needed the labor of women in the fields, and could not afford to maintain this dichotomy. Women who moved, either willingly or unwillingly, outside the established gender roles were made to feel different, or even ashamed of their appearance.

This article is the third in a series by Stine on the effects of social variables on material culture. The interested reader may also refer to her dissertation. KMM

*historical archaeology/class/ethnicity/architecture/ceramic analysis/North Carolina/United States, Southeast*

168. STINE, LINDA F. 1991. Early twentieth century gender roles: Perceptions from the farm. In *The Archaeology of Gender: Proceedings of the Twenty-Second Annual Conference of the Archaeological Association of the University of Calgary,* edited by Dale Walde and Noreen D. Willows, 496-501. Archaeological Association, The University of Calgary, Calgary.

Stine looks at gender roles in an early twentieth century (1910-1940) farming community in piedmont North Carolina. Her research includes oral history, interviews, literature study, and archaeology. She discusses the concept of gender specific activity areas as an outgrowth of Victorian ideas of separate spheres in which female labor was subordinate to male labor. In the early twentieth century this concept developed into the institution of separate but equal activity spheres for men and women.

Stine finds a gender division within farmsteads reflected in both the literature of the time and in the structure of the farmsteads themselves. Her research suggests a pattern similar to that of New England farmsteads in which the house was the female activity sphere, the barn and barnyards the male activity sphere, and the gardens and yards in between were "areas of mutual interaction" (p. 497). Stine shows that the typical pattern was for women and young children to work in the house while men and older children worked in the fields, although she does not elaborate on this interesting age division in gender roles. Field crops had priority and women helped in the fields whenever necessary. Stine also provides evidence of much cross-over between men's work and women's work, due to both necessity and choice.

Stine conducted archaeological excavations at two adjoining farmsteads and was able to delineate specific functional areas. Perhaps because of space limitations, her discussion of the archaeological aspects of her research lacks detail. For instance, it is not entirely clear exactly how she determined separate activities and activity areas archaeologically. She does provide important caveats for anyone attempting gender attribution of activity areas or specific materials. She reminds us that gender, as a social construct, will not necessarily be directly reflected in activity patterns. Stine emphasizes the difference between cultural conceptions of gender roles and the actual performance of activities. Her data, which clearly show that deviation from gender norms may be as much a matter of personal choice as of economic necessity, provide an ideal venue to underscore the complexity of archaeological studies of gender. DLG

*historical archaeology/ethnoarchaeology/agriculture/spatial analysis/North Carolina/United States, Southeast*


169. TALALAY, LAUREN E. 1987. Rethinking the function of clay figurine legs from Neolithic Greece: An argument by analogy. *American Journal of Archaeology* 91:161-169.

This interesting addition to the literature on figurines comes from a classical archaeologist who uses methods and theories from anthropological archaeology to address the function of 18 figurine legs found at five Neolithic communities in the northern Peloponnese of Greece. Talalay argues that although such figurines are often associated with "an ancient cult of a Great Mother Goddess...small, portable figurines were not a unifunctional class of objects but may have served a variety of purposes" (p. 161). After describing the figurine fragments (fired and painted clay female leg and torso forms which seem to have been purposefully separated) and their archaeological context (the sites of Lerna, Franchthi Cave, Akratas, Corinth, and Asea), she presents a hypothesis—these objects "functioned as special contracts or identifying tokens symbolizing social and economic bonds" between communities or groups in these communities (p. 161). Talalay hinges her proposition on three supporting lines of evidence: the construction of the artifacts, classical and historical analogues of similar kinds of split objects, and the structure of Middle Neolithic society as known from other recent research. She also points out the difficulties of testing her hypothesis, stating that "The list of potential and plausible uses in Middle Neolithic society is enormous and until the range of possibilities can be reasonably narrowed, attempts to generate these kinds of test implications may be a futile exercise" (p. 166).

Talalay has done such a thorough job of critiquing her own argument that little more need be added here. As she indicates, matching legs have *not* yet been found in different communities. If and when the separate halves of a set are found in different communities, her hypothesis will gain a tremendous amount of support. Finally, Talalay also raises some questions regarding more general problems of representation and sex or gender, such as why these artifacts have all been "sexed as female" (p. 169). Some other questions that may lead to interesting research can be proffered here. If the leg fragments are all female, what might this imply concerning their suggested function? How does this relate to the contemporaneous gender ideology? How does their decoration relate to their use? Indeed, who made these figurines and what gender or subset of society used them? SLD

*iconography/figurines/representation/Goddess/Neolithic/Greece/Mediterranean*


170. TAYLOR, SARAH 1990. "Brothers" in arms? Feminism, poststructuralism and the "rise of civilisation." In *Writing the Past in the Present,* edited by Frederick Baker and Julian Thomas, 32-41. St. David's University College, Lampeter, England.

Taylor's article examines the relation between feminsim and poststructuralism, identifying three main areas of intellectual overlap: (1) the critique of logocentrism and the use/abuse of binary oppositions; (2) de-mystification of social structures and the "natural," particularly through studies of the role of ideology;

and (3) the attention paid to the "active" individual and to the practice of everyday life. At the same time, Taylor finds substantial differences. Poststructuralists are generally less comfortable with competing and contradictory subjectivities than are feminists (who, according to Taylor, experience them in everyday life). Being mainly academicians, poststructuralists are far more likely to be co-opted by existing power structures. Their embrace of dense writing styles and exclusivity suggest to her that they are really far more interested in changing their status in the academic hierarchy than in changing the world. If for no other reason, feminists should be wary of poststructuralists because they are generally male, and "even well-intentioned men [tend] to end up steering agendas and dominating discussion, including ostensibly feminist discussion" (p. 36).

"Having got this bit of poststructuralist bashing off my chest," as she puts it, (p. 37), she takes up the question of "the rise of civilization" (i.e., rise of state-level polities). Here feminism faces a bit of a dilemma: should feminists accept the view that the rise of the state marks the subjugation of women, and that "civilization" (as far as feminism is concerned) is a bad thing? Or should they instead argue that the role of women in the rise of civilization has been undervalued or overlooked? Taylor neatly resolves the dilemma she had herself posed by concluding that feminists must do both—deplore the effects of "civilization" while redefining it to recognize the place and power of women.

The different portions of the essay are intriguing in their own right, but seem related only by their proximity to one another. Her enumeration of the similarities between poststructuralism and feminism depends on fairly narrow definitions of each, definitions which many proponents of one or the other would reject, and her elucidation of the differences refers less to characteristics of poststructuralism than to the character of its practitioners. Her discussion of the "rise of civilization" seems somewhat out of place, and ultimately uses the modern utility of different views as the major criteria for determining their historical validity. AWB

*feminist critique/state formation/poststructuralism/postprocessualism*


171. TRINGHAM, RUTH E. 1991. Households with faces: The challenge of gender in prehistoric architectural remains. In *Engendering Archaeology: Women and Prehistory*, edited by Joan M. Gero and Margaret W. Conkey, 93-131. Basil Blackwell, Cambridge, MA.

In this complex article, Tringham attempts to show that assigning gender to particular activities or items of material culture in the archaeological record is not necessary or always even desirable. Her argument is presented in many different ways, including stories about personal experiences, summaries of previous research on households, an imaginary dialogue among archaeologists with different research strategies, presentation of her own research data, and a story set in the Neolithic.

Tringham advocates a change in research strategy which allows examination of gender relations without attribution. She criticizes the use of the household as an analytic unit in archaeology, pointing out that most households are faceless and devoid of gender but hold implicit assumptions about gender roles. Actions at the household level are critical in broader social relations, and Tringham advocates the use of ethnography and ethnoarchaeology to understand variability in architecture and the roles and relations of men and women within the household.

Tringham offers her own work at Opovo, a Late Neolithic settlement in Yugoslavia, as an example of how microscale analysis yields interesting information about the use and use-life of the houses. The imaginary dialogue among Marija Gimbutas, Ian Hodder, Andrew Sherratt, and Tringham herself illustrates how different theoretical approaches yield very different interpretations of what went on at Opovo, none of which are a feminist archaeology. Finally, consideration of the information from Opovo leads Tringham to look at household cycles of construction, destruction, and replacement. She concludes that houses were deliberately burned at the end of their use-lives, perhaps at the death of the household head. This destruction and rebuilding of houses also has implications for continuity of land use and land ownership. She ends with a story of how a Neolithic inhabitant at Opovo might have reacted to the destruction of a house.

This article's style can be "disconcerting and unsettling"(p. 99), which is how Tringham predicts many will react to her new research strategy. The inclusion of stories and fictional dialogues, while illustrating some of her points, may also put some readers off. Tringham's discussion of household archaeology is very good, however. It addresses some of the limitations of current household oriented research and points out that gender relations within the household are usually ignored. Her discussion of the importance of microscale domestic architecture, ethnography, and ethnoarchaeology for examining social relations in general, and gender relations in particular, is likewise thought-provoking. Her own architectural analyses at Opovo are a fine illustration of how examination of the microscale can provide detailed information about the building, use, and abandonment of houses.

Ultimately, Tringham is not particularly successful in giving these households faces, except in the illustrations. Her final discussion of house use-lives is an interesting and satisfying explanation for the archaeological evidence from Opovo, but it remains surprisingly gender-free, even using faceless concepts such as "the household cycle" (p. 123) without discussing how household composition or gender dynamics affect the household cycle. The closing story includes gender, yet so could any number of very different stories all purporting to show a gendered prehistory at Opovo. There must be some way of evaluating this story about the past as opposed to other stories. Are all gendered pasts created equal, or are some more equal than others? TVZ

*architecture/household analysis/spatial analysis/Neolithic/Yugoslavia/Europe*

172. TROCOLLI, RUTH 1992. Colonization and women's production: The Timucua of Florida. In *Exploring Gender through Archaeology: Selected Papers from the 1991 Boone Conference,* edited by Cheryl Claassen 95-102. Prehistory Press, Madison.

This paper examines the effects of Spanish colonization on Timucuan women. Trocolli considers gender as a strategic variable to her analysis, viewing it as an important organizing construct in Timucuan production. Using ethnohistoric and archaeological evidence she reconstructs Timucuan culture at the time of contact and suggests that Timucuan women held prominent positions and had access to formal political and ritual power. Women produced considerable amounts of material goods and made important subsistence contributions to the household, complementing those made by the men. With colonization came the demise of Timucuan society and the imposition of a patriarchal Spanish system, including the idea of economically dependent women and the exclusion of women from public, social and ritual spheres. The Spaniards' survival, however, required adopting native subsistence practices. The incorporation of native knowledge and production into the Spanish household was accomplished through the creation of bicultural households, through marriage, concubinage, and servitude of Timucuan women, although initially marriage between cacique's daughters and important Spaniards was viewed as a method of pacification. This process of *mestizaje* also provided a means by which Timucuan women could pass on native traditions to their daughters (e.g., ceramic technology and subsistence practices). This eventually resulted in the development of a creole culture.

The archaeological evidence from sixteenth to seventeenth century households in St. Augustine demonstrates the material differences between those occupied by mestizo, criollo and Spanish-natives. For example, the bicultural households are dominated by native ceramic assemblages for food preparation, non-native ceramics for serving, and Spanish architectural elements whereas the criollo households have the least quantities of native ceramics and food remains. Trocolli concludes that colonization changed the mode and relations of production as well as the products themselves but that the Timucuan women's continued transmission of elements of their cultural heritage "demonstrates the resiliency and adaptiveness of *both* the Spaniards and the native women" (p. 101).

This paper provides an interesting study of changes and continuity in women's social and economic roles pre- and post-colonization. However, the central importance of gender to her analysis warrants a definition of the concept, which unfortunately is not provided. It seems clear that she links gender strictly to biological sex (e.g., "berdaches were between genders" p. 98). This results in an analysis more of the sexual division of labor, albeit those aspects related to women, than of gendered relations of production and the changes in these wrought by colonization. Trocolli's interpretation of the *mestizaje* process as a successful adaptive strategy for Timucuan women and Spanish men seems inconsistent with what she defines as the colonization process—domination, exploitation and disenfranchisement of indigenous peoples by the colonizers. Certainly the acculturation of Spaniards to life in colonial Florida cannot be simply equated to the

## Annotated References

process undergone by the Timucuans to life under the Spanish. Other theoretical frameworks may be more appropriate to understanding the social alliance of Timucuan women and Spanish men. EAB

*historical archaeology/household analysis/division of labor/Timucua/Florida/United States, Southeast*


173. TZACHILI, IRIS 1986. Of earrings, swallows and Theran ladies. In *Archaeology and Fertility Cult in the Ancient Mediterranean: Papers presented at the First International Conference on Archaeology of the Ancient Mediterranean,* edited by A. Bonanno, 97-104. B.R. Grüner Publishing Co., Amsterdam.

This paper attempts to trace the significance of a set of images relating to the depiction of women in Late Bronze Age iconography at the settlement at Thera through associations of visual images with supporting textual references. Tzachili identifies the earrings prominently worn by female personages in Theran wall paintings as one of a series of traits that sets Theran art apart from the more general Minoan iconography that otherwise appears to dominate.

Earrings, unusual in Aegean iconography, are linked with earrings painted on possibly ritual nippled-ewer vases and with depictions of swallows (characteristic on these vases), which in one instance are shown to be wearing earrings. Tzachili's brief analysis of this set of linked items relies on an examination of a very small number of instances in which earrings and swallows are featured in the Homeric poems. She concludes that earrings, worn by young women who with "companions of her own age" may have formed a female community important for social integration, evoke the dangerous ambiguities of (seductive) youth. Swallows, although also related to a broader set of images of spring and renewal, are seen in a reference from the *Odyssey* to represent socially uncontrollable and therefore dangerous youth.

Whatever the difficulties of seeking such detailed symbolic connections between the Theran wall-paintings and the Homeric poems, of which Tzachili is surely aware, the argument is unconvincing primarily because of the paucity of references that contextualize the depictions of earrings and a lack of detailed analysis of the Theran depictions within their own context. In her introductory remarks, Tzachili emphasizes the importance of *not* forcing all details to fall into a Minoan scheme, and refers briefly to prevailing interpretations which assign divergent features of iconography at Thera, thought to be a Minoan colony, either to the older Cycladic tradition or to Mycenean "influences." A detailed analysis of the Theran depictions themselves would seem the logical starting point for a serious attempt to understand the position of Theran iconography and gender within this confusion of external influences. LEF

*iconography/costume/Bronze Age/Crete/Thera/Minos/Greece/Mediterranean*


174. VICTOR, KATHARINE L. AND MARY C. BEAUDRY 1992. Women's participation in American prehistoric and historic archaeology: A comparative look at the journals *American Antiquity* and *Historical Archaeology.* In *Exploring Gender through Archaeology: Selected Papers from the 1991 Boone Conference,* edited by Cheryl Claassen, 11-22. Prehistory Press, Madison.

Victor and Beaudry's paper discusses and compares two preliminary studies (Beaudry and White 1991, Victor 1991) on the representation of women within the journals *Historical Archaeology* and *American Antiquity*, and their respective sponsoring societies. The studies tabulate the occurrence of women as HSA/SAA officers, members of the editorial staffs, authors, book reviewers, and as cited by their colleagues within these journals. Victor developed a statistical ranking scheme, the E-score, to overcome the problem of quantifying the various roles of women as authors using raw counts. Articles were coded "0" if the authors were only men, "1" if a man was senior and a woman junior author, "2" if a woman was senior and a man junior author, and "3" if the authors were only women. The E-score is calculated by multiplying the frequencies within each rank by the coded rank, summing these products and then dividing by the number of articles minus any for which gender could not be determined. An E-score of 1.5 would indicate equality in the representation of women and men as authors in these journals.

Findings from Beaudry and White's (1991) analysis indicate that women's representation in the above categories has improved over time, but that women do not dominate the field of historical archaeology.

Women account for 50% of the membership in SHA, but their representation in the journal is far below that of men. From 1967-90, 29% of the articles had women as sole or senior authors, 19% of the book reviews were authored by women, and 18% of the citations were to women authors. Victor and Beaudry add to the analysis by attempting to delineate research spheres using the E-score test. They find that women are well represented in seven areas (e.g., botanical analysis, ceramic analysis) and absent from others (i.e., military studies, methods, theory, and fur trade/contact).

Analysis of the *American Antiquity*/SAA 1967-91 data indicate: (1) Relatively poor representation of women as officers and as editorial staff, although interestingly in the latter case the figures increased both times the editorship was held by a woman. (2) An increasing (but statistically insignificant) trend in the representation of women authors. The highest E-score is 0.8 (1989) which is far below parity. Over this period, 11% of the articles had women as sole authors, 5% women as senior authors, 7% women as junior authors, and 74% were written by men. (3) A slight, but again statistically insignificant, increase over time of women as book reviewers with a peak E-score of 1.1 in 1987. (4) A consistently low number of women authors reviewed with a peak in 1979 of an E-score of 0.75. (5) E-scores consistently below 1.5 for the representation of women in citations. This was based on a 25% random sample of each volume.

In comparing the results, Victor and Beaudry note that the climate is only slightly less "chilly" overall for women as officers, as authors and as cited authorities in historical archaeology than in prehistoric archaeology. As reviewers, the opposite is the case, but in neither journal do women achieve parity. They also find that except in two cases (textiles/textile manufacture in *AA* and ethnobotany in *HA*) all research spheres are dominated by men.

Victor and Beaudry's paper presents much needed quantitative information on the status of women in prehistoric and historical archaeology. Often this topic is dealt with subjectively. One aspect of their analysis which they need to clarify however is how senior and junior authorship was determined in cases where names were alphabetically listed. There is no category for "co-author" in their study and its inclusion may slightly alter some of their results but presumably not their overall findings. As they themselves conclude, this paper clearly points to a need for an examination of why women remain underrepresented as authors and authorities in archaeology, and how this situation can be changed. EAB

*References cited*
Beaudry, Mary C. and Jacqueline White 1991. Cowgirls with the blues? The experience of women in historical archaeology. Paper presented at the 24th Annual Meeting of the Society for Historical Archaeology, Richmond, Virginia.

Victor, Katharine L. 1991 Women in *American Antiquity*? Ms. on file, Department of Archaeology, Boston University.

*discrimination/sociopolitics of archaeology/American Antiquity/Historical Archaeology*

175. VINSRYGG, SYNNØVE 1987. Sex-roles and the division of labour in hunting-gathering societies. In *Were They All Men? An Examination of Sex Roles in Prehistoric Society*, edited by Reider Bertelsen, Arnvid Lillehammer, and Jenny-Rita Naess, 23-32. Arkeologisk Museum i Stavanger, Stavanger, Norway.

LILLEHAMMER, GRETE 1987. Small scale archaeology. Remarks on Synnøve Vinsrygg's paper. In *Were They All Men? An Examination of Sex Roles in Prehistoric Society*, edited by Reider Bertelsen, Arnvid Lillehammer, and Jenny-Rita Naess, 33-34. Arkeologisk Museum i Stavanger, Stavanger, Norway.

These two papers are described together because Lillehammer's work follows directly from Vinsrygg's article. Vinsrygg begins her discussion by linking the sociopolitics of archaeology in Norway to the nature of ideas about the past. She notes that Stone Age studies tend to be largely male dominated and that they often focus on hunting while ignoring gathering and women's activities. Vinsrygg is particularly interested in the division of labor. In order to obtain a more balanced understanding of the past, and with the goal of developing "a picture of people and society" (p. 24), she draws on cross-cultural ethnographic studies of hunter-gatherers. In doing so, she underscores that an understanding of both male and female roles in such societies is critical to archaeology. Vinsrygg subsequently launches into the question of how to identify women's activities in the archaeological record. Because women are assumed to be associated with children, she argues that children's activities must also be represented in these archaeological remains.

Because Stone Age sites lack plant remains, Vinsrygg is compelled to find an alternative data set linked to women's activities. She focuses instead on one class of artifacts traditionally interpreted as heads of war clubs found at Stone Age (possibly mesolithic and subneolithic) sites in Rogaland (southwestern Norway): perforated stones that she believes were used prehistorically as digging stick weights. She supports this claim with solid ethnographic data. The majority of these, she argues, were used by women gatherers while smaller forms of the tool were possibly used by children. The distribution of this type of artifact is primarily coastal, and Vinsrygg suggests that plant resources, gathered by women, may have been available mostly in these areas.

Vinsrygg's article raises an interesting twist picked up by Lillehammer on how to identify children in the archaeological record. The fact that "children must learn and be able to cope with the world they are born into" (p. 34) leads Lillehammer to the inescapable conclusion that portions of archaeological assemblages were produced by them. Lillehammer argues that parts of assemblages often ignored by archaeologists, such as small and poorly made ("practice") artifact forms (the latter often designated as refuse in archaeologist's classification schemes), may be the products of children's activities.

Both of the articles discussed here address the problem of "finding" prehistoric groups traditionally ignored by archaeologists in Norway and elsewhere. They both also exemplify that a different slant in approaching a data set can radically change the interpretation of how the material record was once used. As a North American archaeologist, I found Vinsrygg's analysis of perforated stones striking, especially because these artifacts resemble some in North America conventionally believed to be atlatl weights and therefore assumed to be associated with hunting technologies. The idea of identifying children's activities archaeologically is also intriguing. One problem that is apparent, especially in Vinsrygg's arguments, however, is the tacit assumption that only women are associated with gathering and child care activities. She does not allow for variability in the division of labor. Although some of Vinsrygg's cross-cultural ethnographic sources are dated (for example, Murdock 1967; Lee 1968), her attempt to bring ethnographic data to bear on an archaeological problem is to be commended. NSG-F

*References cited*
Lee, Richard B.1968. What hunters do for a living, or, how to make out on scarce resources. In *Man the Hunter*, edited by Lee, R. B. and I. DeVore. Aldine, Chicago.

Murdock, George P. 1967. *Ethnographic Atlas*. University of Pittsburgh, Pittsburgh.

*division of labor/children/gatherer-hunters/mothering/Rogaland/Mesolithic/Paleolithic/Europe*


176. WALDE, DALE AND NOREEN D. WILLOWS (editors) 1991. *The Archaeology of Gender: Proceedings of the Twenty-Second Annual Conference of the Archaeological Association of the University of Calgary.* Archaeological Association, The University of Calgary, Calgary.

This large volume brings together many recent papers on gender in archaeology (and anthropology in general) presented at the Chacmool Conference in Calgary in 1989. The archaeological papers are grouped in categories including the concept of gender and feminist and postprocessual approaches (7 papers), ethnoarchaeological studies (5), historical archaeology (5), hunter-gatherer archaeology (4), ideology, art, and material remains (11), gender in agricultural origins (3), gender in complex societies (14--although some of these also fit into another category, such as historical archaeology), and the status of women in archaeology (8). The contributions vary a great deal in both quality and depth. Many of the papers are preliminary reports less than five pages in length. All papers dealing directly with archaeologists or archaeological data are evaluated separately in this bibliography. SLD

177. WALKER, PHILLIP L. AND JON M. ERLANDSON 1986. Dental evidence for prehistoric dietary change on the northern Channel Islands, California. *American Antiquity* 51(2):375-383.

Walker and Erlandson study dental caries in skeletons from Santa Rosa Island, in the Santa Barbara Channel Islands region of California, to examine changes in diet and in the sexual division of labor over time. They use new skeletal evidence to evaluate previous models of dietary change. These studies, which were based on faunal and artifactual studies on the mainland, found widespread evidence for the use of plant resources in the early period, followed by a shift to dependence on marine resources. On the Channel Islands, marine foods were heavily relied upon throughout prehistoric times.

They studied 155 skeletons (82 female, 73 male) from two sites spanning the early (Canada Verde Site, 3000 to 4000 BP), middle (Skull Gulch Site A, 1820 to 900 BP) and late (Skull Gulch Site B, 1100 to 1500 AD) periods. They control for possible biases in their samples (such as different age structures) and conclude that dental caries are nearly twice as frequent in the early period sample than in the middle period sample. Walker and Erlandson point out that a high-protein (e.g., marine-based) diet is unlikely to produce a high caries rate, suggesting that the pattern they observe may indicate a shift over time from a high carbohydrate to a high protein diet. This interpretation conflicts with previous artifactual and faunal studies that show heavy use of marine resources and little plant food processing in all periods on the Channel Islands. They point out that the early period Channel Island sites do contain a significant number of apparent digging stick weights, however, that may indicate an emphasis on roots and tubers in the early period diet. Looking at sex differences in caries ratios, they find that at Canada Verde, females have a much higher rate of carious lesions than males, while at Skull Gulch, males and females have nearly equal rates of dental caries. They suggest that in the early period hunting and gathering economy, men had greater access to high protein foods than did women; the implication is that men ate some of the game at the kill site. With a shift to a marine based economy, men and women would have had approximately equal access to shellfish, resulting in a more evenly distributed caries rate.

Although less than half of their paper is actually focused on sex based dietary differences and the possible implications of these patterns for gender roles, Walker and Erlandson do provide an intriguing example of the study of prehistoric gender roles based on an integration of skeletal and artifactual evidence. DLG

*mortuary analysis/osteology/subsistence/division of labor/Channel Islands/California/United States, Western*

178. WALKER, SUSAN 1983. Women and housing in classical Greece. In *Images of women in antiquity,* edited by Averil Camoon and Amelie Kuhrt, 81-91. Croom Helm, London.

Walker addresses the issue of female seclusion in Classical Greece by combining documentary information with archaeological examples of domestic houses. The documents indicate that seclusion was characteristic of wealthy households, and Walker suggests that men with wealth and citizenship to pass on to their sons would be extremely concerned with the legitimacy of their children and would seclude their wives to secure their paternity.

Relevant documentary information includes the association of women with private homes and men with public buildings. Various sources present homes as architecturally modest, not reflecting actual distinctions of wealth, and Walker suggests that this modesty of housing reflects the ideal modesty of women. The house is described as a production center for food, clothing, and children, where even wealthy women with servants were expected to do some domestic tasks. The *andron*, or male dining room, was a particularly sensitive area where it was important to prevent the meeting of women and male guests. One document describes a two-story house as consisting of male apartments on the lower floor and female ones above, suggesting that household space was in fact conceptually gendered.

Since no second stories have survived in Athens or Attica, there is a potential difficulty in defining gendered space archaeologically. But women in documents are also associated with workrooms, storerooms, and hearths, all of which have been identified in sites. With this in mind, the author examines the floor plans of an Attic and an Athenian house and compares them to one in Euboea and to a modern Islamic house in

Nigeria. All of the Greek houses appear to be well-to-do, judging from the materials found in them. Walker identifies the rooms as either male use areas, female use areas, or unassigned, intermediate areas, based upon the isolation of workrooms from the *andron*, the protected nature of the house entrance, and the visibility of potentially female areas from potentially male ones.

The author concludes that something can be said about the gendered nature of household space even without evidence of the actual "women's quarters," but that this depends on correct functional identification of the rooms and may be muddled by sequential occupations and remodeling of houses.

This article cogently lays out the basic facts of an important issue, and it implicitly raises a number of important archaeological issues of interpretation. First, because this article considers only wealthy households where seclusion is expected, the author focuses on how to divide the space between the sexes rather than whether the house is so divided or what is the nature of the division. Comparison with a poor, presumably unsecluded household seems crucial. If domestic modesty makes it difficult to tell a poor house from a rich one architecturally, there should be consequent difficulties in defining a wealth-related practice like seclusion architecturally. Second, definitions of male and female rooms should be made consistently with regard to factors like visibility and isolation. Walker seems to oscillate in defining both the Athenian house, where the *andron* has a separate entrance, and the Attic house, where alien men would have had to pass the female rooms, with a direct line of sight into them, as secluded. Finally, the author uses several different concepts interchangeably, although it would be useful to separate them. It is unclear whether she is thinking primarily in terms of prohibited areas, activity areas where certain tasks are performed, or conceptual male and female realms (as might be indicated by the upper/lower distinction, for instance). These are gendered spaces in different senses and are not by definition secluded space.

Given a context in which women are secluded, there are at least two realms of gender relationships. Walker's perspective concerns the relation between women of the household and outside men, but it would also be interesting to look at the relationships between men and women of one household, including those between owners and servants. SF

*household analysis/architecture/spatial analysis/classical archaeology/Greece/Mediterranean*


179. WALL, DIANA DIZEREGA 1991. Sacred dinners and secular teas: Constructing domesticity in mid-nineteenth-century New York. *Historical Archaeology* 25(4):69-81.

In this article, Wall presents the results of her analysis of the ceramics from two mid-nineteenth century home sites in Greenwich Village, New York. Wall compares teaware and tableware from two middle class households—one representing the lower middle class and one representing the upper middle class—in order to determine "whether women at the wealthier and poorer ends of the middle class spectrum were using goods to construct similar or different domestic worlds in New York in the mid-19th century" (p. 69).

Wall first briefly discusses the development of the urban middle class in the nineteenth century and the role of women (who took charge of most aspects of domestic life, including shopping for the home, by the mid-nineteenth century) within this system. She then compares the tablewares and teawares found at each of the two sites. She finds that at both houses the tableware is very similar (mostly white granite ironstone in the Gothic pattern) while the teaware is quite different: in the poor middle class household the teaware is quite plain, similar to the tableware, whereas in the richer household a fancier decorated porcelain was used for tea. Wall suggests that her findings indicate that meals (as evidenced by tableware) had the same meaning in both households. She speculates that the Gothic tableware, like the Gothic dining room furniture popular at the time, may indicate a sacredness associated with family meals. The teawares, however, suggest that while both households apparently served tea with meals, only the wealthier family held more elaborate, formal afternoon teas. Wall speculates that the woman of the wealthier household "may well have used her dishes in a series of competitive displays designed to impress her friends and acquaintances with the refined gentility of her family" (p. 79).

As Wall herself points out, this study is a limited one, but it does have interesting implications for future research. Despite a small data set, this is an insightful, theoretical analysis of historic materials. DLG

*historical archaeology/ceramic analysis/New York/United States, Northeast*

180. WATSON, PATTY JO AND MARY C. KENNEDY 1991. The development of horticulture in the eastern Woodlands of North America: Women's role. In *Engendering Archaeology: Women and Prehistory*, edited by Joan M. Gero and Margaret W. Conkey, 255-275. Basil Blackwell, Cambridge, MA.

Watson and Kennedy's article is largely a critique of Bruce Smith's (1987) coevolutionary sequence for the origins of agriculture in eastern North America. Smith suggests that between 8000 and 5000 BP, river systems in eastern North America stabilized, and by 6500 BP anthropogenic localities occupied by both humans and weedy, colonizing plants developed. These localities were characterized by four factors important in the domestication of native plants: (1) increased sunlight in areas of human occupation through removal of portions of the canopy or overstory; (2) fertile soils associated with organic enrichment; (3) continually disturbed soil favoring pioneer plants; and (4) the constant reintroduction of seeds of edible species in areas of human occupation. These conditions selected plants with larger seeds and thinner seed coats. At first humans tolerated edible or useful species while ignoring or removing other species. With time, humans began to more systematically promote the growth of useful plants while excluding other species. Finally, humans began to plant seeds and manage gardens, so that by ca. 3500 BP morphologically distinct domesticates appear.

Using ethnographic evidence and more general comparative data on the sexual division of labor in foraging and farming societies, Watson and Kennedy conclude that it was probably women who were most closely involved with the cultivation and maintenance of plants and gardens. Women have greater expertise regarding plants, they argue, and hence a gradualistic coevolutionary process where the plants all but domesticate themselves robs women of agency in economic change. It plays into the scheme:

women>gather>plants

which in turn fits into the scheme:

women>gather>plants>passive, *whereas* men>hunt>animals>active.

Hence they find Smith's scenario objectionable because it attempts to keep women passive rather than recognizing them as active agents of change. Similarly, Prentice's (1986) suggestion that the adoption of non-native domesticates may have been facilitated by shamans and ritual uses is seen as forcing women into passive roles, since it implies that if active agency and innovation were involved, women did not participate. They characterize his argument with the scheme:

man>trade>ceremony>active>innovation>cultivation>domestication

Watson and Kennedy also suggest that scenarios for the rise of Northern Flint maize ignore the role of women as horticulturalists. Smaller numbers of kernel rows in this important variety have been seen as botanical adaptations to short growing seasons, unchecked competition from weeds, and drought. But Watson and Kennedy reject this suggestion, describing how women horticulturalists adapted this import to new conditions, feeding "many thousands of people for hundreds of years" (p. 266). Attributing the decrease in row numbers to different environmental conditions, they argue, does not recognize the efforts of women who experimented with different tillage practices and genetic strains to produce Northern Flint. Watson and Kennedy note that until conclusive evidence is marshaled to support either Smith's or Prentice's theory, they "prefer to pursue a third alternative: prehistoric women were fully capable not only of conscious action, but also of innovation" (p. 269).

Certainly discussions of the rise of native agriculture in North America are too few in the archaeological literature, and any thoughtful addition to that literature should be welcomed. Watson and Kennedy argue strongly for the consideration of women as active innovators and experimenters, and against a view of women as passive witnesses to change. At the same time, their argument is unfortunate in several respects. First and perhaps foremost, it takes offense where none was given. Smith's article, for example, doesn't assert that one gender or another was responsible for agriculture. Concerned less with the relations between men and women than between humans and plants, it attempts to account for the rise of agriculture and the gradual decrease of seed coats and increases in seed size over several thousand years. It requires a bit of a stretch to see this as insulting the knowledge or agency of either gender, especially since if observed and directly promoted, these morphological changes might have occurred far more rapidly. Smith's account may explain why these changes occurred more slowly without demeaning the intelligence or intentionality of the men or women involved (see Smith #155 for his own rebuttal). If criticisms of other authors' real or imagined views that slight the ingenuity and agency of women are discounted, Watson and Kennedy's article simply says that women domesticated plants in prehistoric North America, and they did it on purpose. AWB

*References cited*
Prentice, Guy 1986. Origins of plant domestication in eastern North America: Promoting the individual in archaeological theory. *Southeastern Archaeology* 5:103-119.

Smith, Bruce 1987. The independent domestication of indigenous seed-bearing plants in eastern North America. In *Emergent Horticultural Economies of the Eastern Woodlands,* edited by William Keegan, 3-47. Center for Archaeological Investigation Occasional Paper 7. Southern Illinois University, Carbondale.

*division of labor/agricultural origins/feminist critique/postprocessualism/trade/United States, Midwest/United States, Southeast/Smith, Bruce D./Prentice, Guy*


181. WEBER, CARMEN A. 1991. The genius of the orangery: Women and eighteenth century Chesapeake gardens. In *The Archaeology of Gender: Proceedings of the Twenty-Second Annual Conference of the Archaeological Association of the University of Calgary,* edited by Dale Walde and Noreen D. Willows, 263-269. Archaeological Association, The University of Calgary, Calgary.

Weber's article is concerned with the relationship of women, gardens and architecture in eighteenth century America. It is Weber's contention that the present day involvement of American women in gardening and garden clubs--including the subsequent excavation of gardens--has a long and varied history, and can be used to provide insight into the roles of women in garden design, and their control over its use. Her premise is that gardening offered a means for women of that time period of establishing a degree of control over their own lives. She further argues that such a relationship can be made manifest through an examination of the historical and archaeological record of the time period.

The article uses a case history approach, focusing on the life history of one Margaret Carroll of Maryland as representative of a class of women who used the vehicle of greenhouses or "orangeries" to assert themselves into their society. To quote Weber, she employs "an anthropological approach utilizing historical research, archaeological and architectural investigation to examine the material culture of the eighteenth century" (p. 268). To a degree she succeeds in presenting a body of data that supports the premise that women played a dominant role in constructing maintaining and, perhaps most important, displaying the products of the greenhouse (oranges and lemons, hence the term "orangery") as a way of symbolizing their status. For example, one of the stronger arguments used is the correspondence from President George Washington to Tench Tilghman regarding the construction and provisioning of a greenhouse at Mount Vernon. Tilghman is presented as deferring to Margaret Carroll as the authority he consults.

It should also be stated that Weber's case history approach has the weakness of being relatively atheoretical; a thesis is presented and facts are brought to bear to support it. Yet there is little or no presentation of an argument about how or why involvement with gardening is, *a priori*, an especially important power relationship *vis* the rest of eighteenth century society. An even more glaring omission is a theoretical discussion of the class aspect of the historical figures under examination. Although Weber clearly indicates the degree of social stratification of the people in her study, how their affiliation with a landed, and monied, gentry relates to their position as women is left unanswered. This is especially critical because there are broader sociocultural, political, economic and ideological concerns that can be addressed using a data base and methodology such as Weber presents. MRF

*historical archaeology/architecture/division of labor/Chesapeake Bay/United States, Northeast*

182. WHELAN, MARY K. 1991. Gender and archaeology: Mortuary studies and the search for the origins of gender differentiation. In *The Archaeology of Gender: Proceedings of the Twenty-Second Annual Conference of the Archaeological Association of the University of Calgary,* edited by Dale Walde and Noreen D. Willows, 358-365. Archaeological Association, The University of Calgary, Calgary.

Whelan's intent is to problematize the origins of gender systems (culturally recognized male and female roles and values) in a way that is not androcentric, and to explore the evidence available to address this issue. She criticizes the reconstruction of early hominid gender roles as reflections of our own gender system. Studies which assume a modern-looking division of labor and public/domestic dichotomy millions of years in the past lend "natural" credence to current social relations. She suggests that it is best to look for evidence of past genders and then question their nature, rather than imposing androcentric constructs.

The fact that gender is a cultural construct creates problems for exploring its origins, since the origin of culture is itself a problem. Whelan asserts that in late *Homo erectus* times, when hominids moved into ecologically different areas but did not speciate, they must have been more dependent on culture than on biological adaptation. Before this period hominid culture could not have been enough like human culture for the concept of gender to be an appropriate one.

Four approaches to studying gender are discussed: ethnographic analogy, mortuary studies, art, and contextual analysis. For *Homo erectus,* mortuary and artistic data do not exist, analogy is deemed inappropriate, and contextual analysis has yet to be tried.

The Middle and Upper Paleolithic are more promising; there is more evidence, and several arguments have been made about the construction of social boundaries that suggest gender might be a relevant category. Harrold's analysis of Middle Paleolithic burials suggested differentiation by sex, grave goods being found with several male burials and no female ones. Two things make this a problematic interpretation. First, skeletons from different populations sexed by only a few elements have been shown to consistently mis-sex females as males. Second, most of Harrold's females were Asian and his males European, so the pattern could be regional rather than gender-linked. In the Upper Paleolithic both male and female burials contain grave goods, but Whelan notes that the problem of mis-sexing burials persists. Artistic data are not available until the Upper Paleolithic. Whelan argues that female figurines, regardless of their function, show that female aspects were being used and emphasized in cultural ways, indicating the existence of gender. She suggests that burial data, if correctly sexed, might support this conclusion. Analogy and contextual analysis are not discussed for these periods.

This paper shows the conceptual and methodological difficulties inherent in the question of the origin of gender, and does not attempt to say more than the evidence indicates. If this is meager, it is also refreshingly free of unwarranted androcentric speculations.

Several issues raised by this article need to be addressed by future research. Given that other primates have sexually differentiated behaviors and even tasks, and that early hominids might be imagined to have had the same, how should one understand the origin of gender out of something that was sexually differentiated, but not gendered? How and under what circumstances did existing differences become culturally elaborated and new ones culturally created? Regarding art and mortuary data, it would also be useful to have some discussion of what burials and figurines might indicate about social identities in general, and how they are expected to relate to gender identities particularly. Contextual analysis, which was introduced early in the paper but then abandoned, could be useful in dealing with data like figurines that are usually very much de-contextualized. SF

*mortuary analysis/art/feminist critique/ethnographic analogy/Paleolithic/Europe*


183. WHELAN, MARY K. 1991. Gender and historical archaeology: Eastern Dakota patterns in the nineteenth century. *Historical Archaeology* 25(4):17-32.

After some introductory statements concerning gender in archaeology, historical archaeology, and how historical archaeology can contribute to Native American histories, Whelan shows how archaeological data from a nineteenth century Sioux cemetery in Minnesota can be approached from an historical perspective that incorporates gender (as opposed to sex) as an organizing principle. First, she describes the Blackdog Burial site, which dates between 1830-1860, and the 24 burials (comprised of 39-41 individuals: 6 male, 6 female, and the rest not definitively assigned to sex) that were excavated as a salvage project.

Next, Whelan takes a few pages to examine "The Archaeology of Sex versus Gender," specifically in regard to mortuary analysis (pp. 22-25). She argues that it is important for archaeologists to make this distinction, since "the Western conflation of sex and gender can lead to the impression that biology, and not culture, is responsible for defining gender roles" (p. 23), and due to the history of alternate gender roles (such as the berdache) in North America, which may be liable to "ethnocentric misinterpretations" by mortuary analysts (p. 24). Whelan takes great care in describing how sex is assigned to the skeletal material ("independently of the artifacts associated with each burial, and multivariate sexing and aging methods were used when possible" [p. 25]).

Whelan does not find perfect correlations between artifacts (of any type) and sex in the preliminary analysis. In her words, "gender defined as isomorphic with sex was not visible at the Blackdog Burial site. This probably indicates that mortuary contexts were not the primary arena in which the Dakota signaled adult gender roles, rather than that such roles were absent from the culture" (p. 26). It is also possible that perishable items were used in mortuary ritual. However, three artifact types (pipestone pipes, mirrors, and pouches) were restricted to seven individuals, six of whom were male. Whelan suggests that "the predominance of one sex (male) in this group suggests that possession of these artifacts did signal a gender category, because sex played an important though not exclusive role in defining membership" (p. 26). She argues that rather than dismissing this woman's burial as exceptional, "it is suggested here that she was a fully participating member of the gender category, as much as any of the men" (p. 26), and provides some ethnographic and ethnohistoric parallels for this practice.

Furthermore, although comparable numbers and types of beads are found with both male and female adults, Whelan did find some correlations between bead color and sex, "most likely related to differences in the types of decorative designs sewn on masculine and feminine garments" (p. 26). Other artifact correlations show that age probably was a significant factor in regard to burial goods, and that differential sexual status (as signified by numbers of categories of artifacts) was not visible.

Whelan pulls together an interesting assortment of historical and archaeological information on the historic Blackdog villages and the cemetery (including some contemporary Euro-American art showing the village in relation to the cemetery), and her careful use of gender as a concept quite different from sex is commendable. The strict methodology used to assign sex to the skeletons (apart from their associated artifacts) may increase the number of individuals of "indeterminate" sex, but this seems to be the only way to avoid confusing gender with sex when the two may not be identical. Whelan reminds us that there is good ethnographic evidence for gender blurring or crossing, or even an alternative gender category (i.e., berdache) in Native North America. The few gender-related artifact distributions Whelan describes are tantalizing, as is the evidence for a woman buried with traditionally "male" accouterments, but her sample is so small (12 individuals) that despite the advantage gained through the use of some very interesting historic documentation, few general conclusions can be drawn. SLD

*historical archaeology/mortuary analysis/ethnohistory/Sioux/Dakota/United States and Canada, Plains*

184. WHITTLESEY, STEPHANIE M. 1991. Beyond anatomy: The sociology of gender in Arizona archaeology. In *The Archaeology of Gender: Proceedings of the Twenty-Second Annual Conference of the Archaeological Association of the University of Calgary,* edited by Dale Walde and Noreen D. Willows, 226-232. Archaeological Association, The University of Calgary, Calgary.

Whittlesey's paper focuses on the sociological effects of personal roles on career advancement and success in archaeology, an issue less widely explored than many other issues related to gender. She argues that responsibilities concomitant with nonprofessional roles explain significant disparities in the career paths of women and men working in academic and cultural resource management archaeology in the United States.

In her attempt to move beyond "anecdote and rhetoric," Whittlesey provides the results of a survey on archaeologists working in Arizona. She mailed questionnaires to all women who participate professionally in archaeology in Arizona, and to an equal number of men, selected to match the professional positions of the women surveyed (p. 226). Students were excluded because their careers are not fully launched. Forty-two individuals, or about 50%, responded to the survey.

Although women and men are nearly equally represented, the numbers of respondents varied greatly between different career categories. People in academic departments replied most frequently. None of the men working for state agencies returned their questionnaires, and women employed by federal agencies and private resource management seldom responded. Whittlesey, however, does not quantify the differential response rates in her discussion. Although these data do not represent all Arizona archaeologists, Whittlesey suggests that they are useful since they identify several trends which warrant further consideration.

The women and men in the sample are classified into four categories based on their marital and parental status: (1) single (including divorced and widowed); (2) married; (3) married, with children living at home; and (4) single, with children living at home. Next, Whittlesey considers relative professional success attained by men and women in each category. For this study, five criteria are used as an index of professional success: (1) a Ph.D. degree; (2) average number of refereed publications (books and articles); (3) mean number of journal articles; (4) funding from agencies (excluding cultural resource management contracts); and (5) attendance at more than three out-of-state conferences per year. These data are summarized in tabular form, along with the average ages of people in each category.

Whittlesey reports three major trends. First, gender influences professional success. Women hold fewer doctorates, publish less frequently, have lower average numbers of journal articles, and obtain grant funding less frequently. Second, martial status influences professional status for both women and men. Single people earn fewer doctorates, have lower average numbers of refereed publications, and are less likely to obtain grant funding. Finally, parental status exerts a significant influence on professional success.

Archaeologists with children hold fewer doctorate degrees, have lower average numbers of journal publications, and are less likely to obtain grants. As a whole, single parents are the least professionally successful group considered.

To provide a greater sociological context, Whittlesey also considers respondents' perceptions of professional success, mobility and nonprofessional roles, job activity, and publication ethics. She suggests that both genders, but especially women, must choose between professional success and personal fulfillment as a parent. Recognizing that measures of professional success in archaeology require an enormous energy commitment at the expense of personal, nonprofessional roles, Whittlesey asks the reader to consider the ultimate effect on the discipline and its practitioners should this trend persist. She suggests that archaeologists need to re-examine and re-evaluate the system of rewards within the discipline. Neither academia nor cultural resource management consider how family responsibilities impinge on professional development of both women and men. Whittlesey suggests "we may do well to examine the idea that *these criteria are themselves male-biased*, created in the years when women were often not members of the professional community, and continue to be employed predominantly by men" (p. 231).

Whittlesey's article is a concise and informative sociological critique of many levels of gender bias manifest by the different professional achievements of a sample of professional archaeologists. Even though her study does not represent all archaeologists employed in Arizona, let alone the entire discipline, it is a useful contribution because of the identification and evaluation of many biases that quietly but substantially affect the professional success. Whittlesey is successful in her attempt to begin a more systematic examination of how personal roles exert pervasive influences which go beyond anatomical differences. She challenges us to decide whether "simple awareness that these biases exist can [possibly] help ease the difficulty" (p. 231). KFA

*discrimination/sociopolitics of archaeology/Arizona/United States, Southwest*

185. WILDESON, L.E. 1980. The status of women in archaeology: Results of a preliminary survey. *Anthropology Newsletter* 21(5):5-8.

Wildeson and the Society for American Archaeology Committee on the Status of Women in Archaeology surveyed 273 female archaeologists, including 164 listed in the *AAA Guide to Departments* and an additional 109 identified through chain letters. Of these, 39% replied, including women holding academic (34%) and non-academic (46%) appointments. Graduate students were not included in the survey, as the Committee wished to focus on "working" archaeologists.

Summaries of background data for the respondents are presented, permitting Wildeson to create a composite of a "representative" woman archaeologist who believes:

> that equality is the major issue facing women today and that she is not getting
> it (especially with respect to salary, tenure, and training opportunities). What
> she considers a really good salary is at least $4000 above the mean for all women
> archaeologists.... She believes that a number of her responses to the questions
> would have been different if she were male. (p. 7)

Data collected included both quantitative information on age, age group, salary, highest degree, etc., as well as qualitative data culled from responses to open-ended questions. The data indicate that women in archaeology face serious impediments both to becoming established in the discipline and to professional advancement.

Wildeson sees her data as revealing several persistent (and unfounded) myths. The idea that academic archaeologists earn less than their public and private sector counterparts is not supported by the information she collected; academics actually enjoy higher mean salaries than their non-academic counterparts. Nor are women forced into lower-status governmental positions. Most respondents indicated that they had chosen their jobs and saw themselves less as devalued than as pioneers. There is a brief suggestion that women archaeologists may be doing better than their counterparts in other subdisciplines. The article also includes references to earlier studies, many not included in these annotations, examining the role and status of women in particular areas of the discipline. AWB

*discrimination/sociopolitics of archaeology/United States*


186. WILK, RICHARD R. AND WILLIAM L. RATHJE 1982. Household archaeology. *American Behavioral Scientist* 25(6):617-639.

"Household archaeology" presents the authors' views on a number of issues of specific interest to archaeology: household size, household composition, and the archaeological implications of differential household forms producing and distributing items in different contexts. These factors are discussed in the context of a proposed model detailing variables such as environment, household demography, social organization, and economic activities, and their linkage to material culture in regard to modeling evolutionary change.

In the case of this article, which is explicitly concerned with broad outlines of domestic composition and productive activities, it is appropriate to address how the authors deal with gender, the division of labor, and the attendant concern with how economic practices are transformed through time. Those looking for a detailed account of gender roles will be disappointed, however. Indeed, gender activities of any kind are rarely specified by Wilk and Rathje; specific attention to female roles is encountered only briefly under the section heading of "reproductive functions" (pp. 630-631). According to the authors, in societies where a woman's contribution to the subsistence base is important, a large cooperative household frees women to work by distributing child care tasks throughout the cooperative. Women's labor is said to be especially important in the transitional stage of hunting and gathering to agriculture and can be expected to be found there in conjunction with the pooling of reproductive labor and cooperative child caring tasks.

Not all discussions of a limited scale can detail everything to be said about social organization. A discussion that takes as its starting point households and associated economic practices, however, may be expected to include a more energetic discussion of how households are differentially organized around gender roles. Wilk and Rathje simply comment on child care tasks by women and assert that women's labor is more important in an initial phase of the introduction of agriculture to a hunting and gathering society. But this point only highlights the major problem area with such evolutionary schemes, even ones painted in the broadest strokes, whereby assumptions and hidden premises are put forth as true assertions of social reality when in fact they may only represent a methodological bias. MRF

*household analysis/division of labor/ethnoarchaeology/ethnographic analogy*


187. WILLIAMS, BARBARA 1981. *Breakthrough: Women in Archaeology.* Walker and Company, New York.

This collection of women's biographies seems to be aimed primarily at high school students, especially women interested in archaeology or in becoming an archaeologist. It highlights "the many difficulties that exist in pursuing that profession" (p. xvii), emphasizing women's problems in combining a successful marriage and career. The sketches outline how and why six women became archaeologists, describing family support (both social and financial), sexism in graduate school and in the discipline, mentors, and how archaeology changed in the 1960s and 1970s. The women described (Cynthia Irwin-Williams, Jane Holden Kelley, Karen Olsen Bruhns, Leslie E. Wildesen, Ernestine Green, and Mary Eubanks Dunn) are shown as exceptional individuals who had special opportunities or who sacrificed or tolerated a great deal.

Although it is interesting to read individual life histories, these stories are deliberately tame and uncontroversial. They lack gritty details about fieldwork or the personal politics and relationships that make up the stories that most archaeologists tell about themselves or each other. Furthermore, although the word "breakthrough" is used in the title, there is little sense that these women were the vanguards of a changing field—perhaps in 1981 it was unclear if female archaeologists had or would change archaeology. In general, *Breakthrough in Archaeology* is traditionally (certainly not feminist) oriented. SLD

*discrimination/graduate training/history of archaeology/sociopolitics of archaeology/United States, Southwest/United States, Southeast*


188. WILLOUGHBY, PAMELA R. 1991. Human origins and the sexual division of labour: An archaeological perspective. In *The Archaeology of Gender: Proceedings of the Twenty-Second Annual Conference of the Archaeological Association of the University of Calgary,* edited by Dale Walde and Noreen D. Willows, 284-291. Archaeological Association, The University of Calgary, Calgary.

In this article, Pamela Willoughby addresses hominid and human origins, with specific focus on the role of sexual division of labor in this evolution. Criticizing the field of paleoanthropology for its overemphasis on "data-free" theory, she challenges the assumptions made by some researchers that a sexual division of labor with male hunting served as the primary lever for bipedalism and encephalization (Washburn and Lancaster 1968), and is equally critical of attempts to explain this early human evolution as a result of mother-child plant foraging groups (Zihlman and Tanner 1978, and see Zihlman 1991, in the same volume). Instead, Willoughby turns to the archaeological evidence from the Lower and Middle Paleolithic. Recognizing that the fossil data base is insufficient to test models for early hominid evolution such as bipedalism and encephalization, she focuses on the potential of Paleolithic archaeology for answering questions about sexual divisions of labor. She contests Isaac's use of ethnographic analogy for identifying such labor divisions in the Paleolithic but allies herself with his concern to identify the strategic contributions of both sexes in adaptive strategies, seeing this as a critical component of human evolution. While Willoughby is skeptical that archaeology will ever be able to identify women's and men's areas or assemblages in the Paleolithic, she suggests that the only way to develop understandings of the role of sexual division of labor in human evolution is by developing models that can identify patterns of relationship deviant from any ethnographically known social configurations. She uses ethnographic and primate studies to identify parallels in sexual divisions of labor (positing that females are normally the plant preparers in both groups), and interprets the spheroids in the Developed Oldowan as female tools.

This article offers a valuable critique of many unsupported assumptions that have been incorporated into paleanthropological and archaeological interpretations of human evolution, and it makes a sane plea for closer attention to data in these lofty attempts. It is unfortunate that the article ends before Willoughby gets into the interesting arena of how to go about studying sexual division of labor. Willoughby notes that it is incorrect to use the ethnographic record uncritically to interpret the Paleolithic, or any other prehistoric situation for that matter, and that the best approach is to generate models that can account for the observed behavioral patterning independent of known analogous situations. Her comparison of ethnographic and primate systems provides a useful technique for building such models but fails to commit to it. Instead of using these data to construct critical models of the evolution of human behavioral systems from primate-like ones and then testing these with the Paleolithic record, she presents an ineffective analysis of a single class of artifacts from the Developed Oldowan.

Willoughby's treatment of Developed Oldowan is ambiguous. She implies that plant processing is a universal female behavior in both primates and humans and then assigns Developed Oldowan spheroids as possible components of female tool kits based on untested functional assumptions about the spheroids. While I do not intend to criticize Willoughby for attempting to recognize sexual division of labor by trying to identify sexually specific classes of artifacts, her analysis is circular, relying on behavioral assumptions to identify functional classes which would then 'reaffirm' the behavioral assumptions. Instead of trying to understand the evolution of sexual division of labor as a fundamental cultural system of social organization (if it is that), she implicitly identifies a universal sexual division of labor presumably shared between primates and human foragers. Why should we be surprised that spheroids were female artifacts if they were plant processing tools and her model is correct? What would it tell us about human evolution in the Developed Oldowan? To be fair, it seems that this analysis was not intended to be a significant part of the article which is predominantly a legitimate critique of unsubstantiated conclusions in paleoanthropological studies of human evolution. This analysis could be better developed and would add considerably to the article by showing how researchers could address questions of human cultural evolution more critically and more carefully than they have before.

We are perhaps overly eager to see "sexual division of labor" in our models of cultural systems of organization. Willoughby, following Isaac, takes this position. This prevents us from considering alternative organizations which may or may not exist at different times and in different social contexts. While there are biological constraints on males and females that perforce divide some tasks and encourage the division of others, there is no *a priori* reason to assume that the salient division of labor in a given society is based on sex. A more productive approach is one that considers "divisions of labor" and explicitly attempts to identify the axes of division in given cultural contexts to construct a more accurate picture of the variability in patterns of social organization and task differentiation. JBF

*division of labor/ethnographic analogy/hominids/Paleolithic/Oldowan/Africa*

189. WOOLFREY, SANDRA, PRINCE CHITWOOD AND NORMAN E. WAGNER 1976. Who made the pipes? A study of decorative motifs on Middleport pipe and pottery collections. *Ontario Archaeology* 27:3-11.

This brief comparison of decorative motifs on Iroquois ceramic pipes and domestic pottery is an early but relatively unknown attempt to attribute gender to artifacts' producers. The authors assume that women made the late prehistoric Middleport period pottery, as women are the only potters described in numerous historic Iroquois accounts. One report from 1644, however, states that men made pipes, although the pipe material—stone or ceramic—is not specified. Woolfrey et al. suggest that if the correlation of pottery designs and ceramic pipe designs is high, "one would expect that, either the pottery makers and pipe makers were one and the same, or, that one of the two had influenced the decorative art of the other" (p. 3).

The design motifs from pottery and pipes from five Middleport period sites in Ontario are presented, along with pipe and pottery motifs from two later prehistoric sites in the same area. In general, many of the pipes have decorative motifs found on some percentage of the sites' ceramics, but "it is clear that the pipe makers were selective in their use of these motifs" (p. 5). The authors conclude that this "makes it tempting to assume that the pipe makers and pottery makers at any one site reflect different cultural traditions perhaps to clan or previous village affiliations" (p. 5-6). In other words, men made the pipes. Woolfrey et al. tenatively suggest the pipe's decoration may reflect designs used by men's matrilineal clans.

An exploration of alternative explanations for the patterns of pottery versus pipe decoration described would strengthen the authors' argument. Although Woolfrey et al. do not need to draw deeply from the ethnohistoric record for this succinct study, there is an extensive literature on women's roles in Iroquois society (Spittal 1990), and archaeologists interested in gender in prehistory may profitably work with that information and more sophisticated analyses to test this report's premises. SLD

*References cited*
Spittal, W. G. (editor) 1990. *Iroquois Women: An Anthology*. Iroqrafts, Ohsweken, Ontario.

*ceramic analysis/ceramic production/division of labor/Iroquois/Ontario/Canada*

190. WRIGHT, RITA P. 1991. Women's labor and pottery production in prehistory. In *Engendering Archaeology: Women and Prehistory*, edited by Joan M. Gero and Margaret W. Conkey, 194-223. Basil Blackwell, Cambridge, MA.

Wright takes issue with the commonly expressed assumption "that labor extensive activities with low economic yields are engaged in by [all] women, whereas labor intensive activities are innovative and lead to commercialization, the [exclusive] domain of men" (p. 195). She contends that this is an expression of the ideology of separate spheres of work for women and men which pervades contemporary western thought and colors our understanding of the organization of labor. Wright adopts the perspective that women as well as men were active in the development of pottery technologies. Her major goal is to "demonstrate how contemporary concepts of gender and the work place have worked to bias not only our understanding of prehistoric pottery production but also our interpretation of its development" (p. 196). To achieve this goal, discussion is organized in three parts: (1) an evaluation of how women have been passively portrayed or marginalized in ethnographies of pottery production; (2) a consideration of the ecological and evolutionary approaches used to address questions of the divisions of labor; and (3) an examination of the development of pottery production with respect to the rise of the Harappan civilization between 6000 and 1800 BC.

In virtually all ethnographies of pottery production and gender, "the word *potter* has been equated with the individual who *forms* pots, that is with the person who shapes the clay while it is in the plastic state" (p. 198, emphasis in original). Individuals who assist with other tasks essential to ceramic manufacture are invisible. Furthermore, because the division of labor in pottery production may be organized by gender, there are many discrepancies in the ethnographic literature with respect to the sex or gender of the producers. Given this oversimplification of the manufacturing process, Wright concludes that pottery may be both a male and female craft, and that women are usually integral to production. There is little basis for the stereotype that women do not participate in ceramic production for consumption outside the household (p. 199).

Next, Wright considers the ecological and evolutionary approaches used to investigate the development and organization of gender-based divisions of labor. Researchers who adopt an ecological approach view a division of labor in pottery production as an adaptive response resulting from scheduling conflicts, for example. Researchers with an evolutionary perspective account for the differentiation of gender roles as an outcome of the ideological factors and changing sociopolitical relations accompanying the development of complex societies (p. 200). Wright demonstrates how both approaches rely on ethnographic sources to establish critical thresholds for significant shifts in the organization of production. Although these studies view gender as socially constructed relationships, they emphasize the more general issue of the women's subordination with the evolution from pre-state to state level society. Wright concludes that this shift in emphasis and revisionist constructs allows a new set of explanatory frameworks to be applied to understanding the origins and development of dramatic changes in divisions of labor.

Wright examines origins, technology, and the cultural context of Harappan pottery manufacture to determine whether revisionist interpretations of the changing organization of labor accompanying state formation are truly free of androcentric bias. She assesses how advances in ceramic technology complement or enhance other cultural developments, especially in regard to women. Wright addresses associated sets of technical achievements, particularly cooking and plant domestication. She also investigates the spatial arrangement of production and the question of commercialization. Wright concludes that the archaeological evidence does not support the exclusion of women from pottery production with the emergence of the state. In fact, she suggests that ceramics were manufactured within at least two, or possibly three, different contexts near the end of the Harappan archaeological sequence: in small-scale workshops in towns, as seen previously in the region; in workshops located in segregated craft quarters administered by a central Mohenjodaro authority; and in workshops administered by kinship groups at Harappa (p. 213). None of these contexts exclude women's participation, and the lack of evidence for formal administrative control at the Harappan workshops suggests that ceramic production did not significantly change with the emergence of the state, which poses a challenge to widely accepted evolutionary models concerning the relationship between the state and kinship groups.

This article is a notable contribution to the study of social divisions of labor. Wright presents a thoughtful evaluation of how women have been passively portrayed or marginalized in ethnographies of pottery production and the ecological and evolutionary approaches used to address the organization of labor. The Harappan case successfully illustrates why archaeologists cannot make the *a priori* assumption that women are removed from pottery production when ceramics are produced for consumption outside the household. Wright is unable to identify women and men in the Harappan record of changing ceramic manufacture, but her paper demonstrates how the explication of gender roles in past production processes is not necessarily hindered by difficulties in recognizing gender in the archaeological record. In fact, Wright's examination of the relationship between states and kinship groups challenges archaeologists to address the ideological underpinnings of the division of labor and gender. KFA

*processualism/division of labor/ceramic analysis/Harappa/Pakistan/Asia*

191. WYLIE, ALISON 1992. The interplay of evidential constraints and political interests: Recent archaeological research on gender. *American Antiquity* 57(1):15-35.

In this article, Alison Wylie expands previous arguments (#192, 193) regarding the role and epistemological implications of feminist political agendas in the recent florescence of an explicit sex/gender focus in North American archaeology. Her purpose is to describe how the feminist movement inspired an interest in women and gender and to show how such a focus can actually "enhance the conceptual integrity and empirical adequacy of archaeological knowledge claims." She details how the archaeology of gender was legitimated by the anti-positivist, anti- and postprocessual archaeologies emerging in the 1980s, and how it has been conceptually maneuvered into the "hyperrelativist" camp associated with postprocessual archaeology. While Wylie takes on and clarifies a number of important epistemological issues in this article, her overall goal is to show that a feminist (politically) inspired archaeology of gender can and *must* be conceived of as engaged in conventional scientific methods which are, in the final analysis, non-relativistic.

Wylie begins by asking why an archaeology of gender has only now begun to take root and why, in the words of skeptics, it should ever develop at all. According to Wylie, a political and analytic focus on women and gender has been slower to develop in archaeology than in many of its related fields such as sociocultural anthropology and history because of the strong hold of "processual" archaeology through the 1970s and 1980s, which rejected the explanatory relevance of internal "ethnographic" variables like gender and class. With the emergence of critical, postprocessual archaeology in the 1980s, which was more receptive to exploration of "internal" causal variables, room was created for the archaeological study of gender. The answer to the second question, "why ever," leads Wylie into a well-developed examination of archaeological epistemology and the positivist/relativist opposition.

Because the archaeological examination of gender was motivated by feminist political agendas to rectify perceived androcentric biases in archaeological theory and practice, Wylie argues, it has naturally drawn on and been equated with postmodern critiques of scientific practice. Postmodern critiques have questioned the validity of all scientific knowledge claims by arguing that every aspect of the scientific process incorporates human biases, from the formulation of research agendas and hypotheses to the selection of "appropriate" data for "testing" them. The natural outcome of such an argument is that science is incapable of even approximating objective "truth" and this view has been incorporated into many of the more extreme "postprocessual" platforms (Hodder 1984; Shanks and Tilley 1987a, 1987b). Feminist-inspired archaeology thus comes to be equated with postprocessual "hyperrelativism" and is viewed suspiciously by all who cling to an "objective" scientific method as a means of studying the past. Following current arguments in general "feminist theory" (e.g., Keller 1989), Wylie rejects this hyperrelativism and argues that if feminist archaeology is to achieve its political goals (equal representation of women and men in the past towards equality in the present), it *must* be able to claim superior interpretations based on "conventional" methods of science. The focus on women and gender is expected to provide *better* interpretations, not just alternatives, by more satisfactorily accounting for the empirical patterns examined. If gender is a fundamental principle of organization, ideology, and cultural agency, the political motivation provided by the feminist movement to consider gender in archaeology can only lead to better archaeological explanation.

Recognizing that the above argument is epistemologically insufficient to justify the limited retreat from the logic of "hyperrelativism," Wylie devotes considerable attention to examining and justifying the philosophical underpinnings of a legitimate scientific methodology. Wylie rejects both extreme positivism and extreme relativism. Positivists claim that science cleanses theory of bias through the objective test process, and Wylie points out that such a position is naive of the pervasively negotiated aspect of what constitutes legitimate hypotheses and legitimate evidence. There is, she argues, considerable latitude for subjective bias to influence scientific research from hypothesis to conclusion. But she also argues that more accurate knowledge claims are nevertheless possible because there is a critical independence between hypotheses and linking arguments. Empirical data can contradict hypothetical predictions and support one hypothetical position better than another. When multiple lines of evidence are brought to bear on a question of interest, stronger knowledge claims are possible as it becomes less likely that empirical support for an hypothesis is a result of built-in tautologies. Finally, when an hypothesis is challenged by an alternative one, the researchers are compelled to examine the empirical record more carefully to resolve the ambiguity.

This article makes a valuable contribution to archaeological philosophy, not only from a feminist/ gender perspective but also in terms of the epistemology of archaeology in general. Wylie manages to show

how politics and human bias interdigitate with scientific procedure, and how it is still possible to make defensible knowledge claims about the past. Despite the importance of her insights, I question several aspects of her argument. First, one can only accept Wylie's argument that a focus on gender will improve archaeological knowledge claims if one accepts the claim that "internal" and "ethnographic" variables are significant causal variables in cultural change. This substantially weakens the argument that an archaeology of gender provides *better* interpretations than other approaches because it rests on a contested foundation never subjected to explicit empirical "testing." Our most immediate goal should be to find a way to generate testable hypotheses about the role of gender in cultural transformations.

While I think that Wylie has properly identified and rejected the polarization of positivist and relativist epistemologies, I am not convinced that her empirical methodology is altogether revolutionary. I suspect that most practicing scientists in fact recognize that their data can be biased by their theoretical positions, and that it is in the self-critical evaluation of hypotheses with multiple lines of evidence, each of which has the capacity to contradict hypothesis predictions, that science gains any claim to approximate "objective truth." Much of the objection to normal archaeology seems to lie more in the scientific terminology than in the actual concepts. Wylie avoids words like *test* and *explanation* in favor of *constrain* and *interpretation*. In normal usage, I would argue, a test of an hypothesis is conceptualized as and performed in accordance with Wylie's vision of evaluating hypotheses against empirical constraints. *Explanation* perhaps implies too much finality and conclusiveness in lay terms, but according to the canons of science, an explanation is an hypotheses that has endured multiple empirical tests, though it can always be replaced by a better hypothesis. *Interpretation* on the other hand is better employed as a pseudonym for an untested hypothesis, a conjectural scenario for which constraining data have not yet been isolated. It seems to me that Wylie has knowingly or not simply rediscovered the philosophy science for gender archaeology.

Finally, while recognizing and welcoming the role of political interests in the orientation of archaeological inquiry, we must resist the *politicization* of archaeological research to the extent that it can introduce its own biases. Wylie writes "politically engaged science is often more rigorous, self-critical, and responsive to the facts than allegedly neutral science, for which nothing much is at stake." This may be the case where politically engaged researchers provide a dialectical tension across a political divide, but the more a researcher has a political stake in the results of an analysis, the less likely she or he will be to reject her/his own politically preferred but unsupported hypothesis. JBF

*References cited*
Hodder, Ian 1984. Archaeology in 1984. *Antiquity* 58:25-32.

Keller, Evelyn Fox 1989. Feminism and science. In *Women, knowledge and reality: Explorations in feminist philosophy*, edited by Ann Garry and Marilyn Pearsall, 175-188. Unwin Hyman, London.

Shanks, M., and C. Tilley 1987a. *Re-constructing archaeology*. Cambridge University Press, Cambridge.

1987b. *Social Theory and Archaeology*. Cambridge University Press, Cambridge.

*epistemology/positivism/relativism/postmodernism/feminist critique/processualism/postprocessualism*


192. WYLIE, ALISON 1991. Feminist critiques and archaeological challenges. In *The Archaeology of Gender: Proceedings of the Twenty-Second Annual Conference of the Archaeological Association of the University of Calgary*, edited by Dale Walde and Noreen D. Willows, 17-23. Archaeological Association, The University of Calgary, Calgary.

Wylie sets out to answer two interrelated questions about the recent "explosion" of "sex/gender" interest in archaeology. The questions are (1) why now and why only now? and (2) isn't sex/gender archaeology "just" political? Wylie's answers provide a clear and insightful analysis of the interrelatedness of feminist politics, androcentric theoretical assumptions, and ecological, critical and individualistic theoretical positions. Wylie argues that not to consider sex/gender theoretically and critically in archaeological model building is to legitimize the uncritical assumptions about gender that we have tolerated and perpetuated in established traditions of analysis. She wonders at the fact that the "New Archaeology" of the 1960s and 1970s, which took itself as a self-critical awakening, did not develop an explicitly sex/gender orientation. According to Wylie, this "explosion" was held back in archaeology, despite its development in many other disciplines, by the predominant emphasis on ecological and macro-structural approaches in "New Archaeology." An archaeology of gender was finally facilitated by the emergence of critical, symbolic and structural archaeologies which focused more closely on internal variables affecting cultural situations. Wylie acknowledges that not all ecosystem approaches deny the importance of internal variables, and she argues that gender can be conceived of as a legitimate systemic variable as it is thought to be "a system-wide dimension of social organization."

But is sex/gender archaeology "just" political? Wylie argues that historically it was indeed the political feminist movement questioning modern sex/gender structures that led some archaeologists to question the application of these assumptions in archaeological contexts, both in the structure of the discipline and in terms of the analytical models employed. But, Wylie argues, the origin of gender interest in a political movement does not make a sex/gender archaeology empirically or scientifically vacuous or lead to a "slide into all out relativism." On the contrary, an archaeology of sex/gender is fundamentally concerned to improve the explanatory power of archaeological models by identifying gender as a critical but previously unconsidered variable in cultural dynamics. If feminist archaeologists are to claim superior explanations, they must, according to Wylie, operate within accepted conventional methods of scientific empirical validation. The linch pin in this argument is the recognition that "the problems we choose to work on, the hypotheses we take seriously, the presuppositions about what variables are relevant to consider, even the methods we think appropriate and the standards by which we judge results, are *all* conventions." Wylie continues, "[t]his is not to say, however, that any of these judgments are arbitrary, or exclusively dictated by received convention." Wylie thus concludes that sex/gender archaeology *is* political in both the sense that it was inspired by a political movement and in its recognition that there is considerable room for untested beliefs and political motivations, both conscious and unconscious, in the process of archaeological theorizing. And yet it is critically empirical in its attempt to "get it right" and provide *better* archaeological models.

While I am refreshed by Wylie's well-articulated analysis, I believe several points could use additional clarification. First, I believe that much of the suspicion surrounding the archaeology of gender springs from its perceived association with critical and postprocessual archaeology and the extreme relativism inherent in some of the more radical positions taken under these labels. While Wylie's point that the challenges these perspectives brought against "ecosystem" archaeology made room for the development of a gender archaeology is well taken, her recognition of the importance of empirical method situates the archaeology of gender back in the mainstream of scientific archaeology (with all of the caveats against an unselfconscious positivism). This includes contradictory or contrasting approaches which take environmental, sociological or ideological variables as the primary structuring units or motivators of change. This mainstream can encompass ecosystemic, Marxist, symbolic, structuralist, or any other empirically-based models.

In addition, I am concerned about Wylie's willingness to castigate ecosystem archaeology as somehow outmoded by a newly recognized "need to take...'internal,' local structuring principles into account." While internal structuring principles seem to play a significant role in shaping specific cultural structures, perceptions/meanings, and many cultural processes, it remains unclear where the significant variables of cultural structure and process lie, and I expect answers will ultimately depend on the questions being asked and the models being tested as to whether "ethnographic" variables are ultimately causal or "mere epiphenomena." JBF

*epistemology/feminist critique/processualism/postprocessualism/structuralism/contextual archaeology/ sociopolitics of archaeology*

193. WYLIE, ALISON 1991. Gender theory and the archaeological record: Why is there no archaeology of gender? In *Engendering Archaeology: Women and Prehistory,* edited by Joan M. Gero and Margaret W. Conkey, 31-54. Basil Blackwell, Cambridge, MA.

Why is there no archaeology of gender? Wylie argues that the commonplace explanation—that the necessary methodological tools for identifying different genders in the archaeological record have yet to be developed—is inadequate. Instead, she looks to the epistemological and paradigmatic approaches dominant in the discipline. She considers several recent or current epistemological stances and theoretical movements, but focuses particularly on the work of Lewis Binford, rejecting his "eco-functionalist" and "objectivist" views as inimical to the kinds of contextualist analyses necessary for the study of "meaning-constituted, history and context specific 'insides' of cultural systems that an archaeology of gender would take as its central object of analysis" (p. 47). In Wylie's view, positivist approaches suppressed precisely those kinds of critical and reflexive questioning, characteristic in her view of postprocessual approaches, necessary to develop an archaeology of gender.

Wylie's study makes a positive contribution to a general understanding of the sociology of archaeology and the linkages between paradigmatic structures of explanation and the assessment of what constitutes fit subjects for research. Some of her criticisms, however, critique less the positions or views presented by other authors than her own extensions or reinterpretations of their views. For example, at the outset she rejects the notion that methodologies for attributing gender, or at least recognizing it in the archaeological record, needed to be developed for an archaeology of gender to gain acceptance. First, she notes that the methods already exist, and discusses the available "conceptual framework" developed by feminists and archaeologists concerned with the role of gender. By conflating conceptual frameworks and the methodological means by which they might be assessed, Wylie runs the real risk of making archaeology a projection of current views onto a passive past. Second, she argues that the methodological hindrance view is internally self-defeating because it requires that disciplines other than archaeology develop the proper methodologies for identifying past genders. This is damning if true, but it is not clear that such methodologies must come from auxiliary disciplines, only that they must be developed if current debates are to be lifted from the level of assertion and counter-assertion to rigorous and closely-reasoned analysis.

Wylie's paper represents an important theoretical statement of contextualist arguments informed by a concern with gender, and is worthy of close and critical reflection. Readers sympathetic to relativistic and contextualist arguments will likely find her approach and conclusions of considerable value, while more skeptical readers may be put off by logical gaps and inconsistencies in the argument itself. AWB

*processualism/postprocessualism/contextual archaeology/sociopolitics of archaeology/feminist critique/ epistemology*


194. YELLEN, JOHN E. 1991. Women, archaeology, and the National Science Foundation. *Society for American Archaeology Bulletin* 9(1):7.

YELLEN, JOHN E. 1991. Women, archaeology and the National Science Foundation: An analysis of Fiscal Year 1989 data. In *The Archaeology of Gender: Proceedings of the Twenty-Second Annual Conference of the Archaeological Association of the University of Calgary,* edited by Dale Walde and Noreen D. Willows, 201-210. Archaeological Association, The University of Calgary, Calgary.

Yellen analyzes data on archaeological proposals (48 dissertation and 111 senior) submitted to the Anthropology Program at the National Science Foundation (NSF) during fiscal year (FY) 1989 and compares them to proposals submitted during FY1978-81 in an attempt to discern gender differences and biases in submission of proposals and success rates. The data indicate that in both fiscal years significantly more men than women applied for senior grants but that the difference in success rates was statistically insignificant. Unlike the earlier fiscal years, the 1989 data demonstrate that women who proposed field research were statistically as likely to receive support as women proposing non-field research.

Following this initial analysis, Yellen focuses on elucidating factors which may account for the smaller number of proposals submitted by senior women, and on examining the evaluation process for gender bias. The data on dissertation proposals suggest equity between men and women in applying for grants, success rates and fieldwork/non-fieldwork ratios. In contrast, only 26% of the senior proposals are submitted by women. He suggests that this is not unexpected given the small number of women in his ad hoc sample of 10 university departments that have archaeologists who frequently submit NSF proposals. The small submission percentage also pertains to women who have 6 years or less postdoctoral experience. Based on the dissertation data, this percentage would be expected to be twice as high. He thus concludes that "women differentially disappear from the researcher pool in the passage from graduate to fully professional status" (p. 202). In examining the characteristics of the senior applicant pool, women who have held their doctorate for 12 or more years have a lower success rate than women who ahve held it less. This contrasts with the success rate of men which increases with their academic rank. Yellen suggests that this may be the result of less mentoring and support provided to women in the earlier decades than to either their male contemporaries or to academically younger women. The data also indicate that senior women submit fewer fieldwork proposals than men.

Yellen's analysis of the review process using ad hoc reviewer ratings and panel ratings indicates: ad hoc male reviewers are slightly tougher than their female counterparts, the average ad hoc male reviewer rating for a male-submitted proposal is higher (by over half a point) than for a female-submitted proposal, panelists give lower ratings than ad hoc reviewers, male-submitted proposals are rated more highly by ad hoc and panel reviewers, and final panel recommendations do not reflect gender bias. EAB

*discrimination/sociopolitics of archaeology/National Science Foundation*

195. YENTSCH, ANNE 1991. Access and space, symbolic and material, in historic archaeology. In *The Archaeology of Gender: Proceedings of the Twenty-Second Annual Conference of the Archaeological Association of the University of Calgary,* edited by Dale Walde and Noreen D. Willows, 252-262. Archaeological Association, The University of Calgary, Calgary.

Anne Yentsch seeks to find ways to make historic archaeology "more responsive to gender-related issues." For her, this attempt is motivated by a feminist concern to "re-enfranchise" women in their past, present, and future. She approaches her goal in two ways: with a critique of the dominant sociopolitics of historic archaeology; and with a case study of symbolically gendered space in an American Revolution period household.

Yentsch argues that historic archaeology has been largely dominated by male "gatekeepers," relegated to a lower prestige than prehistoric archaeology, limited by impersonal theoretical perspectives, and divorced from its historic sources. The lack of women in prestigious positions in historic archaeology has inhibited the field from developing a concern for women in the past, and has fostered a male-centered representation of the past consistent with contemporary androcentric ideology. Instead of making maximal use of both archaeological and historical methods of analysis, Yentsch claims, historic archaeologists have privileged the archaeological record with all of its limitations in an attempt to ally themselves more closely with the more prestigious prehistoric archaeologists. In addition, historic archaeologists have by and large adopted the "impersonal" theoretical positions of the New Archaeology (*a la* Deetz and South) and Marxist perspectives (Leone), thereby foreclosing on any consideration of gender relations. Finally, she criticizes historic archaeologists for their failure to use the historic record to its fullest potential in addressing topics such as gender relations of the past. By taking the position of testing the historic record with the archaeological, Yentsch claims, historic archaeologists greatly diminish the integrative value of these two data sources.

Yentsch presents a case study employing a gendered perspective to examine the historic archaeological record of eighteenth century Revolutionary America. She develops a picture of the eighteenth century English gentry gender ideology utilizing historic sources and structural/symbolic analysis. Specifically, she examines the gender ideology of public and private space, masculine and feminine realms, and, assuming this ideological reconstruction to be valid for colonial eighteenth century Anglo-American gentry, she uses it to examine the layout of the Morven Plantation and to interpret the ideological meaning behind the British troops' desecration of the "public" space with "women's" refuse (food remains and broken cooking utensils). Ultimately, Yentsch argues that historic documents and archaeological remains can be used in conjunction to arrive at more detailed and sophisticated interpretations of the past.

While Yentsch's basic interest in promoting gender equality in part by considering the role of gender in "historic process" is laudable, and I suspect that she is correct to advocate more critical use of the historic record in historic archaeology, I find it hard to agree with many of her specific points and find her case study offers weak support for her program of revitalization. While historic sources should be used to their fullest potential in resolving questions of interest, as should archaeological resources, the two categories of data are considerably different and should not be treated as interchangeable in historical reconstruction. Historic sources are biased by the outlook and agendas of the original authors but tend to provide greater detail concerning *some* aspects of life than do most archaeological sources, especially concerning aspects of ideology, politics, and rules of conduct. These variables must be approached less directly with archaeological remains. But historic documentation is rarely representative of the views of an entire population and typically yields only a few of many perspectives on social relations and other cultural phenomena.

It was unclear how Yentsch got from English structural oppositions to an Anglo-American household, the location of which was never given and which could as easily have been somewhere in England but for a reference to the British occupation of 1776 and a visit by George Washington. Yentsch describes how the Morven household was symbolically marked by earth-tone decorations in the "private" spaces (family and servant areas) and white-toned decorations in the "public" areas (entrance and entertainment areas). Because these two categories of use areas parallel the ideological division of feminine/private domain and masculine/public domain as reconstructed from English historical literature, Yentsch interprets the "desecration" of Morven by the British troops as meaningful in its introduction of "feminine" materials into the public space. However, by her own descriptions, the "private"/"public" division had a class basis as well, where slaves and paid laborers used the "private" entrance and dignitaries used the "public" one. Why isn't the "desecration" interpreted as class based? It is also possible that the public and private spheres were not perceived as gendered and the "desecration" was effective by its mere disruption of the use and discard patterns of the household spaces, or that the "desecration" was a result of the British occupation in the most appropriate space without any premeditated intention to or concern over symbolic desecration. The fundamental problem with this approach is not in Yentsch's plea for a more substantial use of historic records in historic archaeology, but in her lack of consideration of alternative explanations and failure to develop testable predictions to assess the one she chooses to advance. JBF

*historical archaeology/structuralism/symbolic archaeology/class/household analysis/New Jersey/United States, Northeast/Great Britain*


196. YENTSCH, ANNE 1991. Engendering visible and invisible ceramic artifacts, especially dairy vessels. *Historical Archaeology* 25(4):132-155.

This article is composed of two loosely linked lines of argument. One focus of inquiry addresses the transferral of dairying activities from the control of women in a household context to the control of men in a commercialized or industrialized context in the eighteenth to nineteenth century United States. To establish that dairying was traditionally a woman's activity, the author gives a history of dairying in Europe, and draws parallels with colonial America. She points out that this important occupation is largely ignored or not attributed to women in economic histories of the time period. In a second phase, dairying became a major focus of production activities, but still largely within the context of the family. Small-scale dairies were eventually replaced by large-scale, rail-road owned factories. The author indicates that the take-over of dairying by men occurs at a time when the opportunities for sale of dairy products provided significant cash income, and draws parallels with other instances of male appropriation of domestic activities such as beer-making.

The second focus of this article pertains to the analysis of archaeological ceramics. Within a general context of identifying dairying tools, several ceramic methodologies were critiqued, including pattern analysis and ceramic price indices. Yentsch indicates that these methodologies tend to obscure activities of women, and illustrates this by showing that it is difficult to monitor dairying in the archaeological record because ceramics associated with this activity may be placed in several functional categories in analysis. She suggests that another methodology called POTS may be more useful, but does not elaborate on the analytical design.

The subject of shifts in gender-appropriate activities as they are affected by economic activities is a timely one, and it is clear that the author has carefully considered the issues discussed in this paper. However, the author assumes an in-depth knowledge on a variety of subjects on the part of the reader, which may limit the accessibility of this example to researchers outside of the field of historical archaeology. The paper also suffered from a lack of bridging arguments to tie the historical data and the archaeological ceramic data together in more than a general way. Ceramics particular to dairying are not described, nor their relationship to "redwares." The ceramic data are used to illustrate methodological points rather than to test specific propositions concerning the archaeological visibility of gendered activities. KMM

*ceramic analysis/dairying/division of labor/historical archaeology/United States, Northeast*

197. ZAGARELL, ALLEN 1986. Trade, women, class, and society in ancient Western Asia. *Current Anthropology* 27(5):415-430.

This is an interesting analysis of the emergence of the Mesopotamian state in the Early Dynastic Period. As his point of departure, Allen Zagarell charges that state emergence was not precipitated by the development of a merchant class and the establishment of a western-model capitalist economy. Instead, he uses the Mesopotamian archaeological and textual evidence to argue that the state system emerged as result of the deterioration of the "kin-corporate" system of property ownership and production by a "public" mode of production composed of elites and workers in temples, palaces, and estates, who appropriated kin-corporate labor and amassed power and surplus production that would have previously been shared by lineage groups. As these elite amassed more wealth, they branched out and established "colonial administrations" on the fringes of the Mesopotamian realm to engage in trade exchange. This burgeoning trade system encouraged the commoditization of goods and provided a context for the development of a merchant class of entrepreneurs. This commoditization presumably led to a fully developed market system with debtors and debt slavery.

Critical to the purposes of this collection of annotations, Zagarell suggests that women played a primary role in the emergence of an elite independent of the traditional kin-corporate system. Iconographic evidence is cited as evidence for a high proportion of women in the temple production units, and it is posited that the appropriation of female labor, under religious justification, allowed the emergent elites to generate the surplus wealth that would promote their full independence from the leveling effect of the kin-corporate mode of production. Zagarell suggests that despite evidence for female elites, the appropriation of female labor for surplus production under the "temple and palace" modes of production initiated the institutional subordination of women in the subsequent Mesopotamian state (cf. Gailey 1985).

A compelling scenario, this model is marred by a few, perhaps cosmetic, problems. First, is the lack of explicit definition given to the term "state." An implicit definition seems to be that of a complex polity with a market based economy characterized by commoditization, commodity exchange, and debt. As such the state would, by definition, be a capitalistic polity (if not of the western type, whatever that is). On the other hand, Zagarell seems to consider the emergence of the temple/palace modes of production as a period of state development. He avoids all mention of "chiefdom" type organizations, although the "public" temple/palace system seems to fit nicely into such a framework, with the development of hierarchical elites legitimizing tribute (in this case women's labor) through the elites' roles as religious functionaries. A "chiefdom" model of political and administrative organization clarifies the Mesopotamian evolutionary picture still further by separating this period in analytical terms from the subsequent state development corresponding to the emergence of a market system, entrepreneurial capitalism and multi-tiered bureaucratic government (cf. Wright 1977). Although Service's (1962) four-stage model of cultural evolution has been heavily criticized

## *Annotated References*

as a form of typologizing, it is nevertheless a useful framework for analysis of political and economic structure, provided the particular cases fit. In this case, they appear to.

Although Zagarell's main purpose was not to focus on gender in Mesopotamian state formation, his recognition of the gendered aspect of temple labor adds an interesting aspect to his model. It remains to be seen how critical gender was to this sequence of Mesopotamian culture change. JBF

*References cited*
Gailey, Christine 1985. The state of the state in anthropology. *Dialectical Anthropology* 9:65-91.

Service, Elman 1962. *Primitive Social organization: An evolutionary perspective.* Random House, New York.

Wright, Henry T. 1977. Recent research on the origin of the state. *Annual Review of Anthropology* 6:379-397.

*state formation/trade/class/religion/Mesopotamia/Near East*

# *Additional References*

*The following references were in press or unavailable at the time this volume was completed.*


DU CROS, HILARY, and LAURAJANE SMITH (editors) 1992 (in press). Women in Archaeology: A Feminist Critique. Department of Prehistory, Australian National University, Canberra, Australia.

GIFFORD-GONZALEZ, DIANE (in press). Gaps in zooarchaeological analysis: Gender and issue. In *Bones to Behavior,* edited by Jean Hudson, pp. 1-30. Occasional Paper. Center for Archaeological Investigations, Southern Illinois University, Carbondale, IL.

KORNFELD, MARCEL (editor) 1991 (in press). Approaches to Gender Processes on the Great Plains. *Plains Anthropologist* 36(134).

RODRÍGUEZ VALDÉS, MARÍA 1988. *La Mujer Azteca.* Universidad Autonoma del Estado de Mexico, Toluca, Mexico.

RUSSELL, PAMELA M. 1987. *Women in Upper Paleolithic Europe.* M. A. thesis, Auckland, New Zealand.

# Author Index

*(Numbers refer to citations)*

Anati, Emmanuel, 1
Armelagos, George J., 27
Arnold, Bettina, 2
Arnold, Karen, 3
Arsenault, Daniel, 4
Arwill-Nordbladh, Elisabeth, 5
Bahn, Paul G., 6
Barnes, Ramon M., 27
Barrett, John C., 7, 8
Barstow, Ann, 9
Beaudry, Mary C., 174
Bender, Barbara, 10
Bender, Susan J., 11
Bertelsen, Reidar, 12
Biaggi, Cristina, 13
Binford, Sally R., 14
Boardman, John, 15
Bolen, Kathleen M., 16, 17
Booker, Jane E., 27
Boutton, Thomas E., 27
Boye, L., 18
Braidwood, Robert J., 22
Brashler, Janet G., 19
Brendel, Klaus, 27

Bridges, Patricia S., 20, 21
Broman Morales, Vivian, 22
Bruhns, Karen Olsen, 23
Brumfiel, Elizabeth M., 24
Brush, Karen A., 25
Buchanan, Keith, 26
Bumsted, M. Pamela, 27
Burtt, Fiona, 28
Chabot, Nancy Jo, 29, 30
Cheney, Susan Lawrence, 31
Chitwood, Prince, 189
Claassen, Cheryl, 32, 33, 34, 35
Commasnes, Liv-Helga (see Dommasnes)
Conkey, Margaret W., 36, 37, 38, 39, 40
Cordell, Linda S., 41
Crabtree, Pamela J., 42
Crooks, Deborah L., 119
Damm, Charlotte, 43, 44
Danziger, Eve, 45
Deagan, Kathleen, 46
Derry, Linda, 47
Dobres, Marcia-Ann, 48
Dommasnes, Liv Helga, 49, 50, 51
Donley-Reid, Linda W., 52, 53

Draiby, B., 18
Duke, Philip, 54
Ehrenberg, Margaret, 55
Eisner, Wendy R., 56
Engelstad, Ericka, 57, 58
Erlandson, Jon, 177
Eymar, Francis, 59
Feinman, Gary M., 60
Feldman, Lawrence, 129
Flannery, Kent V., 61
Foote, Cheryl J., 62
Francis, Julie, 99
Fratt, Lee, 63
Gero, Joan M., 38, 64, 65, 66, 67, 68, 69, 70, 71
Gibb, James G., 72
Gibbs, Liv, 73
Gilchrist, Roberta, 74, 75
Gimbutas, Marija, 76
Graham, Elizabeth, 77
Grauer, A. L., 78
Graves, Pam, 3
Guillén, Ann Cyphers, 79
Handsman, Russell G., 80
Hastorf, Christine A., 81
Haugen, Inger, 82
Hawkes, Sonia Chadwick, 137
Hayden, Brian, 83, 84
Hill, Warren, 98
Hodder, Ian, 85, 86, 87
Hollimon, Sandra E., 88, 89
Hvenegaard-Lassen, K., 18
Jackson, Thomas L., 90
Jensen, Joan M., 91
Jones, Sian, 92
Joyce, Rosemary, 93
Kehoe, Alice B. ,94, 95, 96, 97
Kelley, Jane, 98
Kennedy, Mary C., 180
King, Julia A., 72
Kleppe Johansen, Else, 51
Kornfeld, Marcel, 99
Kramer, Carol, 100
Larsen, Mary Ann, 101
Latta, Martha A., 102
Lerman, Juan Carlos, 27
Lillehammer, Arnvid, 12
Lillehammer, Grete, 175
Løken, Trond, 103
Loth, Heinrich, 104

Lowell, Julie C.,105
Mandt, Grø, 106, 107
Marshall, Yvonne, 109
Maurer, Bill, 110
McCafferty, Geoffrey G., 111
McCafferty, Sharisse D., 111
McEwan, Bonnie G., 112
McGhee, Robert, 113
Meyers, Carol L., 114
Middleton, William D., 60
Miller, Darlis A., 115
Miller, Virginia E., 115
Mitchell, Christi, 116
Muller, Vianna, 117
Murray, M. A., 118
Naess, Jenny-Rita, 12
Nelson, Margaret C., 119
Nelson, Sarah M., 120, 121, 122
Nichols, Linda M., 59
Niles, Susan, 123
O'Brien, Patricia J., 124
Odegaard, V., 18
Orphanides, Andreas G., 125
Oyuela-Caycedo, Augusto, 126
Paterson, Ann L., 139
Pay, Sharon, 92
Pirie, Victoria, 127
Pohl, Mary DeLand, 128, 129
Pollak, Janet S., 130
Pollock, Susan, 131
Pomeroy, Sarah B., 132
Purser, Margaret, 133
Randsborg, Klavs, 134
Rathje, William, 186
Reed, Linda J., 135
Renfrew, Colin, 136
Reynolds, Nicholas, 137
Rice, Patricia C., 138, 139
Rice, Prudence M., 140
Ridgway, Brunilde Sismondo, 141
Robb, John ,142
Rohrlich, Ruby (Ruby Rohrlich-Leavitt), 143, 144
Roosevelt, Anna C., 145
Root, Dolores, 71
Russell, Pamela M., 146
Samson, Ross, 147
Sassaman, Kenneth E., 148
Schackel, Sandra K., 62

## Author Index

Scott, Elizabeth M., 149, 150
Seifert, Donna J., 151, 152
Sempowski, Martha L., 153
Small, David B., 154
Smith, Bruce D., 155
Spector, Janet D., 39, 156, 157, 158
Spencer-Wood, Suzanne M., 159, 160
Stalsberg, Anne, 161
Stanley, Autumn, 162
Stark, Miriam, 100, 163
Stig-Sørenson, Marie Louise, 164, 165, 166
Stine, Linda France, 167, 168
Talalay, Lauren E., 169
Taylor, Sarah, 3, 170
Tringham, Ruth E., 171
Trocolli, Ruth, 172
Tzachili, Iris, 173
Victor, Katharine L., 174
Vinsrygg, Synnøve, 175
Wagner, Norman E., 189
Walde, Dale, 176

Walker, Phillip, 177
Walker, Susan, 178
Wall, Diana diZerega, 179
Watson, Patty Jo, 180
Weber, Carmen A., 181
Wells, Calvin, 137
Whelan, Mary K., 158, 182, 183
Whittlesey, Stephanie M., 184
Wildeson, L. E., 185
Wilk, Richard R., 186
Williams, Barbara, 187
Williams, Sarah H., 40
Willoughby, Pamela R., 188
Willows, Noreen D., 176
Winter, Marcus C., 61
Woolfrey, Sandra, 189
Wright, Rita P., 190
Wylie, Alison, 191, 192, 193
Yellen, John, 194
Yentsch, Anne, 195, 196
Zagarell, Alan, 197

# Subject Index

*(Numbers refer to citations)*

acculturation, 172
activity areas (see spatial analysis)
Africa, 30, 52, 53, 87, 104, 154, 188
agriculture, 1, 9, 17, 20, 21, 27, 40, 42, 55, 72, 73, 77, 86, 91, 105, 116, 143, 155, 162, 167, 168, 180
agriculture, origins, 9, 17, 20, 21, 40, 42, 55, 86, 155, 162, 180, 190
Akkad, 131
Alabama, 20, 21, 47
Alaska, 101
Albers, Patricia, 116
Alberta, 31
alcohol, 31
Amantaní, 123
Amazonia, 145
*American Antiquity*, 68, 163, 174
American Revolution, 195
Andes, 4, 23, 64, 65, 81, 123, 145
Anglo-Saxons, 25, 137
Ankara, 154
Apache, 62
archaeobotany, 66, 81, 174
Archaic period, southeast U.S., 20, 21, 35, 148, 155
Archaic period, western U.S., 99
architecture, 52, 73, 75, 87, 101, 115, 123, 141, 144, 154, 167, 171, 178, 181
Arctic, 101, 113
Arikara, 88, 116
Arizona, 62, 184
Asia, 26, 120, 121, 190
Athabaskan, 101, 135
Auel, Jean, 130
Aztecs, 24, 111
Barney, William, 47
Barstow, Ann, 143
Belgium, 56
Belize, 77, 93, 128, 129
berdache, 172, 183
biblical archaeology, 114
bibliography, 34
Binford, Lewis, 193
biography (see history of archaeology)
Blackdog Site, 183
bone chemistry (see stable isotope analysis)
bone morphology, 20, 21
botanical analysis (see archaeobotany)

Bourdieu, Pierre, 52
Brazil, 145
Breuil, Abbé Henri, 6, 94
Britain (see Great Britain)
British Museum, 30
Bronze Age, Europe, 7, 55, 73, 106, 107, 117, 164, 166
Bronze Age, Mediterranean, 142, 144, 173
brothels, 31, 152, 160
Bruhns, Karen O., 187
Butler, Mary, 11
C. C. Witt Site, 124
California, 88, 89, 90, 177
Cambodia, 26
Canada, 31, 96, 98, 113, 121, 185, 189
Canada Verde Site, 177
capitalism, 18, 75
Caribbean, 112
caries, 177
cave art, 6, 139, 146
Çatal Hüyük, 9, 86, 143, 144
ceramic analysis, 4, 24, 46, 64, 77, 93, 102, 108, 116, 140, 167, 174, 179, 189, 190, 196
ceramic production, 102, 108, 116, 140, 148, 189, 190
Chalcatzingo, 79
Channel Islands, 177
Chesapeake Bay, 72, 181
chiefdom formation, 145
children, 16, 175
children's literature, 28
China, 120
Christianization, 103
Chumash, 88, 89
class, 47, 52, 64, 93, 117, 120, 131, 143, 144, 149, 152, 160, 167, 179, 195, 197
Classic period, Maya, 93, 128, 129
classical archaeology, 15, 132, 141, 178
cloth (see textiles)
clothing, 79, 149, 150, 152, 164
Colombia, 126
computer disk, 34
conference papers, 34, 60, 70, 176
Conkey, Margaret W., 110, 191
contextual archaeology, 4, 7, 48, 73, 75, 80, 85, 86, 87, 110, 154, 165, 166, 192, 193
Contact period, New World, 62, 63, 93, 153, 174
cooking, 24, 72, 190

Copper Age, 142
cosmology (see religion)
costume, 164, 173
Crete, 23, 55, 136, 144, 173
critical theory, 159, 165, 192
Cro-Magnon, 130
Cueto de la Mina, 37
Czechoslovakia, 97
dairying, 72, 196
Dakota, 156, 183
Deetz, James, 39, 116, 195
DeLivre, A., 40
Denmark, 43, 44, 73, 134, 164
Dincauze, Dena, 11
discrimination, 5, 28, 44, 60, 67, 68, 69, 71, 94, 98, 100, 119, 121, 127, 163, 174, 184, 185, 187, 194
division of labor, 10, 12, 16, 17, 20, 21, 23, 24, 31, 35, 37, 42, 55, 61, 62, 65, 72, 73, 77, 82, 88, 89, 90, 91, 96, 97, 99, 105 108, 128, 129, 135, 140, 148, 149, 156, 157, 168, 172, 175, 177, 180, 186, 188, 189, 190, 196
Dolni Vestonice, 22, 95
Dunn, Mary Eubanks, 187
Dutton, Bertha Pauline, 41
Early Woodland period, U.S., 35, 148
education, 28, 29, 119, 158
eighteenth century, U.S., 46, 149, 150, 181, 195
Ellis, Florence Hawley, 41
Engels, Friedrich, 18, 143, 165
England (see Great Britain)
epistemology, 3, 8, 33, 36, 38, 39, 48, 50, 54, 57, 58, 74, 97, 110, 159, 165, 191, 192, 193
Eskimo (see Inuit)
ethnicity, 46, 47, 52, 132, 149, 150, 160, 161, 167
ethnoarchaeology, 52, 53, 157, 168, 186
ethnographic analogy, 16, 23, 24, 45, 54, 55, 79, 83, 96, 97, 101, 104, 105, 108, 113, 125, 126, 128, 129, 134, 135, 137, 138, 140, 146, 154, 175, 182, 186, 188, 190
ethnohistory, 24, 46, 62, 63, 77, 93, 102, 104, 105, 111, 112, 115, 116, 117, 124, 126, 128, 129, 131, 156, 183
exhibits (see museums)
Europe, 2, 5, 6, 7, 14, 17, 37, 49, 55, 56, 59, 75, 76, 78, 80, 82, 84, 85, 87, 92, 95, 96, 97, 117, 118, 122, 130, 138, 139, 146, 161, 164, 166, 171, 175

## Subject Index

faunal analysis, 66, 152
female seclusion, 154, 178
feminist critique, 3, 5, 12, 18, 36, 38, 39, 40, 42, 44, 48, 50, 57, 58, 63, 65, 66, 71, 74, 92, 110, 111, 116, 132, 147, 158, 159, 160, 165, 170, 182, 191, 192, 193, 195
feminist standpoint theory, 159
fertility cults, 1, 76, 84, 106, 107, 118, 122, 136, 145
fiction, 130, 156, 171
figurines, 13, 14, 22, 55, 79, 93, 95, 104, 109, 118, 122, 125, 128, 138, 145, 169
Flax, J., 36
Florida, 46, 112, 172
Formative period, Mesoamerica, 61, 128, 145
Foster, G., 140
France, 2, 6, 85, 97, 139
fur trade, 135, 149, 150
gatherer-hunters, 1, 17, 20, 21, 28, 35, 42, 54, 55, 83, 88, 89, 96, 106, 135, 138, 146, 175
gender inequality, origins of, 10, 110, 117, 143, 144, 182
Germany, 2, 43, 55, 117
Gero, Joan, 60, 163, 191
Giddens, Anthony, 7, 8, 52
Gimbutas, Marija, 84, 171
Goddess, 9, 13, 14, 76, 84, 106, 107, 118, 125, 136, 169
graduate training, 44, 98, 100, 187
Great Britain, 7, 25, 29, 30, 44, 75, 78, 92, 118, 137, 195
Great Plains (see United States and Canada, Plains)
Greece, 15, 141, 169, 178
Green, Ernestine, 187
Greenwich Village, 179
Guale, 46
Guatemala, 77, 93, 128, 129
Harappa, 190
Hellenistic period, Greece, 141
Henry, Donald O., 42
Hidatsa, 105, 157
Hildebrand, Hans, 51
Hill, James, 39
Hindu, 154
historical archaeology, 19, 31, 46, 47, 62, 63, 72, 102, 109, 112, 114, 133, 149, 150, 151, 152, 156, 160, 167, 168, 172, 174, 179, 181, 183, 195, 196 (see also sixteenth, seventeenth, eighteenth, and nineteenth century, U.S.)
*Historical Archaeology*, 174
history of archaeology, 5, 11, 33, 41, 51, 165, 187
Hocquenghem, Anne Marie, 4
Hodder, Ian, 48, 110, 154, 171, 191
Holidome Site, 124
Homer, 173
hominids, 30, 40, 182, 188
Hongshan, 120
Hopi, 105
Horton, Mark, 52
household analysis, 53, 61, 72, 82, 87, 171, 178, 186, 195
hunter-gatherers (see gatherer-hunters)
Hurlbert, B., 121
Huron, 102
iconography, 4, 6, 12, 14, 15, 26, 76, 84, 106, 115, 118, 131, 136, 142, 144, 145, 146, 169, 173
Inca (see Inka)
individual in prehistory, 12, 83, 147
industrialization, 19
Inka, 64, 81
Inuit, 101, 113
Iran, 22, 95
Iraq, 131
Iron Age, Europe, 2, 49, 55, 103, 117, 166
Iron Age, Near East, 114
Iroquois, 102, 109, 153, 189
Irwin-Williams, Cynthia, 41, 187
Islam, 154, 178
Israel, 42, 114
Italy, 142
Johnson, Gregory, 37
Jorvik Viking Centre, 29, 92
K.A.N., 51
Kagaaba, 126
Kayseri, 154
Kehoe, Alice, 22
Kelley, Jane Holden, 41, 187
Kennedy, Mary C., 155, 162
Kenya, 52, 53
Khmer, 26
kiva, 105
Kramer, Carol, 67, 69, 121, 163
!Kung, 42, 158
*Kvinner i Arkeologi i Norge* (see K.A.N.)
Lambert, Marjorie Ferguson, 41

Lapita, 108
Leone, Mark, 29
Lepenski Vir, 80
Levant, 42
Linear Pottery period, Europe, 17
lithic technology, 59, 65, 66, 124, 148
Little Rapids Site, 156
logging camps, 19
Longacre, William, 39
Lubbock, John, 5
Magdalenian, 37, 96
Malta, 13, 136
marxian, 80
marxism, 10, 18, 40, 64, 80, 111, 143, 144, 160, 192, 195
Maryland, 72, 181
matriarchy, 84, 143, 144
Maya, 45, 77, 93, 128, 129, 145
Medicine, Beatrice, 116
Medicine Crow Site, 116
medieval archaeology, 75, 78, 147
Mediterranean, 1, 15, 84, 114, 118, 136, 141, 142, 144, 169, 173, 178
megaliths, 87, 136
Mellaart, James, 9, 143
Mesoamerica (see Maya and Mexico)
Mesolithic, Europe, 17, 80, 134, 175
Mesopotamia, 131, 197
*mestizaje*, 46, 172
metallurgy, 7, 166
Mexico, 24, 45, 61, 77, 79, 93, 111, 115, 128, 129, 145
Michigan, 149, 150
Michilimackinac, 149
Midwest (see United States, Midwest)
Minnesota, 156, 183
Minoan period, Minos (see Crete)
Middle East (see Near East)
Middle Preclassic, Mexico, 79
Mississippian period, U.S., 20, 21
Moche, 4, 23, 64
Mono, 90
Montelius, Oscar, 5, 51, 165
Morgan, Lewis H., 143
mortuary analysis, 2, 12, 25, 27, 42, 43, 49, 55, 56, 73, 77, 83, 87, 88, 89, 103, 109, 120, 124, 131, 134, 137, 153, 161, 164, 177, 182, 183
Morven Plantation, 195
Moslem (see Islam)

mothering, 16, 111, 138, 175
Murdock, G., 140
museums, 29, 30, 80, 92, 127
myth, 76, 83, 106, 107, 120, 162
National Endowment for the Humanities, 163
*National Geographic*, 71, 163
National Science Foundation, 68, 69, 100, 163, 194
Natufian, 42
Navajo, 62
Neanderthals, 130
Near East, 9, 22, 42, 95, 114, 131, 143, 144, 154, 162, 197
NEH (see National Endowment for the Humanities)
Neolithic, Africa, 87
Neolithic, Europe, 17, 43, 55, 76, 84, 85, 87, 106, 134, 142, 169, 171
Neolithic, Mediterranean, 1, 13, 84, 142, 169
Neolithic, Near East, 9, 22, 42, 86, 95, 144, 162
New Archaeology (see processualism)
New Guinea, 108
New Jersey, 195
New Mexico, 62, 63, 91
New York, 102, 109, 153, 179
nineteenth century, U.S., 19, 31, 47, 133, 160, 179, 183, 196
Niuheliang Site, 120
North Carolina, 167, 168
Northeast (see United States, Northeast)
Norway, 12, 49, 51, 82, 103, 175
NSF (see National Science Foundation)
Oaxaca, 61
Oceania (see Polynesia)
Oldowan, 188
Onion Portage Site, 101
Ontario, 189
Opovo, 171
origins research, 36, 40, 48
osteology, 21, 27, 78, 88, 89, 137, 177
Ottoman, 154
Pacific, 108, 121
Pakistan, 190
paleodemography, 78, 138, 145
paleoethnobotany (see archaeobotany)
Paleoindian period, 99
Paleolithic, Africa, 188
Paleolithic, Europe, 6, 10, 14, 37, 40, 55, 76, 84, 95, 96, 97, 122, 130, 138, 139, 146, 175, 182

## Subject Index

Paleolithic, Mediterranean, 1
paleopathology, 78, 88, 89, 137
paleozoology (see faunal analysis)
Palestine, 114
Parthenon, 15
Pawnee, 124
Peru, 64, 65, 81, 145
Philippines, 140
Pinkley, Jean McWhirt, 41
Plains (see United States and Canada, Plains)
political uses of the past, 28, 30, 40, 92, 94, 147
Pollock, Susan, 144
Polynesia, 108
positivism, 191
postmodernism, 58, 159, 170, 191, 192, 193
postprocessualism, 7, 40, 43, 48, 50, 57, 58, 74, 85, 87, 154, 155, 159, 164, 170, 180, 191, 192, 193, 195
poststructuralism, 170
Preclassic period, Mexico, 78
Prentice, Guy, 180
processualism, 33, 57, 58, 77, 81, 145 155, 159, 190, 191, 192, 193
prostitution (see brothels)
Pueblo, 62, 63, 91
Queyash Alto, 64
Randsborg, Klavs, 44
race (see ethnicity)
rape, 137
Recuay, 64
relativism, 191, 193
religion, 1, 76, 93, 106, 107, 111, 123, 124, 126, 136, 143, 144, 146
representation, theory of, 4, 6, 13, 14, 15, 23, 30, 76, 80, 84, 85, 93, 95, 109, 115, 122, 139
revisionist theory, 40, 48, 74, 147, 159
Rice, Patricia C., 122
rock art, 6, 12, 73, 106, 139, 142, 146
Rogaland, 175
Rogers, J. Daniel, 116
Roman period, 56, 117
Russia, 161
Rydh, Hanna, 51
SAA (see Society for American Archaeology)
Sacks, Karen, 117
Sanday, Peggy, 120
Sausa, 81
Scandinavia, 5, 12, 43, 49, 50, 51, 55, 73, 82, 103, 106, 107, 134, 161, 164, 166

sculpture, 26, 80, 93, 104, 118, 120, 141
semantics, 45
Seneca (see Iroquois)
seventeenth century, U.S., 46, 62, 63, 72, 109, 112, 153
Shang dynasty, 120
Shanks, Michael, 28, 29, 57, 58, 191
shellfishing, 35, 148
shell mounds, 35
Sherrat, Andrew, 171
Shepard, Anna O., 41
Shoshone, 59
Sioux, 183
sixteenth century, U.S., 46, 62, 63, 109, 112, 153
skeletal analysis (see osteology)
Skull Gulch Site, 177
slavery, 112, 143
Smith, Bruce D., 35, 180
social differentiation, 167
Society for American Archaeology, 60, 70, 185
sociobiology, 83
sociology of science, 50, 58, 66, 67, 94
sociopolitics of archaeology, 3, 11, 18, 30, 41, 44, 51, 53, 54, 57, 60, 66, 67, 68, 69, 71, 74, 92, 94, 98, 100, 119, 121, 127, 163, 165, 184, 185, 187, 193, 194
South, Stanley, 46, 152, 195
South America, 4, 59, 64, 65, 69, 81, 115, 123, 126, 145
Southeast (see United States, Southeast)
Southwest Asia (see Near East)
Southwest U. S. (see United States, Southwest)
Spain, 10, 37, 139
Spanish colonization, 62, 63, 112, 129, 172
spatial analysis, 47, 52, 53, 61, 64, 72, 73, 75, 77, 105, 123, 124, 126, 128, 154, 157, 168, 171, 178
Spector, Janet, 39, 105, 110, 149
Spretnak, Charlene, 14
stable isotope analysis, 27, 81
Stark, Miriam, 67, 69 121, 163
state formation, 25, 64, 65, 117, 128, 143, 144, 145, 170, 197
Stone, Merlin, 14
Stone Age (see Paleolithic)
structuralism, 52, 80, 113, 142, 154, 166, 192, 195

structuration theory, 7, 8
Subarctic, 101, 135
subsistence, 24, 27, 35, 64, 77, 81, 88, 89, 90, 91, 128, 129, 135, 149, 152, 177
Sumer, 131, 143, 144
Swahili, 52, 53
Swanscombe, 30
Sweden, 5
task differentiation approach, 39, 72, 110, 156, 157
teaching (see education)
text books, 158
textiles, 24, 96, 164
Thera, 173
Thule, 113
Tilley, Christopher, 28, 29, 57, 58, 191
Timucua, 172
trade, 42, 49, 52, 55, 76, 102, 108, 111, 116, 117, 129, 135, 149, 155, 161, 180, 197
Tunis, 154
Turkey, 9, 143, 144
twentieth century, U.S., 152, 167, 168
United States, 68, 69, 71, 119, 121, 160, 185
United States, Midwest, 27, 149, 150, 180, 183
United States, Northeast, 11, 72, 102, 109, 153, 179, 181, 189, 195, 196
United States, Northwest, 101
United States (and Canada), Plains, 31, 54, 88, 99, 116, 124, 156, 157, 183
United States, Southeast, 19, 20, 21, 35, 46, 47, 112, 148, 155, 167, 168, 172, 180, 187
United States, Southwest, 23, 41, 62, 63, 91, 105, 184, 187
United States, Western, 31, 41, 59, 88, 89, 90, 133, 177
Venus figurines, 1, 14, 22, 76, 95, 122, 130, 138, 145
Victorian ideology, 18, 31, 160, 168
Viking, 49, 134, 161
Washington, D.C., 152
Watson, Patty Jo, 155, 162, 191
weaving, 24, 64
West Virginia, 19
Western society, contemporary, 16, 68, 71, 80, 122, 158
WHAM!, 92, 127
White, Marian, 11
Wildesen, Leslie E., 187
Winters, Howard, 39
Woodland period, U.S., 35, 148
Wormington, Hannah Marie, 41
Yellen, John, 39, 67, 69, 163
Yugoslavia, 80, 171
Yupik, 101
Zihlman, Adrienne, 55, 188
Zuni, 105